365 days with **Spurgeon**

Volume **5**

A further collection of daily readings from sermons preached by
Charles Haddon Spurgeon
from his Metropolitan Tabernacle Pulpit

Selected and arranged by
Terence Peter Crosby

Day One

© Day One Publications 2010
First printed 2010

ISBN 978-1-84625-230-3

Unless otherwise stated, all Scripture quotations are from
the Authorised Version Crown Copyright

British Library Cataloguing in Publication Data available

Published by Day One Publications
Ryelands Road, Leominster, HR6 8NZ
☎ 01568 613 740 FAX 01568 611 473
email—sales@dayone.co.uk
web site—www.dayone.co.uk
North American—e-mail—sales@dayonebookstore.com
North American web site—www.dayonebookstore.com

All rights reserved
No part of this publication may be reproduced, or stored in a retrieval system, or transmitted, in any form or by any means, mechanical, electronic, photocopying, recording or otherwise, without the prior permission of Day One Publications.

Chief Sub-Editor: Trudy Kinloch
Designed by Steve Devane and Printed by Thomson Litho, East Kilbride

Dedication

To John Roberts

upon his retirement

as General Secretary

of Day One Christian Ministries

and with gratitude for his guidance and support

at the start of my writing ministry

INTRODUCTION

This fifth volume of *365 Days with Spurgeon*, covering sermons preached between 4 May 1879 and the end of 1884, deals with a significant period during his later ministry. His pastorate had commenced on 28 April 1854 and his 25th anniversary was commemorated in the sermons preached on 18 May 1879. No. 1525, preached on 29 February 1880, was the second of only three such leap year sermons and the only one on a Sunday morning. Since 1857 the Spurgeons had lived at Nightingale Lane, near Wandsworth Common, but between 1 to 18 August 1880, they moved to a new home at Westwood in Norwood (see Mrs. C.H.Spurgeon—*Ten years of my life*, pp.123–5); there was no interruption to Spurgeon's preaching during this move! A temporary move of a different kind took place when there were major renovations at the Metropolitan Tabernacle—from 12 August to 2 September 1883 the Sunday services were transferred to Exeter Hall (nos. 1734–7, 1740, 1754, 1762), while the Thursday meetings appear to have been held at Christ Church, Westminster Bridge Road. Significant anniversaries were shortly to follow. On 11 November 1883 Spurgeon preached twice at services commemorating the 400th anniversary of Martin Luther's birth the previous day. Then Spurgeon celebrated his own 50th birthday on 19 June 1884 and special services were held around that time.

Charles Haddon Spurgeon at 50

Photograph taken from The Life of Charles Haddon Spurgeon (London: Passmore and Alabaster, 1903); p. 402.

The inclusion of over sixty undated sermons in this volume again draws our attention to the sicknesses and necessary annual visits to Mentone in the South of France, which continued to interrupt Spurgeon's ministry; sick notes and letters accompanied nos. 1504–8, 1510, 1512–14, 1517, 1630–4, 1690, 1755, 1762, 1797, 1820–3, 1826–9 and 1832–4. During one of these periods of absence in 1884 the pulpit was filled by one of Spurgeon's twin sons, Thomas, during a visit home from his pastorate in New Zealand; these sermons were later published as a book entitled *The Gospel of the Grace of God*. Five years earlier Spurgeon's own short sermon no. 1511 had been followed by Thomas' valedictory address on 28 September 1879 before his second voyage to Australia.

The new form of evangelistic outreach on Sunday evenings, when the regular members vacated their seats to make room for others, continued, as indicated by nos. 1489, 1579, 1620, 1691, 1717 and 1746. The last of these was the latest of the fourteen sermons (two published posthumously) between 1876 and 1883 thus identified. According to a note in *The Sword and the Trowel* for 1880, the evening sermon on 9 May 1880 (later published as no. 2000) was another such occasion.

As in earlier volumes of *365 Days with Spurgeon*, the majority of the readings have been allocated to coincide with the actual dates on which the sermons were preached. Each reading indicates Spurgeon's title and text; where necessary long texts have been abbreviated but listed in full in the Scripture index. The reader's attention is drawn to contemporary topics of personal, national and international interest to which Spurgeon sometimes referred. There has been a minimum of sympathetic updating of the original material to remove antiquated language and terminology; occasionally Spurgeon's Scripture quotations (probably from memory) have been corrected to remove inaccuracies. The footnotes for meditation have been added by the compiler, though over half of the readings conclude with a suitable verse from one of the hymns sung on each particular occasion. Part or the whole of Spurgeon's own Scripture readings have been selected for the further suggested reading on 53 days where they were particularly relevant to the chosen sermon extract; otherwise the readings have been selected by the compiler.

In addition to the usual subject, Scripture and location indices, those interested in hymns are directed to the appendix containing details of Spurgeon's 'One hundred best hymns'; this has been compiled from the hymn numbers listed at the end of 1,582 of the 3,563 weekly numbers of the *New Park Street* and *Metropolitan Tabernacle Pulpit* sermons.

Thanks are due once again to all at Day One for their encouragement in producing this volume, also to Digby James for layout arrangements and to Peter Currie for his help with getting started on a new computer! But above all it is fitting for us to remember part of the text with which Spurgeon commenced a short series on Psalm 118 'in connection with the dedication of the Jubilee House, which commemorated the completion of the beloved Pastor's fiftieth year, June 19th, 1884'—'the LORD helped me. The LORD is my strength and song, and is become my salvation' (Psalm 118:13–14).

Terence Peter Crosby
Wandsworth, London

1 JANUARY (1882)

The beginning of months

'And the LORD *spake unto Moses and Aaron in the land of Egypt, saying, this month shall be unto you the beginning of months: it shall be the first month of the year to you.'* Exodus 12:1–2
SUGGESTED FURTHER READING: Acts 8:26–39

Everything is out of joint till a man knows Christ: everything is disorderly and bottom upwards till the gospel comes and turns him upside down, and then the right side is up again. Man is all wrong till the gospel puts him all right. Though grace is above nature it is not contrary to nature, but restores true nature. Our nature is never so truly the nature of a man as when it is no longer man's sinful nature. We become truly men, such as God meant men to be, when we cease to be men such as sin has made men to be. Beginning as our life does at our spiritual passover, and at our feeding upon Christ, we ought always to regard our conversion as a festival and remember it with praise. Whenever we look back upon it the memory of it should excite delight in our hearts. I wonder how long a man ought to thank God for forgiving his sins? Is life long enough? Is time long enough? Is eternity too long? How long ought a man to thank God for saving him from going down to hell? Would 50 years suffice? Oh no, that would never do, the blessing is too great to be all sung of in a millennium. Suppose you and I never had a single mercy except this one, that we were made the children of God and co-heirs with Christ Jesus—suppose we had nothing else to enjoy! We ought to sing about that alone for ever and ever. If we were sick, cast on the bed of pain with a hundred diseases, with the bone wearing through the skin, yet since God's everlasting mercy will sanctify every pain and affliction, should we not still continue to lift up happy psalms to God and praise him for ever and ever? Therefore, be that your watchword all through the year: 'Hallelujah, praise ye the Lord!'

FOR MEDITATION: (*Our Own Hymn Book* no. 1036 vv.5&6—John Newton, 1779)
    'Now through another year, supported by His care,
    We raise our Ebenezer here, "The Lord has helped thus far."
    Our lot in future years, unable to foresee,
    He kindly to prevent our fears, says, "Leave it all to Me."'

SERMON NO. 1637

2 JANUARY (UNDATED SERMON)

The Pastor's life wrapped up with his people's steadfastness. A pleading reminder for the New Year

'Now we live, if ye stand fast in the Lord.' 1 Thessalonians 3:8
SUGGESTED FURTHER READING: Romans 1:7–15

Think of what the effect must be upon a minister's mind if he shall have laboured long and seen no fruit. There may be instances in which a man has been faithful, but not successful, places where, for a time, the dew falls not, and the softening influences of the Spirit are not given. Then the soil breaks the ploughshare, and the weary ox is ready to faint. I began to preach while yet a youth, scarce sixteen years of age, but before I had preached half a dozen times I saw persons affected by those sermons. I pined to find some heart that had looked to Jesus while I had preached him; and I have photographed upon my eye-balls at this very moment a very humble clay-walled cottage which seemed to me to be a sacred spot, for I was told by a venerable deacon that it was the house of a poor woman who had sought and found the Saviour through my ministry. I did not let the week conclude till I had seen her, for I hungered for the joy of meeting with one whom I had brought to Christ. If I found one soul converted I took heart and looked for more. Brother, are you working for Jesus? Then you know what it is to feel the shadow of death when you do not win a soul. Does it not seem hard to be knocking for Christ against a door that never opens, but has fresh bolts put to it to keep it closed? Be not ashamed of yourself because you feel distressed; it proves your capacity for being used. By-and-by God will bless you, and then you will understand the text 'Now we live.' You will find that your pulse is quickened, your heart's blood warmed, your soul filled with a diviner life as you rise nearer to the dignity of a saviour of men, and taste the joys unspeakable for which Christ laid down his life.

FOR MEDITATION: (*Our Own Hymn Book* no. 686 vv.7&8—Paul Gerhardt, 1659; tr. by John Wesley, 1739)
    'Thou seest our weakness, Lord, our hearts are known to Thee:
    Oh lift Thou up the sinking hand, confirm the feeble knee!
    Let us, in life and death, Thy steadfast truth declare;
    And publish, with our latest breath, Thy love, and guardian care.'

SERMON NO. 1758

3 JANUARY (UNDATED SERMON)

Samuel and the young man Saul

'And as they were going down to the end of the city, Samuel said to Saul, Bid the servant pass on before us, (and he passed on,) but stand thou still a while, that I may show thee the word of God.' 1 Samuel 9:27

SUGGESTED FURTHER READING: Revelation 1:1–8

If you will come and think well of the Word of God, you will see in it that which will meet all *the past* of your life, whatever it has been. There may be blots upon it, but in the Word of God you will find that which will wash them all away. You may have wept over your life, and yet you cannot wash away its stains; but the Word of God will tell you how you shall be made whiter than snow, and made to start again in life, delivered from every crimson stain. As to *the present*, does it puzzle you? Ah, well it may, for life is a tangled thread to those who know not God. But you shall find the clue of it, you shall thread the labyrinth, you shall see how even your afflictions work for your good, how your sickness means your health, how your being out of work and in poverty is to make you rich, how even your lying at death's door is sent to give you life, and you shall so understand the present as to feel that with all its apparent evil it is working for your good. And as to *the future*, would you read aright your destiny? My Lord can tell you the future by making you know that, 'Surely goodness and mercy shall follow me all the days of my life, and I will dwell in the house of the LORD for ever.' Oh that men would not neglect the Word of God, either in the hearing of it preached, or in the private reading of it in their homes. For believe me, there is something in the Bible which just suits you. I used to think that a certain text in the Bible was written with a special view to my case. It seemed to me that it might have been penned after I had lived, so accurately did it describe me. Even so, dear friend, there is something in the Bible for you.

FOR MEDITATION: (*Our Own Hymn Book* no. 505 v.1—Samuel F. Smith, 1850)

    'Hark! 'tis the Saviour's voice I hear,
    Come, trembling soul, dispel thy fear;
    He saith, and who His word can doubt?
    He will in no wise cast you out.'

SERMON NO. 1547

4 JANUARY (UNDATED SERMON)

The duty of the present hour

'Break up your fallow ground: for it is time to seek the LORD, till he come and rain righteousness upon you.' Hosea 10:12

SUGGESTED FURTHER READING: Romans 10:5–13

Very much seeking of the Lord is based on ignorance, that there are some who really set about seeking the Lord as if they could not find him, and as if he were a long way off. This is corrected by the apostle in those memorable words, 'Say not in thine heart, Who shall ascend into heaven?... Or, Who shall descend into the deep?... The word is nigh thee'. How nigh thee? 'In thy mouth.' That is how nigh it is. 'In thy mouth.' What hinders a man's receiving that which is in his mouth? Swallow it, man. Swallow! That is all you have to do. It is 'in thy mouth': nothing can be nearer, surely, than to have it 'in thy mouth'. Oh! if I were dying, and I had a live-long lozenge in my mouth, and I knew that it would save my life, do you think I would not suck it down? Ah! would I rest until it was down? I should not care if a critic stood by and said, 'You must not eat that lozenge. You are not worthy of it.' I have got it in my mouth, and your remonstrance comes too late; it is gliding down my throat. 'Oh! But you must not swallow that lozenge: you are not fit to receive it.' I have got it, and I defy anyone to rob me of it, for down it goes. 'But you must not, really, partake of it; it may not be meant for you. Perhaps you are not in the election of grace.' In vain your supposition. I have got it in my mouth, and if possession is nine points of the law, it is all the points of the gospel. I take it into my inward parts, and I will never part with it. That is just the gospel, and a sweet way of putting it, 'The word is nigh thee, even in thy mouth, and in thy heart.' 'If thou shalt confess with thy mouth the Lord Jesus, and shalt believe in thine heart that God hath raised him from the dead, thou shalt be saved.'

FOR MEDITATION: It is possible to taste without swallowing (Matthew 27:34). There is great danger in being a mere taster of God's word (Hebrews 6:4–6), but great blessing is to be obtained by feasting upon it (Psalm 19:10; Jeremiah 15:16), even when it sounds unpleasant (Ezekiel 2:8–3:3).

SERMON NO. 1563

5 JANUARY (UNDATED SERMON)

Tokens for good

'Shew me a token for good; that they which hate me may see it, and be ashamed: because thou, LORD, hast holpen me, and comforted me.'
Psalm 86:17

SUGGESTED FURTHER READING: 2 Peter 1:16–2:3

The Apostle Peter, after he has described Christ upon the mount as manifesting himself to his servants in the transfiguration, declares, 'We have also a more sure word of prophecy'. What, more sure than the transfiguration? Yes, more sure even than the evidence of their eyes when they saw their Lord glorified upon the holy mount. If you have ever been upon the mount with Christ, and if you have seen all his brightness, yet still you are not to compare even the sight of your eyes, when they see the best and brightest that they can see, with the word of testimony which must be sure, 'a light that shineth in a dark place'. All the rapt experiences which we have ever had are not to be trusted in comparison with the word of God. I say it advisedly, even the sweetest communion we have ever had with Christ may after all be suspected, and indeed it is upon such ripe fruit that Satan soon sets his hand that he may rob us of its savour if possible, for he is not slow to cast doubts upon the holiest joys of God's elect. There may come a time when we shall fear that we were carried away by excitement, or deluded by fanaticism; but he who speaks the word of Scripture cannot lie, and when his Spirit speaks that same truth into the soul we have therein a testimony which never can be doubted, but must be accepted over the head of everything. 'Let God be true, but every man a liar', ourselves and all, all liars as compared with the eternal verities of the revelation of God the Holy Spirit. The basis of faith is not our experience, but the testimony of God, and we must mind we do not make the feet of our image partly of God's gold and partly of our clay. Our experience may be in error, but the infallible word of God cannot be, and it is upon that alone which we must stand.

FOR MEDITATION: The bottom line should always be, 'what saith the scripture?' (Romans 4:3; Galatians 4:30). All sources of instruction should be submitted to the test of scripture and rejected, if found wanting (Deuteronomy 13:1–5; Isaiah 8:19–20; Matthew 4:1–11; Colossians 2:6–8).

SERMON NO. 1559

6 JANUARY (UNDATED SERMON)

Commendation for the steadfast

'Thou hast a little strength, and hast kept my word, and hast not denied my name... Because thou hast kept the word of my patience, I also will keep thee from the hour of temptation.' Revelation 3:8,10
SUGGESTED FURTHER READING (Spurgeon): John 17:6–19

Our faith stands not in the wisdom of man, but in the power of God. What is taught in Holy Scripture is sure truth to us, and every other statement must bow to it. Chillingworth said what ought to be true, though I am afraid that it is not—'The Bible and the Bible alone is the religion of Protestants.' I should like to see a few more of such Protestants. Many say that we ought to keep 'abreast of the times,' whatever that may mean, and that there is a certain 'spirit of the age,' to which we should be subject. This to me is treason against sovereign truth. I know of only one spirit to whom I desire to be subject, and that is the Spirit of all the ages, who never changes. By his teaching we are not only nineteen centuries behind the present age, but we come in at the back of all the ages of human history. If we have but little strength, we mean to let the times and the spirits go where they like; we shall keep to the Holy Spirit and to his eternal teachings. Supposing that we have not such big heads as some have, and cannot devise or multiply sophisms and inventions as they do, it will be no small thing to be commended at the last, in these terms—'thou hast a little strength, and hast kept my word'. Brother, cling to God's word; cling to infallible and immutable revelation! Whatever novelty comes up, keep to the word of Jesus! Whatever discovery may be made by the wise men of the age, let Christ be wisdom unto you. Regard the new teachers no more than you would 'the wise men of Gotham', for those who oppose themselves to God's word are fools. Let them cry 'Lo here! or, lo there!' but believe them not. Here is your anchorage. The Book is our ultimatum.

FOR MEDITATION: (*Our Own Hymn Book* no. 669 v.3—Anne Steele, 1760)
   'Eternal life Thy words impart; on these my fainting spirit lives:
   Here sweeter comforts cheer my heart, than all the round of nature gives.'

N.B. Gotham—a Nottinghamshire village, the natives of which had reputedly been very simple-minded according to 17th century legends.

SERMON NO. 1814

7 JANUARY (1883)

A monument for the dead, and a living voice to the living

'That if thou shalt confess with thy mouth the Lord Jesus, and shalt believe in thine heart that God hath raised him from the dead, thou shalt be saved.' Romans 10:9
SUGGESTED FURTHER READING: Acts 20:17–21:14

Look at our dear, departed brother, Mr Higgs. His children will tell you that his death was sad to them, but not to him. He suffered agonizing pain, but his peace was as deep as the sea. He had no uncertainty; he was as sure of his safety as if it had been a matter of calculation by the rules of arithmetic. He knew whom he had believed, and what the Lord had done for him, and could not see a weak point in it all. He spent the night trying to cheer and comfort others: he had no trembling thought about himself. He did not say, 'Have pity upon me, O ye my friends; for the hand of God hath touched me.' No, he knew that Christ was the resurrection and the life, and he was ready to depart. He wished his beloved ones to go to their beds; since they would stop with him, he desired them to sing. 'What shall we sing?' 'Sing' said he, *'For ever with the Lord, Amen, so let it be.'* It is hard singing when your father is dying, but it was not hard to him. He bade them read that chapter, 'Let not your heart be troubled'; he did not apply the verses to himself, but directed the comfort to his dear wife, for she had greater need of it than he: his faith was firm. It was for her he cared, and for those about him; as for himself, all was rest. One said to him a fortnight before, 'Don't be down-hearted; you may get better yet.' 'Stop' said he. 'What do you mean? I have never been down-hearted at anything in my life; certainly not at the thought of dying. If it was the Lord's will that I should die in the street at this moment, I would cheerfully go.' He never said a word more than he felt. God send us more like him.

FOR MEDITATION: (*Our Own Hymn Book* no. 912 v.5—Philip Doddridge, 1755)
    'O long-expected day, begin;
    Dawn on these realms of woe and sin:
    Fain would we leave this weary road,
    And sleep in death, to rest with God.'
N.B. William Higgs, a beloved deacon, died on 3 January 1883, aged 58.

8 JANUARY (1882)

Men without heart, sight, or hearing

'Yet the LORD *hath not given you an heart to perceive, and eyes to see, and ears to hear, unto this day.'* Deuteronomy 29:4
SUGGESTED FURTHER READING: Amos 5:1–15

Your eyes will be opened one day, in another sense. The rich man 'seeth Abraham afar off, and Lazarus in his bosom.' Who was that? That was a Jew, who had everything in this life, being clothed in purple, and faring sumptuously every day, but he had no heart to perceive nor eyes to see. 'In hell he lift up his eyes, being in torments'. Oh, my hearers, hell's torments will open your eyes. Will you wait till then? O you ungodly ones, you will think then. I pray God you may have sense enough to think now, while thinking will be of use to you. If there be a heaven, seek it; if there be a hell, escape it; if there be a God, love him; if there be a Christ, trust him; if there be sin, seek to be washed from it; if there be pardon, rest not till you have it. Oh do not mock your Saviour! Do not make game of eternal realities! Be in earnest about this, and in earnest at once. If you must play the fool, trifle with something less precious than your souls. Procure toys less expensive than your own immortal destinies. Oh, that God would bless this word to you careless ones, that you may feel at once that you do not feel as you should, and begin to cry to God to give you feeling; that you may see that you do not see, and begin to cry, 'Lord, open my eyes;' that you may hear a voice which shall make you feel that you do not hear as you ought to hear, and therefore must cry to God to give you hearing. Remember that spiritual life is from God only. It is his gift, and it is not bestowed according to merit, but is given by pure grace to the unworthy. Seek it, and you shall have it.

FOR MEDITATION: (*Our Own Hymn Book* no. 461 v.5—Anne Steele, 1760)
'Oh change these wretched hearts of ours,
And give them life divine!
Then shall our passions and our powers,
Almighty Lord, be Thine.'

SERMON NO. 1638

9 JANUARY (PREACHED 8 JANUARY 1882)

The touch

'And Jesus, immediately knowing in himself that virtue had gone out of him, turned him about in the press, and said, Who touched my clothes? And his disciples said unto him, Thou seest the multitude thronging thee, and sayest thou, Who touched me?' Mark 5:30–31

SUGGESTED FURTHER READING: 1 Corinthians 6:9–11

I have seen the proud man, who could not otherwise have been cured of his haughtiness, come and sit at Jesus' feet and learn of him, until he has been made meek and lowly. I have seen the obstinate man come to Jesus and gladly take Christ's yoke upon him, and become willingly and joyfully obedient to the supreme will of him who bought him with his blood. Often have I seen the unclean and the lascivious enticed to Jesus by his gentleness, and they have been made pure. How often have these eyes seen the despairing that have been on the verge of madness cheered and comforted till they have sung for joy of heart. How frequently have I seen the coward made brave, the morose made gentle, the revengeful made forgiving, by coming into contact with Jesus. You cannot love my Lord and love sin. You cannot trust my Lord and yet delight yourselves in iniquity. Only get near to him, and he will begin a cure upon your character, and, before long, will perfect it. If your malady should be a delight in the pleasures and the pursuits of the world, he will teach you not to love the world, nor the things of it. Do you suffer from selfishness? He shall teach you to deny yourselves. His lance and nails and cross shall crucify you with himself till self-seeking shall die. Are you afflicted with a sloth that will not let you be active? My Master's zeal shall fire your soul till, like him, you shall be consumed with energy. I do not mind what your fault is, my brother or my sister; but this I know, there is power in my divine Lord and Master to redeem you from that fault. He can destroy evil and create good. Behold, he makes all things new!

FOR MEDITATION: (*Our Own Hymn Book* no. 538 v.7—Amelia Matilda Hull, 1860)

'There is life for a look at the Crucified One;
There is life at this moment for thee:
Then look, sinner—look unto Him and be saved,
And know thyself spotless as He.'

10 JANUARY (UNDATED SERMON)

Beloved, and yet afflicted

'Lord, behold, he whom thou lovest is sick.' John 11:3
SUGGESTED FURTHER READING: James 5:13–16

Jesus may give healing. It would not be wise to live by a supposed faith, and cast off the physician and his medicines, any more than to discharge the butcher, and the tailor, and expect to be fed and clothed by faith; but this would be far better than forgetting the Lord altogether, and trusting to man only. Healing for both body and soul must be sought from God. We make use of medicines, but these can do nothing apart from the Lord, 'who healeth all thy diseases'. We may tell Jesus about our aches and pains, and gradual declinings, and hacking coughs. Some persons are afraid to go to God about their health: they pray for the pardon of sin, but dare not ask the Lord to remove a headache: and, yet, surely, if the hairs outside our head are all numbered by God it is not much more of a condescension for him to relieve throbs and pressures inside the head. Our big things must be very little to the great God, and our little things cannot be much less. It is a proof of the greatness of the mind of God that while ruling the heavens and the earth, he is not so absorbed by these great concerns as to be forgetful of the least pain or want of any one of his poor children. We may go to him about our failing breath, for he first gave us lungs and life. We may tell him about the eye which grows dim, and the ear which loses hearing, for he made them both. We may mention the swollen knee, and the sore finger, the stiff neck, and the sprained foot, for he made all these our members, redeemed them all, and will raise them all from the grave. Go at once, and say, 'Lord, behold, he whom thou lovest is sick.'

FOR MEDITATION: In healing, as in everything else, God usually employs means—Luke was a physician (Colossians 4:14). But in healing, as in everything else, we are to trust in God himself, not in the means he employs (Psalm 146:3–4; Jeremiah 17:5–8). To ignore this can be a risky business (2 Chronicles 16:12–13; Mark 5:25–26). Always remember that God does not always choose to heal the sick (2 Timothy 4:20).

N.B. This sermon was 'preached before an audience of invalid ladies at Mentone'.

SERMON NO. 1518

11 JANUARY (UNDATED SERMON)

A woman of a sorrowful spirit

'Hannah answered and said, No, my lord, I am a woman of a sorrowful spirit.' 1 Samuel 1:15
SUGGESTED FURTHER READING: Jeremiah 45:1–5

Affliction and suffering are not proofs of sonship, for 'Many sorrows shall be to the wicked'; and yet, where there are great tribulations, it often happens that there are great manifestations of the divine favour. There is a 'sorrow of the world' that 'worketh death', a sorrow which springs from self-will, and is nurtured in rebellion, and is therefore an evil thing, because it is opposed to the divine will. There is a sorrow which 'will eat as doth a canker', and breeds yet greater sorrows, so that such mourners descend with their sorrowful spirits down to the place where sorrow reigns supreme, and hope shall never come. Think of this, but never doubt the fact that a sorrowful spirit is in perfect consistency with the love of God, and the possession of true godliness. It is freely admitted that godliness ought to cheer many a sorrowful spirit more than it does. It is also admitted that much of the experience of Christians is no Christian experience, but a mournful departure from what true believers ought to be and feel. There is very much that Christians experience which they never ought to experience. Half the troubles of life are homemade, and utterly unnecessary. We afflict ourselves perhaps, ten times more than God afflicts us. We add many thongs to God's whip: when there would be but one we must make nine. God sends one cloud by his providence, and we raise a score by our unbelief. But taking all that off, and making the still further abatement that the Gospel commands us to rejoice in the Lord always, and that it would never bid us do so if there were not abundant causes and arguments for it, yet, for all that, a sorrowful spirit may be possessed by one who most truly and deeply fears the Lord. Never judge those whom you see sad, and write them down as under the divine anger, for you might err most grievously and most cruelly in making so rash a judgment. Fools despise the afflicted, but wise men prize them.

FOR MEDITATION: (*Our Own Hymn Book* no. 703 v.4—Horatius Bonar, 1856)
    'Take Thou my cup, and it with joy or sorrow fill;
    As ever best to Thee may seem, choose Thou my good and ill.'

SERMON NO. 1515

12 JANUARY (UNDATED SERMON)

The sitting of the refiner

'*And he shall sit as a refiner and purifier of silver: and he shall purify the sons of Levi, and purge them as gold and silver, that they may offer unto the* LORD *an offering in righteousness.*' Malachi 3:3
SUGGESTED FURTHER READING: Hebrews 12:5–11

I once heard a Welshman preach in his own native tongue. It was a sermon in which he got into the spirit of his subject, and spoke as one inspired. He used a very simple illustration when he said, 'The mother has her dear babe upon her knee. It is time for washing; she washes its face. The little one cries; it loves not the soap; it loves not the water; and therefore it cries. Here is a great sorrow! Listen to its lamentations! It is ready to break its heart! What does the mother do? Is she sorrowful? Does she weep? No; she is singing all the while, because she understands how good it is that the child should suffer a little temporary inconvenience in order that its face, all smeared and foul, should become bright and beautiful again. Thus does the great Father rest in his love, and rejoice over us with singing while we are sighing and crying.' Ours is but a child's sorrow, sharp and shallow, of which the greatest source is our own ignorance of the great designs of the Perfecter of men. The Lord pities our childish sorrow, but he does not so regard it as to stay his hand from his cleansing work. 'Let not thy soul spare for his crying', said Solomon; and our wise Father when he is chastening us does not spare us for our crying. What if the metal that is put into the furnace should feel when the crucible is hot, and should cry out, 'Oh, take me out; the fire is too hot; I cannot bear it. I am dissolving; I am melting; take me out.' Would the assayer regard the entreaties of the metal? Ah, no! The refiner sits still. Why should he be flurried? He knows what he is at, and he knows that his divine methods are wise and infallible. He is not hurting the silver, but doing it lasting service.

FOR MEDITATION: (*Our Own Hymn Book* no. 731 v.2—John Mason, 1683)
> 'His thoughts are high, His love is wise,
> His wounds a cure intend;
> And though He does not always smile,
> He loves unto the end.'

SERMON NO. 1575

13 JANUARY (UNDATED SERMON 1882)

The use of the bow

'And David lamented with this lamentation over Saul and over Jonathan his son: (Also he bade them teach the children of Judah the use of the bow: behold, it is written in the book of Jasher.)' 2 Samuel 1:17–18
SUGGESTED FURTHER READING (Spurgeon): Psalm 66:8–20

Nothing is more healthy than to have work to do. I have seen persons of leisure give way most terribly in the case of the loss of children; while I have known labouring people, who, I believe, have been as sensitive in heart, who have kept up bravely. Under God, I have attributed the difference to the fact that the poor woman must go to earn her daily bread, or must get about her domestic duties whatever happens, and the poor man must do his daily task, or else the family will be in need; thus toil has proved to be a blessed necessity by withdrawing the mind from the sorrow which would have engrossed it. You have heard of Alexander Cruden. Perhaps you do not know that he was crossed in love, and met with certain other trials which drove him nearly mad; and yet Alexander Cruden did not become insane, for he engaged upon the immense work of forming a concordance of sacred Scripture, which concordance has become the great instrument by which we search the word of God. This work kept him from becoming altogether insane. If I had to prescribe to 'a mind diseased,' I would say, 'Enter upon good work, and keep at it.' Dear friends, if you are in trouble, and Satan tempts you to get alone, and to cease from the work of the Lord, resist the injurious suggestion. God the Holy Spirit is most likely to comfort you, and to apply the precious promises of his word to your soul, if you pursue your Master's work with all your heart. Attend to his business, and he will attend to your business. Tell poor sinners about his wounds, and he will bind up yours. Forget your cross in his. Forget your griefs in the griefs of the sons of men who are perishing for lack of knowledge; and you shall find the readiest way to consolation.

FOR MEDITATION: (*Our Own Hymn Book* no. 66 song 1 v.3—Isaac Watts, 1719)
  'Oh bless our God and never cease, ye saints, fulfil His praise;
  He keeps our life, maintains our peace, and guides our doubtful ways.'

SERMON NO. 1694

14 JANUARY (1883)

Gladness for sadness

'Make us glad according to the days wherein thou hast afflicted us, and the years wherein we have seen evil... And let the beauty of the LORD our God be upon us.' Psalm 90:15,17
SUGGESTED FURTHER READING: Psalm 27:1–14

What a beauty is this which the Lord gives—'the beauty of the LORD our God'! This comeliness is the beauty of his grace; for our covenant God is the God of all grace. If the Lord makes us to know that we are his, our faces shine. If he fills us with his life and love, then brightness flashes from the eyes, and there is a grace about every movement. This 'beauty' means holiness; for holiness is the beauty of God. If the Holy Spirit works in you the beauty of holiness, you will rise superior to your afflictions. If this church shall be made the holier by its bereavements, we shall gain much by our losses. This beauty of the Lord must surely mean his presence with us. As the sun beautifies all things, so does God's presence. When we know that Jesus is with us, when we feel that he is our helper, when we bask in his love, when he abides with us in power, this is the beauty of the saints. If we have Christ in us, Christ with us, we can bear any amount of trouble. *'I can do all things, or can bear all suffering if my Lord be there.'* This beauty gives to the believer an attractiveness in the eyes of men: they perceive that we have been with Jesus, and they behold our faces shining like the faces of angels. It is a great thing when a Christian is so happy, so holy, and so heavenly that he attracts others to Christ, and people seek his company because they perceive that he has been in the company of the blessed Lord. God give you this, and if you have it, dear friend, you may forget your sorrows: they are transfigured into joy.

FOR MEDITATION: (*Our Own Hymn Book* no. 92 part 1 v.3—Isaac Watts, 1719)
  'My heart shall triumph in the Lord,
  And bless His works, and bless His word.
  Thy works of grace, how bright they shine!
  How deep Thy counsels, how divine!'

N.B. Two days after the funeral of William Higgs (see 7 January) a second beloved deacon, William Mills, had died on 12 January 1883, aged 62.

SERMON NO. 1701

15 JANUARY (1882)

Acceptable service

'Wherefore we receiving a kingdom which cannot be moved, let us have grace, whereby we may serve God acceptably with reverence and godly fear: for our God is a consuming fire.' Hebrews 12:28–29
SUGGESTED FURTHER READING: Hebrews 10:26–31

The Lord God who is to be served by us, even as our covenant God, is a 'consuming fire.' In love he is severely holy, sternly just. We hear people say, 'God out of Christ is a consuming fire,' but that is an unwarrantable alteration of the text. The text is 'our God', that is God in Christ 'is a consuming fire.' 'Our God' means God in covenant with us; it means our Father God, our God to whom we are reconciled, even our God, is still a 'consuming fire.' A large proportion of nominal Christians do not believe in this God. They profess to reverence a merciful God, but the moment you preach his justice they are indignant; the God who is a consuming fire is not accepted by this proud 'nineteenth century.' I do this day most solemnly declare my faith in the God of the Hebrews, who will by no means spare the guilty. The God of Abraham, and Isaac, and Jacob is the one and only God, and I avouch him this day to be my God. Jehovah is the Holy One of Israel; the God of the whole earth shall he be called. He that smote Pharaoh at the Red Sea, he that smote kings and slew mighty kings, is my God, and I believe in him as the God and Father of our Lord and Saviour Jesus Christ. I know no God but Abraham's God, Jehovah, the I AM. Under the New Testament God is not an atom less severe than under the old; and under the covenant of grace the Lord is not a particle less righteous than under the law. We are so saved by mercy that no sin goes unpunished: the law is as much honoured under the gospel as under the law. The substitution of Jesus as much displays the wrath of God against sin as even the flames of hell would do. While the Lord is merciful, infinitely so, and his name is love, yet still 'our God is a consuming fire', and sin shall not live in his sight.

FOR MEDITATION: (*Our Own Hymn Book* no. 189 v.4—Basil Manly jun., 1850)
  'How shall sinners worship Thee, God of spotless purity?
  To Thy grace all hope we owe; Thine own righteousness bestow.'

SERMON NO. 1639

16 JANUARY (UNDATED SERMON)

Salvation by knowing the truth

'God our Saviour; who will have all men to be saved, and to come unto the knowledge of the truth.' 1 Timothy 2:3–4
SUGGESTED FURTHER READING: 2 John 1–4

I have heard of a man who knew how to swim, but, as he had never been in the water, I do not think much of his knowledge of swimming: in fact, he did not really know the art. I have heard of a botanist who understood all about flowers, but as he lived in London, and scarcely ever saw above one poor withered thing in a flowerpot, I do not think much of his botany. I have heard of a man who was a very great astronomer, but he had not a telescope, and I never thought much of his astronomy. So there are many persons who think they know and yet do not know because they have never had any personal acquaintance with the thing. A mere notional knowledge or a dry doctrinal knowledge is of no avail. We must know the truth in a very different way from that. How are we to know it, then? Well, we are to know it, first, by *a believing knowledge*. You do not know a thing unless you believe it to be really so. If you doubt it, you do not know it. If you say, 'I really am not sure it is true,' then you cannot say that you know it. That which the Lord has revealed in Holy Scripture you must devoutly believe to be true. In addition to this, your knowledge, if it becomes believing knowledge, must be *personal knowledge*, a persuasion that it is true in reference to yourself. It is true about your neighbour, about your brother, but you must believe it about yourself, or your knowledge is vain; for instance, you must know that you are lost, that you are in danger of eternal destruction from the presence of God, that for you there is no hope but in Christ, that for you there is hope if you rest in Christ, that resting in Christ you are saved. Yes, you. You must know that because you have trusted in Christ you are saved, and that now you are free from condemnation, and that now in you the new life has begun.

FOR MEDITATION: (*Our Own Hymn Book* no. 556 v.1—Charles Wesley, 1739)

'Jesus, the sinner's Friend, to Thee,
Lost and undone, for aid I flee;
Weary of earth, myself, and sin,
Open Thine arms and take me in.'

SERMON NO. 1516

17 JANUARY (UNDATED SERMON)

Taught that we may teach

'And the man said unto me, Son of man, behold with thine eyes, and hear with thine ears, and set thine heart upon all that I shall shew thee; for to the intent that I might shew them unto thee art thou brought hither: declare all that thou seest to the house of Israel.' Ezekiel 40:4

SUGGESTED FURTHER READING: Matthew 13:9–17

First, he says, 'behold with thine eyes.' What are the eyes for but to see with? He means this: look, pry, search with your eyes. Do not let the truth flit before you and then say, 'Yes, I have seen it.' No. Stop it. Hold it by meditation before the mind's eye, and see with your eyes. Look, look, look into it. Remember what is said of the angels: 'which things the angels desire to look into'; not 'to look *at*', but 'to look *into*.' Looking *to* Christ will save you, but it is looking *into* Christ that gives joy, peace, holiness, heaven. Look into the gospel: let your eyes be intent and steadfastly fixed upon every truth, especially at choice times when God favours you with the noontide light of his face. Then be doubly intent upon his word. And then he puts it, 'hear with thine ears'. Well, a man cannot use his ears for anything else, can he? Yes, but *hear* with your ears. Listen with all your might. You are to spy out the meaning with the mind's eye; but, besides that, try to catch the very tone in which the promise or precept has been uttered. Treasure up the exact words, for though cavillers call it folly to speak of verbal inspiration, I believe that we must have verbal inspiration or no inspiration. If any man shall say to you, 'The sense of what your Father said is true, never mind his words', you would reply, 'Yes, but I would like to know precisely what he said, word for word.' I know that it is so in legal documents. It is not merely the sense that you look to, but every word must be right. God's word, as it came from him, came in such perfection that, even to the syllables in which the sense was clothed, there was infallibility about it. When I get God's word I would desire to hear it with my ears as well as see it with my eyes.

FOR MEDITATION: (*Our Own Hymn Book* no. 764 v.4—George Burden Bubier, 1856)

'Oh, this is life! Oh, this is joy, my God, to find Thee so;
Thy face to see, Thy voice to hear, and all Thy love to know.'

SERMON NO. 1578

18 JANUARY (UNDATED SERMON)

Knowledge. Worship. Gratitude.

'So that they are without excuse: because that, when they knew God, they glorified him not as God, neither were thankful.' Romans 1:20–21
SUGGESTED FURTHER READING: 1 Corinthians 8:1–13

Our Saviour could plead for some, 'Father, forgive them; for they know not what they do.' But what plea is to be used for those who know what they do, and yet do evil, who know what they ought to do, and do it not? These have the light, and close their eyes; or, to use another figure, they have the light, and use it to sin by. They take the golden candlestick of the Sanctuary into their hands, and by its help they perform their evil deeds the more dexterously, and run in the way of wickedness the more swiftly. Accursed is that man who heaps to himself knowledge till he becomes wise as Solomon, and then prostitutes it to base ends by using it to aggrandize his wealth, to pamper his appetites, to bolster his unbelief, or to conceal his vices. A man may by knowing more become all the more a devil. His growing information may only increase his condemnation. It is clear, then, that knowledge is not a possession of such unmingled good that we may grow vain of it; better far will it be if the more we know the more we watch and pray. Go on and read, young man. Go on and study with the utmost diligence. The more of knowledge you can acquire the better; but take care that you do not, like Sardanapalus, heap up your treasures to be your own funeral pile. Do not by a rebellious pride curdle the sweet milk of knowledge, and sour your precious blessing into an awful curse. It is soon done, but not so soon undone. It was the eating of the fruit of the tree of knowledge of good and evil which brought all this evil upon us which you see this day. You may eat of that tree still, if so it please you; but if you taste not of the tree of life at the same time, your knowledge shall only open to you the gates of hell.

FOR MEDITATION: Knowledge is a privilege and a responsibility which brings blessings if acted upon (John 13:17). However, we replace the blessing with a curse if we fail to do what we know to be right (Luke 12:47), give our approval to what we know to be wrong (Romans 1:32), or allow our supposed knowledge to go to our heads (1 Corinthians 8:1–2).

N.B. Sardanapalus—a king of Assyria.

SERMON NO. 1763

19 JANUARY (UNDATED SERMON)

John and Herod

'For Herod feared John, knowing that he was a just man and an holy, and observed him; and when he heard him, he did many things, and heard him gladly.' Mark 6:20

SUGGESTED FURTHER READING: 2 Chronicles 24:1–22

'Herod feared John,' and yet he beheaded him. A person may be evangelical and Calvinistic, and so on, and yet, if he is placed under certain conditions, he may become a hater and a persecutor of the truth he once avowed. Herod went a step lower, however; for this Herod Antipas was the man who afterwards mocked the Saviour. It is said, 'Herod with his men of war set him at nought, and mocked him, and arrayed him in a gorgeous robe'. This is the man that 'did many things' under the leading of John. His course is altered now. He spits on the Redeemer and insults the Son of God. Certain of the most outrageous blasphemers of the gospel were originally Sunday-school scholars and teachers, young men who were 'almost persuaded,' yet they halted and hesitated, and wavered until they made the plunge and became much worse than they possibly could have become if they had not seen the light of truth. If the devil wants raw material to make a Judas, 'the son of perdition', he takes an apostle to work upon. When he takes a thoroughly bad character like Herod, it is necessary to make him plastic as Herod had been in the hands of John. Somehow or other, border men are the worst enemies. In the old wars between England and Scotland, the borderers were the fighting men; and so the border people will do more harm than any until we get them on this side of the frontier. Oh that the grace of God may decide those who now hesitate! I may mention to you that, before long, Herod lost all the power he possessed. He was a foxy man, and always tried to win power, but in the end he was recalled by the Roman emperor in disgrace. That was the end of him. Many a man has given up Christ for honour, and has lost himself as well as lost Christ.

FOR MEDITATION: (*Our Own Hymn Book* no. 992 v.2—Charles Wesley, 1767)
'We bow before Thy gracious throne, and think ourselves sincere;
But show us, Lord, is every one Thy real worshipper?'

SERMON NO. 1548

20 JANUARY (UNDATED SERMON)

Men bewitched

'O foolish Galatians, who hath bewitched you, that ye should not obey the truth, before whose eyes Jesus Christ hath been evidently set forth, crucified among you?' Galatians 3:1
SUGGESTED FURTHER READING: Galatians 1:1–12

In many parishes the Church of England is slightly to be distinguished from the church of Rome, and yet nobody is astonished; and, if we make a remark about it, we are set down as bigoted. Who has bewitched this Protestant land? With Smithfield scarcely yet swept of the ashes of her martyrs, they set up the crucifix again! What would Oliver Cromwell say if he and his Ironsides could come back again to see what they are making of this land? As I cannot speak such vigorous words as he would have uttered, I leave the subject with words borrowed from Paul, which well suit the case; 'O foolish Englishmen, who hath bewitched you, that ye should thus turn aside?' Nor is this all. You see this witchery in another way among our dissenting churches. At a time not yet forgotten Unitarianism and Socinianism gradually crept into Nonconforming congregations, and the pulpits lost their testimony for Christ; the meeting-houses were deserted, and true religion seemed dying out of the land. Then came Whitefield and Wesley, and all their troop of Methodists, and the blessed flame that was almost quenched burned up again, and we, of this generation, have said one to another, 'That experiment will never be repeated: the Nonconformist churches will never go in that direction again: they know better. They see the ill-effect of this modern teaching, and they will stick to the grand old gospel now.' So I dreamed; but I dream in that way no longer, for scarcely do I look anywhere without finding the gospel of Christ diluted, the milk of the word adulterated, and the grand gospel, as Luther and Calvin would have thundered it out, seldom enough to be heard. O foolish Nonconformists, 'who hath bewitched you, that ye should not obey the truth', but should seek after this novelty and the other, this refinement and the other, and let your God and Saviour go?

FOR MEDITATION: Three safeguards enabled the apostle Paul to maintain a pure gospel: he was not ashamed of it (Romans 1:16), he fully preached it (Romans 15:19) and he defended it (Philippians 1:17). The lay believer is urged to do likewise (Philippians 1:27; Colossians 1:23; Jude 3).

SERMON NO. 1546

21 JANUARY (1883)

On laying foundations

'And why call ye me, Lord, Lord, and do not the things which I say?' 'He that heareth, and doeth not, is like a man that without a foundation built an house upon the earth; against which the stream did beat vehemently, and immediately it fell; and the ruin of that house was great.' Luke 6:46,49
SUGGESTED FURTHER READING: Acts 8:9–24

Kind, good, Christian friends often, without a thought of doing so, help to mislead seeking souls. 'Yes,' they say, 'you are converted,' and so perhaps the person would be if all he said was true; but it is said without feeling; it comes from the lip only, and not from the heart; and therefore it is ruinous to encourage him. A kindly assurance from a Christian friend may breed false confidence, if that assurance was mistakenly given. In these days we do not meet with many Christians who err by dealing too severely with converts; the shot strikes the other target. Our forefathers were possibly too suspicious and jealous; but nowadays we nearly all err in the opposite direction: we are so anxious to see everybody brought to Christ, that our wish may tend to delude us into the belief that it is so. We are so willing to cheer and comfort those who seek the Lord, that we may fall into the habit of prophesying smooth things, and thus shun everything which tends to probe and test, lest it should also discourage. Let us beware lest we cry, 'Peace, peace,' where there is no peace. It will be a sad thing to breed hypocrites when we were looking for converts. I have heard of one who had been into the Enquiry Room a dozen times, and when on another occasion she was invited to go there she said, 'I really do not know why I should go, for I have been told that I was saved twelve times already, and I am not a bit better than before they told me so.' It would be better to send some home weeping rather than rejoicing. Many a wound needs the lancet more than the plaster. You may be comforted by well-meant assurances, and yet that comfort may be all a lie.

FOR MEDITATION: (*Our Own Hymn Book* no. 668 v.2—Mary Bowly, 1847)
  'We have no fear that Thou shouldst lose
  One whom eternal love could choose;
  But we would ne'er this grace abuse.
  Let us not fall. Let us not fall.'

SERMON NO. 1702

22 JANUARY (1882)

Great spoil

'*I rejoice at thy word, as one that findeth great spoil.*' Psalm 119:162
SUGGESTED FURTHER READING: Psalm 19:7–14

In dividing the spoil there is profit, pleasure, and honour. I am not about to justify the deeds of war, for these I hate: as to plunder and rapine, such as have been indulged in by the general run of conquerors, they are detestable crimes. Men have made themselves worse than devils to men. No calamities have ever befallen nations that are so much to be deplored as the atrocities of war. I use the warlike metaphor, but condemn the fact. Men conceive when they divide the spoil that there is honour in it. Look at the crowds that gathered along the Via Sacra when the Roman conquerors came down from the Appian Way, passed under the arch, and marched towards the Capitol. Then did the populace crowd the house roofs, and the chimney tops, that they might see a Scipio or a Caesar expose his captives and display his spoils. They shouted till they were hoarse, and wearied themselves with applause at the sight of the *spolia opima* which were borne in the procession. Thus men judge of plunder in war. See how Napoleon thought to glorify himself by placing in Paris the works of art which he had taken from the capitals of Europe. What are most trophies but stolen goods, or that which is purchased by them? But when you and I lay hold on Holy Scripture then have we grasped a prey more precious than royal treasures, a prey which we may hold with justice and honour. When we can say that the things which God has revealed are ours, then we are rich beyond a miser's dream; and when we can hold them against all comers, then that which we believe becomes our honour and gives glory to us, and glory to faith, and chief glory to him who wrought our faith in us by his almighty Spirit.

FOR MEDITATION: Do you value God's word in the same way as the Psalmist did? Consider some of the other descriptions given in Psalm 119—God's word is to be rejoiced in 'as much as in all riches' (v.14), is better 'than thousands of gold and silver' (v.72), is 'sweeter than honey' (v.103) and is to be loved 'above gold' (v.127).

N.B. Spolia opima—the spoils taken from the enemy's general when killed by the commander of the army himself.

SERMON NO. 1641

23 JANUARY (UNDATED SERMON)

The spirit of bondage and of adoption

'For ye have not received the spirit of bondage again to fear; but ye have received the Spirit of adoption, whereby we cry, Abba, Father. The Spirit itself beareth witness with our spirit, that we are the children of God.' Romans 8:15–16

SUGGESTED FURTHER READING: Luke 12:1–12

'The spirit of bondage again to fear.' There are five sorts of fears, and it is well always to distinguish between them. There is the *natural fear* which the creature has of its Creator, because of its own insignificance and its Maker's greatness. From that we shall never be altogether delivered; for with holy awe we shall bow before the divine majesty, even when we come to be perfect in glory. Secondly, there is a *carnal fear*: that is, the fear of man. May God deliver us from it! May we never cease from duty because we dread the eye of man! 'Who art thou, that thou shouldest be afraid of a man that shall die?' From this cowardice God's Spirit delivers believers. The next fear is a *servile fear*, the fear of a slave towards his master, lest he should be beaten when he has offended. That is a fear which should rightly dwell in every unregenerate heart. Until the slave is turned into a child he ought to feel that fear which is suitable to his position. By means of this fear the awakened soul is driven and drawn to Christ, and learns the perfect love which casts it out. If servile fear be not cast out it leads to a fourth fear, namely, a *diabolical fear*; for we read of devils, that they 'believe, and tremble.' This is the fear of a malefactor towards the executioner, such a fear as possesses souls that are shut out for ever from the light of God's countenance. But, fifthly, there is a *filial fear* which is never cast out of the mind. This is to be cultivated. This is 'the fear of the LORD' which is 'the beginning of wisdom.' This is a precious gift of grace: 'Blessed is the man that feareth the LORD'. This makes the saints fearful of offending, lest they should grieve infinite love; it causes them to walk before the Lord with the fear of a loving child who would not in anything displease his parent.

FOR MEDITATION: 'The fear of man bringeth a snare' (Proverbs 29:25), but 'the fear of the LORD' brings knowledge (Proverbs 1:7), wisdom (Proverbs 9:10), prolonged days (Proverbs 10:27), confidence (Proverbs 14:26) and life (Proverbs 14:27; 19:23).

SERMON NO. 1759

24 JANUARY (UNDATED SERMON)

Loved and loving

'My beloved is mine, and I am his: he feedeth among the lilies.' Song of Solomon 2:16
SUGGESTED FURTHER READING: Jonah 2:1–9

The evident intent of the language is to set forth the delicacy of the highest form of holy fellowship. The Lord our God is a jealous God, and that jealousy is most seen where his love is most displayed. The least sin, wilfully indulged in, will grieve the Holy Spirit; slights, forgetfulnesses, and neglects will cause him to turn away. If we would remain positively and joyously assured that the Beloved is ours and that we are his, we must use the utmost circumspection and holy vigilance. No man gains full assurance by accident, or retains it by chance. As the gentle hind wanders in lovely spots where the pure white lilies grow, and as he shuns the places profaned by strife, and foul with rank weeds and nettles, so does the Lord Jesus come to holy minds perfumed with devotion and consecrated to the Lord, and there in sacred quiet he finds solace and abides with his saints. May the Lord preserve us from pride, from self-seeking, from carnality, and wrath, for these things will chase away our delights even as dogs drive off the hind of the morning. Both our inward and outward walk must be eagerly watched lest anything should vex the Bridegroom. A word, a glance, a thought may break the spell, and end the happy rest of the heart, and long may it be before the blessing is regained. Some of us have learned by bitter experience that it is hard to establish a settled peace, and easy enough to destroy it. The costly vase, the product of a thousand laborious processes, may be broken in a moment; and so the supreme delight of communion with the Lord Jesus, the flower of ten thousand eminent delights, may be shattered by a few moments' negligence.

FOR MEDITATION: God can have no fellowship with sin (2 Corinthians 6:14–16). While it is the Christian's privilege to enjoy fellowship with God and with God's people (1 John 1:3,7), sin only serves to interrupt it and any who claim to enjoy fellowship with God while living in sin are downright liars (1 John 1:6; 2:4), who would do far better to repent and seek God afresh (Hosea 5:15–6:3).

SERMON NO. 1634(B)

25 JANUARY (UNDATED SERMON)

For the candid and thoughtful

'And when Jesus saw' ['saw him,' so it should be (Spurgeon)] 'that he answered discreetly, he said unto him, Thou art not far from the kingdom of God.' Mark 12:34

SUGGESTED FURTHER READING: Deuteronomy 30:1–20

This man knew the law, and knew it well. He had a spiritual appreciation of its range, meaning, and spirituality. Notice how he puts it: he puts it well. He says that to love God 'with all the heart, and with all the understanding, and with all the soul, and with all the strength,' is the first commandment. Here we see, first, that he mentions *sincere love*, in the words 'to love him with all the heart'. God is to be loved, not in name, not with lip language, not with mere pretence, but with the heart. God requires by his law the hearty obedience of his creatures. Next, the scribe puts it, 'with all the understanding'; that is, God deserves and demands the *intelligent love* of his creatures. He does not ask blind love of them: he desires them to know something of him, and of his works, and of his claims upon them, so as to love him because he deserves their affection. The understanding must justify and impel the affections. Then, he puts it, 'with all the soul'; that is, with the *emotional nature*. Love God with feeling, not coolly, but with the whole force of your feeling. Love him with your soul, for soul love is the soul of love. And then he adds, 'and with all the strength'; that is to say, *intensity* is to be thrown into our love to God. We are to serve him with our might, and throw all our whole energy into his worship. Thus he gives us, under four heads, a description of the kind of love which the law of God requires of us: sincere—'with all the heart'; intelligent—'with all the understanding'; emotional—'with all the soul'; intense and energetic—'with all the strength.' This the scribe knew, and it was most valuable knowledge.

FOR MEDITATION: Examine your love towards God. Is it sincere (Ezekiel 33:30–31; Ephesians 6:24; 1 John 3:18; 4:20)? Is it intelligent (Psalm 116:1; 1 John 4:19)? Is it emotional (Psalm 119:97; 1 Peter 1:8)? Is it intense and energetic (Joshua 23:11; John 21:15)?

26 JANUARY (UNDATED SERMON)

Expected proof of professed love

'Shew ye...the proof of your love.' 2 Corinthians 8:24
SUGGESTED FURTHER READING: John 14:21–31

The text says, 'shew ye to them, and before the churches, the proof of your love'. What proof shall we show? There are so many forms of action which would prove love to Christ that I cannot possibly go through them all, especially as each person, I believe, will give a different proof of his love. There is (to use a difficult word) an idiosyncrasy about each believer. He is a man by himself, and his love, if it is genuine, will take a form peculiar to himself in the proof which it gives. Certain proofs look towards God and the Lord Jesus. If you love him, you will 'keep his commandments: and his commandments are not grievous.' If you love him, you will seek to honour him, to spread the savour of his glorious name. If you love God in Christ Jesus, you will be anxious to extend his rule over the hearts of men. If you love God, you will long for communion with him: you will not be satisfied to live for days without speaking with him. If you love him, you will grieve yourself when you grieve him; your heart will smite you when you have gone astray. If you love God, you will long to be like him; you will strive after holiness. If you love God, he will reign over you; Christ will be your King; your mind will be under subjection to him; your thoughts will be guided by him; your opinions will be taken from his word; your whole life will be seasoned by his Spirit who dwells in you. Do you not see that there are hundreds of ways in which you can show proof of your love towards God? Oh, that we may not be found wanting in any of these things!

FOR MEDITATION: (*Our Own Hymn Book* no. 639 v.7—Philip Doddridge, 1755)
   'Thou know'st I love Thee, dearest Lord;
   But oh, I long to soar
   Far from the sphere of mortal joys,
   And learn to love Thee more.'

27 JANUARY (UNDATED SERMON)

At school

'Teach me to do thy will; for thou art my God.' Psalm 143:10
SUGGESTED FURTHER READING: Hebrews 13:17–21

The Lord's will should be done *immediately*. As soon as a command is known it should be obeyed. Lord, suffer me not to consult with flesh and blood. Make me prompt and quick of understanding in the fear of God. 'Teach me to do thy will' as angels do, who no sooner hear thy word than they fly like flames of fire to fulfil thy behests. His will should be done *cheerfully*. Jehovah seeks not slaves to grace his throne. He would have us delight to do his will: yea, his law should be in our heart. Oh! brothers and sisters, you need to pray this: 'Teach me to do thy will', or else you will miss the mark. Teach me to do it *constantly*. Let me not sometimes be thy servant, and then run away from thee. Keep me to it. Let me never weary. When the morning wakes me may it find me ready, and when the evening bids me rest may I be serving thee until I fall asleep. Teach me to do it also, Lord, *universally*, not some part of it, but all of it, not one of thy commands being neglected, nor one single part of my daily task being left undone. I am thy servant; make me to be what a good servant is to her mistress, neglecting none of the cares of the household. May I be watchful in all points. 'Teach me to do thy will' *spiritually*, not making the outside of cups and plates clean, but obeying thee within my soul. May what I do be done with all my heart. If I pray, help me to pray in the spirit. If I sing, let my heart make music unto thee. When I am talking to others about thy name, and trying to spread the savour of Jesus, let me not do it in my own strength, or in a wrong spirit, but may the Holy Spirit be upon me. 'Teach me to do thy will' *intensely*. Let the zeal of thy house eat me up. Oh that I might throw my whole self into it. This little prayer grows, does it not? Pray it, brothers and sisters, and may the Lord answer you.

FOR MEDITATION: (*Our Own Hymn Book* no. 143 v.5—Anne Steele, 1760)
  'Teach me to do Thy sacred will;
  Thou art my God, my hope, my stay;
  Let Thy good Spirit lead me still,
  And point the safe, the upright way.'

SERMON NO. 1519

28 JANUARY (1883)

Hands full of honey

'*And he turned aside to see the carcase of the lion: and, behold, there was a swarm of bees and honey in the carcase of the lion. And he took thereof in his hands, and went on eating, and came to his father and mother, and he gave them, and they did eat: but he told not them that he had taken the honey out of the carcase of the lion.*' Judges 14:8–9
SUGGESTED FURTHER READING: Isaiah 25:1–9

The particular part of the incident which is recorded in these two verses appears to have been passed over by those who have written upon Samson's life: I suppose it appeared to be too inconsiderable. They are taken up with his festive riddle, but they omit the far more natural and commendable fact of his bringing forth the honey in his hands and presenting it to his father and mother. This is the little scene to which I direct your glances. It seems to me, that the Israelitish hero with a slain lion in the background, standing out in the open road with his hands laden with masses of honeycomb and dripping with honey, which he holds out to his parents, makes a fine picture, worthy of the greatest artist. And what a type we have here of our Divine Lord and Master, Jesus, the conqueror of death and hell. He has destroyed the lion that roared upon us and upon him. He has shouted 'victory' over all our foes. 'It is finished' was his note of triumph and now he stands in the midst of his church with his hands full of sweetness and consolation, presenting them to those whom he calls, 'my brother, and sister, and mother.' To each one of us who believe in him he gives the luscious food which he has prepared for us by the overthrow of our foes; he bids us come and eat that we may have our lives sweetened and our hearts filled with joy. To me the comparison seems wonderfully apt and suggestive: I see our triumphant Lord laden with sweetness, holding it forth to all his brethren, and inviting them to share in his joy.

FOR MEDITATION: (*Our Own Hymn Book* no. 145 part 1 v.5—Isaac Watts, 1719)
'Thy glorious deeds of ancient date
Shall through the world be known;
Thine arm of power, Thy heavenly state,
With public splendour shown.'

SERMON NO. 1703

29 JANUARY (1882)

'Verily, verily'

'Verily, verily, I say unto you, He that heareth my word, and believeth on him that sent me, hath everlasting life, and shall not come into condemnation; but is passed from death unto life.' John 5:24
'Verily, verily, I say unto you, He that believeth on me hath everlasting life.' John 6:47
SUGGESTED FURTHER READING: Matthew 17:14–21

Here is a person standing right in the middle of a railway track, and I say to him, 'My dear fellow, if you do not come out of that you will be smashed to atoms within the next five minutes, for an express train is thundering along the line.' He laughs and answers, 'Do you mean to say that my shifting the position of my body a couple of feet will make all that difference? Do you tell me that if I move I shall be safe, and that if I stand here I shall be cut to pieces?' 'Yes, I do say it with tears, begging you to believe me, and come out of the track.' 'Then,' he says, 'you are very uncharitable.' 'Yes,' I reply, 'and you are very insane.' What more can I say? It is never uncharitable to speak the truth for the good of the person concerned. A small matter may suffice to shape the destiny of an immortal soul. In those ill times, when there were slaves across the Atlantic, a lady went down to one of our ships, accompanied by her negro servant. The lady remarked to the captain that if she were to take this black woman with her to England, she would become free as soon as she landed. The captain replied, 'Madam, she is free already. The moment she came on board a British vessel she was free.' When the negro woman knew this, do you think she went on shore with her mistress? By no means; she chose to keep her liberty. But what made her rise from a slave to a free woman? Why, only a few inches of separation from the shore. I do not know how far the ship was from land; the distance may have been very little; still it made all the difference; she was free on board, and a slave on land. How slight the change of place; but how great the difference involved; marvel not that faith involves such great things.

FOR MEDITATION: Material things teach us that small changes make big differences (1 Corinthians 5:6; James 3:3–5). The same applies to matters of faith (Luke 17:5–6). Our faith or lack of faith in the Lord Jesus Christ is going to make an eternal world of difference (John 3:16,18,36).

SERMON NO. 1642

30 JANUARY (1881)

Silver sockets: or, redemption the foundation

'When thou takest the sum of the children of Israel after their number, then shall they give every man a ransom for his soul unto the LORD, *when thou numberest them; that there be no plague among them.' 'And thou shalt take the atonement money of the children of Israel; ... to make an atonement for your souls.'* Exodus 30:12,16
SUGGESTED FURTHER READING: Ephesians 1:3–14

When the account was taken of the number of the children of Israel the Lord commanded that every male over twenty years of age should pay half a shekel as redemption money, confessing that he deserved to die, owning that he was in debt to God, and bringing the sum demanded as a type of a great redemption which would by-and-by be paid for the souls of the sons of men. The truth was thus taught that God's people are a redeemed people: they are elsewhere called 'the redeemed of the LORD'. If men reject the redemption which he ordains, then they are not his people; for of all his chosen it may be said—'The LORD hath redeemed Jacob, and ransomed him from the hand of him that was stronger than he.' Whenever we attempt to number up the people of God it is absolutely needful that we count only those who at least profess to have brought the redemption price in their hands, and so to have taken part in the atonement of Christ Jesus. David, when he numbered the people, did not gather from them the redemption money, and hence a plague broke out amongst them. He had failed in obedience to the Lord's ordinance, and counted his subjects, not as redeemed people, but merely as so many heads. Let us always beware of estimating the number of Christians by the number of the population of the countries called Christian; for the only true Christians in the world are those who are redeemed from iniquity by the blood of the Lamb, and have personally accepted the ransom which the Lord has provided, personally bringing their redemption money in their hands by taking Christ to be theirs and presenting him by an act of faith to the great Father.

FOR MEDITATION: (*Our Own Hymn Book* no. 440 v.2—Madan's Collection, 1763)
  'Ye, who see the Father's grace beaming in the Saviour's face,
  As to Canaan on ye move, praise and bless redeeming love.'

SERMON NO. 1581

31 JANUARY (UNDATED SERMON)

Rare fruit

'I create the fruit of the lips; Peace, peace.' Isaiah 57:19
SUGGESTED FURTHER READING: Romans 5:1–11

When the last great war was over (I mean the great war of all, in which we were so long engaged with the Bonapartes) news of the peace came to a certain town. It was only gently whispered that there was peace, but it was all over the town in a few minutes. Everybody ran through the streets. Bread had been sent up to an awful price by the war, and everybody was weary with the taxes, the slaughter of soldiers, and the perpetual fear of invasion. A man ran down the street shouting, 'Peace, peace, peace, peace,' and everybody was glad. All manner of good things were wrapped up in the one word 'peace': families would no more be divided, trade would no longer be crippled, famine would no more devour the land. Now the loaf would be within the reach of the poor and the hungry; and the widow might keep her sons at home, safe from the cannon's mouth. 'Peace, peace,' they cried; and within an hour there were bells ringing from every steeple, and as the sun went down there were candles in every window. Everybody must have an illumination because peace had come. Now, if peace be so precious as to temporal things, it is equally precious as to eternal things; and if a man has once seen Jesus Christ, it is the joy of his life to sing, 'Peace, peace.' Here stands the reconciled man, and he looks up to heaven through the pure blue air, past the stars, endless leagues beyond imagination's utmost stretch: he looks up, and his mind conceives of God, and his heart feels, 'I am at peace with him. Though he is a consuming fire, I am at peace with him. With the great Father I am at peace. Though it is very tempestuous round about him, yet I am at peace with him. I am at peace with the eternal Son: though he shall break his enemies with a rod of iron, he will never break me; I am at peace with him. I am at peace with the Holy Spirit, for though to blaspheme him is death without hope of mercy, yet I am at peace with him: he will never destroy me.' What a peace is this!—peace with God, the peace of God, perfect peace.

FOR MEDITATION: (*Our Own Hymn Book* no. 722 v.4—Isaac Watts, 1709)
   'In vain the tempter frights my soul, and breaks my peace in vain;
   One glimpse, dear Saviour, of Thy face revives my joys again.'

1 FEBRUARY (PREACHED 3 FEBRUARY 1881)

Four choice sentences

'Behold, I am with thee.' Genesis 28:15
'I will be with thee.' Genesis 31:3
'The God of my father hath been with me.' Genesis 31:5
'Behold, I die: but God shall be with you.' Genesis 48:21
SUGGESTED FURTHER READING: Isaiah 41:8–14

When God is with a man there is a familiarity of condescension that is altogether unspeakable: it ensures an infinite love. 'I am with thee'. God will not dwell with those he hates. He puts 'away the wicked of the earth like dross'. He says to them, 'I never knew you: depart'; but to each one of his people he says, 'I have called thee by thy name; thou art mine.' And, more than that, 'I am with thee.' As a man delights to be with a friend, so are the delights of Christ with the sons of men, whom he has chosen and redeemed with blood. 'I am with thee'- it means practical help. Whatever we undertake, God is with us in the undertaking; whatever we endure, God is with us in the enduring; whithersoever we wander, God is with us in our wandering. 'If God be for us, who can be against us?' If God be with us, can we ever be exiled or banished? If God be with us, what can we not do? If God be with us, what can we not endure? Well said the apostle, as if answering that question, 'I can do all things through Christ which strengtheneth me.' 'I am with thee'. Come, brother or sister, if you would get the fullness of this privilege, believe that God is near you now, near to you as he that sits at your side; no, nearer; for he is so with you as to be in you. And do you know that his whole Godhead is with you? 'I am with thee': as if there were not another, the whole Godhead is with you. You do not have to cry aloud like Baal's priests, or cut yourself with knives, that you may attract his eye; for he says, 'I am with thee'. Your sighs he hears; your tears he puts into his bottle. 'I am with thee'.

FOR MEDITATION: (*Our Own Hymn Book* no. 732 v.3—George Keith, 1787)
 'Fear not, I am with thee, oh, be not dismayed!
 I, I am thy God, and will still give thee aid;
 I'll strengthen thee, help thee, and cause thee to stand,
 Upheld by My righteous omnipotent hand.'

SERMON NO. 1630

2 FEBRUARY (PREACHED 3 FEBRUARY 1884)

The rocky fortress (and its inhabitant)

'He that walketh righteously, and speaketh uprightly; he that despiseth the gain of oppressions, that shaketh his hands from holding of bribes, that stoppeth his ears from hearing of blood, and shutteth his eyes from seeing evil; he shall dwell on high: his place of defence shall be the munitions of rocks.' Isaiah 33:15–16
SUGGESTED FURTHER READING: Psalm 20:1–9

I leave to others the task of showing the beauty of groaning, or the delightfulness of murmuring: it is mine to urge you to shake yourselves from the dust, and put on your beautiful garments. Why are you so cast down? Dear people of God, you go out in the streets in rags, and yet you have royal robes provided for you; why do you not put them on? 'Oh,' say you, 'but I have great sorrow.' Yes, but it is written, 'As sorrowful, yet alway rejoicing.' Why tell everybody of your grief? Is there any good to be done thereby? What does our Lord say? 'But thou, when thou fastest, anoint thine head, and wash thy face; that thou appear not unto men to fast.' It is a Christian's duty to be happy. What a blessed religion is that in which joy is a matter of precept—'Rejoice in the Lord alway: and again I say, Rejoice.' I have been so long away from England that I do not know where our Queen is residing just now; but if I had the wings of a dove, and could mount into the upper air, I would soon find out. I should look for the Royal Standard. I should see it floating over Windsor or Osborne, and by this token I should espy the royal abode. Fling out the banner to the breeze when the king is within. Is the king at home with you, dear brother? Do not forget to display the standard of holy joy. Hoist it, and keep it flying. When the Bridegroom is not with us we will mourn; but so long as we see his face no man can make us fast. Rejoice, and yet again rejoice, and thus let the Royal Standard fly at the top of the tower: the King is within us! The Prince of Peace is enthroned in our hearts!

FOR MEDITATION: (*Our Own Hymn Book* no. 18 version 2 v.4—Tate and Brady, 1696)
    'Therefore to celebrate His fame
    My grateful voice to heav'n I'll raise;
    And nations, strangers to His name,
    Shall thus be taught to sing His praise.'

SERMON NO. 1764

3 FEBRUARY (1884)

First King of righteousness, and after that King of peace

'First being by interpretation King of righteousness, and after that also King of Salem, which is, King of peace.' Hebrews 7:2
SUGGESTED FURTHER READING: Matthew 5:6–20

That is the kind of king that God would have every one of us to be. We ought all to be, first, kings of righteousness, and then kings of peace. The Lord has appointed each man his kingdom: let us see to it that we reign for good and not for evil. On all sides we hear voices inviting us to peace apart from righteousness. 'Oh,' they say to us, 'a confederacy, a confederacy.' What do you mean? You are to preach a lie, and we are to preach the truth, and yet we are to call each other brothers. We are no brothers, and we will not by our silence aid the fraud. 'Oh, but,' they say, 'be charitable.' Charitable with what? Charitable with God's truth, flinging it down into the mire of error? Charitable by deceiving our fellowmen? That we cannot be. Brethren, we must so hold and love the truth as to hate every false way, for the way of error is ruinous to the souls of men, and it will go hard with us if even by our silence we lead men to run therein. If any man shall say to you, 'Come and let us sin together,' reply to him, 'I cannot enter into association with you, for I must first be pure and then peaceable, since I serve a Lord who is first King of righteousness, and after that King of peace.' 'Hold your tongue,' says the world. 'Do not fight against error. Why need you speak so fondly against a wrong thing?' We must speak, and speak sharply too, for souls are in danger. We must uplift the banner of truth, or we shall be meanest of all cowards. God has made us kings, and we must be first kings of righteousness, and after that kings of peace.

FOR MEDITATION: Righteousness and peace can live happily together (Psalm 85:10; Isaiah 32:17; 60:17; Romans 14:17; Hebrews 12:11; James 3:18), but not if joined by a third party such as sin (1 Corinthians 15:34), unrighteousness (2 Corinthians 6:14), iniquity (Hebrews 1:9) or the wrath of man (James 1:20).

SERMON NO. 1768

4 FEBRUARY (1883)

All joy in all trials

'*My brethren, count it all joy when ye fall into divers temptations; knowing this, that the trying of your faith worketh patience. But let patience have her perfect work, that ye may be perfect and entire, wanting nothing.*' James 1:2–4

SUGGESTED FURTHER READING: 1 Peter 4:12–19

Our own looking within seldom yields solid comfort. Actual trial is far more satisfactory; but you must not try yourself. The effectual proof is by trials of God's sending. The way of trying whether you are a good soldier is to go down to the battle: the way to try whether a ship is well built is, not merely to order the surveyor to examine her, but to send her to sea: a storm will be the best test of her staunchness. They have built a new lighthouse upon the Eddystone: how do we know that it will stand? We judge by certain laws and principles, and feel tolerably safe about the structure; but, after all, we shall know best in after-years when a thousand tempests have beaten upon the lighthouse in vain. We need trials as a test as much as we need divine truth as our food. Admire the ancient types placed in the ark of the covenant of old: two things were laid close together,—the pot of manna and the rod. See how heavenly food and heavenly rule go together: how our sustenance and our chastening are equally provided for! A Christian cannot live without the manna nor without the rod. The two must go together. It is as great a mercy to have your salvation proved to you under trial as it is to have it sustained in you by the consolations of the Spirit of God. Sanctified tribulations work the proof of our faith, and this is 'more precious than' that 'of gold that perisheth, though it be tried with fire'. Now, when we are able to bear it without starting aside, the trial proves our sincerity.

FOR MEDITATION: (*Our Own Hymn Book* no. 750 v.3a—William Cowper, 1779)

'Did I meet no trials here, no chastisement by the way,
Might I not, with reason, fear I should prove a castaway?'

N.B. In 1882 the fourth Eddystone lighthouse, fourteen miles out to sea off Plymouth, replaced Smeaton's Tower of 1759, which was reassembled on Plymouth Hoe, where it is now open to the public.

SERMON NO. 1704

5 FEBRUARY (1882)

A home question and a right answer

'From that time many of his disciples went back, and walked no more with him. Then said Jesus unto the twelve, Will ye also go away? Then Simon Peter answered him, Lord, to whom shall we go?' John 6:66–68
SUGGESTED FURTHER READING: 2 Peter 2:17–22

We know some that used to walk with Christ, who walk no more with his people; their hearts have gone away from Christ. The Sabbath is ignored; the house of God is forsaken; the Bible is put away; prayer is neglected and perhaps despised. They walk no more with Christ, for they prefer a broader or smoother road. If anybody mentions what they used to be, they slink away, and seem to say, 'Never mention it again: we wish it to be ignored.' I remember a household where the sons and daughters all professed to be converted to Christ; but some of them were fond of amusements that were not consistent with the profession of religion. When they were found in such engagements, they blushed a little; but by-and-by they boldly averred that they had never been converted, that they were forced into it by persuasion, and hurried on by excitement to do that which their better sense led them to regret. Their excuse was as false as their former profession. They knew that they acted of their own accord, and willingly professed Christ. Alas, just as willingly, when temptation came, they forsook him. Ah, apostate, it is all very well to say that you were persuaded; but you know that you deliberately confessed your faith, or you would never have been baptized by us; you deliberately sought membership with the church of God, or you would not have been received. If you have gone back from Christ you yourself must bear the shame in time and eternity. But when any openly sever themselves from the companionship of the Crucified One, well may the question pass from heart to heart, 'Will ye also go away?'

FOR MEDITATION: (*Our Own Hymn Book* no. 666 vv.1&7—John Newton, 1779)
   'When any turn from Zion's way, (alas, what numbers do!)
   Methinks I hear my Saviour say, "Wilt thou forsake Me too?"
   What anguish has that question stirred, if I will also go;
   Yet, Lord, relying on Thy word, I humbly answer, No.'

SERMON NO. 1646

The fruit of the Spirit: joy

'*But the fruit of the Spirit is ... joy.*' Galatians 5:22
SUGGESTED FURTHER READING (Spurgeon): Philippians 4:1–13

Our joy is sadly diminished by our *unbelief*. If you will not believe neither shall you be established. *Ignorance* will do the same to a very large extent. Many a Christian has a thousand reasons for joy which he knows nothing of. Study the Word and ask for the teaching of the Spirit of God that you may understand it; so shall you discover wells of delight. Joy is diminished, also, by *walking at a distance from God*. If you get away from the fire you will grow cold: the warmest place is right in front of it, and the warmest place for a believing heart is close to Christ in daily fellowship with him. It may be that *sin indulged* is spoiling our joy. 'This little hand of mine,' as Mr Whitefield once said, 'can cover up the sun as far as my eyes are concerned.' You have only to lift a naughty, rebellious hand, and you can shut out the light of God himself: any known sin will do it. Trifling with sin will prove a kill-joy to the heart. I believe that many lose the joy of the Lord because *they do not put it in the right place*. See where it lives. Look at my text: 'the fruit of the Spirit is love, joy, peace'. There joy stands in the centre; 'love' is on one side and 'peace' on the other. Find a man who never loved anybody and you have found a joyless man. This man's religion begins and ends with looking to his own safety. The only point he longs to know is, is he himself saved? He never knows joy, poor creature; how can he? As to peace, where is it? He has none, because wherever he goes he growls, grumbles, snarls and barks at everybody. There is no peace where he is; he is always quarrelling, and then he says, 'I have little joy.' He does not live in the right house for joy. Joy dwells at no. 2. 'Love' is no. 1; 'joy' is no. 2; 'peace' is no. 3; and if you pull down either of the houses on the side, no. 2 in the middle will tumble down. Joy is the centre of a triplet, and you must have it so or not at all:—'love, joy, peace'.

FOR MEDITATION: (*Our Own Hymn Book* no. 774 v.6—Isaac Watts, 1709)
'Nor earth, nor all the sky,
Can one delight afford;
No, not a drop of real joy,
Without Thy presence, Lord.'

7 FEBRUARY (1884)

The singular origin of a Christian man

'We are his workmanship, created in Christ Jesus unto good works, which God hath before ordained that we should walk in them.' Ephesians 2:10
SUGGESTED FURTHER READING: Acts 9:36–43

What are good works? I should say that they are works such as God commands—*works of obedience*. When we heartily keep the divine precepts, we must be right; for it can never be evil for a man to do what God bids him. Next, I should say that they are *works of love*, of love to God, and love to man, works done out of a pure affection to the great Father, and out of unselfish regard to men. That which we do to display our own liberality is done unto self, and so is spoiled; but where there is a single eye to God's glory, the work is good. Works done out of love to Christ, and love to saints, and love to the poor, and love to lost sinners, are good works. Furthermore, I should say that *works of faith* are good works; works done in confidence in God, undertaken in reliance upon his help, and in the firm belief that he will accept them even though men might censure them. The proclamation of his gospel with faith in its power, the pleading of the promise with expectation of its fulfilment, the sacrifice of personal gain for the service of truth, works such as these are good, and pleasing to God; for 'without faith it is impossible to please him'. I am bound to add that good works include the necessary *acts of common life* when they are rightly performed. We are to produce good works in our home, in our shop, in our work-room, in our travel abroad, or on our sickbed: everywhere we are to be filled with good works to God's glory. All our works should be good works, and we may make them so by sanctifying them with the Word of God and prayer, according to that precept, 'Whether therefore ye eat, or drink, or whatsoever ye do, do all to the glory of God.'

FOR MEDITATION: Good works cannot save us, but once we are saved they should characterise us (Matthew 5:16). We should be fruitful in them (Colossians 1:10), established in them (2 Thessalonians 2:17), rich in them (1 Timothy 6:18), prepared for them (2 Timothy 2:21; 3:17), patterns of them (Titus 2:7), zealous of them (Titus 2:14), ready for them (Titus 3:1), careful to maintain them (Titus 3:8,14) and provoking one another to do them (Hebrews 10:24). Being unfit for them is a disgrace (Titus 1:16).

SERMON NO. 1829

8 FEBRUARY (PREACHED 5 FEBRUARY 1882)

Our Lord's trial before the Sanhedrim

'And they all condemned him to be guilty of death.' Mark 14:64
SUGGESTED FURTHER READING: Acts 5:27–42

How ready should we be to bear slander and ridicule for Jesus' sake. Do not get into a huff, and think it a hard thing that people should mock at you. Who are you, dear sir? Who are you? What can you be if compared with Christ? If they spat upon him, why should they not spit upon you? If they buffeted him, why should they not buffet you? Shall your Master have all the rough of it? Shall he have all the bitter, and you all the sweet? A pretty soldier you, to demand better fare than your Captain! How earnestly, next, ought we to honour our dear Lord. If men were so eager to put him to shame, let us be ten times more earnest to bring him glory. Is there anything we can do today by which he may be honoured? Let us set about it. Can we make any sacrifice? Can we perform any difficult task which would glorify him? Let us not deliberate, but at once do it with our might. Let us be inventive in modes of glorifying him, even as his adversaries were ingenious in the methods of his shame. Lastly, how surely and how sweetly may all who believe in him come and rest their souls in his hands. Surely I know that he who suffered this, since he was verily the Son of the Blessed, must have ability to save us. Such griefs must be a full atonement for our transgressions. Glory be to God, that spittle on his countenance means a clear, bright face for me. Those false accusations on his character mean no condemnation for me. That putting him to death proves the certainty of our text last Sabbath morning, 'Verily, verily, I say unto you, He that believeth on me hath everlasting life.' Let us sweetly rest in Jesus, and if ever our faith is agitated, let us get away to the hall of Caiaphas, and see the Just standing for the unjust, the Faultless One bearing condemnation for sinners.

FOR MEDITATION: (*Our Own Hymn Book* no. 275 v.2—Bernard of Clairvaux, 1153, tr. Paul Gerhardt, 1659)
'O Lord of life and glory, what bliss till now was Thine!
I read the wondrous story, I joy to call Thee mine.
Thy grief and Thy compassion were all for sinners' gain;
Mine, mine was the transgression, but Thine the deadly pain.'

SERMON NO. 1643

9 FEBRUARY (UNDATED SERMON)

Faith among mockers

'He trusted on the LORD *that he would deliver him: let him deliver him, seeing he delighted in him.'* Psalm 22:8
SUGGESTED FURTHER READING: Mark 4:35–41

What ought a child of God to do in order to show that he really does trust in the Lord? How did Jesus do this? Well, I think that in our Lord's case it was his wonderful calmness which compelled everybody to see that 'he trusted in the LORD'. You never find him in a flurry; he is never worried nor confused. He is beset behind and before with men who try to catch him, but he is as self-possessed as if he spoke among friends. He does not appear to be the least upon his guard, and yet instead of their catching him, before long he either catches them, or else they retire saying, 'Never man spake like this man.' He was always cool, peaceful, ready, self-composed. You notice his inward quietude not only when enemies are round about him, but when he is surrounded by a great mob of people all hungry, starving, famishing: he breaks the bread and multiplies it, but not before he has made them all sit down on the green grass by hundreds and by fifties. He will have them in companies, arranged in ranks, for convenient distribution; and when they are all placed in order, as if it had been a well-marshalled royal entertainment, then it is that he takes the bread, and, looking up to heaven, with all deliberation asks a blessing, and breaks and gives the food to the disciples. The disciples make no scramble of it: it is an orderly festival, and the thousands are all fed in due order, in majestic decorum, for Christ was calm, and therefore master of the situation. He never looks as if he had fallen into difficulties, and then adopted expedients to get out of them, but his whole life is pre-arranged and ordered in the most prudent and peaceful manner.

FOR MEDITATION: (*Our Own Hymn Book* no. 56 v.3—Isaac Watts, 1719)
   'In Thee, most holy, just and true,
   I have reposed my trust;
   Nor will I fear what man can do,
   The offspring of the dust.'

10 FEBRUARY (1884)

An astounding miracle

'And they went into Capernaum; and straightway on the sabbath day he entered into the synagogue, and taught. And they were astonished at his doctrine: for he taught them as one that had authority, and not as the scribes.' Mark 1:21–22

SUGGESTED FURTHER READING: Matthew 22:15–22

Why was it that the Saviour's teaching had such a remarkable power about it? Was it not, first, because he preached the truth? There is no power in falsehood except so far as men choose to yield to it because it flatters them, but there is great force in truth; it makes its own way into the soul. As long as men have consciences they cannot help feeling when the truth is brought to bear upon them. Even though they grow angry their very resistance proves that they recognize the force of what is spoken. Moreover, the Saviour spoke the truth in a very natural, unaffected manner: the truth was in him, and it flowed freely from him. His manner was truthful as well as his matter. There is a way of speaking truth so as to make it sound like a lie. Perhaps there is no greater injury done to truth than when it is spoken in a doubtful manner, with none of the accent and emphasis of conviction. Our Saviour spoke as the oracles of God: he spoke truth as truth should be spoken, unaffectedly and naturally, as one who did not preach professionally, but out of the fullness of his heart. You all know how sermons from the heart go to the heart. Moreover, our great Exemplar delivered his teaching as one who most heartily believed what he was speaking, who spoke what he knew, who spoke of things which were his own. Jesus had no doubts, no hesitancy, no questions, and his style was as calmly forcible as his faith. Truth seemed to be reflected from his face just as it shone forth from God in all its native purity and splendour. He could not speak otherwise than he did, for he spoke as he was, as he felt, and as he knew. Our Lord spoke as one whose life supported all that he taught.

FOR MEDITATION: 'His word was with power' (Luke 4:32). What else made the preaching of the Lord Jesus Christ so effective? Others were able to testify that he spoke with authority (Matthew 7:29), unlike any other man (John 7:46) and plainly (John 16:29). 'And the common people heard him gladly' (Mark 12:37). Preachers, take note!

SERMON NO. 1765

11 FEBRUARY (1883)

The hearing of faith

'This only would I learn of you, Received ye the Spirit by the works of the law, or by the hearing of faith?' Galatians 3:2
SUGGESTED FURTHER READING: Acts 15:1–11

The safety of the weak and of the strong believer rests upon the same foundation. This may be seen in a figure. On board one of the fine steamboats which flit between England and America I see a strong, hardy, vigorous man. Will he get to America safely? Yes, if the ship does. But see, yonder is a little child which cannot walk, and has to be carried in its mother's arms. Will it reach America safely? Yes, if the ship does. Both the robust man and the whimpering infant, all being well, will reach their journey's end, if the ship does. Their safety lies in the same place. Their condition does not affect their transit. But is there no difference between the child and the man? Assuredly, a great deal of difference as to many things, but there is no difference about the fact that their passage across the ocean depends upon the steamboat rather than upon themselves. The strong man could not walk across the Atlantic any more than the child could: they are alike incompetent for the passage if left alone, and alike capable of it if placed on board the same vessel. So, if you meet with a great saint, say to yourself, 'My honoured brother will get to heaven through Jesus Christ; and I, a poor babe in grace, shall get to heaven in the same way.' I want you children of God to feel this. Are you on board the Covenant transport? Does the blood-red flag fly at the mast head? Then, if the meanest believer is not safely carried into port, neither will the strongest child of God reach the fair havens. If that ship of free grace goes down, Peter and Paul must sink as well as ourselves; for we are at sea in the same vessel. Our confidence is in no measure or sense in what we are, but altogether in what Christ is on our behalf; we depend on Jesus and rest in Jesus by a simple faith.

FOR MEDITATION: (*Our Own Hymn Book* no. 546 v.5—Charlotte Elliott, 1836)
'Just as I am—Thou wilt receive,
Wilt welcome, pardon, cleanse, relieve;
Because Thy promise, I believe,
O Lamb of God, I come.'

SERMON NO. 1705

12 FEBRUARY (1882)

Our Lord's first appearance before Pilate

'Pilate ... saith unto them, I find in him no fault at all.' John 18:38
SUGGESTED FURTHER READING: John 8:34–47

'I find in him no fault at all.' Pilate, you have spoken well. Your verdict is typical of the verdict of all who have ever examined Christ. Some have examined him with an unfriendly eye, but in proportion as they have been candid in the observation of facts, they have been struck with his life and spirit. It is a very rare thing to hear even the infidel rail at the character of Jesus; in fact, some of the foremost sceptics as to our Lord's teaching have been remarkably impressed with admiration of his life. No character like that of Jesus is to be seen in history, no, not even in romance. If anyone says the four gospels are forgeries, let him try to write a fifth, which shall be like the other four. Why, you cannot add an incident to the life of Christ; its details are unique; the fancy cannot imagine a fresh incident which could be safely joined on to that which is recorded. Every critic would cry out, 'This is not genuine.' The life of Jesus is a roll of cloth of gold, of the manufacture of which the art is utterly lost. His spotless character stands alone and by itself, and all true critics are compelled to say they find no fault at all in him. Let me add that this verdict of Pilate is the verdict of all that have ever associated with Christ. One disciple who was with Christ betrayed him, but he spoke nothing against him. No, the last witness of Judas before he hanged himself was this, 'I have sinned in that I have betrayed the innocent blood.' If there had been a fault in Jesus, the traitor would have spied it out; his unquiet conscience would have been glad enough to find therein a sedative, but even he was compelled to say, 'I have betrayed the innocent blood.' 'Which of you convinceth me of sin?' is the challenge of Jesus, to which there is no reply.

FOR MEDITATION: The perfect sinless purity of the Lord Jesus Christ was prophesied before his birth (Isaiah 53:9; Luke 1:35), testified by those who were close to him (Matthew 27:4; 1 Peter 1:19; 2:22) and admitted even by those who had been no friends of his (Matthew 27:19; Luke 23:4,14–15,22,41; John 19:4,6). What he himself claimed was no vain boast (John 8:29).

13 FEBRUARY (PREACHED 6 FEBRUARY 1881)

A greater than Solomon

'Behold, a greater than Solomon is here.' Luke 11:31
SUGGESTED FURTHER READING (Spurgeon): Colossians 1:11–23

In his *nature* the Lord Jesus is greater than Solomon. Alas, poor Solomon! The strongest man that ever lived, namely Samson, was the weakest of men; and the wisest man that ever lived was, perhaps, the greatest, certainly the most conspicuous fool. How different is our Lord! There is no infirmity in Christ, no folly in the incarnate God. The backsliding of Solomon finds no parallel in Jesus, in whom the prince of this world found nothing though he searched him through and through. Our Lord is greater than Solomon because he is not mere man. He is man, perfect man, man to the utmost of manhood, sin excepted; but still he is more, and infinitely more, than man: 'in him dwelleth all the fullness of the Godhead bodily.' He is God himself: 'the Word was God.' God dwells in him, and he himself is God. As in nature he was infinitely superior to Solomon, and not to be compared with him for a moment, so was he in *character*. Look at Christ and Solomon for a minute as to real greatness of character, and you can hardly see Solomon with a microscope, while Christ rises grandly before you, growing every moment till he fills the whole horizon of your admiration. Principally let me note the point of self-sacrifice. Jesus lived entirely for other people; he had never a thought about himself. Solomon was, to a great extent, wise unto himself, rich unto himself, strong unto himself; and you see in those great palaces, and in all their arrangements, that he seeks his own pleasure, honour, and profit; alas! that seeking of pleasure leads him into sin, and that sin into a still greater one. Solomon, wonderful as he is, only compels you to admire him for his greatness, but you do not admire him for his goodness. You see nothing that makes you love him, you tremble before him rather than feel gladdened by him. Oh, but look at Christ. He does not have a thought for himself. He lives for others.

FOR MEDITATION: (*Our Own Hymn Book* no. 389 v.1—John David Chambers, 1857)
   'Exult all hearts with gladness at sound of Jesu's Name;
   What other hath such sweetness, or such delight can claim?'

SERMON NO. 1600

14 FEBRUARY (1884)

Before day-break with Christ

'*And in the morning, rising up a great while before day, he went out, and departed into a solitary place, and there prayed. And Simon and they that were with him followed after him. And when they had found him, they said unto him, All men seek for thee. And he said unto them, Let us go into the next towns, that I may preach there also.*' Mark 1:35–38
SUGGESTED FURTHER READING: 2 Corinthians 11:5–33

If the Lord Jesus Christ, who preached by his own authority and power, and who wrought miracles really by his own might, yet fled away as much as he could from the applause of men, much more let each one of us do so. Oh, to walk before the Lord, and be blind and deaf to all the censures and the plaudits of the poor creatures around us! I have seen men whom God has greatly blessed, who have been highly honoured by their brethren, and yet they have been cast down, and have therefore been made to lie low in their own esteem. On the other hand, I have observed others whose usefulness in the church has not appeared to anybody but themselves, and yet they have been so tall that they almost needed St Paul's Cathedral to stand upright in: their self-esteem has been ten times taller than the esteem of their wiser brethren. Let us prefer to be found among the useful and lowly, rather than among the self-conceited and useless. God will not greatly bless us if we grow great. We may soon become too big to be used to win souls. I notice that soul-winning is generally accomplished by humble instruments. It is a delicate task, and the Lord who does it will not use those who are great, and strong, and mighty in their own esteem. When the Lord finds his servants lowly, like the Lord Jesus Christ, then they shall be used. The longer I live the more do I see that, as a rule, pride is the death of all true spiritual usefulness. As you love God, and would desire to honour him by a useful life, put far from you the temptation to sip of the intoxicating cup of human honour. Draughts of worldly glory are not for the priests of the Most High.

FOR MEDITATION: The 'meek and lowly' (Matthew 11:29) Lord Jesus Christ came not to be served but to serve (Mark 10:45; Philippians 2:7). He shunned earthly fame and power (Luke 4:5–8; 5:15–16; John 6:15) and humbled himself (Philippians 2:8). His followers are expected to take him, not the world, as their model (Mark 10:42–45; Philippians 2:3–5).

SERMON NO. 1769

15 FEBRUARY (1880)

The royal prerogative

'He that is our God is the God of salvation; and unto GOD the Lord belong the issues from death. But God shall wound the head of his enemies, and the hairy scalp of such an one as goeth on still in his trespasses.' Psalm 68:20–21

SUGGESTED FURTHER READING: Jeremiah 14:10–22

A new god has been lately set up among men, the god of modern Christianity, the god of modern thought, a god made of honey or sugar of lead. He is all leniency, gentleness, mildness, and indifference in the matter of sin. Justice is not in him, and as for the punishment of sin, he knows it not. The Old Testament, as you are, no doubt, made aware by the wise men of this world, takes a very harsh view of God, and therefore modern wisdom sets it on one side; one half of the word of God is out of date, and turned to waste paper. Although our Lord Jesus did not 'come to destroy the law or the prophets', 'but to fulfil' them, yet the advanced thinkers of these enlightened times tell us that the idea of God in the Old Testament is a false one. We are to believe in a new god, who does not care whether we do right or wrong, for by his arrangement all will come to the same end in the long run. There may be a little twisting about for awhile for some who are rather incorrigible, but it will all come right at last. Live as you like, go and swear and drink, go and oppress the nations, and make bloody wars, and act as you will; by jingo you will be all right at last. This is roughly the modern creed which poisons all our literature. But let me say, by Jehovah this shall not be as men dream. Jehovah, the Judge of all the earth, must do right. The God of Abraham, and of Isaac, and of Jacob is the God of our Lord and Saviour Jesus Christ: the God of the whole earth shall he be called. He has not changed at all in the stern integrity of his nature, and he will by no means spare the guilty. Read, then, the last verse of our text, and believe that it is as true today as when it was first written.

FOR MEDITATION: Modern thought is not quite as modern as some would have us think. There have always been those who would deny the justice and judgment of God, albeit at their own expense (2 Chronicles 36:15–16; Jeremiah 5:12–14; 14:13–15). Remember who first told such lies (Genesis 3:1–4).

SERMON NO. 1523

16 FEBRUARY (1882)

Freshness

'My glory was fresh in me, and my bow was renewed in my hand.' Job 29:20
'I shall be anointed with fresh oil.' Psalm 92:10
SUGGESTED FURTHER READING: Job 33:19–28

It is well to have a freshness about our feelings. I know that we do not hope to be saved by our feelings, neither do we put feeling side by side with faith; yet I should be very sorry to be trusting and yet never feeling. Surely it would be a dead faith. It would be a strange thing to be a living child of God and to have no feelings. I will tell you about feelings as they strike me. Sometimes I have deplored the condition of my heart before God, and thought my feelings to be the worst that could be; but what a foolish judge I have been, for in a week's time I have wanted to have those despised feelings over again, and thought that now at last I had fallen into a worse state than before. I am persuaded that we are very poor judges of the value of our own inward feelings. Maybe, when we are lowest in our own esteem, we are really highest in the sight of God, and when we feel as if we did not pray, we are praying; the heart may be wrestling with God more when it fears that it does not pray than when you come down complacently out of your closet and say, 'I know that I have had a good time, for I feel perfectly self-satisfied.' I long for truth in the inward parts, and wisdom in the secret places of the soul. Anything is good which rids us of pretence. Oh to be broken to shivers by the hand of God, and for every grain of dust to cry out to him! I believe this mode of praying often prospers beyond any other. At any rate, give me not stereotyped pretension to feeling, but fresh feeling. Whether it is joy or sorrow, let it be living feeling, fresh from the deep fountains of the heart. Whether it is exultation or depression, let it be true, and not superficial or simulated.

FOR MEDITATION: (*Our Own Hymn Book* no. 676 v.4—Isaac Watts, 1709)
  'From Thee, the overflowing spring,
  Our souls shall drink a fresh supply,
  While such as trust their native strength,
  Shall melt away, and droop, and die.'

SERMON NO. 1649

17 FEBRUARY (1884)

Recruits for King Jesus

'And David went out to meet them, and answered and said unto them, If ye be come peaceably unto me to help me, mine heart shall be knit unto you: but if ye be come to betray me to mine enemies, seeing there is no wrong in mine hands, the God of our fathers look thereon, and rebuke it.' 1 Chronicles 12:17

SUGGESTED FURTHER READING: Proverbs 26:17–28

Some people might be compared to hedgehogs; they cannot be touched by anybody; they are all spines and prickles. Such people may think well of themselves, but it is to be feared that the loving Jesus does not think well of them. The man with a hot head and a bitter heart, is he a friend of Jesus? I cannot imagine that such a head as that will lie in Jesus Christ's bosom. Oh, no; he 'that loveth is born of God,' but not the man of hate and spite. Give me the eyes of the dove, and not those of a carrion crow. When the dove soars aloft into the air, what does she look for? Why, for her dovecote, and when she discovers the beloved abode she uses her wings with lightning speed, for there is her delight. If you were to throw a raven or a carrion-crow into the air, it would be looking for something foul which it could feed upon; and there are men and women in every Christian church who are always trying with far-reaching and greatly-magnifying eyes to find out some wretched scandal or another. If you want to go to your bed uncomfortable, and to lie awake all night, if you are a pastor of a church, have a few minutes' talk with a friend of this order. These are the folks who have just sniffed out a matter that ought to be inquired into. When it is inquired into there is nothing to discover, and great heart-burning is caused in the process of investigation. These same scandalmongers will have something fresh tomorrow morning with which to keep their dear tongues going. May we be favoured with very few of these irritating beings. May those that come among us always be those that can say, 'peace be to thine helpers'.

FOR MEDITATION: Whispering and gossiping, whether in the world (Romans 1:28–31) or in the church (2 Corinthians 12:20) are spoken of in the same breath as other evils. The Christian is supposed to rise above all this (Ephesians 4:31). Any charge against another requires the evidence of witnesses (Matthew 18:16; 2 Corinthians 13:1; 1 Timothy 5:19).

SERMON NO. 1770

18 FEBRUARY (1883)

'Herein is love'

'Herein is love, not that we loved God, but that he loved us, and sent his Son to be the propitiation for our sins. Beloved, if God so loved us, we ought also to love one another.' 1 John 4:10–11
SUGGESTED FURTHER READING: Psalm 89:1–8

Our love to God, even when it does exist, and even when it influences our lives, is not worthy to be mentioned as a fountain of supply for love. The apostle points us away from it to something far more vast, and then he cries, 'Herein is love'. I am looking for 'the springs of the sea', and you point me to a little pool amid the rocks which has been filled by the flowing tide. I am glad to see that pool: how bright! how blue! how like the sea from whence it came! But do not point to this as the source of the great water-floods; for if you do I shall smile at your childish ignorance, and point you to that great rolling ocean which tosses its waves on high. What is your little pool to the vast Atlantic? Do you point me to the love in the believer's heart, and say, 'Herein is love'? You make me smile. I know that there is love in that true heart; but who can mention it in the presence of the great rolling ocean of the love of God, without bottom and without shore? The word *not* is not only upon my lip but in my heart as I think of the two things, 'not that we loved God, but that he loved us'. What poor love ours is at its very best when compared with the 'love wherewith he loved us'! Let me use another figure. If we had to enlighten the world, a child might point us to a bright mirror reflecting the sun, and he might cry, 'Herein is light!' You and I would say, 'Poor child, that is but borrowed brightness; the light is not there, but yonder, in the sun.' The love of saints is nothing more than the reflection of the love of God. We *have* love, but God *is* love.

FOR MEDITATION: (*Our Own Hymn Book* no. 803 v.5—William Williams, 1772)
    'Love to miserable sinners,
    Love unfathomed, love to death,
    Was the only end and motive,
    To resign His gracious breath.'

19 FEBRUARY (1882)

Our Lord before Herod

'When Herod saw Jesus, he was exceeding glad: for he was desirous to see him of a long season, because he had heard many things of him; and he hoped to have seen some miracle done by him. Then he questioned with him in many words; but he answered him nothing.' Luke 23:8–9
SUGGESTED FURTHER READING: Jeremiah 11:1–17

Herod had already silenced the Voice, and no marvel that he could not hear the Word. For what was John? He said, 'I am the voice of one crying in the wilderness'. What was Jesus but the Word? He that silences the Voice may well be denied the Word. Had not Herod's shallow soul been moved to its depths, such depths as they were? Had he not been admonished by one of the greatest of the children of men? 'Among them that are born of women there' had not then been 'a greater than John the Baptist'. Had not a burning and shining light shone right into his very eyes? And if he refused to hear the greatest of the sons of men, and to see the brightest light that God had then kindled, it was only right that the Saviour should refuse him even a ray of light, and let him perish in the darkness which he had himself created. You cannot trifle with religious impressions with impunity. God thinks it no trifle. He who has once been moved in his soul and has put away the heavenly word from him, may fear that it will be said of him, 'My Spirit shall not always strive with man'. 'Ephraim is joined to idols: let him alone.' May not some conscience here, if it has but a little life in it, be alarmed at the memory of former rejections of the gospel, frequent quenchings of the Spirit, repeated tramplings upon the blood of Jesus? If God never speaks to you again in the way of mercy, you have no right to expect that he should do so; and if from this day to the day of judgment the Lord should never give you another word of mercy, who shall say that you have been treated harshly? Have you not deserved it at his hands as Herod had done?

FOR MEDITATION: The sin of silencing the voice that had spoken to Herod (Mark 6:20,27) began when he stopped John preaching to others (Luke 3:18–20). Jesus warned those who tried this (Matthew 23:13; Luke 11:52); the Jews who did learnt that, if they would not listen to God, he would divert his messengers to others who would (Acts 13:44–49; 18:5–6). When we hear God's voice, we must not harden our hearts (Hebrews 3:7–11).

SERMON NO. 1645

20 FEBRUARY (1881)

The heroic in Christianity

'*For if ye love them which love you, what thank have ye? For sinners also love those that love them. And if ye do good to them which do good to you, what thank have ye? For sinners also do even the same. And if ye lend to them of whom ye hope to receive, what thank have ye? For sinners also lend to sinners, to receive as much again.*' Luke 6:32–34
SUGGESTED FURTHER READING: Luke 22:31–62

He went into Gethsemane, and there he knelt and prayed for you and me until he was covered with a gory sweat, and great drops of blood followed each other to the ground. Is there any pain that we would not face, is there any reproach we could not bear after this for his dear sake? Does that not rouse you? Will you after this be proud and claim honour of your brethren, and grow angry if it be refused? Come with me once again, for he goes to the cross, and there he hangs. It is your Lord, remember! See, the iron passes through his hand: it is your Lord who is thus maimed! The nails tear through his feet, the feet of your Lord! He wears a diadem as monarch, but it is a coronet of thorns: it is your Lord who is thus crowned! He wears crimson, too; but it is his own blood; and he is your own Lord! He has not a rag else, for they have stripped him, yes, stripped and scourged your Lord! And they are hissing at him, jesting at his prayers, and scoffing at his cries—all this at your Lord! And what of you? The other day you were ashamed to own that you were his disciple. Are you not disgusted at such cowardice? You were silent the other day when sinners were blaspheming him: you were niggardly when his poor people needed help; you refused to give when his church and his cause knocked at your door. You would not forgive a fellow Christian the other day, and you parted company with one who had been your friend for years, and all for a hot word; and yet you call yourself a Christian! Yes, and I, too, am a Christian, and have my own private cause for self-humiliation; and that is our Master bleeding there. How can we bear to look him in the face? What sorry disciples we are!

FOR MEDITATION: (*Our Own Hymn Book* no. 263 v.2—John Hampden Gurney, 1851)
   'Help us, through good report and ill, our daily cross to bear;
   Like Thee, to do our Father's will, our brethren's griefs to share.'

SERMON NO. 1584

21 FEBRUARY (PREACHED 17 FEBRUARY 1884)

A waiting God and a waiting people

'And therefore will the LORD *wait, that he may be gracious unto you, and therefore will he be exalted, that he may have mercy upon you: for the* LORD *is a God of judgment: blessed are all they that wait for him.'*
Isaiah 30:18
SUGGESTED FURTHER READING: James 5:7–11

Frequently we may have to wait for temporal blessings. It may not be safe for us to obtain the desire of our heart, because our heart is as yet too much occupied with the world and the things thereof. We may have to wait for deliverance from trouble, for as yet the furnace may not have accomplished its refining work. You may be ill, and you may pray God to make you well, but he may still allow his beloved to be sick; to you sickness may be healthier than health. You are very poor, and you would like to struggle out of abject poverty. By all means struggle on; but do not murmur if you should not be successful; poverty may be a richer state for you than wealth. There may be somewhat in your character which cannot be perfected except by suffering and labour; and it is better that your character be perfected than your substance increased. None of us can come to the highest maturity without enduring the summer heat of trials. As the sycamore fig never ripens if it is not bruised, as the corn does not leave the husk without threshing, and as wheat makes no fine flour till it be ground, so are we of little use till we are afflicted. Why should we be so eager to escape such benefits? We shall have to wait with patience, saying, 'The will of the Lord be done.' He waited to give grace to us, let us wait to give glory to him. Brother, wait cheerfully. If God sees fit to say, 'Wait,' do not be angry with him. Why give way to hurry and worry? O rest in the Lord. Your strength is to sit still. One of the most lovely flowers of the new creation is entire submission to the divine will.

FOR MEDITATION: The partners of patience are rest in God (Psalm 37:7), comfort in the scriptures (Romans 15:4), consolation (Romans 15:5), hope (1 Thessalonians 1:3) and faith (2 Thessalonians 1:4; Hebrews 6:12). The products of patience include experience (Romans 5:4) and inheriting God's promises (Hebrews 6:12; 10:36). Read David's testimony (Psalm 40:1–3).

SERMON NO. 1766

22 FEBRUARY (1880)

Your personal salvation

'*Receiving the end of your faith, even the salvation of your souls. Of which salvation the prophets have enquired and searched diligently, who prophesied of the grace that should come unto you.*' 1 Peter 1:9–10
'*Let thy mercies come also unto me, O* LORD, *even thy salvation, according to thy word.*' Psalm 119:41
SUGGESTED FURTHER READING: Psalm 25:1–22

Tell out your case in all its terrible truthfulness. Say, 'O Lord, I feel that nobody in all this world needs thy mercy more than I do: let my need plead with thee; give me thy salvation. I am no impostor; I am a sinner: let thy mercy and thy truth visit me in very deed.' Your soul's wounds are not such as sham beggars make with chemicals: they are real sores; plead them with the God of all grace. Your poverty is not that which wears rags abroad and fine linen at home; you are utterly bankrupt, and this you may urge before the Lord as a reason for his mercy. Next plead this: 'Lord, thou knowest, and thou hast made me to know somewhat of what will become of me if thy mercy does not come to me: I must perish; I must perish miserably. I have heard the gospel, and have neglected it; I have been a Sabbath breaker, even when I thought I was a Sabbath keeper; I have been a despiser of Christ, even when I stood up and sang his praises, for I sang them with a hypocrite's lips. The hottest place in hell will surely be mine unless thy mercy comes to me. Oh, send that mercy, now.' This is good and prevalent pleading: hold on to it. Then plead, 'If thy mercy shall come to me it will be a great wonder, Lord. I have not the confidence to do more than faintly hope it may come; but, oh, if thou dost ever blot out my sin I will tell the world of it; I will tell the angels of it: through eternity I will sing thy praises, and claim to be of all the saved ones the most remarkable instance of what thy sovereign grace can do.' Do you feel like that?

FOR MEDITATION: Have you experienced God's mercy, the removal of his anger, which you deserve on account of your sin? The reception of God's mercy can only follow confessing to him your sin (Psalm 51:1–2; Proverbs 28:13; Luke 18:13–14) and should then be followed by confessing to others your salvation (1 Timothy 1:16; 1 Peter 2:9–10).

23 FEBRUARY (UNDATED SERMON 1882)

My solace in my affliction

'*For ever, O* LORD, *thy word is settled in heaven. Thy faithfulness is unto all generations: thou hast established the earth, and it abideth. They continue this day according to thine ordinances: for all are thy servants. Unless thy law had been my delights, I should then have perished in mine affliction.*' Psalm 119:89–92

SUGGESTED FURTHER READING (Spurgeon): Psalm 143:1–12

'Unless', said the Psalmist, 'thy law had been my delights, I should then have perished in mine affliction.' We know by experience what he means. The trouble is a thing of the past, but the trembling is still present to our memory. We were mercifully delivered when we might have been utterly destroyed. My brethren, that same word which has made the earth to keep its place has hitherto been sufficient to make you keep your place. Some of you have passed through deep waters, and yet you have not been drowned. I have a sympathy with young people when they are doubting, because they have not seen the mighty works of which their fathers have told them; but if you have been sustained for forty years in the wilderness you ought to know the faithfulness of God, and I am ashamed of you when you get disheartened, and discourage your brethren. Most of all, I am ashamed of myself whenever I fall into despondency. Admiral Drake had been round the world. He had survived all sorts of storms and battles. One day, when coming up the Thames, he was caught in such an ugly wind that he was likely to be wrecked, and the admiral cried, 'No, no, I have been round the world, and I do not intend to be drowned in a ditch.' I want you to be animated by a like courage, for the Lord will not leave you. Surely he who has preserved you in all your previous distresses will not desert you in your present adversities. If you had not taken delight in God's word, you would long ago have perished in your affliction; look back upon the past, then, and see that God has been sufficient for you up till now. What reason have you for the suspicion that he will not befriend you even to the end?

FOR MEDITATION: (*Our Own Hymn Book* no. 670 v.2—Isaac Watts, 1709)
   'Jesus, my God! I know His name, His name is all my trust;
   Nor will He put my soul to shame, nor let my hope be lost.'

SERMON NO. 1656

24 FEBRUARY (PREACHED 26 FEBRUARY 1882)

My hourly prayer

'Hold thou me up, and I shall be safe: and I will have respect unto thy statutes continually.' Psalm 119:117
SUGGESTED FURTHER READING: Deuteronomy 33:26–29

'Hold thou me up'. Every morning before you see the face of men, register this prayer in heaven, 'Hold thou me up, and I shall be safe: and I will have respect unto thy statutes continually.' Are you going downstairs without that prayer? Then you may fall into sin at the breakfast table. You may lose your temper, and a trifle not worth noticing may put you off the tram lines for the day. Therefore pray before the car moves. You have taken your hat and your gloves, and you are going off to the City. Does it happen that there you meet careless, godless men? Are you tempted there? Then as you get into your train, or as you trudge along the pavement, breathe the prayer, 'Hold thou me up, and I shall be safe'. You can meet the worst of men without fear. You have your shield on your arm, and the two-edged sword of God at your side. You are prepared for all hazards now that the upholding prayer has been breathed before the Most High. Did you say that you are not going to the City today? It is a day's excursion, is it? You are going into the country to see friends, or you are to make holiday with a few companions? All well and good. You may have such recreations very properly; but now is a special time for the prayer, 'Hold thou me up'. Your friends will not all be saints, probably, and when they go a little way in mirth perhaps they will run a little too far. Therefore, now entreat the Keeper of Israel, 'Hold thou me up, and I shall be safe', safe at my play as well as at my work. The child of God in his recreation should prove that he has undergone a re-creation, which has made him a new creature in Christ Jesus. Grace should enter into all our enjoyments as well as into all our employments.

FOR MEDITATION: (*Our Own Hymn Book* no. 626 v.3—Josiah Conder, 1836)
    'Lord! uphold me day by day;
    Shed a light upon my way;
    Guide me through perplexing snares;
    Care for me in all my cares.'

SERMON NO. 1657

25 FEBRUARY (1883)

The Holy Spirit's threefold conviction of men

'*And when he is come, he will reprove the world of sin, and of righteousness, and of judgment: of sin, because they believe not on me; of righteousness, because I go to my Father, and ye see me no more; of judgment, because the prince of this world is judged.*' John 16:8-11

SUGGESTED FURTHER READING: Ephesians 5:3-14

Here we see as in a map the work of the Spirit upon the hearts of those who are ordained unto eternal life. Those three effects are all necessary, and each one is in the highest degree important to true conversion. First, the Holy Spirit 'is come' to convince men of sin. It is absolutely necessary that men should be convinced of sin. The fashionable theology is, 'Convince men of the goodness of God: show them the universal fatherhood and assure them of unlimited mercy. Win them by God's love, but never mention his wrath against sin, or the need of an atonement, or the possibility of there being a place of punishment. Do not censure poor creatures for their failings. Do not judge and condemn. Do not search the heart or lead men to be low-spirited and sorrowful. Comfort and encourage, but never accuse and threaten.' Yes, that is the way of man; but the way of the Spirit of God is very different. He comes on purpose to convince men of sin, to make them feel that they are guilty, greatly guilty, so guilty that they are lost, ruined and undone. He comes to remind them not only of God's loveliness, but of their own unloveliness, of their own enmity and hatred to this God of love, and, consequently, of their terrible sin in thus ill-using one so infinitely kind. The Holy Spirit does not come to make sinners comfortable in their sins, but to cause them to grieve over their sins. He does not help them to forget their sin, or think little of it, but he comes to convince them of the horrible enormity of their iniquity. It is no work of the Spirit to pipe to men's dancing: he does not bring forth flute, harp, dulcimer, and all kinds of music to charm the unbelieving into a good opinion of themselves; but he comes to make sin appear sin, and to let us see its fearful consequences. He comes to wound so that no human balm can heal: to kill so that no earthly power can make us live.

FOR MEDITATION: (*Our Own Hymn Book* no. 544 v.3—Joseph Hart, 1759)
  'We all have sinned against our God, exception none can boast;
  But he that feels the heaviest load will prize forgiveness most.'

SERMON NO. 1708

26 FEBRUARY (1882)

The dream of Pilate's wife

'When he was set down on the judgment seat, his wife sent unto him, saying, Have thou nothing to do with that just man: for I have suffered many things this day in a dream because of him.' Matthew 27:19

SUGGESTED FURTHER READING: Jeremiah 44:1–30

Am I addressing any who are purposing to do some very sinful thing, but have lately received a warning from God? The warning is not put to you in some mysterious and obscure way, but it comes point blank to you in unmistakable terms. God has sent conscience to you, and he has enlightened that conscience, so that it speaks very plain English to you. This morning's discourse stops you on the highway of sin, puts its pistol to your ear, and demands that you 'Stand and deliver.' Stir an inch, and it will be at your own soul's peril. Do you hear me? Will you regard the heaven-sent expostulation? Oh, that you would stand still awhile and hear what God shall speak while he bids you yield yourself to Christ today. It may be now or never with you, as it was with Pilate that day. He had the evil thing which he was about to do fully described to him, and therefore if he ventured on it, his presumption would be great. His wife had not said, 'Have nothing to do with that man', but 'with that just man', and that word rang in his ears, and again and again repeated itself till he repeated it too. Read the twenty-fourth verse. When he was washing his wicked hands he said, 'I am innocent of the blood of this just person', the very name his wife had given to our Lord. The arrows stuck in him! He could not shake them off! Like a wild beast, he had the javelin sticking in his side, and though he rushed into the forest of his sin, it was evidently rankling in him still—'that just man' haunted him. Sometimes God makes a man see sin as sin, and makes him see the blackness of it; and if he then perseveres in it, he becomes doubly guilty, and pulls down upon himself a doom intolerable beyond that of Sodom of old.

FOR MEDITATION: Examine the sad behaviour of some who neglected warnings and insisted on going their own way (Genesis 4:6–8; 2 Samuel 18:10–15; 2 Chronicles 26:16–19; Jeremiah 36:21–25), the strange behaviour of one who was double-minded (Numbers 22:12–22) and the sensible behaviour of those who were prepared to take notice (Genesis 20:3–9; 31:22–29; 1 Samuel 25:21–35; Acts 5:33–40).

SERMON NO. 1647

27 FEBRUARY (1881)

Holy longings

'*My soul breaketh for the longing that it hath unto thy judgments at all times.*' Psalm 119:20
SUGGESTED FURTHER READING: 2 Chronicles 34:1–33

The longings of a man are a pretty sure index of what he will be: they cannot create capacity, but they develop it; they lead to the use of means for its increase, and they make the mind keen to seize on opportunities. By some means or other a man usually becomes what he intensely longs to be, especially if those desires are formed in early youth while yet the world is all before him where to choose. Hence our proverb: 'The child is father to the man.' Even in little children tastes and pursuits have been prophetic—the young artist sketches his sister in the cradle, the youthful engineer is busy with his boyish inventions. If his longings deepen, strengthen, and become vehement with the increase of his years, the young man's character is being surely moulded from within, and this is often a greater force than that of circumstances acting from without. Thus is it in spiritual things: we may form forecasts as to what we shall be from our burning and pressing desires. Desires are the buds out of which words and deeds will ultimately be developed. Spiritual desires are the shadows of coming blessings. What God intends to give us he first sets us longing for. Hence the wonderful efficacy of prayer, because prayer is the embodiment of a longing inspired of God because he intends to bestow the blessing. What are your longings, then, my hearer? Do you long to be holy? The Lord will make you holy. Do you long to conquer sin? You shall overcome it by faith in Jesus. Are you pining after fellowship with Christ? He will come and make his abode with you. Does your soul thirst, even pant after God as 'the hart ... after the water brooks'? Then you shall be filled with all his fullness; for all these longings are prophetic of that which is to be, even as the snowdrop, crocus and anemone foretell the approach of spring.

FOR MEDITATION: (*Our Own Hymn Book* no. 119 song 6 v.3—Isaac Watts, 1719)

'How would I run in Thy commands, if Thou my heart discharge
From sin and Satan's hateful chains, and set my feet at large!'

28 FEBRUARY (UNDATED—probably August 1880 during move)

The singing pilgrim

'Thy statutes have been my songs in the house of my pilgrimage.' Psalm 119:54
SUGGESTED FURTHER READING: Deuteronomy 6:1–9

The Bible is a wonderful book. It serves a thousand purposes in the household of God. I recollect a book my father used to have, entitled 'Family Medicine', which was consulted when any of us fell sick with juvenile diseases. The Bible is our book of family medicine. In some houses, the book they most consult is a 'Household Guide.' The Bible is the best guide for all families. This Book may be consulted in every case, and its oracle will never mislead. You can use it at funerals. There are no such words as those which Paul has written concerning the resurrection of the dead. You can use it for marriages—where else can you find such holy advice to a wedded pair? You can use it for birthdays. You can use it for a lamp at night. You can use it for a screen by day. It is a universal Book; it is the Book of books, and has furnished material for mountains of books; it is made of what I call bibline, or the essence of books. I am preaching to you tonight as a man without books. I cannot get at any of my books, for they are all packed away; but I have a library here in having this one volume, which is, in fact, a number of books bound together. This one Book is enough to last a man throughout the whole of his life, however diligently he may study it. It seems that David, when he was a pilgrim, used the part which he had of this blessed Book as a songbook. It was nearly all history. What could he find to sing of there? He sang the wars and victories of the God of Israel. You and I have a bigger book than David had; can we say that, as pilgrims, we use this blessed Book for songs? Truly we ought to do so, for this is the book that started us on pilgrimage. The blessed teachings of this Book, sent home by the Holy Spirit, made us flee from the City of Destruction, and made us seek the road that leads to life eternal. We sing about this Book, for it is 'perfect, converting the soul'.

FOR MEDITATION: The Bible is relevant to every situation (2 Timothy 3:16). Recall some passages which relate to family life (Ephesians 6:1–4), funerals (1 Thessalonians 4:13–18), marriages (Ephesians 5:22–33), birthdays (Psalm 139:13–18) and to all hours (Psalm 91:5–6; 121:5–6).

SERMON NO. 1652

29 FEBRUARY (1880)

The lily among thorns

'As the lily among thorns, so is my love among the daughters.' Song of Solomon 2:2
SUGGESTED FURTHER READING (Spurgeon): Matthew 10:5–16

A true Christian knows not how to harm his fellow men. He is like the lily which stings no one, and yet he lives among those who are full of sharpness. He aims to please, and not to provoke, and yet he lives among those whose existence is a standing menace. The thorn tears and lacerates: it is all armed from its root to its topmost branch, defying all comers. But there stands the lily, smiling, not defying; charming, and not harming. Such is the real Christian, holy, harmless, full of love and gentleness and tenderness. Therein lies his excellence. The thorn pierces, but the lily soothes: the very sight of it gives pleasure. Who would not stop and turn aside to see a lily among thorns, and think he reads a promise from his God to comfort him amid distress? Such is a true Christian: he is a consolation in his family, a comfort in his neighbourhood, an ornament to his profession, and a benediction to his age. He is all tenderness and gentleness, and yet it may be he lives among the envious, the malicious, and the profane, a lily among thorns. The thorn says, 'Keep away; no one shall touch me with impunity.' The lily cries, 'I come to you; I shed my soul abroad to please you.' The sweet odours of the lily of the valley are well known; perhaps no plant has so strong a savour about it of intense and exquisite sweetness as that lily of the valley which is found in Palestine. Such is the sanctified believer. There is a secret something about him, a hallowed savour which goes out from his life, so that his graciousness is discovered; for grace, like its Lord, 'cannot be hid.' Even if the regenerate man is not known as a professor, yet does he reveal himself by the holiness of his life: 'thy speech bewrayeth thee.'

FOR MEDITATION: A true Christian, living in the world amongst unbelievers, should function as salt (Matthew 5:13), light (Matthew 5:14; Philippians 2:15) and a fragrance (2 Corinthians 2:14–16). Godly behaviour will have a variety of effects (Matthew 5:16; Romans 12:18–20; 1 Peter 3:1–2, 15–16; 4:3–4) but it is bound to make some difference.

SERMON NO. 1525

1 MARCH (UNDATED SERMON)

The value and rank of the believer

'Since thou wast precious in my sight, thou hast been honourable, and I have loved thee: therefore will I give men for thee, and people for thy life.' Isaiah 43:4

SUGGESTED FURTHER READING: 2 Timothy 2:15–22

The child of God is too honourable to take what other people would take, if thereby he would stain his dignity. He may often feel it unbecoming his dignity to do that which is lawful; he may therefore choose a more excellent way. Lions will not be found stealing little bits of meat like cats, or feeding on carrion like dogs. It is not for eagles to hawk for flies and it is not for children of God to stoop below the glorious level of their new birth. 'Since thou wast precious in my sight, thou hast been honourable'. Oh, you right honourables, take care to act honourably. My brethren, we do not wish to be called 'reverend', any one of us, but God has called us honourable, and it would be a fairer title by far for us to wear. Reverence, surely, we can never claim; that belongs but to one. But if he calls us 'honourable', I venture at least to call you 'right honourable.' O you right honourables, always live as right honourables. Do not let us hear of you that you spoke in a sulk, for that is to act like a spoiled child. One of God's honourables in a passion, uttering burning words! This will never do. One of God's children doubting God, afraid to trust his heavenly Father, and trying by little tricks of trade to get on, instead of being honest! Is this a conversation such as becomes the household of faith? Is not this the reverse of what becomes us? There is one that cannot forgive his brother: is that seemly? He will not speak to his friend because of some small offence; is that honourable? Some that profess to be God's children seem to think it a poor business to be a Christian? Brethren, think not so. Have a high idea of what a Christian ought to be; and then pray the Spirit of God to raise you up to it.

FOR MEDITATION: Receiving honour from other people is nothing compared to receiving honour from God (John 5:44). God honours those who honour him (1 Samuel 2:30), who call upon him (Psalm 91:15) and who serve the Lord Jesus Christ (John 12:26). Can God honour you?

SERMON NO. 1671

2 MARCH (1882)

God's fatherly pity

'Like as a father pitieth his children, so the LORD *pitieth them that fear him.'* Psalm 103:13

SUGGESTED FURTHER READING: Isaiah 63:7–16

In the former part of this psalm the Psalmist sang of God's deeds of love, his gifts, his benefits, and his acts of kindness; but here he goes deeper into the divine motive, and hence he finds sweeter incentives to devout gratitude. There is a fullness of consolation in the fact that the heart of God is towards his people. He not only dispenses blessings—so does the sun, so do the clouds, so do the fruitful fields—but he takes a warm interest in our welfare, and has a feeling towards us of kindly, gentle affection, and that of such intensity that one of the highest forms of earthly love is here used as a figure to set forth the tender mercy of our God towards us. I have always been taught as a principle in theology that God has no griefs—that he is 'without parts or passions' I think was the definition; but I have often inwardly objected to such statements; they seemed to me so inconsistent with the tone and tenor of Scripture; for he appears to take pleasure in his people, and to be 'grieved' with their ill-manners. Surely, metaphors that are inspired must have a meaning that is instructive. If the Father's 'bowels are troubled', if our Lord and Saviour is 'moved with compassion', and if the Holy Spirit is 'vexed', there must be something analogous to what we call emotion among ourselves in the acknowledged attributes of the Most High. At least he appears to sympathize with his people, so that 'in all their affliction he was afflicted,' and he pities us 'as a father pitieth his children.'

FOR MEDITATION: Scripture warns of the danger of grieving God the Father (Genesis 6:6; Psalm 78:40; Hebrews 3:10,17), God the Son (Mark 3:5), and God the Holy Spirit (Ephesians 4:30). Wouldn't you rather have God rejoicing over you instead (Deuteronomy 30:9–10; Isaiah 62:5; Jeremiah 32:41; Zephaniah 3:17; Luke 10:21)?

SERMON NO. 1650

3 MARCH (1881)

The believer's deathday better than his birthday

'A good name is better than precious ointment; and the day of death than the day of one's birth.' Ecclesiastes 7:1
SUGGESTED FURTHER READING: Philippians 1:19–26

'Better is the end of a thing than the beginning thereof'. When we are born we begin life, but what will that life be? Friends say, 'Welcome, little stranger.' Ah, but what kind of reception will the stranger get when he is no longer a newcomer? Very likely he is not long in the world before he begins to feel the poverty of his parents, and perhaps the misery of an unholy home. A troop of infantile diseases are waiting around him; and the little candle that is newly lit is in great danger of being blown out. Infancy is a very dangerous passage for a tiny boat unfitted to bear rough buffetings. Those first few years are full of rocks and quicksands, and many scarce begin life before they end it. He who is newly born and is ordained to endure through a long life is like a warrior who puts on his harness for battle; and is not he in a better case who puts it off because he has won the victory? Ask any soldier which he likes best, the first shot in the battle or the sound which means 'Cease firing, for the victory is won.' The soldier does not deliberate a moment; there is no room for question. Since the day of a believer's death is his time of triumph and of victory, it is better than the day of the first shot, the day of one's birth. When we were born we set out on our journey, but when we die we end our weary march in the Father's house above. Surely it is better to have come to the end of the tiresome pilgrimage than to have commenced it. We wave the handkerchief, and bid goodbye to those who start upon a long voyage, and it is fitting that they should be made as cheerful as they can be; but, surely, it is a better day when at last they reach their port, all danger over, and come to their desired haven. So, then, it is better to die than to begin to live, if we are indeed the Lord's people.

FOR MEDITATION: (*Our Own Hymn Book* no. 828 v.1—From the French; George W. Bethune, 1847)
 'It is not death to die,
 To leave this weary road,
 And, 'midst the brotherhood on high,
 To be at home with God.'

SERMON NO. 1588

4 MARCH (1883)

The best war-cry

'The LORD *his God is with him, and the shout of a king is among them.'*
Numbers 23:21
SUGGESTED FURTHER READING: Psalm 46:1–11

There is no worship like that which proceeds from a man when he feels the Lord is here. What a hush comes over the soul! Here is the place for the bated breath, the unsandalled foot, and the prostrate spirit. Now are we on holy ground. When the Lord descends in the majesty of his infinite love to deal with the hearts of men, then it is with us as it was in Solomon's temple when the priests could not stand to minister by reason of the glory that filled the place. Man is set aside, for God is there. In such a case the most fluent think it better to be silent; for there is at times more expressiveness in absolute silence than in the fittest words. 'How dreadful is this place! this is none other but the house of God, and this is the gate of heaven.' Why? Because Jacob had said, 'Surely the LORD is in this place.' We regard the lowliest assemblies of the most illiterate people with solemn reverence if God is there: we regard the largest assemblies of the wealthiest and most renowned with utter indifference if God is not there. This is the one necessity of the church: the Lord God must be in the midst of her, or she is nothing. If God be there, peace will be within her walls and prosperity within her palaces; but if the Lord is not there woe unto the men that speak in his name, for they shall cry in bitterness, 'Who hath believed our report?' Woe unto the waiting people, for they shall go away empty! Woe unto the sinners in a forsaken Zion; for them comes no salvation! The presence of God makes the Church to be a joyful, happy, solemn place: this brings glory to his name and peace to his people; but without it all faces are pale, all hearts are heavy.

FOR MEDITATION: (*Our Own Hymn Book* no. 907 v.2—Isaac Watts, 1709)
'The King Himself comes near,
And feasts His saints to-day;
Here may we sit and see Him here,
And love, and praise, and pray.'

SERMON NO. 1709

5 MARCH (1882)

Pilate and ourselves guilty of the Saviour's death

'*When Pilate saw that he could prevail nothing, but that rather a tumult was made, he took water, and washed his hands before the multitude, saying, I am innocent of the blood of this just person: see ye to it. Then answered all the people, and said, His blood be on us, and on our children.*' Matthew 27:24–25
SUGGESTED FURTHER READING (Spurgeon): John 19:1–16

Some of us have sincerely and intelligently pleaded guilty of the death of our Lord Jesus Christ. We know that he not only suffered for our transgressions, but by our iniquities. This is not clear to a great many; and I would not have them pretend that it is. They cannot see that they have anything to do with the matter of Jesus' death, and therefore they are not moved to repentance by hearing thereof; indeed, they imitate the example of Pilate in our text, when he took water and washed his hands before the multitude, and said, 'I am innocent of the blood of this just person.' We aim to arouse slumbering consciences. Without going into any questions as to whether such a man did or did not actually have a share in the particular action by which Jesus died, I maintain that in many ways men practically commit a like crime, and so prove that they have similar dispositions to those ancient Kill-Christs. Though they repudiate the crucifixion, they repeat it, if not in form, yet in spirit. Though Jesus is not here in flesh and blood, yet the cause of holiness and truth and his divine Spirit are still among us, and men act towards the kingdom of Christ, which is set up among them, in the same way as the Jews and Romans acted towards the incarnate God. True, all men are not alike inveterate against him, for the Lord spoke of some who have 'the greater sin'; and few are as guilty as the traitor Judas, that son of perdition; but in every form of it the rejection of Christ is a great sin, and it will be a great gospel blessing if it be repented of after the fashion of the prophet when he said, 'they shall look upon me whom they have pierced, and they shall mourn for him, as one mourneth for his only son, and shall be in bitterness for him, as one that is in bitterness for his firstborn.'

FOR MEDITATION: (*Our Own Hymn Book* no. 581 v.4—Isaac Watts, 1709)
"'Twas you, my sins, my cruel sins, His chief tormentors were;
Each of my crimes became a nail, and unbelief the spear.'

SERMON NO. 1648

6 MARCH (1881)

Jesus at a stand

'And Jesus stood still.' Mark 10:49
SUGGESTED FURTHER READING: Matthew 9:10–31

'Son of David, have mercy'. If you ask our Lord for anything on the ground of merit, you will find him deaf as a stone: if you think yourself a very good body, deserving favour at his hands, he will pass on and never regard you, for he has 'not come to call the righteous, but sinners to repentance.' Change that plea for a better, for when your prayer is for mercy you will touch the Saviour's heart directly, and mercy shall be yours. The proud man prays, and he thinks his eloquent prayer must prevail, but the winds carry away his supplications; the humble man does no more than smite on his breast and say, 'God be merciful to me a sinner', and that cry for mercy wins the day. When the messenger of mercy was travelling through the world he asked himself at what inn he should alight and spend the night. Lions and Eagles were not to his mind, and he passed by houses wearing such warlike names; so, too, he passed by places known by the sign of 'The Waving Plume' and 'The Conquering Hero', for he knew that there was no room for him in these inns. He hastened by many a hostelry and tarried not, till at last he came to a little inn which bore the sign of 'The Broken Heart'. 'Here,' said mercy's messenger, 'I would stay, for I know by experience that I shall be welcome here.' 'A broken and a contrite heart, O God, thou wilt not despise.' Now, beloved friends, if you plead for mercy, being deeply conscious that nothing but the grace of God can save you, even though you cannot put pretty words together or offer a long prayer, you shall prevail with God. You need not be an orator in order to be mighty in pleading with the Lord. Only appeal on the ground of free grace and dying love and Jesus will stand still and listen to you.

FOR MEDITATION: (*Our Own Hymn Book* no. 598 v.1—Henry Francis Lyte, 1833)
> 'When at Thy footstool, Lord, I bend,
> And plead with Thee for mercy there,
> Think of the sinner's dying Friend,
> And for His sake receive my prayer.'

7 MARCH (1880)

The fair portrait of a saint

'*My foot hath held his steps, his way have I kept, and not declined. Neither have I gone back from the commandment of his lips; I have esteemed the words of his mouth more than my necessary food.*' Job 23:11–12

SUGGESTED FURTHER READING (Spurgeon): Psalm 119:27–35

Let us consider Job's first sentence. He says: 'My foot hath held his steps'. This expression sets forth great carefulness. He had watched every step of God, that is to say, he had been minute as to particulars, observing each precept, which he looked upon as being a footprint which the Lord had made for him to set his foot in, observing, also, each detail of the great example of his God; for in so far as God is imitable he is the great example of his people, as he says, 'Be ye holy; for I am holy': and again, 'Be ye therefore perfect, even as your Father which is in heaven is perfect.' Job had observed the steps of God's justice, that he might be just, the steps of God's mercy, that he might be pitiful and compassionate, the steps of God's bounty, that he might never be guilty of churlishness or want of liberality, and the steps of God's truth, that he might never deceive. He had watched God's steps of forgiveness, that he might forgive his adversaries, and God's steps of benevolence, that he might also do good and communicate, according to his ability, to all that were in need. In consequence of this he became 'eyes to the blind, and feet ... to the lame'; he 'delivered the poor that cried, and the fatherless, and him that had none to help him. The blessing of him that was ready to perish came upon' him, and he 'caused the widow's heart to sing for joy.' 'My foot', he says, 'hath held his steps': he means that he had laboured to be exact in his obedience towards God, and in his imitation of the divine character. Beloved, we shall do well if we are to the minutest point hourly observant of the precepts and example of God in all things. We must follow not only the right road, but his footprints in that road.

FOR MEDITATION: 'Order my steps in thy word' (Psalm 119:133). In addition to the word of God being a lamp to our feet and a light to our path (Psalm 119:105), the recorded behaviour of the Lord Jesus Christ provides the Christian with footprints in which to follow (1 Peter 2:21).

SERMON NO. 1526

8 MARCH (UNDATED SERMON)

A hasty expression penitently retracted

'I said in my haste, I am cut off from before thine eyes: nevertheless thou heardest the voice of my supplications when I cried unto thee.' Psalm 31:22

SUGGESTED FURTHER READING: 1 Corinthians 11:1–22

Behold a written confession, dictated by the penitent heart of David, who here withdraws the curtain from his own innermost life. I should not wonder if his experience should turn out to be very like your own, for 'As in water face answereth to face, so the heart of man to man'; this is the reason why the experience of one man is his best means of interpreting the feelings of another. Take heed, however, when you are reading the histories of the saints that you use them with prudence, for it is not all the experience of a Christian that is Christian experience. A believer may experience much not as a believer, but because his believing is failing him. Sometimes we are to regard the experiences of good men as beacons to warn us from rocks rather than as lighthouses to show us where the harbour may be. Rheumatism is a human disease, but I would not recommend a person to seek after it in order to prove his manhood. We can well do without some things which were characteristic of certain eminent men, since they did not adorn or strengthen them, but rather disfigured and weakened them. It is well to follow David, but it is better to follow David's son; for David sometimes went astray like a lost sheep, but David's son was 'that great shepherd of the sheep' whose every step it is safe for the flock to follow. Do not let us imitate David in speaking in haste, or in saying, 'I am cut off from before thine eyes'; but let us take care that we closely copy him in confessing conscious fault, as he here does, in crying to God in the hour of trouble, as he tells us he did, and in bearing witness to the exceeding goodness of God, notwithstanding our faultiness, as he here bears witness when he says, 'nevertheless thou heardest the voice of my supplications when I cried unto thee.'

FOR MEDITATION: The presence of both the flesh and the Spirit ensures that the Christian will face internal contradictions (Galatians 5:16–17). Even the greatest of saints have experienced this (Matthew 16:15–23; Romans 7:15–24). When it comes to imitating them, the bottom line must always be the example of the Lord Jesus Christ (1 Corinthians 11:1).

SERMON NO. 1589

9 MARCH (1880)

Fear not

'Fear not.' Revelation 1:17
SUGGESTED FURTHER READING: Matthew 10:16–31

My dear brothers and sisters in Christ, do not be afraid, though you are nothing but poor sheep, and you are sent out into the midst of wolves. Does it not seem as if our Lord could hardly have known what he was at when he said, 'Behold, I send you forth as sheep in the midst of wolves'? Yet he made no mistake. Just think for a minute; how many wolves are there in the world now? They have been eating up the sheep ever since they had a chance; but are there more wolves or more sheep alive at this day? Why, the wolves get fewer and fewer every day, till when a wolf comes down into the inhabited lands in France we have it reported in the paper, and we have not one animal of the kind in this country wild, though they used to abound here. The fact is that the sheep have driven out the wolves. It looked as if they would eat the sheep up, but the sheep have exterminated them. So it will be in the end with defenceless believers and raging persecutors; patient weakness will overcome passionate strength. Only be patient. You have an anvil in the shop: and you know how hard the hammer comes down on it. What does the anvil do? Why, bears it. You never saw the anvil get up and fight the hammer. Never. It stands still and takes the blows. Down comes the hammer. But now listen. How many hammers have been worn out to one anvil? The old block of iron remains where it has stood for years, ready to bear more strokes. The hammers will break, but not the anvil. Be an anvil, brother. Be the sheep, brother, still; for heavenly submission shall win the victory, and patient non-resistance shall come off more than a conqueror.

FOR MEDITATION: God's sheep should always take seriously the threat posed by spiritual wolves (Matthew 7:15; Acts 20:28–31), but this should always be done in the context of confidence in the good shepherd (John 10:11–15, 27–29).

10 MARCH (UNDATED SERMON)

Cheer up, my comrades

'And Josiah set the priests in their charges, and encouraged them to the service of the house of the LORD.' 2 Chronicles 35:2
SUGGESTED FURTHER READING: 1 Samuel 17:12–58

The smallest slight chafes those who are over-sensitive. They murmur, 'I do my best, and nobody thanks me.' You think yourself a martyr and complain that you are misrepresented. Be it so; that was your Master's lot and it is the lot of all his servants. This is a cross we must all carry, or we shall never wear the crown. Do you fancy that this is a new experience? Look at Joseph. His brethren could not bear him, and yet it was he that saved the family and fed them in time of famine. Look at David. His brothers asked why he had left the charge of the sheep to come down to the battle, suspecting that the pride of his heart had brought him among the soldiers and standards. Yet nobody could bring back Goliath's head but that young David. Take a lesson from the ruddy hero; take no notice of what your brethren say about you. Go and bring back the giant's head. A good adventure is the best answer to evil accusations. If you are serving the Master let their scandal stir you up to more self-consecration. If they cry out against you as too forward, serve the Lord with more vigour, and you will antidote the venom of their tongues. Did you enter into Christ's work in order to be honoured among men? Then retire from it, for you came with a bad motive. But if you enlisted purely to bring honour to him and to win his smile, what more do you want? Be not disheartened because you are not applauded; to be kept in the rear rank is often necessary to future eminence. If you take a man, put him in front, pat him on the back and say, 'What a great man he is', he will make a false step before long, and there will be an end of your hero; but when a man is brought forward by God, he is often one whom everybody criticises, finds fault with and declaims as an impostor, but the banter he is exposed to serves as ballast for his mind. When he has success he will not be spoiled with conceit, for the grace of God will make him bow with gratitude.

FOR MEDITATION: Premature praise and prominence can foster the pride which goes before a fall (Proverbs 16:18). Those who aspire to be church leaders must first be tested and prove themselves (1 Timothy 3:6–7,10). They are then more likely to make good progress (1 Timothy 3:13).

SERMON NO. 1513

11 MARCH (1883)

Incense and light

'And Aaron shall burn thereon sweet incense every morning: when he dresseth the lamps, he shall burn incense upon it. And when Aaron lighteth the lamps at even, he shall burn incense upon it, a perpetual incense before the LORD throughout your generations.' Exodus 30:7–8
SUGGESTED FURTHER READING (Spurgeon): Hebrews 10:11–22

The more divine knowledge you get, all things being equal, the more complete will your prayers become. 'Grow in grace, and in the knowledge of our Lord and Saviour Jesus Christ': light the lamp at the same time that you kindle the incense. For instance, when you pray, what prayer can there be without knowing God our Father? How can you pray aright to an unknown God? The more knowledge of God the more correct does prayer become. 'He that cometh to God must believe that he is, and that he is a rewarder of them that diligently seek him.' What prayer can there be apart from the knowledge of the Lord Jesus Christ? If we know nothing of him by whom we pray, how full of sins of ignorance will our prayers be! It is well also to have a deep, sensible knowledge of sin. Penitential prayers are impossible without this, and how can prayers be accepted if penitence is not mixed with our petitions? We want, at the same time that we have the knowledge of sin, to have also a knowledge of our own weakness. The man who is consciously weak prays for strength, but he who dreams that he is strong will not do so. You need to study yourselves before you pray, so as to ask for those things in which you are most deficient, and for protection against those constitutional tendencies or besetting sins to which you are most subject. The prayer of ignorance is like an arrow shot by a blind man, which is not likely to hit the mark. In proportion as petitions arise from a heart fully instructed in its own necessities they will be likely to ask for the right blessings, and to be prepared aright before the Lord. David wished his prayers to be accepted, and hence he cried, 'Let my prayer be set forth before thee as incense'.

FOR MEDITATION: 'I will pray with the understanding also' (1 Corinthians 14:15). Notice how Solomon used prayer to request and acquire understanding (1 Kings 3:9–12) and how understanding led Daniel into prayer and further understanding (Daniel 9:2–3,20–25).

SERMON NO. 1710

12 MARCH (UNDATED SERMON)

Renewing strength

'They that wait upon the LORD *shall renew their strength.'* Isaiah 40:31
SUGGESTED FURTHER READING: Acts 9:8–19

When a man wants his bodily strength renewed his purpose may be effected *by eating a good meal*. He has grown empty through hunger, and there is nothing in him; he must be filled up with substantial nourishment, and then the human engine will generate fresh force. Oh, you who are weak in spirit, come and feed upon Christ! 'They that wait upon the LORD' in that way, by feeding upon the body and blood of Christ, shall find him to be 'meat indeed', and 'drink indeed', and so they 'shall renew their strength.' Sometimes a man may renew his strength *by taking a little rest*. He has grown weak through stern labour and long fatigue, and he must be quiet, and repose till he recovers. Oh, you weary, heavy-laden ones, where is there rest for you except in the Christ of God? Oh, come to God, and rest in him, and wait patiently for him! Then shall your peace be as a river, and then shall your strength be restored speedily. We have known strength to be restored *by a bath*. A weary one has plunged himself into the cool flood, and he has risen quite another man. Oh, for a baptism into the Spirit of God! Oh, to plunge into the Godhead's deepest sea, to throw oneself into the might and majesty of God, to swim in love, upborne by grace! We have known men's strength renewed *by breathing their native air*. They have risen out of a hot atmosphere into the cool breeze of the mountain side, and the bracing breeze has made them strong again. Oh, to have the breath of the Spirit blowing upon us once again! By him we were born, by him we were quickened, by him we have been revived from former faintness, and it is by breathing his divine life that we shall be filled with life again.

FOR MEDITATION: (*Our Own Hymn Book* no. 677 v.5—Isaac Watts, 1709)
 'The saints shall mount on eagles' wings,
 And taste the promised bliss,
 Till their unwearied feet arrive
 Where perfect pleasure is.'

SERMON NO. 1756

13 MARCH (UNDATED SERMON)

The hunger-bite

'His strength shall be hunger-bitten.' Job 18:12
SUGGESTED FURTHER READING: Psalm 119:145–152

In this age we are all busy, and through being busy we are apt to neglect the soul-feeding ordinances; I mean the reading of Scripture, the hearing of the word, meditation upon it, prayer and communion with God. Some of you do not rise as soon as you might in the morning, and prayer is hurried over; and too often at eventide you are half-asleep with the many cares of the day, and prayer is offered in a slovenly way. Nor is this all, for during the day when, if you were as you should be, you would be praying without ceasing, there is this to think of, and that, and the other, and such a pressure of business that ejaculations are few. How can you pray? You did at one time get a text of Scripture in the morning and chew it all day, and you used to get much sweetness out of it, and your soul grew; but now, instead of a text of Scripture, you have pressing engagements as soon as you are out of bed. You would, now and then, steal into a mid-day prayer meeting, perhaps, or get two or three minutes alone, but you have gradually dropped that habit, and you have felt justified in doing so for 'really, time is so precious, and there is so much to do in this age of competition.' Dear friend, I am no judge for you, but let me ask you whether you are not becoming hunger-bitten through not feeding upon the word of God. Souls cannot be strong without spiritual meat any more than bodies can be well when meals are neglected. There is a good rule I have heard mothers say about children and chickens—'little and often'; and I think it is true with Christians. They want little and often during the day; not a long passage of Scripture (perhaps memory would fail), but a short passage now and a short passage then, and a little prayer here and a little prayer there. It is wonderful how souls grow in that way. Alas! I fear all this is neglected, and spiritual strength is hunger-bitten. Let us begin from this time forward to give attention to the sustenance of our souls. Let us daily feed upon the word of God, that we may grow thereby; so shall our strength no more be hunger-bitten.

FOR MEDITATION: The Psalmist knew all about the importance of the means of grace. Consider when and how often he sought God in prayer (Psalm 119:62,147,164) and in his word (Psalm 119:55,97,148).

SERMON NO. 1510

14 MARCH (1880)

'They were tempted'

'They ... were tempted.' Hebrews 11:37
SUGGESTED FURTHER READING: Deuteronomy 8:1–20

It is certain that under temptation of the more insidious kind more professed Christians have been led away than ever were frightened from the faith by racks, or torments, or fear of death. It is a very sad fact that when Queen Mary died there were people lying in prison condemned for heresy, who had some of them been great sufferers for the faith, and bold confessors of it, and yet when released they did not abide in their steadfastness. Queen Mary died and Elizabeth ascended the throne, and they obtained their liberty, but, alas, some of them, returning to the comforts of home, became altogether worldly people, and forsook the faith for which once they would have even dared to die. I have known some unhappy cases of the same kind, where people have been persecuted by their families for following Christ, and have stood up for him right manfully, so that I have felt great admiration for them for their consistent courage. I have lived to see these very individuals delivered from the yoke of bondage, able to start in life for themselves and to do exactly as they pleased, but, alas, soon after persecution ceased they have grown cold, and have forsaken the ways of God. What a strange creature is man! Lord, what a deceitful heart I have! O that thou wouldst search it and try it, lest it be so that I follow thee in stormy weather, but leave thee when the south wind blows. I think the apostle put in this clause just where we find it because more deadly to the church have been the blandishments of the world's wealth than all the ragings of her cruelty. Her stakes, her racks and her gibbets have never injured the church so much as her witcheries, her smiles, her fashions and her patronage. Yet this was borne by saints of old, for 'they ... were tempted.'

FOR MEDITATION: Which would be better and safer for the Christian—hardship with persecution or ease with man's praise? Read what the Lord Jesus Christ had to say on the subject (Luke 6:20–26).

SERMON NO. 1528

15 MARCH (UNDATED SERMON)

The sheep before the shearers

'As a sheep before her shearers is dumb, so he openeth not his mouth.' Isaiah 53:7

SUGGESTED FURTHER READING: Mark 14:53–15:5

Our Lord was dumb and opened not his mouth against his adversaries, and did not accuse one of them of cruelty or injustice. They slandered him, but he replied not; false witnesses arose, but he answered them not. He did not say, like Paul, 'God shall smite thee, thou whited wall.' I am not going to condemn Paul, but I am not going to commend him. In contrast with the Master how differently he behaves! Jesus does not let fall a word against anybody, though they are doing everything that malice can invent against him. For Pilate he even makes a half apology; 'he that delivered me unto thee hath the greater sin.' One would have thought he must have spoken when they spat in his face. Might he not have said, 'Friend, why are you doing this? For which of all my works do you insult me?' But the time for such protests was over. When they smote him on the face with the palms of their hands, it would not have been wonderful if he had said, 'Why do you smite me so?' But no, he does not speak. He brings no accusation to his Father. He had only to lift his eye to heaven, or to feel a wrathful wish, and legions of angels would have chased out the ribald soldiery; one flash of a seraph's wing and Herod would have been eaten by worms, and Pilate would have died the death he well deserved as an unjust judge. The hill of the cross might have become a volcano's mouth to swallow up the multitude who stood there jesting and jeering at him: but there was no display of power, or rather there was so great a display of power over himself that he did not use his might against his bitterest foes; he restrained Omnipotence itself with a strength which can never be measured, for his mighty love availed even to restrain divine wrath.

FOR MEDITATION: When the Lord Jesus Christ was on the cross passers-by and one of the crucified thieves challenged him to save himself (Matthew 27:39–40; Luke 23:39), the religious leaders mockingly invited God to save him (Matthew 27:41–43) and others mistakenly thought he was calling upon Elijah to save him (Matthew 27:46–49). He could have done 'exceeding abundantly above all that' they asked or thought (Matthew 26:53)! But he held his peace in order to save us (1 Peter 2:23–24).

SERMON NO. 1543

16 MARCH (1884)

Putting the hand upon the head of the sacrifice

'And he shall put his hand upon the head of the burnt offering; and it shall be accepted for him to make atonement for him. And he shall kill the bullock before the LORD.' Leviticus 1:4-5
SUGGESTED FURTHER READING: Hebrews 10:1-10

'We thus judge, that if one died for all, then were all dead.' Believer, you died there in Christ. When your substitute rendered to the law of God the penalty which it demanded, you virtually rendered it. 'The soul that sinneth, it shall die', and you have died, believer; you have paid the debt in the person of the Lord Jesus Christ whom, by the laying on of your hands, you have accepted to be your substitute. You know that story—it is a capital one, well worth telling a thousand times. In the great French war a person was drawn for a conscript, but as he could not leave his family, he paid a very heavy sum for a substitute. That substitute went to the war and was killed. After a time Napoleon called out the rest of the conscription and the man was summoned because he had been formerly drawn; but he refused to serve. He said, 'No, by my substitute I have served, and I am dead and buried: I cannot be made to serve again.' It is said that the question was carried up to the highest court, and laid before the Emperor himself, and the Emperor decided that the man's claim of exemption was a just one. He had fulfilled the conscription by a substitute; that substitute had served for life, and could not be called upon to do more; and therefore the person for whom he was the substitute could not further be summoned under that conscription. This sets forth our joy and glory; we are identified with Christ, we are crucified with him, buried with him, and in him raised to newness of life. 'I am crucified with Christ: nevertheless I live'; 'ye are dead, and your life is hid with Christ in God.'

FOR MEDITATION: (*Our Own Hymn Book* no. 555 v.3—Isaac Watts, 1706)
'My faith would lay her hand
On that dear head of Thine,
While like a penitent I stand,
And there confess my sin.'

SERMON NO. 1771

17 MARCH (PREACHED 23 MARCH 1884)

Slaying the sacrifice

'And he shall kill the bullock before the LORD.*'* Leviticus 1:5
SUGGESTED FURTHER READING (Spurgeon): Hebrews 9:11–28

Think, dear friends, of the nature of the death of Christ, and you will be helped to see how effectual it must be. It was not a death by disease, or old age, but a death of violence, well symbolized by the killing of the victim at the altar. He did not die in his bed, sleeping himself out of the world, but he was taken by wicked hands, and scourged, and spit upon, and then fastened up to die a felon's death. His was a cruel doom; human malice could scarcely have invented any method of execution more sure to create pain and anguish than death by hanging on a tree, fastened by nails driven through hands and feet. In addition to his physical pain, our Lord was sore vexed in spirit. His soul sufferings were the soul of his sufferings: he was 'exceeding sorrowful, even unto death'. Heaven refused its smile: his mind was left in darkness. To be frowned upon by God was a part of the punishment of our sin, and he was not spared that direst and bitterest woe. God himself turned away his face from him, and left him in the dark. He died a dishonourable death, a cursed death—'for it is written, Cursed is every one that hangeth on a tree.' Now, for the Son of God to die, and die in such a manner, was a marvel. Never martyr died crying that he was forsaken by his God: that desertion was the lowest depth of the Saviour's grief, and since he died thus I can well understand that he has thereby made an ample atonement for the sins of all who believe in him. Oh, great atonement of my blessed Lord, my sins are swallowed up in thee! Looking to the cross and to the pierced heart of Jesus my Lord, I am assured that if I am washed in his blood I shall be whiter than snow.

FOR MEDITATION: (*Our Own Hymn Book* no. 291 v.2—Isaac Watts, 1709)
'How dreadful was the hour
When God our wanderings laid,
And did at once His vengeance pour
Upon the Shepherd's head.'

SERMON NO. 1772

18 MARCH (1883)

A sermon to the Lord's little children

'I write unto you, little children, because your sins are forgiven you for his name's sake.' 1 John 2:12
'I have written unto you, little children, because ye know the Father.' 1 John 2:13 *(Revised Version)*
SUGGESTED FURTHER READING: Galatians 4:19–31

Observe that our text is addressed to the 'little children'. It is thought by many wise interpreters that under this term John includes the whole church of God, and that afterwards he divides that church into two companies, the fathers and the young men: those who under one aspect are all 'little children', are under another regarded as young men or fathers. There is very much to support this view in several instances in this epistle. John is evidently addressing all the saints when he speaks of them as 'My little children,' as, for instance, in 1 John 3:18 and also in the closing verse, 'Little children, keep yourselves from idols.' Surely, all the saints are included in these exhortations. There is a sense in which every Christian is still a little child, a sense in which he ought to be so, ever dependent upon the great Father, ever ready to receive the word of the Father without questioning, ever teachable, ever restful in the Father's care, and full of love to him who is his all in all. Of necessity we must ever be 'children before God' for our finite capacity is so limited that we are mere babes in knowledge in the presence of Infinite wisdom, and babes in understanding when contrasted with the great Father of spirits. We know enough to make us know that we know very little. The most advanced intellects in the church are infants compared with the Ancient of Days; 'we are but of yesterday, and know nothing': with all our experience, with all our study, with all our meditation, with all our illumination, we remain 'little children' when measured by the boundless knowledge of the Lord.

FOR MEDITATION: Spurgeon went on to study the passages in 1 John where all the recipients of the letter were called 'little children': they were discouraged from sinning (2:1), instructed about the last time (2:18), urged to abide in Christ (2:28), warned against being deceived (3:7), commanded to be genuine in their love (3:18), reminded that in God they have the victory (4:4) and forbidden to touch idolatry (5:21), otherwise they would remain naughty, fickle, straying, credulous, timid and idolizers.

19 MARCH (UNDATED SERMON)

On humbling ourselves before God

'Humble yourselves therefore under the mighty hand of God, that he may exalt you in due time.' 1 Peter 5:6
SUGGESTED FURTHER READING: Luke 5:17–32

Many years ago a certain prince visited the Spanish galleys, where a large number of convicts were confined, chained to their oars to toil on without relief. I think nearly all of them were condemned to a life sentence. Being a great prince, the King of Spain told him that he might in honour of his visit set free any one of the galley slaves he chose. He went down among them to choose his man. He said to one, 'Man, how did you come here?' He replied that false witnesses swore away his character. 'Ah!' said the prince and passed on. He went to the next, who stated that he had done something that was wrong certainly, but not very much, and that he never ought to have been condemned. 'Ah!' said the prince, and again passed on. He went the round, and found that they were all good fellows, all convicted by mistake. At last he came to one who said, 'You ask me why I came here. I am ashamed to say that I richly deserve it. I am guilty, I cannot for a moment say that I am not: and if I die at this oar, I thoroughly deserve the punishment. In fact, I think it a mercy that my life is spared.' The prince stopped and said, 'It is a pity that such a bad fellow as you should be placed amongst such a number of innocent people. I will set you free.' You smile at that; but let me make you smile again. My Lord Jesus Christ has come here at this time to set somebody free. He has come here at this time to pardon somebody's sins. You that have no sins shall have no pardon. You good people shall die in your sins. But, you guilty ones, who humble yourselves under the hand of God, my Master thinks that it is a pity that you should be among these self-righteous people. So come right away, trust your Saviour and obtain life eternal through his precious blood.

FOR MEDITATION: (*Our Own Hymn Book* no. 605 v.1—John Morrison, 1781)

    'Come, let us to the Lord our God
    With contrite hearts return;
    Our God is gracious, nor will leave
    The desolate to mourn.'

SERMON NO. 1733

20 MARCH (PREACHED 'IN THE SUMMER OF 1884')

Concerning saints

'All thy works shall praise thee, O LORD; *and thy saints shall bless thee.'*
Psalm 145:10
SUGGESTED FURTHER READING: Philippians 3:8–16

I should not think he was much of a saint who did not confess that he was somewhat of a sinner still. I should be afraid that he did not know himself, and that his standard of sainthood was not as high as it ought to be. When a man is so good that he cannot be better, I perceive that in some respects he is so bad that he could hardly be worse; for instance, in the matter of pride, he has gone some few degrees beyond Lucifer himself. When a soul is thoroughly saturated with the belief that it can be no better, it will be no better. That holy restlessness which makes a man lament his imperfections, and pine after something more Christlike, is part of the force by which we move upward towards higher degrees of spirituality and grace. Self-satisfaction is the death of progress, and at the same time the discovery of falsehood. The very power to become sanctified has departed from the man who boasts that he is so. A certain great painter had been accustomed to perform great feats with his brush, but one day, having finished a picture, he laid down his palette, and said to his wife, 'My power to paint is gone!' 'Oh,' said she, 'how is that?' 'Well,' he answered, 'up to this day I have always been dissatisfied with my productions; but the last picture I have painted perfectly satisfies me, and therefore I am certain that I shall never be able to paint anything worth looking at again.' As long as a man is dissatisfied with himself, he will be capable of great things; but when he feels that he has attained, and is perfectly satisfied, depend upon it nothing will come of him during the rest of his life. He has lost the very faculty of progress.

FOR MEDITATION: (*Our Own Hymn Book* no. 221 v.4—S-P-R-, 1777)
'Since that love had no beginning,
And shall never, never cease;
Keep, oh keep me, Lord, from sinning!
Guide me in the way of peace!
Make me walk in
All the paths of holiness.'

SERMON NO. 1796

21 MARCH (1880)

A powerful reason for coming to Christ

'A great multitude, when they had heard what great things he did, came unto him.' Mark 3:8
SUGGESTED FURTHER READING: Acts 4:1–31

The opposition of the great ones of the earth did not, after all, hinder the cause of Christ. The Pharisees, who were the leaders of religious thought, combined with the Herodians, who were the court party, to destroy Jesus; but at the very moment when their wrath had reached its highest pitch the crowd about the Saviour's person was greater than ever. Let us not, therefore, dear friends, be at all dismayed if great men and learned men, and nominally religious men, should oppose the simple gospel of Christ. All the world is not bound up in a Pharisee's phylactery, nor held in chains by a philosopher's new fancy. If some will not have our Saviour, others will: God's eternal purpose will stand, and the kingdom of his Anointed shall come. If our Lord Jesus be rejected by the great, nevertheless the common people hear him gladly. To the poor the gospel is preached, and it is his joy and his delight that out of them he still gathers a company who, though poor in this world, are rich in faith, and give glory to God. I would have you, beloved, count upon opposition, and regard it as a token of coming blessing. Dread not the black cloud; it only forecasts a shower. March may howl and bluster, and April may damp all things with its rains, but the May flowers and the autumn's harvest of varied fruits will come, and come by this very means. Go on and serve your God in the serenity of holy confidence and you shall live to see that the hand of the Lord is not to be turned back, though the kings of the earth set themselves, and the rulers take counsel together.

FOR MEDITATION: Opposition to the gospel tends to go hand in hand with new opportunities for evangelism (Acts 18:5–8; 1 Corinthians 16:8–9). Believers who endure such opposition can look forward to a bright future, but the same cannot be said for their opponents (1 Thessalonians 2:13–16; 2 Thessalonians 1:3–7).

22 MARCH (UNDATED SERMON)

Roads cleared

'Cast ye up, cast ye up, prepare the way, take up the stumblingblock out of the way of my people.' Isaiah 57:14
SUGGESTED FURTHER READING: Acts 16:16–34

What is the way, the way of salvation, the way to heaven? Jesus Christ says, 'I am the way.' He is the Son of God, and he left the glories of heaven and took upon himself our nature and lived here. In due time he took upon himself our sin, and made atonement for it, and now he has gone up into heaven, and sits at the right hand of God, even the Father, whence he will shortly come to judge the living and the dead. The way to be delivered from sin, the way to heaven, is simply to trust in Jesus Christ. God has set him forth to be a propitiation for sin, and whosoever believes in Jesus Christ has his sin put away at once, whatever he may have done. Before Christ went to heaven he said to his disciples, 'Go ye into all the world, and preach the gospel to every creature. He that believeth and is baptized shall be saved; but he that believeth not shall be damned.' This is the way of salvation which we preach, unaltered and unalterable, 'Believe on the Lord Jesus Christ, and thou shalt be saved.' In other words, trust him and you are saved. This is the entrance into the way of salvation, and this is the track of that way even to the end: trust in Christ. 'Are not good works needed?' says one. They always flow from faith in Christ. The man that would be saved from sin trusts Christ, and his nature is changed, and so he hates the sin that once he loved, and endeavours to honour the Christ who has saved him; but in the matter of our salvation, the ground and bottom of it is not our works, or tears, or prayers, but simple reliance upon the finished work of Jesus Christ. He is A and he is Z in the alphabet of grace. He is the beginning and he is the ending. 'He that believeth on the Son hath everlasting life'. 'He that believeth on him is not condemned', and never shall be, for he has 'passed from death unto life.'

FOR MEDITATION: (*Our Own Hymn Book* no. 531 v.4—Thomas Gibbons, 1769)

'That Jesus saves from sin and hell,
Is truth divinely sure;
And on this rock our faith may rest
Immovably secure.'

SERMON NO. 1579

23 MARCH (1884)

The horns of the altar

'And he said, Nay; but I will die here.' 1 Kings 2:30
SUGGESTED FURTHER READING: 1 Corinthians 10:1–12

How common it is to find, when an irreligious man is dying, that someone will say, 'Oh, he is all right; for a clergyman has been, and given him the sacrament.' I often marvel how men calling themselves the servants of God can dare thus to profane the ordinance of the Lord. Did he ever intend the blessed memorial of the Lord's Supper to be something upon which ungodly men may depend in their last hour, as if it could put away sin? I do not one half so much blame the poor ignorant and superstitious people who seek after the sacrament in their dying hours, as I do the men who ought to know better, but who pander to what is as downright a superstition as anything that ever came from the Church of Rome, or, for that matter, from the fetish worship of the most deluded African tribe. Do they conceive that grace comes to men by bits of bread and drops of wine? These things are meant to remind us of the Lord Jesus Christ, and, as far as they do that, and quicken our thoughts of him, they are useful to us; but there is no wizardry or witchcraft linked with these two emblems, so that they convey a form of grace. If you do rely upon such things, I can only say that this error is all of a piece: it is a superstition which begins with, 'In my baptism, wherein I was made a member of Christ, a child of God, and an inheritor of the kingdom of heaven'; which statement is altogether false; and then it continues the delusion by prostituting an ordinance meant for the living child of God, and giving it to the ungodly, the ignorant, and the superstitious, as though it could make them fit for entering heaven. I charge you, as before the Lord, cleanse yourselves of this superstition. There is no salvation apart from faith in the Lord Jesus Christ; and you might as well trust in your sins as in sacraments.

FOR MEDITATION: The Children of Israel in the wilderness experienced types of both baptism and the Lord's Supper, but most of them died there through God's displeasure (1 Corinthians 10:2–5). Simon the magician was baptized, but was still not right with God (Acts 8:13,18–24). Many of the Corinthians incurred God's judgment and suffered as a direct result of abusing the Lord's Supper (1 Corinthians 11:29–30). We are not to trust in sacraments, only in the sacrificial death of the Lord Jesus Christ.

SERMON NO. 1826

24 MARCH (UNDATED SERMON)

Perfect sanctification

'By the which will we are sanctified through the offering of the body of Jesus Christ once for all.' Hebrews 10:10
SUGGESTED FURTHER READING: Hebrews 7:23–28

This offering was made once, and only once. The pith of the text lies in the finishing words of it, 'through the offering of the body of Jesus Christ once for all.' Those words 'for all' are very properly put in by the translators; but you must not make a mistake as to their meaning. The text does not mean that Christ offered himself up once for all, that is, for all mankind. That may be a doctrine of Scripture, or it may not be a doctrine of Scripture, but it is not the teaching here. The passage means 'once for all' in the sense of all at once, or only once. As a man might say, 'I gave up my whole estate once for all to my creditors, and there was an end of the matter,' so here our Lord Jesus Christ is said to have offered himself up as a sacrifice once for all, that is to say, only once, and there was an end of the whole matter. His sacrifice on behalf of his people was for all the sins before he came. Think of what they all were. Ages had succeeded ages, and there had been found amongst the various generations of men criminals of the blackest dye, and crimes had been multiplied; but the prophet said in vision concerning Christ, as he looked on all the multitude, 'All we like sheep have gone astray; we have turned every one to his own way; and the LORD hath laid on him the iniquity of us all.' That was before he came. Reflect that there has been no second offering of himself ever since, and never will be, but it was once, and that once did the deed. Let your mind conceive of this; nearly two thousand years have passed since the offering, and if the prophet were to stand here tonight and look back through those eighteen hundred years and more, he would still say, 'All we like sheep have gone astray; we have turned every one to his own way; and the LORD hath laid on him the iniquity of us all.'

FOR MEDITATION: (*Our Own Hymn Book* no. 406 v.2—John Kent, 1803)
  'Shout, believer, to thy God,
  He hath once the winepress trod;
  Peace procured by blood divine,
  Cancelled all thy sins and mine.'

SERMON NO. 1527

25 MARCH (1883)

Other sheep and one flock

'*And other sheep I have, which are not of this fold: them also I must bring, and they shall hear my voice; and they shall be one fold, and one shepherd [or more correctly, one flock, and one shepherd (Spurgeon)].*' John 10:16
SUGGESTED FURTHER READING: Matthew 15:21–28

'I have much people in this city', was said to the apostle when as yet nobody was converted there. 'I have them,' says Christ though as yet they had not sought him. Our Lord Jesus has an elect redeemed people all over the world at this time, though as yet they are not called by grace. I know not where they are, nor where they are not; but for certain he has them somewhere, since still it stands true, 'other sheep I have, which are not of this fold.' This is a part of our authority for going out to find the lost sheep; for we brethren have a right to go anywhere to ask after our Master's sheep. I have no business to go hunting after other people's sheep; but if they are my Master's sheep who shall stop me going over hill or dale enquiring, 'Have you seen my Master's sheep?' If any say, 'You intrude in this land,' let the answer be, 'We are after our Master's sheep which have strayed here! Excuse our pushing further than politeness might allow; we are in haste to find a lost sheep.' This is your excuse for going into a house where you are not wanted, to try and leave your tract and speak a word for Christ: say, 'I think my Master has one of his sheep here, and I have come after it.' You have received a search-warrant from the King of kings, and therefore you have a right to enter and search after your Lord's stolen property. If men belonged to the devil we would not rob the enemy himself; but they do not belong to him; he neither made them nor bought them, and therefore we seize them in the King's name whenever we can lay hands on them.

FOR MEDITATION: The Lord Jesus Christ came to seek out his lost sheep (Matthew 15:24) and told a parable to that effect (Luke 15:3–7), but his concern for the lost sheep is so great that he expects his followers to join in the search (Matthew 9:36–10:6).

SERMON NO. 1713

26 MARCH (PREACHED 25 MARCH 1883)

Our Great Shepherd finding the sheep

'Until he find it. And when he hath found it ... And when he cometh home.' Luke 15:4–6
SUGGESTED FURTHER READING: 1 Thessalonians 3:11–4:10

The love of Jesus, the Great Shepherd, is very *practical* and active. There is a sheep lost, and the Lord regrets it; but his love does not spend itself in regrets; he arises, and goes forth 'to seek and to save that which was lost.' The love of Jesus Christ is love not in word only, but in deed and in truth. The love of Jesus is *prevenient*. He does not wait until the sheep is willing to return, or until it makes some attempt to come back; but no sooner is its lost estate known to the Shepherd than he starts off, that he may find that which was lost. The love of Jesus to the lost sheep is *pre-eminent*. He leaves the ninety-and-nine in their pasturage, and for a while forgets them, that all his heart, his eye and his strength may be given to the one that has gone astray. O sweet love of Christ, so practical, so pre-eminent, so prevenient! Let us ask for grace that we may imitate it, especially those of us who are called to be shepherds of men. Among God's people most of the saints have a charge to watch over. However little the flock may be, even if it is restricted to our own family, or to the little class that gathers about us on the Sabbath, yet we are all our brother's keeper in some measure. Let us learn the love of Christ, that we may be wise in shepherding. Let us not talk about our friends, and say we love them, but let us show it by earnest, personal, speedy endeavours to do them good. Let us not wait until we see some goodness in them, until they seek after instruction. But

> 'Oh, come, let us go and find them,
> In the paths of death they roam.'

And long before they have a thought of coming home, let us be on their track, eager to grasp them, if by any means we may save some.

FOR MEDITATION: (*Our Own Hymn Book* no. 373 v.5—Horatius Bonar, 1861)
'True lover of the lost, from heaven Thou camest down,
To pay for souls the righteous cost, and claim them for Thine own.'

27 MARCH (1881)

The barrier

'And there shall in no wise enter into it any thing that defileth, neither whatsoever worketh abomination, or maketh a lie: but they which are written in the Lamb's book of life.' Revelation 21:27
SUGGESTED FURTHER READING: Matthew 25:1–13

Suppose we should never enter there! No, start not, for the supposition will soon be a fact with many of you except you repent. Suppose we should be in the next world what some of us are now, defiled and untruthful; what remains? That is an awful text in the parable of the virgins—'and the door was shut.' You read of those who said, 'Lord, Lord, open to us', to whom he answered, 'I know you not.' You have read of them; will any one of us be among them? Will anyone of us who has a lamp, and is thought to be a virgin soul, be among the shut out ones, on whose ear shall fall the words, 'I know you not whence ye are'. You see you cannot be anywhere else but out unless you are in; and you must be shut out if you are defiled and defiling. Dear heart, this is a question I beg you to look to at once. You do not know how short a time you have left to you in which you may look into it. Some who were here but a Sabbath-day or so ago are now gone from us. Eleven deaths reported at one church-meeting among our members! We are a dying people; we shall all be gone within a very short time. I charge you by the living God, and as you are dying men and women, see to it that you are not shut out, so as to hear the fatal cry, 'Too late, too late, you cannot enter now.' There shall be no purgation in eternity, and no possible way of entering in among the perfected, for it is written, 'there shall in no wise enter into it any thing that defileth'. No crying, 'Lord! Lord!', no striving to enter in, no tears, no, not even the pangs of hell itself, shall ever purge the soul so as to make it fit to join with the holy church above, should it pass into the future state uncleansed. Shut out! shut out! May that never be true of any among us.

FOR MEDITATION: (*Our Own Hymn Book* no. 51 version 2 v.3—Isaac Watts, 1719)
   'Behold I fall before Thy face,
   My only refuge is Thy grace;
   No outward forms can make me clean;
   The leprosy lies deep within.'

28 MARCH (EASTER 1880)

Following the risen Christ

'If ye then be risen with Christ, seek those things which are above, where Christ sitteth on the right hand of God. Set your affection on things above, not on things on the earth.' Colossians 3:1–2
SUGGESTED FURTHER READING: John 20:1–26

The resurrection of Christ is commemorated frequently. There is no ordinance in Scripture of any one Lord's day in the year being set apart to commemorate the rising of Christ from the dead, for this reason, that every Lord's day is the memorial of our Lord's resurrection. Wake up any Lord's day you please, whether in the depth of winter, or in the warmth of summer, and you may sing

> 'To-day he rose and left the dead, and Satan's empire fell;
> To-day the saints his triumph spread, and all his wonders tell.'

To set apart an Easter Sunday for special memory of the resurrection is a human device, for which there is no Scriptural command, but to make every Lord's day an Easter Sunday is due to him who rose early on the first day of the week. We gather together on the first rather than upon the seventh day of the week, because redemption is even a greater work than creation, and more worthy of commemoration, and because the rest which followed creation is far outdone by that which ensues upon the completion of redemption. Like the apostles, we meet on the first day of the week, and hope that Jesus may stand in our midst, and say, 'Peace be unto you.' Our Lord has lifted the Sabbath from the old and rusted hinges whereon the law had placed it long before, and set it on the new golden hinges which his love has fashioned. He has placed our rest-day, not at the end of a week of toil, but at the beginning of the rest which 'remaineth ... to the people of God.' Every first day of the week we should meditate upon the rising of our Lord, and seek to enter into fellowship with him in his risen life.

FOR MEDITATION: (*Our Own Hymn Book* no. 306 v.1—Charles Wesley, 1739)
> '"Christ, the Lord, is risen to-day," sons of men and angels say!
> Raise your joys and triumphs high; sing, ye heavens; and earth reply.'

SERMON NO. 1530

29 MARCH (UNDATED SERMON)

'Without carefulness'

'I would have you without carefulness.' 1 Corinthians 7:32
SUGGESTED FURTHER READING: 1 Timothy 6:6–12

I wish to say a word to some whose occupations prevent their attendance at the house of God. I am not going to censure or judge any, but I will say this: whenever I hear of a young man who has a situation with a moderate salary, who is able to get out to worship, and has the whole Sabbath-day to himself, so that he can help in the Sunday-school, and perhaps in some week-evening engagements, if I hear that he is offered twice as much money in a place where he must be shut out from worship and service, I hope he will look long before he makes the bargain. If part of the Sabbath must go, and all week-night privileges must go, I would in most cases say, 'My brother, forego the temporal advantage for the sake of the spiritual.' There may be exceptions to rules, and I lay down nothing as a hard-and-fast rule, but still let this be the general guide in such matters, 'I would have you without carefulness.' If it be so that he who has less has less care, let me have less. He who has a moderate income, with small responsibility, is a richer man than he who has twice as much, with twice as much responsibility, and only half as much opportunity of serving his God. For you, Christians, the best place you can have is where you can do most for Jesus; and the worst place you can have is where you are denied Christian privileges. No amount of salary can make up to you the disadvantage of being kept from the assemblies of the saints, or can make up to your soul the loss sustained by excessive labour in the house of bondage. 'I would have you without carefulness.'

FOR MEDITATION: (*Our own Hymn Book* no. 699 v.4—Charlotte Elliott, 1834)
  'Renew my will from day to day:
  Blend it with Thine, and take away
  All that now makes it hard to say,
  "Thy will be done!"'

SERMON NO. 1692

30 MARCH (1884)

What is your life?

'For what is your life? It is even a vapour, that appeareth for a little time, and then vanisheth away.' James 4:14
SUGGESTED FURTHER READING (Spurgeon): Psalm 39:1–13

I know of nothing that is too little to slay the greatest king. It is a marvel that man lives at all. So unstable is our life that the apostle says, 'what is your life?' So frail, so fragile is it, that he does not call it a flower of the field, or the snuff of a candle, but asks, 'what is your life?' It is as if he had said, 'Is it anything? Is it not a near approach to nothing?' Have you ever noticed how David answers this question in the thirty-ninth Psalm? He says in the fifth verse of that psalm that *man is vanity*. What is vanity? It is nothing in reality; it is merely the presence of something; it is an idle dream, an empty conceit, a delusion, a make-believe. Such is man. But he says more than that: he declares that *every man* is vanity. Princes, kings, philosophers, the strongest, the healthiest, the ablest, the most virtuous—every man is vanity: among the millions of mankind none rises above this dreary state of nothingness. He says more than that: he writes—*every man at his best state is vanity*: when he is in the prime and glory of his life, when he is most healthy and vigorous, when his eye is clearest, and his muscles are firmest, he is still no better than sheer vanity. David goes even further, for thus he speaks—*'every man at his best state is altogether vanity'*, that is, he is nothing but vanity, there is nothing more enduring about him. He is gone with a puff; he spends his years as a tale that is told. Do not overlook one more emphatic word which David sets in the forefront of the sentence; *'verily'*, as if he was quite sure of it, and could not tolerate a question upon the subject— *'verily every man at his best state is altogether vanity.'*

FOR MEDITATION: (*Our Own Hymn Book* no. 39 v.2—Charles H. Spurgeon, 1866)
 'Then teach me, Lord, to know mine end, and know that I am frail;
 To heaven let all my thoughts ascend, and let not earth prevail.'
N.B. This sermon was 'suggested by the sudden death of H.R.H. the Duke of Albany' in Cannes on 28 March 1884, a few days before his thirty-first birthday. Prince Leopold was the youngest of Queen Victoria's four sons.

SERMON NO. 1773

31 MARCH (UNDATED SERMON)

The throne of God and of the Lamb

'The throne of God and of the Lamb shall be in it.' Revelation 22:3
SUGGESTED FURTHER READING: Hebrews 11:8–16

There is a text that I have been turning over in my mind for many years. I want to preach from it, but I cannot understand it clearly enough at present. I hope to preach from it one day before I go to heaven. If not, I will preach from it up there when I shall have realized its full significance. Ah! do not smile. Some opportunities we shall have in heaven to testify of Christ, for we shall make known 'unto the principalities and powers in heavenly places ... the manifold wisdom of God.' It is difficult to imagine that we ever can be able to explore the whole of the unsearchable riches of Christ. The passage I am referring to is that in which Jesus says, 'In my Father's house are many mansions: if it were not so, I would have told you. I go to prepare a place for you.' Like Thomas, I am prone to ask questions. What is there to be prepared, and in what respect does heaven as a place need to be made ready? I do not like to think of heaven as a half-built habitation, or as fully built, yet only partly furnished. What does this preparing of a place for us mean? Perhaps our Lord's going there made heaven ready, and its mansions fit for the occupation of his disciples. Heaven would hardly be a home for saints in the absence of the Saviour. As I do not know the angels, and never was acquainted with any one of them, I doubt very much whether I should feel at home in their company if Jesus were not there too. There are a few saints up yonder whom I once knew and dearly loved. But one wants to be introduced to the whole of the residents, to 'the general assembly and church of the first-born' in heaven. How can this happy familiarity be brought about? Now that Jesus is there we have a friend on high whom we have known, and who has known us, who can introduce us to all its inhabitants and acquaint us with all its joys. His presence is the light and the glory of the celestial city. My place will be prepared when I am safe in his arms.

FOR MEDITATION: (*Our Own Hymn Book* no. 373 v.6—Horatius Bonar, 1861)
   'Rest of the weary, Thou! to Thee, our rest, we come;
   In Thee to find our dwelling now, our everlasting home.'

SERMON NO. 1576

1 APRIL (1883)

Earnest expostulation

'*Or despisest thou the riches of his goodness and forbearance and longsuffering; not knowing that the goodness of God leadeth thee to repentance?*' Romans 2:4
SUGGESTED FURTHER READING: Acts 2:37–42

The apostle is intensely personal in his address. This verse is not spoken to us all in the mass, but to someone in particular. The apostle fixes his eyes upon a single person, and speaks to him as 'Thee' and 'Thou.' 'Despisest thou the riches of his goodness and forbearance and longsuffering; not knowing that the goodness of God leadeth thee to repentance?' It should ever be the intent of the preacher to convey his message to each hearer in his own separate individuality. It is always a very happy sign when a man begins to think of himself as an individual, and when the expostulations and invitations of the gospel are seen by him to be directed to himself personally. I will give nothing for that indirect, essay-like preaching which is as the sheet lightning of summer, dazzling for the moment, and flaming over a broad expanse, but altogether harmless, since no bolt is launched from it, and its ineffectual fires leave no trace behind. I will give nothing for that kind of hearing which consists in the word being heard by everybody in general, and by no one in particular. It is when the preacher can 'Thee' and 'Thou' his hearers that he is likely to do them good. When each man is made to say, 'This is for me,' then the power of God is present in the word. One personal, intentional touch of the hem of Christ's garment conveys more blessing than all the pressure of the crowd that thronged about the Master. The laying of his healing hand upon the individual who was suffering had more virtue in it than all those heavenly addresses which fell from his lips upon minds that did not receive the truth for themselves. I do pray that we may come to personal dealings with the Lord each one for himself.

FOR MEDITATION: (*Our Own Hymn Book* no. 516 v.1—Ann Beadley Hyde, 1825)
   'And canst thou, sinner, slight
   The call of love divine?
   Shall God with tenderness invite,
   And gain no thought of thine?'

SERMON NO. 1714

2 APRIL (PREACHED 9 MAY 1880)

Number two-thousand; or, Healing by the stripes of Jesus

'With his stripes we are healed.' Isaiah 53:5
SUGGESTED FURTHER READING: Colossians 2:8–15

The remedy for your sins and mine is found in the substitutionary sufferings of the Lord Jesus and in these only. These 'stripes' of the Lord Jesus Christ were on our behalf. Do you enquire, 'Is there anything for us to do, to remove the guilt of sin?' I answer: There is nothing whatever for you to do. By the stripes of Jesus we are healed. All those stripes he has endured, and left not one of them for us to bear. 'But must we not believe on him?' Yes, certainly. If I say of a certain ointment that it heals, I do not deny that you need a bandage with which to apply it to the wound. Faith is the linen which binds the plaster of Christ's reconciliation to the sore of our sin. The linen does not heal; that is the work of the ointment. So faith does not heal; that is the work of the atonement of Christ. Does an enquirer reply, 'But surely I must do something, or suffer something?' I answer: You must put nothing with Jesus Christ, or you greatly dishonour him. For your salvation, you must rely upon the wounds of Jesus Christ, and nothing else; for the text does not say, 'his stripes help to heal us', but, 'with his stripes we are healed.' 'But we must repent,' cries another. Assuredly we must, and shall, for repentance is the first sign of healing; but the stripes of Jesus heal us, and not our repentance. These stripes, when applied to the heart, work repentance in us: we hate sin because it made Jesus suffer.

FOR MEDITATION: (*Our Own Hymn Book* no. 534 v.1—Horatius Bonar, 1856)
    'Christ has done the mighty work;
    Nothing left for us to do,
    But to enter on His toil,
    Enter on His triumph too.'

Honey from a lion

'*But not as the offence, so also is the free gift. For if through the offence of one many be dead, much more the grace of God, and the gift by grace, which is by one man, Jesus Christ, hath abounded unto many.*' Romans 5:15

SUGGESTED FURTHER READING: 1 Timothy 2:1-7

All this grace comes to us through the one man, Jesus Christ. I sometimes hear people talking about a 'one man ministry.' I know what they mean, but I know also that I am saved by a one man ministry, even by one who trod 'the winepress alone; and of the people there was none with' him. I was lost by a one man ministry, when father Adam fell in Eden; but I was saved by a one man ministry, when the blessed Lord Jesus Christ bore my sin 'in his own body on the tree'. O matchless ministry of love, when the Lord from heaven came into the world and took upon himself our nature, and became in all respects human, and 'being found in fashion as a man,' was 'obedient unto death, even the death of the cross'! It is through the one man, Christ Jesus, that all the grace of God comes streaming down to all the chosen. Mercy flows to no man save through the one appointed channel, Jesus, the Son of man. Get away from Christ, and you leave the highway of God's everlasting love; pass this door, and you shall find no entrance into life. You must drink from this conduit-pipe, or you must thirst for ever, and ask in vain for a drop of water to cool your parched tongue. 'In him dwelleth all the fulness of the Godhead bodily.' All the infinite mercy of God and love of God—and God himself is love—is concentrated in the person of the well-beloved Son of the Highest, and unto him be glory for ever. Sing unto him, you angels! Chant his praise, you redeemed! For by the one man Christ Jesus the whole company of the elect have been delivered from the wrath to come, to the praise of the glory of the grace of God.

FOR MEDITATION: (*Our Own Hymn Book* no. 909 v.4—Isaac Watts, 1719)
  'Blest be the Lord, who comes to men,
  With messages of grace;
  Who comes in God His Father's name,
  To save our sinful race.'

4 APRIL (1880)

On whose side are you?

'Then Moses stood in the gate of the camp, and said, Who is on the LORD's side? Let him come unto me.' Exodus 32:26
SUGGESTED FURTHER READING: Isaiah 47:8–11

I would to God we were on the Lord's side in view of the sinful amusements which appear to have such charms for many that even Christian people go quite as far as they should in reference to them. When they had bowed before this golden calf they 'rose up to play', and very pretty play it was. It does not bear explanation. There is about the world a good deal of this 'playing.' Beware, I pray you, of every amusement which prevents your redeeming the time, or tends to pollute the mind. There are recreations of a healthy, manly, refreshing kind, but those which are of no possible service to you are unprofitable. The same spirit which made the Puritan refuse to reverence the so-called holy days and holy things of superstition led him so to reverence God and his sacred law that he would not join in the debasing amusements of the period, which were, indeed, so gross as a rule that even irreligious people would not in these times endure them. We have somewhat of the same protest to bear, and we must not flinch from it. We have better joys than the wanton and the foolish can bring to us. We say of a pastime, if this is pure and clean, if this is health-giving to the body, or restful and invigorating to the mind, we are not led by any old-fashioned whim to denounce it, and we do not denounce it: but if about it there is a taint of vice or a temptation that way, or if it be mere folly, we cannot endure it. We venture not where Jesus could not have gone. We would not go where we should be afraid to die, or should tremble to hear the trumpet announcing the coming of the Lord. Stern teaching this. Are you enough on the Lord's side to bear it? I pray God to put backbones into modern professors.

FOR MEDITATION: Worldly pleasures do a great deal of damage (Proverbs 21:17; Luke 8:14; 1 Timothy 5:6). The pleasures of sin can be enjoyed only for a season (Hebrews 11:25), but at God's right hand there are pleasures for evermore (Psalm 16:11).
   N.B. This sermon was preached at the time of a general election.

5 APRIL (PREACHED 11 MAY 1879)

Forts demolished and prisoners taken

'Casting down imaginations, and every high thing that exalteth itself against the knowledge of God, and bringing into captivity every thought to the obedience of Christ.' 2 Corinthians 10:5
SUGGESTED FURTHER READING: Isaiah 55:6–13

The text runs thus, 'bringing into captivity every thought'. The word translated 'thought' has a very broad meaning, but its best explanation is that which is placed first in the lexicon, 'everything which comes from the mind.' The mind is like a city, and when it is captured the inhabitants which swarm its streets are the thoughts, and these are taken prisoners. Look at the process, which I will rapidly describe. The gospel comes with power to the heart of a man, and he begins to fear the wrath of God and the judgment to come. See how he trembles. Christ has captured his *thoughts of self-security*. He no more says, 'Though I add drunkenness to thirst, it shall surely be well with me.' On the contrary he cries, 'I am guilty; I have broken God's law, and I am condemned.' The Lord has captured his *thoughts of self-righteousness*. This is the man who yesterday boasted in himself that he was righteous: the pure and holy law of God has come near his conscience, and he feels himself guilty, and therefore sues for mercy. Now he begins to pray, 'God be merciful to me a sinner', and it is clear that his *thoughts of independence*, his ideas that he could do without his God, are made prisoners. His *thoughts of pleasure* in alienation from the Great Father are now slain, for he desires to draw near to the Most High. See! A little hope begins to dawn; he hopes that there may be salvation for him. His *thoughts of rebellious despair* are led captive in fetters of iron. Praise the Lord! Watch him still further. The Spirit of God encourages him, and he comes to believe in Jesus: his self-trust is a prisoner. That Jesus died for sinners is a truth, which he accepts, and he casts himself upon it; his proud intellect is a captive, and he gladly bows at the Redeemer's feet.

FOR MEDITATION: (*Our Own Hymn Book* no. 515 v.7—Joseph Grigg, 1765)
  'Yet know (nor of the terms complain)
  Where Jesus comes, he comes to reign;
  To reign, and with no partial sway;
  Thoughts must be slain that disobey.'

SERMON NO. 1473

6 APRIL (1884)

God's work upon minister and convert

'*I have appeared unto thee for this purpose, to make thee a minister and a witness both of these things which thou hast seen, and of those things in the which I will appear unto thee; delivering thee from the people, and from the Gentiles, unto whom now I send thee, to open their eyes, and to turn them from darkness to light, and from the power of Satan unto God, that they may receive forgiveness of sins, and inheritance among them which are sanctified by faith that is in me.*' Acts 26:16–18

SUGGESTED FURTHER READING: Luke 8:26–39

If you want to win souls follow up this line of things. Soul-winning is generally accomplished not by argument, but by testimony. The best minister is a witness-bearer. Butler's *Analogy* is one of the most notable works in defence of revelation, and it is eminently calculated to impress the student with the truthfulness of our holy religion; but I should like to know whether there ever was a man, woman, or child truly converted to the Lord Jesus by Butler's *Analogy*. I do not think it. Nor do I depreciate the work on that account, for it has other uses which it admirably serves. This, however, I am certain of, that a little book like *The Dairyman's Daughter*, by Legh Richmond, which is not worthy for a moment to be compared with Butler's *Analogy* as a display of intellectual power, has led thousands to saving faith in the Lord Jesus. That little biography of a peasant girl, a mere nothing as to thought compared with the wonderful *Analogy*, has brought tens of thousands to the Saviour's feet, where the other has brought few, if any. What is the reason? The *Analogy* is a very clear and admirable argument, but *The Dairyman's Daughter* is a witness of what has been seen, and tasted and handled by one like ourselves. Heads are won by reasoning, but hearts are won by witness-bearing. Our lines of things should be that of David—'I will declare what he hath done for my soul.' Paul frequently repeated the story of his own conversion, for he knew of nothing more likely to convince and convert.

FOR MEDITATION: Reasoning has its place and in the course of time powers of persuasion may bear fruit (Acts 17:2–4; 18:4,19–20), but the Christian's priority is to be a witness and to give personal testimony to the truth (Luke 24:48; John 15:27; Acts 1:8; 5:32; 10:39–41; 22:15; 1 Peter 5:1; 1 John 1:2).

SERMON NO. 1774

7 APRIL (PREACHED 1 JUNE 1879)

Jesus admired in them that believe

'When he shall come to be glorified in his saints, and to be admired in all them that believe (because our testimony among you was believed) in that day.' 2 Thessalonians 1:10

SUGGESTED FURTHER READING: Jude 24–25

Perhaps the chief point in which Christ will be glorified will be the absolute perfection of all the saints. They shall then be without 'spot, or wrinkle, or any such thing'. We have not experienced what perfection is, and therefore we can hardly conceive it; our thoughts themselves are too sinful for us to get a full idea of what absolute perfection must be; but, dear brethren, we shall have no sin left in us, 'for they are without fault before the throne of God', and we shall have no remaining inclination to sin. There shall be no bias in the will towards that which is evil, but it shall be fixed for ever upon that which is good. The affections will never be wanton again; they will be chaste for Christ. The understanding will never make mistakes. You shall never 'put bitter for sweet, and sweet for bitter'; you shall be 'perfect, even as your Father which is in heaven is perfect': and truly, brethren, he who works this in us will be a wonder. Christ will be admired and adored because of this grand result. O mighty Master, with what strange moral alchemy didst thou work to turn that morose dispositioned man into a mass of love! How didst thou work to lift that selfish Mammonite up from his hoarded gains to make him find his gain in thee? How didst thou overcome that proud spirit, that fickle spirit, that lazy spirit, that lustful spirit; how didst thou contrive to take all these away? How didst thou destroy the very roots of sin, and every little rootlet of sin, out of thy redeemed, so that not a tiny fibre can be found? 'The iniquity of Israel shall be sought for ... and the sins of Judah, and they shall not be found ... saith the LORD'. Both the guilt of sin and the inclination to sin shall be gone, and Christ shall have done it, and he will be 'glorified in his saints, and ... admired in all them that believe'.

FOR MEDITATION: (*Our Own Hymn Book* no. 861 v.3—Richard Lee, 1794)
   'All the chosen of the Father,
   All for whom the Lamb was slain,
   All the church appear together,
   Washed from every sinful stain.'

SERMON NO. 1477

8 APRIL (1883)

A description of young men in Christ

'I have written unto you, young men, because ye are strong, and the word of God abideth in you, and ye have overcome the wicked one.'
1 John 2:14

SUGGESTED FURTHER READING: Ephesians 6:10–17

When a man resists Satan, he is victorious over Satan in that very resistance. Satan's empire consists in the yielding of our will to his will; but when our will revolts against him, then already we have in a measure overcome him. Albeit that sometimes we are much better at willing than we are at doing, as the Apostle Paul was; for he said, 'to will is present with me; but how to perform that which is good I find not'; yet, still, the hearty will to be clean from sin is a victory over sin; and as that will grows stronger and more determined to resist the temptations of the evil one, in that device we have overcome sin and Satan. What a blessed thing this is for us to fail not to remember, that Satan has no weapons of defence, and so, when we resist him, he must flee. A Christian man has both defensive and offensive weapons; he has a shield as well as a sword: but Satan has fiery darts, and nothing else. I never read of his having any shield whatever: so that when we resist him he is bound to run away. He has no defence for himself, and the fact of our resistance is in itself a victory. But, brothers and sisters, besides that, some of us who are young men in Christ have won many a victory over Satan. Have we not been tempted, fearfully tempted? But the mighty grace of God has come to the rescue, and we have not yielded. Cannot you look back, not with Pharisaic boasting, but with gracious exultation, over many an evil habit which once had the mastery over you, but which is master of you no longer? It was a hard conflict. How you bit your lip sometimes, and feared that you must yield! In certain moments your steps had almost gone, your feet had well-nigh slipped; but here you are conqueror yet! 'Thanks be to God, which giveth us the victory through our Lord Jesus Christ.'

FOR MEDITATION: (*Our Own Hymn Book* no. 678 v.3—Isaac Watts, 1709)
   'What though thine inward lusts rebel?
   'Tis but a struggling gasp for life;
   The weapons of victorious grace
   Shall slay thy sins, and end the strife.'

9 APRIL (EASTER 1882)

The resurrection of our Lord Jesus

'Remember that Jesus Christ of the seed of David was raised from the dead according to my gospel.' 2 Timothy 2:8
SUGGESTED FURTHER READING: Romans 6:1–11

When our Lord Jesus rose from the dead, after having died, he had fully paid the penalty that was due to justice for the sin of his people, and his new life was a life clear of penalty, free from liability. You and I are clear from the claims of the law because Jesus stood in our stead, and God will not exact payment both from us and from our Substitute: it would be contrary to justice to sue both the Surety and those for whom he stood. And now, joy upon joy, the burden of liability which once did lie upon the Substitute is removed from him also, seeing he has by the suffering of death vindicated justice and made satisfaction to the injured law. Now both the sinner and the Surety are free. This is a great joy, a joy for which to make the golden harps ring out a loftier style of music. He who took our debt has now delivered himself from it by dying on the cross. His new life, now that he has risen from the dead, is a life free from legal claim, and it is the token to us that we whom he represented are free also. Listen! 'Who shall lay any thing to the charge of God's elect? It is God that justifieth. Who is he that condemneth? It is Christ that died, yea rather, that is risen again'. It is a knockdown blow to fear when the apostle says that we cannot be condemned because Christ has died in our stead, but he puts a double force into it when he cries, 'yea rather, that is risen again'. If Satan, therefore, shall come to any believer and say, 'What about your sin?' tell him Jesus died for it, and your sin is put away. If he comes a second time and says to you, 'What about your sin?' answer him, 'Jesus lives, and his life is the assurance of our justification; for if our Surety had not paid the debt he would still be under the power of death.'

FOR MEDITATION: (*Our Own Hymn Book* no. 309 v.3—Thomas Kelly, 1804)
    '"The Lord is risen indeed;"
    He lives to die no more;
    He lives the sinner's cause to plead,
    Whose curse and shame He bore.'

10 APRIL (1881)

The common salvation

'The common salvation.' Jude 3
SUGGESTED FURTHER READING: 2 Timothy 4:1–18

We are all Englishmen, and we all sing, 'Britons never will be slaves'; so, in this case, when the gospel of Jesus Christ is assailed, it does not matter by whom, I feel I may call upon all Christians to take action for the common salvation. Brothers, rouse you to the fight, for more than our hearths and homes is now attacked. Do they deny the deity of Christ? It is not only my religion that is assailed, but yours as well. Do they turn 'the grace of our God into lasciviousness'? It is not this branch of the church that is now endangered. The entire church is placed in jeopardy. This gospel is not my heritage or yours; it is the common domain of all the faithful, and I beseech you feel it to be so. In your own spheres and in your own ways hold the truth, and hold it firmly. You who can neither preach nor write in defence of sound doctrine can at least give negative help by refusing to countenance error. Do not go to hear those who preach false doctrine; do not encourage them in any way; do not bid them God speed. Love 'all them that love our Lord Jesus Christ in sincerity', but if a word be spoken against the Lord or against the gospel which he has revealed, turn your back upon the speaker. Be like the loving John, who, when he went to take a bath, found Cerinthus, the heretic, there, and departed at once with all speed. I want to see more backbone in all professors, more determination never to stultify their faith by pretending to believe that black is white and that white is a shade of black. Love: do I not preach it with all my heart, and do I not bid you manifest it in your deeds? But with that love mingle a firm adherence to the truth as it is in Jesus, and a zealous resolve that it shall not lose its honour while you are capable of upholding it.

FOR MEDITATION: (*Our Own Hymn Book* no. 674 v.2—George Duffield, 1858)
> 'Stand up! Stand up for Jesus! The trumpet-call obey;
> Forth to the mighty conflict, in this His glorious day;
> Ye that are men, now serve Him, against unnumbered foes;
> Your courage rise with danger, and strength to strength oppose.'

SERMON NO. 1592

11 APRIL (1880)

The Holy Spirit's intercession

'Likewise the Spirit also helpeth our infirmities: for we know not what we should pray for as we ought: but the Spirit itself maketh intercession for us with groanings which cannot be uttered. And he that searcheth the hearts knoweth what is the mind of the Spirit, because he maketh intercession for the saints according to the will of God.' Romans 8:26–27
SUGGESTED FURTHER READING: Acts 13:1–4

The Spirit of God is not sent merely to guide and help our devotion, but he himself 'maketh intercession for the saints according to the will of God.' By this expression it cannot be meant that the Holy Spirit ever groans or personally prays, but that he excites intense desire and creates unutterable groanings in us, and these are ascribed to him. Even as Solomon built the temple because he superintended and ordained all, and yet I know not that he ever fashioned a timber or prepared a stone, so does the Holy Spirit pray and plead within us by leading us to pray and plead. This he does by arousing our desires. The Holy Spirit has a wonderful power over renewed hearts, as much power as the skilful minstrel has over the strings among which he lays his accustomed hand. The influences of the Holy Spirit at times pass through the soul like winds through an Aeolian harp, creating and inspiring sweet notes of gratitude and tones of desire, to which we should have been strangers if it had not been for his divine visitation. He knows how to create in our spirit hunger and thirst for good things. He can arouse us from our spiritual lethargy, he can warm us out of our lukewarmness and he can enable us, when we are on our knees, to rise above the ordinary routine of prayer into that victorious importunity against which nothing can stand. He can lay certain desires so pressingly upon our hearts that we can never rest till they are fulfilled. He can make the zeal for God's house to eat us up, and the passion for God's glory to be like a fire within our bones; and this is one part of that process by which in inspiring our prayers he helps our infirmity. True Advocate is he, and Comforter most effectual. Blessed be his name.

FOR MEDITATION: We are commanded to pray in the Holy Spirit at all times (Ephesians 6:18; Jude 20). Is this what you do? Or do you regard him only as your back-up or last resort when you find praying hard work?

SERMON NO. 1532

12 APRIL (PREACHED 10 JUNE 1883)

Imitators of God

'Be ye therefore followers of God, as dear children.' Ephesians 5:1
SUGGESTED FURTHER READING: 3 John 1–12

It is a fine thing for a man to know what he has to do, for then he is led 'in a plain path, because of' his 'enemies.' What a help it is to have a clear chart, and a true compass! We have only to ask, 'What would our heavenly Father do in such a case?' and our course is clear. As far as we are capable of imitating the Lord our pathway is plain. We cannot imitate God in his power, or omnipresence, or omniscience; certain of his attributes are incommunicable, and of them we may say they are high and we cannot attain to them: but these are not intended in the precept. Creatures cannot imitate their Creator in his divine attributes, but children may copy their Father in his moral attributes. By the aid of his divine Spirit we can copy our God in his justice, righteousness, holiness, purity, truth, and faithfulness. We can be tenderhearted, kind, forbearing, merciful, forgiving; in a word, we may 'walk in love, as Christ also hath loved us'. To know what to do is a great aid to a holy life. This puts us into the light, while the poor heathen gropes in darkness, for his false gods are monsters of vice which he may not dream of imitating. Another blessing is that it backs us up in our position; for if we do a thing because we are imitating God, and any raise an objection, it does not trouble us, much less are we confounded. We did not expect when we commenced a holy life that everybody would applaud us, but we reckoned that they would criticize us; and so, when their censure comes, we are supported by the consideration that those who blame the imitation find fault with the copy, if indeed the imitation be well done. He who follows God minds not what the godless think of his way of life.

FOR MEDITATION: (*Our Own Hymn Book* no. 645 vv.1&4—Charles Wesley, 1742)
   'Oh for a heart to praise my God, a heart from sin set free!
   A heart that always feels Thy blood, so freely spilt for me!
   A heart in every thought renewed, and full of love divine;
   Perfect, and right, and pure, and good, a copy, Lord, of Thine!'

13 APRIL (EASTER 1884)

'My Lord and my God'

'Thomas answered and said unto him, My Lord and my God.' John 20:28
SUGGESTED FURTHER READING: Leviticus 24:10–23

Some who denied our Lord's Deity had the effrontery to charge Thomas with breaking the third commandment by uttering such a cry of surprise as is common among profane talkers. Just as thoughtless persons take the Lord's name in vain and say, 'Good God!' or 'O Lord!' when they are astonished, so certain ancient heretics dared to interpret these words, 'My Lord and my God.' It is clear to any thoughtful person that this could not have been the case. Firstly, it was not the habit of a Jew to use any such exclamation when surprised or amazed. An irreligious Gentile might have done so, but it was the last thing that would occur to a devout Israelite. If there is one thing about which the Jews in our Lord's times were particular beyond everything, it was about using the name of God. Why, even in their sacred books they have omitted the word 'Jehovah,' and have only written 'Adonai,' because of a superstitious reverence for the very letters of the divine name. How can we, then, believe that Thomas would have done what no Jew at that time would have dreamed of? Israel after the Babylonian captivity had many faults, but not that of idolatry or irreverence to the divine name. I do not know what an Israelite might have said when greatly surprised, but I am certain that he would not have said, 'My Lord and my God.' Secondly, it could not have been a mere exclamation of surprise, or an irreverent utterance, because it was not rebuked by our Lord, and we may be sure he would not have allowed such an unhallowed cry to have gone without a reprimand. Observe, too, that it was addressed to the Lord Jesus: 'Thomas answered and said unto him, My Lord and my God.' It was not a mere outburst of surprise addressed to no one, but an answer directed to the Lord who had spoken to him. It was also such a reply that our Lord Jesus Christ accepted it as an evidence of faith, for in John 20:29 he says, 'thou hast believed'. The slander proposed by the Arian must, therefore, be rejected with derision.

FOR MEDITATION: The misuse of God's name, of which Thomas has been falsely accused, would have incurred guilt (Exodus 20:7) and judgment (Matthew 12:36). He was actually magnifying God's name (Psalm 34:3) by voicing his belief in the name of the Son of God (John 20:31; 1 John 5:13).

SERMON NO. 1775

14 APRIL (1881)

That horrible east wind!

'And let the peace of God rule in your hearts, to the which also ye are called in one body; and be ye thankful.' Colossians 3:15
SUGGESTED FURTHER READING: 2 Corinthians 13:1–14

I am grieved when I receive members from other churches, who come because they say that they are weary of the incessant bickerings and jealousies which have disturbed their rest. I am sure that there can be no blessing where there is no peace. A house divided against itself cannot stand. A church disputing is a church committing suicide. Many a church has come to its death by bleeding inwardly through strife; otherwise it might have defied the whole world, and hell itself. It is generally the little churches that squabble most: if they cannot excel in anything else, they certainly claim the first rank in quarrelling. A few Christian people get together to serve God, and the devil comes in at once and sets them by the ears: they are good men and true, but Satan bewitches them so that they dispute about nothing at all. Whenever I have to settle a dispute, I always like to have some big, bad thing in it. This I can point out, and we soon agree to set the matter right. When I cannot with microscopes on my eyes find out what it is all about, I find that brothers and sisters are hardest to be reconciled. It is easier to shoot an owl than a gnat. Little differences rankle like tiny thorns, and you cannot get them out of the flesh. Oh, that the Spirit of God would come upon the churches, and turn them into masses of fire; then they would not fall to pieces through intestine strife! When souls are being won, when the gospel is being enjoyed, when Christ is being glorified, when the church is marching on, conquering and to conquer through the divine power that is in her, then is there peace within her borders, and her citizens are filled with the finest of the wheat. But let the life of God run low, and let the Spirit of God depart, then peace departs too.

FOR MEDITATION: Disputes in the early church involved leaders (1 Corinthians 1:10–12; 3:3–4), lawsuits (1 Corinthians 6:1–8), the Lord's Supper (1 Corinthians 11:18–22) and ladies (Philippians 4:2–3). Left unchecked, such things can get totally out of hand (2 Corinthians 12:20; Galatians 5:15).

SERMON NO. 1693

15 APRIL (1883)

The bridegroom's parting word

'Thou that dwellest in the gardens, the companions hearken to thy voice: cause me to hear it.' Song of Solomon 8:13
SUGGESTED FURTHER READING: Isaiah 32:1–8

It is a dreadful thing when Christian people have almost to dread their Sabbath days; I have known this to be the case. When you are called to hard toil through the six days of the week you want a good spiritual meal on the Sabbath, and if you get it, you find therein a blessed compensation and refreshment. Is it not a heavenly joy to sit still on the one day of rest and to be fed with the finest of the wheat? I have known men made capable of bearing great trials—personal, relative, pecuniary, and the like—because they have looked backward upon one Sabbatic feast, and then forward to another. They have said in their hour of trouble, 'Patience, my heart; the Lord's day is coming, when I shall drink and forget my misery. I shall go and sit with God's people, and I shall have fellowship with the Father and with the Son, and my soul shall be satisfied as with marrow and fatness, till I praise the Lord with joyful lips.' But what a sorry case to dread the Sunday and mutter, 'I shall get nothing next Sunday any more than I did last Sunday, except some dry philosophical essay, or a heap of the childish toys and fireworks of oratory, or the same dull mumbling of a mechanical orthodoxy.' Oh, brethren and sisters, my text is scarcely meant for those who dwell in such deserts, but it speaks with emphasis to those who dwell where sweet spiritual fruits are plentiful, where odours and perfumes load the air, where the land flows with milk and honey. If any of you happen to dwell where Christ is 'evidently set forth, crucified among you', and where your hearts leap for very joy because the King himself comes near to feast his saints and make them glad in his presence, then it is to you that my text has a voice and a call: 'Thou that dwellest in the gardens,' in the choicest places of all Immanuel's land, 'the companions hearken to thy voice: cause me to hear it.'

FOR MEDITATION: Congregations need to be fed (John 21:15–17; Acts 20:28; 1 Peter 5:2). The apostle Paul steered well clear of wordy wisdom (1 Corinthians 1:17; 2:1). He knew that he ought to preach boldly (Ephesians 6:19–20) and clearly (Colossians 4:4) and asked for prayer to that end. Pray that your preachers will be like those in Nehemiah 8:7–8.

SERMON NO. 1716

16 APRIL (1882)

'At thy word'

'And Simon answering said unto him, Master, we have toiled all the night, and have taken nothing: nevertheless at thy word I will let down the net.' Luke 5:5

SUGGESTED FURTHER READING: 2 Thessalonians 3:6–13

If I am speaking to those who are out of work just now, searching for some place where they can provide bread for themselves and for their families, as is their duty, let them hear and ponder. If any man does not do his best to provide for his own household he comes not under a gospel blessing, but he is said to be worse than a heathen man and a publican,— it is the duty of us all to labour with our hands at that which is good, that we may have to give to the needy as well as to those dependent on us. If after having gone about this city till your feet are blistered you can find nothing to do, do not sit at home next Monday sulkily saying, 'I will not try again.' Apply my text to this painful trial, and yet again sally forth in hope, saying with Peter, 'we have toiled all the night, and have taken nothing: nevertheless at thy word I will let down the net.' Let men see that a Christian is not readily driven to despair; let them see that when the yoke is made more heavy the Lord has a secret way of strengthening the backs of his children to bear their burdens. If the Holy Spirit shall make you calmly resolute, you will honour God much more by your happy perseverance than the talkative by his fine speeches, or the formalist by his outward show. Common life is the true place in which to prove the truth of godliness and bring glory to God. Not by doing extraordinary works, but by the piety of ordinary life is the Christian known and his religion honoured. At God's word hold on even to the end. 'Trust in the Lord, and do good; so shalt thou dwell in the land, and verily thou shalt be fed.'

FOR MEDITATION: The labourer has a right to his wages and food (Matthew 10:10; 1 Timothy 5:18); those who deliberately refuse to work forfeit such rights (2 Thessalonians 3:10). If you are currently out of work through no fault of your own, take comfort from David's words (Psalm 37:23–25) and be encouraged that Jesus even told a parable about the unemployed finding work (Matthew 20:1–16).

SERMON NO. 1654

17 APRIL (1881)

Rejecters of the gospel admonished

'*To whom he said, This is the rest wherewith ye may cause the weary to rest; and this is the refreshing: yet they would not hear.*' Isaiah 28:12
SUGGESTED FURTHER READING: Galatians 4:12–20

Have you not heard folks say in these days concerning a true gospel preacher that he is always preaching about sovereign grace or the blood of Christ, or crying out, 'Believe, believe and you shall be saved'? They sneer and say, 'It is the old ditty over and over again.' I am not a Hebrew scholar, but those who are tell us that the passage translated 'precept upon precept; line upon line', was uttered in ridicule, and sounded like a ding dong rhyme with which they mocked Isaiah. You would smile if I read you the Hebrew according to the sound with which, in all probability, it was pronounced. They said, 'This is the way Isaiah preaches; "Tzav latzav, tzav latzav; kav lakav, kav lakav: zeeir sham, zeeir sham."' The words were intended to caricature the preacher; though they do not suggest the idea when translated, 'precept upon precept, precept upon precept; line upon line, line upon line', they do suggest it readily enough in the Hebrew. There are people now living who, when the gospel is plainly and simply preached, exclaim, 'We want progressive thought, we want'—they do not quite know what they do want. They are something like the congregation who, when a certain Bishop of London was preaching to them, were utterly inattentive, whereupon the good man took up his Hebrew Bible and read them five or six verses in the Hebrew tongue, and at once they were all awake. Then he rebuked them by saying, 'Verily, I perceive that when I preach you good doctrine you do not care about it, but when I read to you in a tongue which you do not comprehend, straightway you open your ears.' Too many wish for a map to heaven so mysteriously drawn that they may be excused from following it.

FOR MEDITATION: The apostle Paul pronounced woe upon himself if he failed to preach the gospel (1 Corinthians 9:16) and a curse upon any who perverted it (Galatians 1:6–9), but rejoiced when it was preached in truth even from bad motives by some who wished to harm him (Philippians 1:15–18). Those who tired of the true gospel and lapped up a false one left him afraid (2 Corinthians 11:3–4) and astonished (Galatians 1:6).

SERMON NO. 1593

Salvation by works, a criminal doctrine

'I do not frustrate the grace of God: for if righteousness come by the law, then Christ is dead in vain.' Galatians 2:21
SUGGESTED FURTHER READING: Philippians 3:2–9

No one was ever saved under the covenant of works, nor ever will be, and the new covenant is introduced for that reason; but if there be salvation by the first, then what need was there of the second? Self-righteousness, as far as it can, disannuls the covenant, breaks its seal, and does despite to the blood of Jesus Christ which is the substance, the certificate, and the seal of that covenant. If you hold that a man can be saved by his own good works, you pour contempt upon the testament of love which the death of Jesus has put in force, for there is no need to receive as a legacy of love that which can be earned as the wage of work. O sirs, this is a sin against each person of the sacred Trinity. It is a sin against the Father. How could he be wise and good, and yet give his only Son to die on yonder tree in anguish, if man's salvation could be wrought by some other means? It is a sin against the Son of God: you dare to say that our redemption price could have been paid somehow else, and that therefore his death was not absolutely needful for the redemption of the world, or, if needful, yet not effectual, for it requires something to be added to it before it can effect its purpose. It is a sin against the Holy Spirit, and beware how you sin against him, for such sins are fatal. The Holy Spirit bears witness to the glorious perfection and unconquerable power of the Redeemer's work, and woe to those who reject that witness. He has come into the world on purpose that he may convince men of the sin of not believing in Jesus Christ: and therefore if we think that we can be saved apart from Christ we do despite to the Spirit of his grace.

FOR MEDITATION: (*Our Own Hymn Book* no. 554 v.1—Isaac Watts, 1709)
   'No more, my God, I boast no more
   Of all the duties I have done;
   I quit the hopes I held before,
   To trust the merits of Thy Son.'

19 APRIL (PREACHED 12 JUNE 1881)

What the farm labourers can do, and what they cannot do

'And he said, So is the kingdom of God, as if a man should cast seed into the ground; and should sleep, and rise night and day, and the seed should spring and grow up, he knoweth not how. For the earth bringeth forth fruit of herself; first the blade, then the ear, after that the full corn in the ear. But when the fruit is brought forth, immediately he putteth in the sickle, because the harvest is come.' Mark 4:26–29
SUGGESTED FURTHER READING: Ecclesiastes 11:1–6

The seed must be sown everywhere, for there are no choice corners of the world that you can afford to let alone, in the hope that they will be self-productive. You may not leave the rich and intelligent under the notion that surely the gospel will be found among them, for it is not so: the pride of life leads them away from God. You may not leave the poor and illiterate, and say, 'Surely they will of themselves feel their need of Christ.' Not so: they will sink from degradation to degradation unless you uplift them with the gospel. No tribe of man, no peculiar constitution of the human mind, may be neglected by us, but everywhere we must preach the word, in season and out of season. I have heard that Captain Cook, the celebrated circumnavigator, was in one respect an admirable example to us. Wherever he landed, in whatever part of the earth it might be, he took with him a little packet of various English seeds, and he was often observed to scatter them in suitable places. He would leave the boat and wander up from the shore. He said nothing, but quietly scattered English seeds wherever he went, so that he belted the world with the flowers and herbs of his native land. Imitate him wherever you go; sow spiritual seed in every place that your foot shall tread upon. Some of you will before long be at the seaside, or amidst the mountains of Switzerland, or in some other regions of the earth, in the search of variety and beauty; carry the heavenly seeds with you, and do not be satisfied unless in every place you let fall a grain or two that may bring forth fruit unto your God. This is what you can do; mind that you do it.

FOR MEDITATION: Read Matthew 24:14. The Lord Jesus Christ commanded that the gospel be preached in all the world to every creature in every nation (Matthew 28:19; Mark 16:15; Luke 24:47; Acts 1:8). Sowing beside all waters brings with it God's blessing (Isaiah 32:20).

20 APRIL (1884)

Unbinding Lazarus

'*And when he thus had spoken, he cried with a loud voice, Lazarus, come forth. And he that was dead came forth, bound hand and foot with graveclothes: and his face was bound about with a napkin. Jesus saith unto them, Loose him, and let him go.*' John 11:43–44

SUGGESTED FURTHER READING: Psalm 116:1–16

Let us consider what are these bands which often bind newly regenerated sinners. Some of them are blindfolded by the napkin about their head; they are very *ignorant*, sadly devoid of spiritual perception, and moreover the eye of faith is darkened. Yet the eye is there, and Christ has opened it; and it is the business of the servant of God to remove the napkin which bandages it, by teaching the truth, explaining it, and clearing up difficulties. This is a simple thing to do, but exceedingly necessary. Now that they have life we shall teach them to purpose. Besides that, they are bound hand and foot, so that they are compelled to *inaction*; we can show them how to work for Jesus. Sometimes these bands are those of *sorrow*; they are in an awful terror about the past; we have to unbind them by showing that the past is blotted out. They are wrapped about by many a yard of *doubt*, mistrust, anguish, and remorse. 'Loose them, and let them go.' Another hindrance is the band of *fear*. 'Oh,' says the poor soul, 'I am such a sinner that God must punish me for my sin.' Tell him the grand doctrine of substitution. Unwrap this by the assurance that Jesus took our sin, and that 'with his stripes we are healed.' It is wonderful what liberty comes by that precious truth when it is well understood. The penitent soul fears that Jesus will refuse its prayer; assure it that he 'will in no wise cast out' any that come to him. Let fear be taken from the soul by the promises of Scripture, by our testimony to their truth, and by the Spirit bearing witness to the doctrine which we endeavour to impart.

FOR MEDITATION: (*Our Own Hymn Book* no. 35 song 1 vv.3&6—Joseph Irons, 1847)

'Inbred sin my soul annoys, unbelief my peace destroys,
Fiery darts the tempter flings, every day its battle brings.
Lord, I will rejoice in Thee, Thy salvation makes me free;
Plead my cause and all is well, I shall ever with Thee dwell.'

SERMON NO. 1776

21 APRIL (PREACHED 8 JUNE 1882)

One lion: two lions: no lion at all

'The slothful man saith, There is a lion without, I shall be slain in the streets.' Proverbs 22:13

'The slothful man saith, There is a lion in the way; a lion is in the streets.' Proverbs 26:13

SUGGESTED FURTHER READING: Luke 14:15–24

This man, using both his imagination and his tongue, gives me the opportunity of saying that he took great pains to escape from pains. He had to use his inventive ability to get himself excused from doing his duty. It is an old proverb that lazy people generally take the most trouble, and so they do; and when men are unwilling to come to Christ it is very wonderful what trouble they will take to keep away from him. Hear how they argue. Mark their ingenuity in avoiding the narrow way. Oh, if they were to argue half as well upon the question why they should be saved as they do upon the question why they should not be saved, their logic would be put to a much more useful purpose. When we have talked with them we have seen them invent all kinds of difficulties and doubts, disputes and dilemmas. They are ever ready with hard doctrines and texts that are hard to be understood. They seem as if they raked heaven and earth and hell to find reasons why they should be lost, and yet the only reason that they have for this is, that they do not want to give up their sins; they do not want to give up their self-righteousness; they do not want to come to Jesus and be washed in his blood, and owe everything to the charity of God through the Redeemer. They cannot be troubled with repenting and so they leave that doleful business, as they call it. They do not like to work out their own salvation with fear and trembling, and so they invent the lions. They do not care for faith; they do not delight in Christ and so they invent difficulties, and take a world of trouble to avoid trouble, storing up for themselves hereafter a heap of misery in order to escape from the blessedness of being found in Christ both now and at the last great day.

FOR MEDITATION: (*Our Own Hymn Book* no. 520 v.5—Thomas Scott, 1773)
   'Lord, do Thou the sinner turn! Rouse him from his senseless state;
   Let him not Thy counsel spurn, rue his fatal choice too late!'

22 APRIL (PREACHED 8 JUNE 1884)

Unbelief condemned and faith commended

'They are a very froward generation, children in whom is no faith.'
Deuteronomy 32:20
'Blessed is that man that maketh the LORD *his trust.'* Psalm 40:4
SUGGESTED FURTHER READING: Matthew 27:1–26

Dream not that because you do not happen to be an avowed atheist, or deist, or agnostic, that therefore your own form of unbelief is harmless. We read of Israel in the wilderness that 'they could not enter in because of unbelief', yet they were not atheists. A passive unbelief will ruin a man as surely as an active infidelity. Suppose that an enemy is on this side of a river destroying everybody. To find safety the river has to be crossed, and there is only one bridge. Yonder man declares that he will never go over such a bridge; he does not believe in it; he asserts that it is a rotten old thing, which would break down under his weight. He hates the structure; he will not call it a bridge at all; he ridicules all who venture upon it. It is clear that he will stay on this side of the river and die by the pursuer's sword. He is the type of the avowed sceptic. *But where are you?* You say with unfeigned distress, 'I am horrified to hear that man talk so of that excellent bridge; I believe that it is well constructed and that it has carried hundreds of thousands over. I cannot bear to hear a word said against it, for my dear father and mother found refuge by crossing it, and they are now in the land of peace.' Yet you do not escape by that bridge yourself, though well aware of your danger! Do you answer, 'Well, I do not feel worthy to go over it.' Why, that is nonsense; it is as if you should say, 'I cannot swim, and therefore will not cross over the river by means of the bridge.' Your unworthiness cannot be a reason for refusing to accept a free salvation; on the contrary, it is a reason why you should accept it at once. However, it matters little what your excuse may be; you will perish for ever if you do not believe in Jesus.

FOR MEDITATION: Whether unbelief is blatant (Acts 14:2), or masquerades as licence (Luke 12:45–46), ignorance (1 Timothy 1:13) or even fearfulness (Revelation 21:8), it still counts as unbelief in God's eyes and will not go unpunished.

23 APRIL (1882)

The blessed guest detained

'*And they drew nigh unto the village, whither they went: and he made as though he would have gone further. But they constrained him, saying, Abide with us: for it is toward evening, and the day is far spent. And he went in to tarry with them.*' Luke 24:28–29
SUGGESTED FURTHER READING: Song of Solomon 5:1–8

It was toward evening, and night was lowering, and therefore they said, 'Abide with us: for ... the day is far spent.' It would have been very cruel to have allowed him to journey on in the dark and the dews. Would we thus treat any friend of ours? Could we allow a beloved one to abide abroad all night? Was not that his own argument in the Golden Canticle, when he knocked, and said, 'Open to me, my sister, my love, my dove, my undefiled: for my head is filled with dew, and my locks with the drops of the night'? It would have been inhospitable on their part, inhuman for them to leave him to prosecute his journey in the darkness of the gathering night when they had a home in which they could entertain him. And so I charge it upon my own soul never to let Jesus be left unhoused, a stranger who has 'not where to lay his head.' All hearts are cold in every place towards the Well-beloved: it is a cold world for Jesus today even as at the time of his life below. Then 'He came unto his own, and his own received him not.' Let not that be said over again, and said of us who are in a more special sense his own than were his brethren according to the flesh. 'Be not forgetful to entertain strangers' is a gospel command, but be especially eager to entertain your Lord. Shall your Lord ever say to any of you who are called Christians, 'I was a stranger, and ye took me not in'? Oh, no, let us invite him, beg him, entreat him, constrain him to abide with us for his own dear sake, and let us give him in our warm hearts the best entertainment that we can. We never received such a guest before, and another such we shall never see again.

FOR MEDITATION: (*Our Own Hymn Book* no. 1028 v.3—John Keble, 1827)
   'Abide with me from morn to eve,
   For without Thee I cannot live;
   Abide with me when night is nigh,
   For without Thee I dare not die.'

24 APRIL (1881)

The candle

'Neither do men light a candle, and put it under a bushel, but on a candlestick; and it giveth light unto all that are in the house. Let your light so shine before men, that they may see your good works, and glorify your father which is in heaven.' Matthew 5:15–16
SUGGESTED FURTHER READING (Spurgeon): Luke 8:4–18

A bushel is a good and useful article. In almost every eastern house there was a corn-measure, here called a bushel, though it did not generally measure much more than a peck; this measure was commonly in every house because they ground their own corn, and so were generally dealing with the neighbours. That useful corn-measure to me represents the pursuits of ordinary life, the proper and natural occupations of the household. Many men and women hide the candle that God has lit under the bushel of business and domestic cares. But, you ask, is not a housewife to be a housewife? Certainly; but not so a housewife as to conceal her godliness. Is not the labouring man to work with his hands? Certainly, but not so to work for the bread that perishes as to miss life eternal. Is not the man of business to give his best attention thereto? Of course he is, but he must see to it that he does not lose his own soul, or injure the souls of others. Keep your bushel; nobody asks you to burn it, but do keep it in its place. Subordinate all worldly things to the glory of God. Do not allow your possessions or your desires, your pleasures or your cares to act as a bushel hiding his light. This happens with a great many. I must ask conscience to be so kind as to preach for me for a minute or two. Will you look at home, dear friends, and see where you place your business and your religion? Which is uppermost? Which is foremost? Is religion your business, or is business your religion? Does your candle shine upon the bushel, or does the bushel hide the candle? I will not dwell upon the question, because it will be well for you to answer it in quiet, each man for himself.

FOR MEDITATION: (*Our Own Hymn Book* no. 652 v.3—John Fawcett, 1782)

'Preserve me from the snares of sin
Through my remaining days;
And in me let each virtue shine
To my Redeemer's praise.'

SERMON NO. 1594

25 APRIL (1880)

Christ's universal kingdom, and how it cometh

'*Ask of me, and I shall give thee the heathen for thine inheritance, and the uttermost parts of the earth for thy possession. Thou shalt break them with a rod of iron; thou shalt dash them in pieces like a potter's vessel.*' Psalm 2:8–9
SUGGESTED FURTHER READING: Acts 24:1–21

Frequently do we meet with the idea that the world is to be converted to Christ by the spread of civilization. Now, civilization always follows the gospel, and is in a great measure the product of it, but many people put the cart before the horse, and make civilization the first cause. According to their opinion trade is to regenerate the nations, the arts are to ennoble them, and education is to purify them. Peace Societies are formed, against which I have not a word to say, but much in their favour; still, I believe the only efficient peace society is the church of God, and the best peace teaching is the love of God in Christ Jesus. The grace of God is the great instrument for uplifting the world from the depths of its ruin, and covering it with happiness and holiness. Christ's cross is the Pharos of this tempestuous sea, like the Eddystone lighthouse flinging its beams through the midnight of ignorance over the raging waters of human sin, preserving men from rock and shipwreck, piloting them into the port of peace. Tell it out among the heathen that the Lord reigns from the cross; and, as you tell it out, believe that the power to make the peoples believe it is with God the Father, and the power to bow them before Christ is in God the Holy Spirit. Saving energy lies not in learning, nor in wit, nor in eloquence, nor in anything except in the right arm of God, who will be exalted among the heathen, for he has sworn that surely all flesh shall see the salvation of God. The might of the Omnipotent One shall work out his purposes of grace, and as for us, we will use the simple processes of prayer and faith. 'Ask of me, and I shall give thee'.

FOR MEDITATION: Obedience to the gospel will not necessarily change the outward social status (1 Corinthians 7:17–24), but it will utterly transform the inward spiritual state with profound outward effects (1 Corinthians 6:9–11).

SERMON NO. 1535

26 APRIL (PREACHED 27 APRIL 1884)

Esther's exaltation; or, who knoweth?

'Mordecai commanded to answer Esther, Think not with thyself that thou shalt escape in the king's house ... who knoweth whether thou art come to the kingdom for such a time as this?' Esther 4:13–14
SUGGESTED FURTHER READING (Spurgeon): Psalm 116:12–19

Why has the Lord brought you where you are? Has he done it for your own sake? Does he intend all this merely that you may practice self-indulgence? Can this be the design of God? Do not think so. Has he done all this merely to give you pleasure? No: God's work is like a net of many meshes, all connected with each other. We are links of the same chain and cannot move without moving others. We are members of one body and God acts towards us with that fact in view. He does not bless the hand for the hand's sake, but for the sake of the whole body. You are saved that you may save; you are taught that you may teach; you are confirmed in the faith that you may confirm others; talents are allotted to you that you may turn them over and bring in heavenly interest for your Lord. Whatever you have is yours not to hoard for yourself, or to spend upon yourself, but that you may use it as a good steward of God. 'Who knoweth whether thou art come to the kingdom' which God has given you 'for such a time as this', when there is need of you and all that you have? Consider, next, at what a time it is that you have been thus advanced. You have been instructed in the faith at a time when unbelief is rampant; you have been confirmed in full assurance at a time when many are weak and trembling; you have been entrusted with talent at a time when multitudes are perishing for lack of knowledge. What for? You are found in the church when valued brethren are dying or moving off; you have wealth when many are starving. Why? You hold a high position when many master spirits are leading men into infidelity, ritualism or communism. Why are you placed where you are? Your answer must be that God has put you where you are for some good purpose, which must be connected with his own glory and with the extension of his kingdom in the world.

FOR MEDITATION: (*Our Own Hymn Book* no. 663 v.2—James George Deck, 1837)
    'I am Thine, and Thine alone, this I gladly, fully own;
    And, in all my works and ways, only now would seek Thy praise.'

SERMON NO. 1777

27 APRIL (1881)

Hearken and look; or, encouragement for believers

'*Look unto Abraham your father, and unto Sarah that bare you: for I have called him alone, and blessed him, and increased him.*' Isaiah 51:2
SUGGESTED FURTHER READING (Spurgeon): Romans 4:13–25

There is a capacity about faith for *grasping divine promises and purposes*, a width, a breadth, a height, a depth, which can hold the infinite truth as no other power can do. Love alone can rival it, for it embraces the infinite God himself. With the far-reaching plans and promises of God faith alone is fit to deal; carnal reason is altogether out of the lists. Faith, too, has a *great power of reception*, and therein lies much of her adaptation to the divine purpose. Self-confidence, courage, resolution, cool reasoning, whatever else they are good at, are bad at humbly receiving. Those vessels which are full already are of no use as receivers; but faith presents her emptiness to God, and opens her mouth that God may fill it. Mercy needs not a jewel, but a casket into which to put her gems, and faith is exactly what she wants. Then, again, faith always *uses the strength that God gives her*. Pride would vapour with it, and doubt would evaporate it; but faith is practical, and economically uses the talent entrusted to her. Faith has already spent all her own strength, and she so yearns to achieve her purposes that she uses all the power that God will lend her. Faith eats her manna and leaves not a morsel for worms to breed in. Faith, too, can *wait the Lord's time and place*. When faith is weak men are in a dreadful hurry, but strong faith does not judge the Lord to be slack concerning his promise. As God achieves his purpose with infinite leisure, he loves a faith that is patient and looks not for its reward this day or the next. 'He that believeth shall not make haste': that is to say, he shall not be ashamed or confounded by present trials so as to rush upon unbelieving actions. Faith leaves times and seasons with God to whom they belong.

FOR MEDITATION: Faith is God's gift (Ephesians 2:8). By it we can enjoy life (Habakkuk 2:4; Galatians 2:20), purification (Acts 15:9), sanctification (Acts 26:18), righteousness (Romans 3:22; Galatians 5:5; Philippians 3:9; Hebrews 11:7), justification (Romans 3:28; 5:1; Galatians 2:16; 3:24), access (Romans 5:2; Ephesians 3:12), standing (Romans 11:20; 2 Corinthians 1:24), walking (2 Corinthians 5:7), sonship (Galatians 3:26) and Christ's indwelling (Ephesians 3:17).

28 APRIL (1881)

Sarah and her daughters

'Look unto Abraham your father, and unto Sarah that bare you.' Isaiah 51:2
'Even as Sara obeyed Abraham, calling him lord: whose daughters ye are, as long as ye do well, and are not afraid with any amazement.' 1 Peter 3:6.
SUGGESTED FURTHER READING (Spurgeon): Genesis 18:1–15

Sarah did well: 'whose daughters ye are, as long as ye do well'. She did well as *a wife*. She was all her husband could desire, and when, at the age of one hundred and twenty-seven, she at last fell asleep, Abraham not only mourned for her, but wept for her true and genuine tears of sorrow. He wept for the loss of one who had been the life of his house. As a wife she did well. All the duties that were incumbent upon her as the queen of that travelling company were performed admirably, and we find no fault mentioned concerning her in that respect. She did well as *a hostess*. It was her duty, as her husband was given to hospitality, to be willing to entertain his guests; the one instance recorded is, no doubt, the representation of her common mode of procedure. Though she was truly a princess, yet she kneaded the dough and prepared the bread for her husband's guests. They came suddenly, but she had no complaint to make. She was indeed always ready to lay herself out to perform that which was one of the highest duties of a God-fearing household in those times. She did well also as *a mother*. We are sure she did, because we find that her son Isaac was so excellent a man; you may say what you will, but in the hand of God the mother forms the boy's character. Perhaps the father unconsciously influences the girls, but the mother has evidently most influence over the sons. There are exceptions, of course, but, for the most part, the mother is the queen of the son, and he looks up to her with infinite respect if she be at all such as can be respected. Sarah by faith did her work with Isaac well, for from the very first, in his yielding to his father when he was to be offered up as a sacrifice, we see in him evidence of a holy obedience and faith in God which were seldom equalled.

FOR MEDITATION: Read the description of the godly woman in Proverbs 31:10–31. Notice how well she does as a wife (vv.10–12,28–29), as a hostess (vv.15,20) and as a mother (vv.21,27–28). For a summary on the importance of such godly behaviour see also Titus 2:3–5.

SERMON NO. 1633

29 APRIL (PREACHED 1 MAY 1881)

The priest ordained by the oath of God

'*(Those priests were made without an oath; but this with an oath by him that said unto him, The Lord sware and will not repent, Thou art a priest for ever after the order of Melchisedec:) by so much was Jesus made a surety of a better testament.*' Hebrews 7:21–22
SUGGESTED FURTHER READING (Spurgeon): Hebrews 8:1–6

The Levitical priesthood dealt with the shadows of good things to come, not with the substance of them. The sacrificial bullock was not actually a sacrifice, but the representation of the sacrifice that was to come. The morning and evening lambs did not take away sin, but mirrored the great blood-shedding of 'the Lamb of God, which taketh away the sin of the world.' The men of the house of Aaron who attended at the visible altar were not actual priests before the real altar of the Lord, but shadows of the true. The real altar is the person of Christ, the real sacrifice the death of Christ, and the real priest Christ himself. The images of heavenly things were glorious, but the glory of the things themselves dwells in Christ, and we behold that glory 'full of grace and truth.' Fly, shadows, for God did not establish you as abiding things. You predicted and foreshadowed, but you were not the blessings which you pictured. In Christ is the actual putting away of sin, the effectual atonement, the real and efficacious substitution for guilty men, the redemption which actually redeems, the sacrifice which reconciles. In him dwells the truth of the matter: he is not prediction but fact, not promise but fulfilment. Never listen to those who spiritualize Christ himself, and make out his person and work to be a shadow. Certain teachers seem to look upon our Redeemer's life as a sort of allegory, an instructive parable, or a myth, out of which minds like theirs may spell mystic truth. It cannot be so: Christ Jesus is a fact: God was on earth in human flesh: that mysterious person the Son of God, the Son of Mary, lived, loved, died and rose again: his sacrifice once offered has for ever put away sin, and has bestowed upon him the power by his intercession 'to save them to the uttermost that come unto God by him'.

FOR MEDITATION: (*Our Own Hymn Book* no. 383 v.1—Isaac Watts, 1709)
  'Jesus, my great High Priest, offered His blood, and died;
  My guilty conscience seeks no sacrifice beside.
  His powerful blood did once atone; and now it pleads before the throne.'

SERMON NO. 1597

30 APRIL (1884)

A heavenly pattern for our earthly life

'Thy will be done in earth, as it is in heaven.' Matthew 6:10
SUGGESTED FURTHER READING: Colossians 2:20–3:5

Suppose that a man here has come fresh from heaven. Some would be curious to see what his bodily form would be like. They would expect to be dazzled by the radiance of his countenance. However, we will let that pass. We want to see how he would live. Coming newly from heaven, how would he act? Oh, sirs, if he came here to do the same as all men do on earth, only after a heavenly sort, what a father he would be, what a husband, what a brother, what a friend! I would sit down and let him preach this morning, most assuredly; and when he had done preaching, I would go home with him and have a chat. I should be careful to observe what he would do with his substance. His first thought would be, if he had a shilling, to lay it out for God's glory. 'But,' says one, 'I have to go to shop with my shilling.' Be it so, but when you go say, 'Oh! Lord, help me to lay it out to thy glory.' There should be as much piety in buying your necessaries as in going to a place of worship. I do not think this man coming fresh from heaven would say, 'I must have this luxury; I must have this goodly raiment; I must have this grand house', but he would say, 'How much can I save for the God of heaven? How much can I invest in the country I came from?' I am sure he would be pinching and screwing to save money to serve God with; and he himself, as he went about the streets and mingled with ungodly men and women, would be sure to find out ways of getting at their consciences and hearts; he would be always trying to bring others to the bliss he had enjoyed. Think that over, and live as he did, who really did come down from heaven. For after all, the best rule of life is, what would Jesus do if he were here to-day?

FOR MEDITATION: God's will for us on earth takes in many related aspects, such as our sonship (Ephesians 1:5), our salvation (Matthew 18:14; John 6:40; 1 Timothy 2:4; 2 Peter 3:9), our sanctification (1 Thessalonians 4:3), our service (Ephesians 6:5–7), our self-sacrifice (Acts 21:13–14), and our satisfaction (1 Thessalonians 5:18). Pray as the Saviour did: 'not my will, but thine, be done' (Luke 22:42).

SERMON NO. 1778

1 MAY (1884)

Trembling at the word of the Lord

'To this man will I look, even to him that is poor and of a contrite spirit, and trembleth at my word.' Isaiah 66:2
SUGGESTED FURTHER READING (Spurgeon): Isaiah 54:11–17

It is marvellous that God should take delight in the man that trembles at his word. The Lord has no such pleasure in the careless and carnally secure. He that goes tramping through his Christian career as if he was somebody, and all was safe, is no favourite of heaven. The man who takes things easily and self-confidently, with a kind of happy-go-lucky feeling that all must end well with him, has no consideration from God. Have you seen the fine professor who has despised the tender in heart? Mark that man, for the end of that man will be a crash. Have you heard the boastful preacher, self-sufficient as to his own knowledge and eloquence? Mark that man also, for his end is confusion. But watch that trembling one, whose only hope is in Christ, whose only strength is in the Lord, for he shall be sustained. Watch the self-distrustful one who never pounces upon a privilege as if it were his by right of merit, but humbly accepts it as a gift to the unworthy; he is the man that shall stand in the evil day. He that goes through life fearing is the man who has nothing to fear. 'Happy is the man that feareth alway', says the Word of the Lord. He that is afraid of falling under trial, and cries, 'lead me not into temptation, but deliver me from evil', he shall be kept from sin; but he who rashly rushes into temptation shall fall by it. He who watches by day as well as by night, puts on his armour when there seems no war, and carries his sword always drawn even when there is no enemy visible: oh, that is the man who shall cope with the deadly enemy of souls! The Holy Spirit is in him, and the Lord has regard unto him; he shall not fall by the hand of the enemy. Though he often trembles, he shall be safe at last.

FOR MEDITATION: (*Our Own Hymn Book* no. 649 v.1—Charles Wesley, 1749)
'I want a principle within
Of jealous, godly fear;
A sensibility of sin,
A pain to feel it near.'

SERMON NO. 2071

2 MAY (1880)

Sentence of death, the death of self-trust

'But we had the sentence of death in ourselves, that we should not trust in ourselves, but in God which raiseth the dead.' 2 Corinthians 1:9
SUGGESTED FURTHER READING: Acts 22:1–16

Suppose that a poor man had fallen into such a state of mind that he could not bear the sun, but lived in perpetual candle light. He dreamed that no light could equal his poor candles, and he despised the sun: candles for him; he hated daylight. Our poor, weak-minded friend is prejudiced against the sun, and we aim to bring him into brightness. How shall we proceed? I think we had better blow out his candles, and leave him in the dark; then, perhaps, he will be willing to try the light of heaven. Then I would take him out of doors, and let him see the sun; after he had once beheld its superior light, he would never be able to praise his poor candles again. The first thing is to blow his candles out; and the first thing to bring a man to Christ, the divine light, is to put out his own feeble candles of self-trust. I have heard of one who fell into the water and sank, and a strong swimmer standing on the shore did not at the same instant plunge in, though fully resolved to rescue him. The man went down the second time, and then he who would rescue him was in the water swimming near him, but not too near, waiting very cautiously till his time came. He who was drowning was a strong, energetic man, and the other was too prudent to expose himself to the risk of being dragged under by his struggles. He let the man go down for the third time, and then he knew that his strength was quite exhausted, and swimming to him he grasped him and drew him to shore. If he had seized him at first, while the drowning man had strength, they would have gone down together. The first part of human salvation is the sentence of death upon all human power and merit. When all hope in self is quite gone, Christ comes in, and with his infinite grace rescues the soul from destruction. As long as you think you can swim, you will kick, and struggle, and drown; but when you see the futility of all your own efforts, and perceive that you are without strength, you will leave yourselves with Jesus, and be saved.

FOR MEDITATION: Saul of Tarsus was one who trusted in himself that he was righteous (Luke 18:9; Philippians 3:4–6). How he changed when God knocked him off his high horse and killed his self-trust (Philippians 3:7–9)!

SERMON NO. 1536

3 MAY (PREACHED 4 MAY 1884)

Grappling irons

'Quicken me after thy lovingkindness; so shall I keep the testimony of thy mouth.' Psalm 119:88

SUGGESTED FURTHER READING: Psalm 80:1–19

This is a prayer which met David's condition. Carefully read the octave of verses with 'Caph' at the head of them [Psalm 119:81–88], and see how well it fits in at the end of each. 'My soul fainteth ... Quicken me'. 'Mine eyes fail ... Quicken me'. 'I am become like a bottle in the smoke ... Quicken me'. 'How many are the days of thy servant?' I seem near to death—'Quicken me'. 'The proud have digged pits for me ... Quicken me', that I may spy out their pitfalls and avoid them. 'They persecute me wrongfully ... Quicken me', Lord, for they cannot hurt me, though they pour death upon me, if thou pourest life into me. 'They had almost consumed me ... Quicken me', and then I may burn with fire, but I shall not be consumed. You see, the blessing of quickening meets all these conditions. I believe that the best preservative under trial is increased spiritual life. Did I hear you complain, 'I am very poor'? Brethren, if your soul is quickened and you become rich in faith, poverty will be a light burden. 'But I am very depressed in spirit.' Truly, this is sad; but if you are more fully quickened, you will shake it off as living men put from them the grave-clothes of the tomb. But you cry, 'I have such hard work to do!' If you have stronger life, the task will be easier. 'But I have been disappointed and defeated.' You will have few defeats, or you will bear them joyfully when your spiritual life is vigorous and full. 'Quicken me'. I suggest that this prayer be presented all over the place by every child of God. Breathe it before God in the silence of your hearts. 'Quicken me: quicken me'.

FOR MEDITATION: (*Our own Hymn Book* no. 119 song 3 v.3—Isaac Watts, 1719)
'When sore afflictions press me down,
I need Thy quickening powers;
Thy word that I have rested on
Shall help my heaviest hours.'

4 MAY (1879)

The glory, unity, and triumph of the church

'*And the glory which thou gavest me I have given them; that they may be one, even as we are one: I in them, and thou in me, that they may be made perfect in one; and that the world may know that thou hast sent me, and hast loved them, as thou hast loved me.*' John 17:22–23
SUGGESTED FURTHER READING: 1 John 4:1–17

The word 'world' has many shades of meaning, ranging from that jet black meaning in which the 'world lieth in wickedness' and that other, 'Love not the world, neither the things that are in the world', upward to the milder senses in John 1:10, 'He was in the world, and the world was made by him, and the world knew him not', and yet higher to the brighter meaning, 'The kingdoms of this world are become the kingdoms of our Lord, and of his Christ'. It is not in the worst sense that our text speaks of the world, but in the same manner as we find it used in such passages as these: 'The Lamb of God, which taketh away the sin of the world'; 'God was in Christ, reconciling the world unto himself, not imputing their trespasses unto them'; and again in 1 John 2:2 'And he is the propitiation for our sins: and not for ours only, but also for the sins of the whole world.' It is certain that 'God so loved the world, that he gave his only begotten Son, that whosoever believeth in him should not perish, but have everlasting life', and we cannot suppose that the great Redeemer would refuse to pray for those for whom he was given. I understand in this particular place by the word 'world' the whole mass of mankind upon the face of the earth who are not as yet converted; among them there is an elect part, for our Lord speaks of some men who shall yet believe on him through the word of his servants, but these at this present moment are undistinguished from the rest. I understand here by the word 'world' all as yet unrenewed out of the whole living family of man; on account of these our Lord would have his believing people brought into this admirable condition. For the sake of the world he would have the church in a high state of holy beauty and strength.

FOR MEDITATION: Christians are not supposed to love the ways of the world (2 Timothy 4:10; 1 John 2:15–17) or to become like the world, but to be so different (Romans 12:2) that they shine out as lights to the people of the world (Matthew 5:14–16; Philippians 2:15–16).

SERMON NO. 1472

5 MAY (PREACHED 7 MAY 1882)

Healed or deluded? Which?

'They have healed the hurt of the daughter of my people slightly, saying, Peace, peace; when there is no peace.' Jeremiah 8:11
'Heal me, O LORD, *and I shall be healed; save me, and I shall be saved: for thou art my praise.'* Jeremiah 17:14
SUGGESTED FURTHER READING (Spurgeon): Psalm 51:1–19

Out-of-the-way sinners, outrageous sinners, black sinners, scarlet sinners may pray, 'Heal me … and I shall be healed; save me, and I shall be saved'. If it be of grace, then surely hope is encouraged where otherwise despair might reign supreme. If it be of pure mercy, then the utmost guilt need not shut out a soul from heaven. Come and try the unfailing grace of God in Christ Jesus, which is unto all and upon all that believe. I know while I am preaching that certain of you say, 'He does not mean me: I am too great a sinner.' On the other hand, another class imagine that they are not sinful enough, so they also fancy that the discourse is not meant for them, Oh that you would give up this wicked perversity, and know that all truth that applies to you is meant for you. I have heard of Robert Burns that, on one occasion when at church, he sat in a pew with a young lady whom he observed to be much affected by certain terrible passages of Scripture which the minister quoted in his sermon. The wicked wag scribbled on a piece of paper a verse which he passed to her. I fear that the substance of that verse has been whispered into many of your ears full often:-
'Fair maid, you need not take the hint, nor idle texts pursue;
'Twas only sinners that he meant, not Angels such as you.'

This sermon is meant for those who think themselves angels as well as for those who know themselves to be sinners. Cease from all dreamy confidences; arouse yourselves from proud self-content, and come to Jesus the Saviour, who alone can save from sin and death.

FOR MEDITATION: The outrageous sinner and the comparatively righteous are in exactly the same boat (Ecclesiastes 9:2). They are both in God's debt and need his forgiveness (Luke 7:40–47) and they both need saving (1 Peter 4:18), otherwise they will perish (Luke 13:1–5). Which is in a better position to hear and heed the call to salvation (Matthew 9:10–13)?

SERMON NO. 1658

The tent dissolved and the mansion entered

'For we know that if our earthly house of this tabernacle were dissolved, we have a building of God, an house not made with hands, eternal in the heavens.' 2 Corinthians 5:1

SUGGESTED FURTHER READING: John 13:31–14:6

When I was a boy it would have seemed odd to me to meet with a man who gloried in being an ignoramus, and yet that is the Latin for that Greek word 'agnostic.' Is it not singular to hear a man boastfully say, 'I am an ignoramus'? How different is our apostle! He says 'we know'. How did he know? First, Paul knew that he had a Father in heaven, for he felt the spirit of sonship; he knew also that his Father had a house, and he was certain that if ever he lost the tent in which he lived he should be sure to be welcomed into his own Father's house above. How do our children know that if ever they are in need of a house they can come home to us? Did they learn that from their tutors at school? No, their childhood's instinct teaches them that our house is their home, just as chickens run under the mother-hen without needing to be trained. Because they are our children they feel that as long as we have a house they have a house too; Paul, therefore, unhesitatingly said, 'We know'; and we know the same through like confidence in our Father's love. In the house of the many mansions we feel quite sure of a hearty welcome in due time. Shut out from our Father's home we cannot be! Houseless wanderers while our royal Father dwells in his palace we cannot be! We are not merely hopeful on this matter, but certain; and therefore we say, 'I know.' Paul knew, again, that he had an elder brother, and that this brother had gone before to see to the lodging of the younger brethren. Paul remembered that Jesus had said, 'I go to prepare a place for you. And if I go and prepare a place for you, I will come again, and receive you unto myself; that where I am, there ye may be also.' So Paul had no question whatever.

FOR MEDITATION: (*Our Own Hymn Book* no. 846 v.3—James Montgomery, 1835)

'My Father's house on high,
Home of my soul! How near,
At times, to faith's foreseeing eye,
Thy golden gates appear!'

7 MAY (1884)

The children and their hosannas

'*And when the chief priests and scribes saw the wonderful things that he did, and the children crying in the temple, and saying, Hosanna to the son of David; they were sore displeased, and said unto him, Hearest thou what these say? And Jesus saith unto them, Yea; have ye never read, Out of the mouth of babes and sucklings thou hast perfected praise?*'
Matthew 21:15–16
SUGGESTED FURTHER READING (Spurgeon): Psalm 78:1–8

Dear Sunday-school teachers, let me congratulate you upon the blessed work in which you are engaged. It is very hard work if you do it thoroughly, especially to you who are busy all the week and really want the Sabbath for rest. You teach the children while suffering from a headache, and they do not always behave as you would wish; but work on for poor London's sake, for the church's sake, for Christ's sake and for the children's sakes. For the love of them never give up Sunday-school teaching. 'Oh, but I am getting into middle life!' Do you think that Sunday-school teaching ought to be done by nobody but boys and girls? 'Oh, but I have done enough!' It is a mercy for you that the sun does not say that he has done enough, or else he would not shine tomorrow, or that God and his Christ do not say they have done enough. What would become of you if the Lord ceased blessing you? We want Sunday-school teachers almost everywhere. Our people who get on in the world are too respectable to teach children. What a wretched pride is this! Those who talk so are disreputable creatures; I am sick of them! In America a president has taught a Sunday-school: it was to his honour. In England chancellors and prime ministers have thought such service no disgrace. Let queens and princes teach Sunday-school; it shall be for their renown. If you are the wealthiest man in London you are the person who should take a class, if you are a true Christian. You of knowledge, you of understanding, you of intelligence, you should come to encourage the rest.

FOR MEDITATION: Jewish parents were to teach their children God's ways (Deuteronomy 4:9–10; 6:6–7; 11:18–21); Christian parents are to do the same (Ephesians 6:4). Timothy reaped the benefits (2 Timothy 3:14–15). But who will teach children from non-Christian families? Those who teach children require high standards of holiness (Romans 2:19–22).

SERMON NO. 1785

8 MAY (1884)

An inscription for the mausoleum of the saints

'These all died in faith, not having received the promises, but having seen them afar off, and were persuaded of them, and embraced them, and confessed that they were strangers and pilgrims on the earth.' Hebrews 11:13

SUGGESTED FURTHER READING: Genesis 49:22–26

These good people—Abel, Noah, Enoch, Abraham, Isaac, Sarah—did they never get beyond faith? We have heard of some who think they have done so. Having begun in the Spirit, they are afterwards made perfect by the flesh. First it is the sinner's simple trust; but they get beyond that, and reach 'the second blessing.' I wish that they would get beyond that also, and reach the third blessing, and then they would feel more deeply than ever the deep depravity of the old nature, and cling still more closely to Christ. To go on from a second to a third, and a fourth, and a fifth, and a sixth, and a seventh, and an eighth, and a ninth, and a tenth blessing, is the thing for a child of God to do; but to get into a state of pride, and cry that he has got a second blessing, is a poor way of growing. There are ten thousand times ten thousand blessings after which believers are constantly ready to reach; but, reach what they may, 'The just shall live by faith'; he shall never get beyond trusting in the faithful promise of a gracious God, living out of himself upon Christ who must be our all in all. 'These all died in faith', the very best of them. They never got beyond that. How could they? Those who get above faith are like the man who went up so high on the ladder that he came down on the other side. They get to be so good that they trust in themselves instead of resting in him who is the Lord our Righteousness. The Lord save us from self-conceit! But then, while they did not get beyond faith, the mercy is that they never got below it. They still had faith. They were sometimes troubled with suspicions of themselves and doubts as to whether the Lord had really wrought a work in their souls, but they never quite gave up faith.

FOR MEDITATION: The big blessing to be sought is the forgiveness of sins by faith in the Lord Jesus Christ (Romans 4:6–8; Galatians 3:9). If God gives to all his saved people 'all things' with his Son (Romans 8:32), 'all spiritual blessings' in Christ (Ephesians 1:3) and baptism by his Spirit into one body (1 Corinthians 12:13), there is no room for a specific second blessing.

SERMON NO. 1825

9 MAY (1880)

Samuel, an example of intercession

'God forbid that I should sin against the LORD *in ceasing to pray for you: but I will teach you the good and the right way.'* 1 Samuel 12:23
SUGGESTED FURTHER READING: Colossians 4:2–12

It would be a sin to cease to pray for those who have been the subjects of your petitions. Samuel confesses that it would have been sinful on his part to abstain from intercession. How so? Why, if he ceased to pray for that people, he would be neglecting his office, for God had made him a prophet to the nation, and he must intercede for them or neglect his duty. It would show a want of love to the Lord's chosen people if he did not pray for them. How could he teach them if he was not himself taught of God? How could he possibly hope to sway them if he had not enough affection for them to cry to God on their behalf? It would be in his case, too, a sin of anger. It would look as if he were in a pet with them and with God too, because he could not be all that he would wish to be. 'God forbid', he said, 'I should harbour such anger in my heart as to cease to pray for you.' It would have been a neglect of the divine glory; for whatever the people might be, God's name was wrapped up in them, and if they did not prosper, the Lord would not be glorified in the eyes of the heathen. He could not give up praying for them, for their cause was the cause of God. It would have been a cruelty to souls if he who possessed such power in prayer had restrained it. Now, brethren and sisters, it will be sin on your part if you neglect the mercy seat. You will grieve the Holy Spirit, you will rob Christ of his glory, you will be cruel to souls dead in sin, and you will be false and traitorous to the Spirit of grace, and to your sacred calling. You are 'kings and priests unto God', and what are you to offer as priests if you do not present before the Lord prayers and supplications for the children of men?

FOR MEDITATION: By not ceasing to pray for them, Samuel remained faithful to an earlier request of the people (1 Samuel 7:8). The apostle Paul's command 'Pray without ceasing' (1 Thessalonians 5:17) was backed up by his own example which included thanksgiving (Ephesians 1:16; 1 Thessalonians 2:13), intercession (Colossians 1:9–10) and remembrance (1 Thessalonians 1:3; 2 Timothy 1:3). He could call upon God as his witness (Romans 1:9). Could you?

SERMON NO. 1537

10 MAY (1883)

The first setting up of the brazen serpent

'And they journeyed from mount Hor by the way of the Red sea, to compass the land of Edom: and the soul of the people was much discouraged because of the way. And the people spake against God, and against Moses, Wherefore have ye brought us up out of Egypt to die in the wilderness? for there is no bread, neither is there any water; and our soul loatheth this light bread.' Numbers 21:4-5
SUGGESTED FURTHER READING: Exodus 15:19–16:12

Are you so discouraged that you do not want to live by faith any longer? Does it seem too unsubstantial? Are you tired of praying, 'Give us day by day our daily bread'? You would like a nice lump sum in the bank instead, and plenty of the cares and snares of wealth. And is it so that you are no longer content with the old gospel? It is so easy to digest that you pine for a hard morsel, a piece of cast-iron philosophy to lie on your mind for years to come. You want a bit of indigestible modern thought that will remain within you like the cucumbers of Egypt, which were not so soon gone as the manna of heaven. You crave for leeks, garlic, and onions, something sensational, remarkable, though by no means comfortable to the pure taste of those who are born of the Spirit. Is it not strange how men who call themselves Christians run after that kind of meat? Of the real good gospel, which is able to save the soul, and to build it up, they begin to say, 'It is worn out; we have heard this one thing so often. You see it is just the same old-fashioned manna; we want more variety. We demand that which is novel, which will commend itself to our advanced intellectual condition by its metaphysical subtlety.' That is the style. I see the spirit everywhere, and it comes across us all in some form or other, complaining of what God provides in providence, complaining of what God provides in the Bible, complaining of what the Holy Spirit provides in his divine operations. We look out, like the Athenians, for 'some new thing': we do not know what we want. When the grumbling humour is on us we complain of anything and everything, as did these Israelites.

FOR MEDITATION: (*Our Own Hymn Book* no. 699 v.1—Charlotte Elliott, 1834)
   'My God and Father! while I stray far from my home, in life's rough way,
   Oh! Teach me from my heart to say, "Thy will be done!"'

SERMON NO. 1722

11 MAY (1884)

The sprinkling of the blood of the sacrifice

'And the priest shall dip his finger in the blood, and sprinkle of the blood seven times before the LORD, *before the vail of the sanctuary. And the priest shall put some of the blood upon the horns of the altar of sweet incense before the* LORD, *which is in the tabernacle of the congregation; and shall pour all the blood of the bullock at the bottom of the altar of the burnt offering, which is at the door of the tabernacle.'* Leviticus 4:6–7
SUGGESTED FURTHER READING (Spurgeon): Isaiah 53:1–12

Continue to look to the blood of Jesus, and draw hope from it. Do not go away from that; where else can you go? The devil's desire will be to keep you from thinking upon Christ; but remember that thoughts about anything else will do you very little good. Your hope lies in thinking upon Jesus, not upon yourself. Masticate and digest such a text as this every morning: 'he is able also to save them to the uttermost that come unto God by him'. Go to bed at night with this verse upon your tongue: 'the blood of Jesus Christ his Son cleanseth us from all sin.' Or this: 'him that cometh to me I will in no wise cast out.' That dear man of God, Mr Moody Stuart, tells us that he once talked with a woman who was in great trouble about her sins. She was well-instructed and knew the Bible thoroughly, so that he was in a little difficulty what to say to her, as she was so accustomed to all-saving truth. At last he urged upon her very strongly that passage, 'This is a faithful saying, and worthy of all acceptation, that Christ Jesus came into the world to save sinners', and he noticed that she seemed to find a quiet relief in a gentle flow of tears. He prayed with her, and when she rose from her knees she seemed much comforted. Meeting her the next day, seeing her smiling face and finding her full of rest in the Lord, he asked, 'What was it wrought you deliverance?' 'Oh,' she said, 'it was that text, "Christ Jesus came ... to save sinners."' 'Did you not know that before?' said Mr Stuart. Yes, she knew the words before, but found that in her heart of hearts she had believed that Jesus came to save saints, not sinners. Do not many awakened persons abide in the same error?

FOR MEDITATION: (*Our Own Hymn Book* no. 285 v.3—Augustus M. Toplady, 1759)
  'For me the Saviour's blood avails, almighty to atone;
  The hands He gave to piercing nails shall lead me to His throne.'

SERMON NO. 1780

12 MAY (PREACHED 11 MAY 1884)

Understandest thou what thou readest?

'And Philip ran thither to him, and heard him read the prophet Esaias, and said, Understandest thou what thou readest? And he said, How can I, except some man should guide me? And he desired Philip that he would come up and sit with him. The place of the scripture which he read was this, He was led as a sheep to the slaughter; and like a lamb dumb before his shearer, so opened he not his mouth.' Acts 8:30–32
SUGGESTED FURTHER READING: 1 Corinthians 9:16–23

I heard of a congregation the other day that was so very small that hardly anyone came to listen to the preacher. Instead of blaming himself and preaching better, the minister said he thought he was not doing much good by sermons and prayer meetings, and therefore he would found a club, and if the fellows came in and played draughts, that might do them good. What a lot of that sort of thing is now being tried! We are going to convert souls on a new system, are we? Are we also to have a substitute for bread and healthier drink than pure water? We cannot save men by faith in Jesus Christ, and so it seems we are going to try new dodges of our own. We shall reap small, scant sheaves from such wretched seed. If you can do good anyhow, do good anyhow; but to hope ever to bring sinners to holiness and heaven by any teaching except that which begins and ends in Jesus Christ is a sheer delusion. 'None other name' is 'given among men whereby we must be saved.' If you have to deal with highly learned and educated people, nothing is as good for them as preaching Jesus Christ; and if the people are ignorant and degraded, nothing is better for them than the preaching of Jesus. A young man said to another the other day, 'I am going down to preach at So-and-so; what sort of people are they there? What kind of doctrine will suit them?' Having heard of the question, I gave this advice; 'You preach Jesus Christ, and that will suit them, I am sure; if they are learned people it will suit them; if they are ignorant it will suit them, God blessing it.'

FOR MEDITATION: (*Our Own Hymn Book* no. 486 v.5—Isaac Watts, 1709)
 'Should all the forms that men devise
 Assault my faith with treacherous art,
 I'd call them vanity and lies,
 And bind the gospel to my heart.'

13 MAY (1883)

Christ in you

'Christ in you, the hope of glory.' Colossians 1:27
SUGGESTED FURTHER READING: John 12:20–36

I have been trying to think what we should do if our Lord were gone. Suppose that a man has heard of a great physician who understands his complaint; he has travelled a great many miles to see this celebrated doctor, but when he gets to the door they tell him that he is out. 'Well,' says he, 'then I must wait till he is in.' 'You need not wait,' they reply, 'his assistant is at home.' The suffering man, who has been often disappointed, answers, 'I do not care about his assistant; I want to see the man himself: mine is a desperate case, but I have heard that this physician has cured the like; I must, therefore, see him. No assistants for me.' 'Well,' say they, 'he is out, but there are his books; you can see his books.' 'Thank you,' he says, 'I cannot be content with his books; I want the living man and nothing less. It is to him that I must speak, and from him I will receive instructions.' 'Do you see that cabinet?' 'Yes.' 'It is full of his medicines.' The sick man answers, 'I dare say they are very good, but they are of no use to me without the doctor: I want their owner to prescribe for me, or I shall die of my disease.' 'But see,' cries one, 'here is a person who has been cured by him, a man of great experience, who has been present at many remarkable operations. Go into the inquiry-room with him, and he will tell you all about the mode of cure.' The afflicted man answers, 'I am much obliged to you, but all your talk only makes me long the more to see the doctor. I came to see him, and I am not going to be put off with anything else. I must see the man himself, for myself. He has made my disease a speciality; he knows how to handle my case, and I will stop till I see him.' Now, dear friends, if you are seeking Christ, imitate this sick man, or else you will miss the mark altogether.

FOR MEDITATION: (*Our Own Hymn Book* no. 793 vv.1&2—John Berridge, 1785)
   'Soon as faith the Lord can see bleeding on a cross for me,
   Quick my idols all depart, Jesus gets and fills my heart.
   None among the sons of men, none among the heavenly train,
   Can with Jesus then compare, none so sweet, and none so fair!'

SERMON NO. 1720

14 MAY (1882)

A feast for the upright

'For the LORD *God is a sun and shield: the* LORD *will give grace and glory: no good thing will he withhold from them that walk uprightly. O* LORD *of hosts, blessed is the man that trusteth in thee.'* Psalm 84:11–12
SUGGESTED FURTHER READING: John 4:16–26

In this sweet Sabbatic Psalm the writer rejoices in the house of God. He evidently loves the place of godly assembly, the place where prayer and praise were offered by the united tribes of his people. But, brethren, there was no superstition in this love. He loved the house of God because he loved the God of the house. His heart and flesh cried out, not for the altar and the candlestick, but for his God. True, his soul fainted for the courts of the Lord, but the reason was that he cried out for the living God, saying, 'When shall I come and appear before God?' Brethren, it is well to take an interest in the place where you gather for worship. I am always glad when brethren are moved to contribute towards the necessary maintenance of the building and the provision for its cleanliness and propriety. I hate that God should be served in a slovenly way. Even the place where we meet to worship should show some sign of reverence for his name. But still our respect for our place of assembly must never degenerate into a superstitious reverence for the mere structure, as though there were some peculiar sanctity about the spot, and prayer offered there would be more acceptable than elsewhere. The great object of our desire must be to meet with God himself. In hearing, the point is to hear the voice of God. In singing, the charm is truly to praise the Most High. In prayer, the main object is to plead with God, and so to speak that our cry comes up before him, even into his ears. Let us always recollect this, and never rest content with merely going to a set place. Let us reckon that we have failed if we have not met with God. Let us come up hither with strong desire for communion with the Lord 'in spirit and in truth.'

FOR MEDITATION: God took harsh measures to teach the Jews the folly of trusting in a 'place of worship' instead of walking with him (Jeremiah 7:3–4,12–14). The Lord Jesus Christ is greater than the 'holiest' of buildings (Matthew 12:6; John 2:19–21) and God is not confined to man-made structures (Acts 7:48–49; 17:24). Jacob found that unexpected places can serve as the house of God and a place to meet him (Genesis 28:11–17).

SERMON NO. 1659

15 MAY (1881)

The substance of true religion

'*But ye should say, Why persecute we him, seeing the root of the matter is found in me?*' Job 19:28
SUGGESTED FURTHER READING: 1 John 5:13–21

Job says to his teasing friends, 'ye should say, Why persecute we him, seeing the root of the matter is found in me?' Notice the curious change of pronouns. The words would naturally run, 'ye should say, Why persecute we him, seeing the root of the matter is found in him?' But Job is so earnest to clear himself from Bildad's insinuation that he is a hypocrite, that he will not speak of himself in the third person, but plainly declares, 'The root of the matter is found in me'. Job seems to say, 'The vital part of the matter may or may not be in you, but it is in me, I know. You may not believe me, but I know it is so, and I tell you to your faces that no argument of yours can rob me of this confidence; for as I know that my redeemer liveth, I know that the root of the matter is found in me.' Many Christian people are afraid to speak in that fashion. They say, 'I humbly hope it is so, and I trust it is so.' That sounds prettily, but is it right? Is that the way in which men speak about their houses and lands? Do you possess a little freehold? Did I hear you answer, 'I humbly hope that my house and garden are my own'? What, then, are your title-deeds so questionable that you do not know? Is this the way in which you speak of your wages at the end of the week, 'I sometimes have a hope that these shillings are mine'? Is that the way you talk about your wife? Is that the manner in which you speak of your own life? Are you afraid even to call your soul your own? No; we demand certainties in reference to things of value, and so it ought to be with regard to Christ and eternity; we cannot put up with mere hopes and surmises in reference to them. Believers should aim at certainty about eternal things, and learn to say, like Job, 'I know that my redeemer liveth,' and, 'the root of the matter is found in me'.

FOR MEDITATION: (*Our Own Hymn Book* no. 326 v.1—Anne Steele, 1760)
   'He lives, the great Redeemer lives,
   (What joy the blest assurance gives!)
   And now before His Father God,
   Pleads the full merit of His blood.'

SERMON NO. 1598

16 MAY (1880)

Divine surprises

'When thou didst terrible things which we looked not for, thou camest down, the mountains flowed down at thy presence.' Isaiah 64:3
SUGGESTED FURTHER READING: Ephesians 3:20–21

How is it that we continue to be surprised at what God does? I answer, first, because our largest conceptions of God fall short of the truth. The man who has, like Enoch, walked with him for years, yet knows little of him. Ah, my brother, you do not know the heights and depths, the lengths and breadths of his wondrous liberality yet. God is infinite. We are as a tiny shell on the beach, we cannot hold the ocean, and therefore the measureless sea must always be a marvel to us. We shall always be in a measure ignorant, and as the unknown is gradually revealed it will take us aback with absolute astonishment. Besides, our experience of God is very brief. We have lived as yet only for a span, or a hand's breadth. Even you old men of sixty or seventy years, what are you? Your life has gone like the winking of an eye: it is nothing as compared with the life of God. Therefore there must be in God's dealings a great deal yet to come of which poor, short-lived insects like us can have no idea. Besides that, I am sorry to say our faith is shamefully weak, and does not look out for great things. We have never had such faith in God as he deserves at our hands. We have never believed him for more than twopence, when we ought to have believed in him for all the gold of Ophir. He is worthy of a trust boundless as the sea, and we have scarcely relied upon him beyond the mere drop of a bucket. By doing 'exceeding abundantly above all that we ask or think,' the Lord puts us into an amazed state. It will always be so.

FOR MEDITATION: Doubting Moses had to learn to expect great things from God (Exodus 5:22–6:1), but this stood him in great stead when he faced a doubting people (Exodus 14:10–14). Considering the great things God has done for us (1 Samuel 12:24; Psalm 126:2–3; Mark 5:19–20) should help us expect even greater things from him (John 1:50; 14:12).

N.B. Spurgeon went on to tell the story of William Haslam, the Church of England clergyman surprisingly converted while preaching. Haslam had been present a fortnight earlier (no.1536—see 2 May) and had sent Spurgeon his book *From death into life: or, Twenty years of my ministry*.

SERMON NO. 1538

17 MAY (1883)

In him: like him

'He that saith he abideth in him ought himself also so to walk, even as he walked.' 1 John 2:6
SUGGESTED FURTHER READING: 1 Peter 2:18–25

The first thing about a Christian is initiation, initiation into Christ: the next thing is imitation, the imitation of Christ. We cannot be Christians unless we are in Christ; and we are not truly in Christ unless 'in him we live, and move, and have our being', and the life of Christ is lived over again by us according to our measure. 'Be ye therefore followers of God, as dear children'. It is the nature of children to imitate their parents. Be imitators of Christ as good soldiers, who cannot have a better model for their soldierly life than their Captain and Lord. Ought we not to be very grateful to Christ that he condescends to be our example? If he were not perfectly able to meet all our other wants, if he were an expiation and nothing else, we should glory in him as our atoning sacrifice (for we always put that to the front, and magnify the virtue of his precious blood beyond everything), but at the same time we need an example, and it is delightful to find it where we find our pardon and justification. They that are saved from the death of sin need to be guided in the life of holiness, and it is infinitely condescending on the part of Christ that he becomes an example to such poor creatures as we are. It is said to have been the distinguishing mark of Caesar as a soldier that he never said to his followers 'Go!' but he always said 'Come!' Of Alexander, also, it was noted that in weary marches he was sure to be on foot with his warriors, and in fierce attacks he was always at the front. The most persuasive sermon is the example which leads the way. This certainly is one characteristic of the Good Shepherd: 'when he putteth forth his own sheep, he goeth before them'. If Jesus bids us do anything, he first does it himself.

FOR MEDITATION: (*Our Own Hymn Book* no. 262 v.4—Isaac Watts, 1709)
   'Be Thou my pattern; make me bear
   More of Thy gracious image here;
   Then God the Judge shall own my name
   Amongst the followers of the Lamb.'

SERMON NO. 1732

18 MAY (1879)

The middle passage

'*O* LORD, *revive thy work in the midst of the years, in the midst of the years make known; in wrath remember mercy.*' Habakkuk 3:2
SUGGESTED FURTHER READING: Psalm 85:1–13

'Revive us! Help us to begin again; start us anew in life.' That is the petition, and it seems to me to be one of the wisest requests that ever fell even from prophetic lips. Let us use it. 'Lord, now that we have been twenty-five years together, let us feel as fresh as if the race were now beginning. Give us back the dew of our youth that we may do our first works, and something more. Let us have with the maturity of age the freshness of youth, and let us run without weariness in thy ways, because thy Spirit has quickened us. Our dependence is upon thee even for life itself; breathe thou on us once more.' That life, as I understand it, is to come upon God's people themselves: 'revive thy work'. What is God's work? Why, it is God's people, 'For we are his workmanship'. True revival must first come upon the churches themselves. In all churches there is much that is not God's work, and we do not ask to have it revived, but rather that it may be put away: but wherever there is anything that is God's work, any of the mind of Christ, any sincere prayer, any faith, any hope, any love, any consecration, we earnestly cry, 'O LORD, revive thy work'. Living saints alone are, in the exact sense of the word, capable of revival; we can only revive those in whom life is already found. 'O Lord, quicken thy people!' He means God's work in each one of us, for we each want revival; may the Lord send it to us now, so that if grey hairs are upon us, and we know it not, we may become young again through his free Spirit. If the fountain of our life runs low, may the Lord touch the secret springs and flood us again with holy zeal. To save us from the perils of 'the midst of the years' we need to have life anew imparted to us.

FOR MEDITATION: (*Our Own Hymn Book* no. 957 v.1—Albert Midlane, 1861)
   'Revive Thy work, O Lord, Thy mighty arm make bare;
   Speak with the voice that wakes the dead, and make Thy people hear.'
N.B. The sermons on 18 May 1879 (see also tomorrow's reading) commemorated Spurgeon's twenty five years of ministry in London.

SERMON NO. 1474

19 MAY (PREACHED 18 MAY 1879)

Crowning blessings ascribed to God

'Thou crownest the year with thy goodness.' Psalm 65:11
SUGGESTED FURTHER READING: 1 Thessalonians 2:13–20

What is the crown of a church? Well, some churches have one crown and some another. I have heard of a church whose crown was its organ, the biggest organ, the finest organ ever played, and the choir the most wonderful choir that ever was. Everybody in the district said, 'Now, if you want to go to a place where you will have fine music, that is the spot.' Our musical friends may wear that crown if they please. I will never pluck at it or decry it; I feel no temptation in that direction. I have heard of others whose crown has been their intellect. There are very few people indeed, not as many people by one-tenth as there are seats, but then they are such a select people, the *elite*, the thoughtful and intelligent! The ministry is such that only one in a hundred can possibly understand what is said, and the one in the hundred who does understand it is therefore a most remarkable person. That is their crown. Again I say I will not filch it. Whatever there may be that is desirable about it, the brother who wears it shall wear it all his days for me. I have heard of other crowns, amongst the rest, that of being 'a most respectable church.' All the people are respectable. The minister of course is respectable. I believe he is 'Reverend,' or 'Very Reverend,' and everybody and everything about him is to the last degree 'respectable.' Cotton jackets and gowns are warned off by the surpassing dignity of everything in and around the place. As for a working man, such a creature is never seen on the premises, and could not be supposed to be; and if he were to come he would say, 'The preacher preaches double Dutch or Greek, or something of the sort'; he would not hear language which he could understand. This is not a very brilliant crown, this crown of respectability; it certainly never flashed ambition into my soul. But our crown under God has been this; 'the poor have the gospel preached to them', souls are saved, and Christ is glorified.

FOR MEDITATION: (*Our Own Hymn Book* no. 420 v.1—John Cennick, 1742)
'Not unto us, to Thee alone, blessed Lamb, be glory given!
Here shall Thy praises be begun, but carried on in heaven.'

20 MAY (1883)

Glory!

'Who hath called us unto his eternal glory.' 1 Peter 5:10
SUGGESTED FURTHER READING: 1 Corinthians 2:6–13

'Eye hath not seen, nor ear heard, neither have entered into the heart of man, the things which God hath prepared for them that love him.' Yet the eye has seen wonderful things. There are sunrises and sunsets, Alpine glories and ocean marvels which, once seen, cling to our memories throughout life; yet even when nature is at her best she cannot give us an idea of the supernatural glory which God has prepared for his people. The ear has heard sweet harmonies. Have we not enjoyed music which has thrilled us? Have we not listened to speech which has seemed to make our hearts dance within us? And yet no melody of harp nor charm of oratory can ever raise us to a conception of the glory which God has laid up 'for them that love him.' As for the heart of man, what strange things have entered it! Men have exhibited fair fictions, woven in the loom of fancy, which have made the eyes to sparkle with their beauty and brightness; imagination has revelled and rioted in its own fantastic creations, roaming among islands of silver and mountains of gold, or swimming in seas of wine and rivers of milk; but imagination has never been able to open the gate of pearl which shuts in the city of our God. No, it has not yet entered the heart of man. Yet the text goes on to say, 'But God hath revealed them unto us by his Spirit', so that heaven is not an utterly unknown region, not altogether an inner brightness shut in with walls of impenetrable darkness. God has revealed joys which he has prepared for his beloved; but mark you, even though they be revealed by the Spirit, yet it is no common unveiling, and the reason that it is made known at all is ascribed to the fact that 'the Spirit searcheth all things, yea, the deep things of God.' So we see that the glory which awaits the saints is ranked among the deep things of God.

FOR MEDITATION: (*Our Own Hymn Book* no. 92 part 1 v.7—Isaac Watts, 1719)

> 'Then shall I see, and hear, and know
> All I desired or wished below;
> And every power find sweet employ
> In that eternal world of joy.'

SERMON NO. 1721

21 MAY (1882)

The perpetuity of the law of God

'For verily I say unto you, Till heaven and earth pass, one jot or one tittle shall in no wise pass from the law, till all be fulfilled.' Matthew 5:18
SUGGESTED FURTHER READING: Mark 2:23–3:6

Jesus did not come to change the law, but he came to explain it, and that very fact shows that it remains, for there is no need to explain that which is abrogated. Upon one particular point in which there happened to be a little ceremonialism involved, namely, the keeping of the Sabbath, our Lord enlarged, and showed that the Jewish idea was not the true one. The Pharisees forbade even the doing of works of necessity and mercy, such as rubbing ears of corn to satisfy hunger, and healing the sick. Our Lord Jesus showed that it was not at all according to the mind of God to forbid these things. In straining over the letter, and carrying an outward observance to excess, they had missed the spirit of the Sabbath law, which suggested works of piety such as truly hallow the day. He showed that Sabbatic rest was not mere inaction, and he said, 'My Father worketh hitherto, and I work.' He pointed to the priests who laboured hard at offering sacrifices, and said of them, 'the priests in the temple profane the sabbath, and are blameless'. They were doing divine service, and were within the law. To meet the popular error he took care to do some of his grandest miracles upon the Sabbath-day; and though this excited great wrath against him, as though he were a law-breaker, yet he did it on purpose that they might see that 'The sabbath was made for man, and not man for the sabbath', and that it is meant to be a day for doing that which honours God and blesses men. O that men knew how to keep the spiritual Sabbath by a ceasing from all servile work, and from all work done for self. The rest of faith is the true Sabbath, and the service of God is the most acceptable hallowing of the day. Oh that the day were wholly spent in serving God and doing good! The sum of our Lord's teaching was that works of necessity, works of mercy, and works of piety are lawful on the Sabbath.

FOR MEDITATION: The Pharisees' unwillingness to help others on the Sabbath did not stop them assisting their own animals on the same day (Matthew 12:11–12; Luke 13:15–16; 14:3–5). They were skilled at avoiding other duties by putting on a show of godliness (Matthew 23:23; Mark 7:9–13). Do you misuse the things of God to get out of other responsibilities?

SERMON NO. 1660

22 MAY (1881)

Everyday religion

'The life which I now live in the flesh I live by the faith of the Son of God.' Galatians 2:20
SUGGESTED FURTHER READING: James 2:14–26

It is a mark of faith that, whenever it comes into the soul, even in its lowest degree, it suggests activity. Look at the prodigal, and note his early desires. The life of grace begins to gleam into his spirit, and its first effect is the confession of sin. He cries, 'Father, I have sinned against heaven, and before thee, and am no more worthy to be called thy son'. But what is the second effect? He desires to be doing something. 'Make me as one of thy hired servants.' Having nothing to do had helped to make him the prodigal he was. He had 'wasted his substance with riotous' idleness, seeking enjoyment without employment. He had plunged into the foulest vices because he was master of money but not master of himself. It was not an ill thing for him when he was sent into the fields to feed swine: the company which he met with at the swine trough was better than that which he had kept at his banquets. One of the signs of the return of his soul's sanity was his willingness to work, although it might be only as a menial servant in his father's house. In actual history observe how Saul of Tarsus, even before he had found peaceful faith in Christ, cried, 'Lord, what wilt thou have me to do?' Faith arouses the soul to action. It is the first question of believing anxiety, 'Sirs, what must I do to be saved?' Hence faith is such a useful thing to men in the labour and travail of this mortal life, because it puts them into motion and supplies them with a motive for work. Faith does not permit men to lie upon the bed of the sluggard, listless, frivolous and idle, but it makes life appear real and earnest.

FOR MEDITATION: (*Our Own Hymn Book* no. 116 song 3 v.1—Henry Francis Lyte, 1834)
    'Redeemed from guilt, redeemed from fears,
    My soul enlarged, and dried my tears,
    What can I do, O love divine,
    What, to repay such gifts as Thine?'

23 MAY (1880)

'The disciple whom Jesus loved'

'The disciple whom Jesus loved ... which also leaned on his breast at supper.' John 21:20
SUGGESTED FURTHER READING: John 13:21–35

Our Lord loved all his disciples: 'having loved his own which were in the world, he loved them unto the end.' He said to all the apostles, 'I call you not servants; for the servant knoweth not what his lord doeth: but I have called you friends.' And yet within that circle of love there was an innermost place in which the beloved John was favoured to dwell: upon the mountain of the Saviour's love there was a knoll, a little higher than the rest of the mount, and there John was made to stand, nearest to his Lord. Let us not, because John was specially loved, think less, even in the slightest degree, of the love which Jesus Christ gave forth to the rest of his chosen. I take it that those who display an extraordinary love to one are all the more capable of great affection to many; therefore, because Jesus loved John most, I have an enhanced estimate of his love to the other disciples. It is not for a moment to be supposed that any one suffered from his supreme friendship for John. John was raised, and they were not lowered, but raised with him. All believers are the dear objects of the Saviour's choice, the purchase of his blood, his portion and inheritance, the jewels of his crown. If in John's case one is greater in love than another, yet all are eminently great, and therefore if it should so happen that you dare not hope to reach the height of John, and cannot look to be distinguished above others as 'the disciple whom Jesus loved', yet be very thankful to be among the brotherhood who can each say, 'He loved me, and gave himself for me.' If you have not attained 'unto the first three', be happy to belong to the host of those who follow the Son of David.

FOR MEDITATION: (*Our Own Hymn Book* no. 798 v.3—Gerhard Tersteegen, 1731, tr. by John Wesley, 1739)
   'Each moment draw from earth away
   My heart, that lowly waits Thy call;
   Speak to my inmost soul, and say,
   "I am thy Love, thy God, thy all!"
   To feel Thy power, to hear Thy voice,
   To taste Thy love, be all my choice.'

SERMON NO. 1539

24 MAY (PREACHED 22 MAY 1879)

The withered hand

'And, behold, there was a man which had his hand withered.' 'Then saith he to the man, Stretch forth thine hand. And he stretched it forth; and it was restored whole, like as the other.' Matthew 12:10,13
SUGGESTED FURTHER READING: Matthew 14:22–33

Christ's way of doing his work is generally this: first to give the command, then to help the heart to turn the command into a prayer, and then to answer that prayer by a promise. Take these specimens. The Lord says, 'make you a new heart'. That is clearly a command. But by-and-by you find the psalmist David, in the fifty-first psalm, saying, 'Create in me a clean heart, O God'. And then, if you turn again to Ezekiel, you get the promise, 'A new heart also will I give you'. First, he commands you; next he sets you praying for the blessing; and then he gives it to you. Take another; the command is, 'Turn ye, turn ye … why will ye die, O house of Israel?' Then comes the prayer, 'turn thou me, and I shall be turned'; and then follows the blessed turning of which the apostle Paul speaks when he says that God has sent his Son to bless us by turning every one of us from his iniquity. Take another case, and let it refer to purging. We find the Lord commanding us to 'purge out … the old leaven'; and straightway there comes the prayer, 'Purge me with hyssop, and I shall be clean'; and then on the heels of it comes the promise, 'I will … purely purge away thy dross'. Or, take another kind of precept, of a sweeter sort, belonging to the Christian. You are continually told to sing: 'Sing praises to God, sing praises: sing praises unto our King, sing praises.' In another place we meet with the prayer, 'open thou my lips; and my mouth shall shew forth thy praise'; and in a third Scripture we have the divine promise, 'This people have I formed for myself; they shall shew forth my praise.' See, then, the Master's way of going to work: he commands you to believe, or repent; he then sets you praying that you may be enabled to do it, and then he gives you grace to do it.

FOR MEDITATION: (*Our Own Hymn Book* no. 394 v.5—Charles Wesley, 1740)
  'Thou seest me deaf to Thy command, open, O Lord, mine ear;
  Bid me stretch out my withered hand, and lift it up in prayer.'

SERMON NO. 1485

25 MAY (1879)

Jesus, the Judge

'And he commanded us to preach unto the people, and to testify that it is he which was ordained of God to be the Judge of quick and dead.' Acts 10:42
SUGGESTED FURTHER READING: John 5:19-30

If we could have the election of a judge, what being could we suppose more impartial or as impartial as the Lord, who, though he counted it 'not robbery to be equal with God', yet 'made himself of no reputation, and took upon him the form of a servant, and was made in the likeness of' sinful flesh? O blessed Judge, be thou at once enthroned by the choice of the whole creation! This person is peculiarly suitable to be judge because he has a perfect knowledge of the law. 'Thy law is my delight', says he. 'He put on righteousness as a' garment. The Lord Jesus Christ from his youth up was an exceedingly deep scholar of the law of God: he grew, as a child, in wisdom concerning the will of God: his ear was opened to hear as the learned, that he might 'know how to speak a word in season to him that is weary'. He knows the law, for he made himself subject to it and kept it in all its parts. This is the first requisite in a judge, to be thoroughly well acquainted with the statute-book. Yet further, he knows also the evil of law-breaking. What a Judge is this whom God has appointed, who, strange to say, has himself suffered for sin! Though in him was no sin, for he was 'holy, harmless, undefiled, separate from sinners,' yet the sting of sin, which is death, he has endured, and the curse of sin has passed upon him, as it is written, 'Cursed is every one that hangeth on a tree'. With what precision, then, can he judge who, being both God and man, and knowing well the law, has also an intimate acquaintance with all the heinousness and wickedness of law-breaking! Well did the Father choose him to be the Judge of the 'quick and dead.' It puts judgment beyond objection when he who is the Friend of sinners is made the Judge of sinners.

FOR MEDITATION: (*Our Own Hymn Book* no. 364 v.3—Reginald Heber, 1811; Thomas Cotterill, 1815)
  'The Lord shall come! A dreadful form,
  With rainbow wreath and robes of storm;
  On cherub wings, and wings of wind,
  Appointed Judge of all mankind.'

SERMON NO. 1476

26 MAY (PREACHED 25 MAY 1884)

The first fruit of the Spirit

'But the fruit of the Spirit is love.' Galatians 5:22
SUGGESTED FURTHER READING: John 15:1–17

'The fruit of the Spirit is love'. It is first because in some respects it is best; first, because it leads the way; first, because it becomes the motive principle and stimulant of every other grace and virtue. You cannot conceive of anything more forceful and more beneficial, and therefore it is the first. But see what follows at its heel. Two shining ones attend it like maids of honour, waiting upon a queen: 'the fruit of the spirit is love, joy, peace': he that has love has joy and peace. What choice companions! To love much is to possess a deep delight, a secret cellar of the wine of joy which no man else may taste. He that loves is like God, who is the God of peace. Truly the meek and loving shall inherit the earth, and delight themselves in the abundance of peace. He is calm and quiet whose soul is full of love; in his boat the Lord stands at the helm, saying to the winds and waves, 'Peace, be still.' He that is all love, though he may have to suffer, yet shall 'count it all joy when' he falls 'into divers' trials. See then what a precious jewel it is that has so many shining brilliants set at its side. Love has this for its excellence, that it fulfils the whole law: you cannot say that of any other virtue. Yet, while it fulfils the whole law, it is not legal. Nobody ever loved because it was demanded of him; a good man loves because it is his nature to do so. Love is free; it 'bloweth where it listeth,' like the Spirit from which it comes. Love, indeed, is the very essence of heart liberty. Well may it be honoured; for while it is a true grace of the gospel, it nevertheless fulfils the whole law. If you would have law and gospel sweetly combined, you have it in the fruit of the Spirit, which is love. Love, moreover, is godlike, for 'God is love.' Love it is which prepares us for heaven, where everything is love.

FOR MEDITATION: Love, sometimes translated 'charity' (A.V.), not only comes first but is also unfailing, abiding and greatest (1 Corinthians 13:8,13). It should be in all that we do (1 Corinthians 16:14) and above all that we are (Colossians 3:14; 1 Peter 4:8). Love is to be our goal (1 Timothy 1:5).

SERMON NO. 1782

27 MAY (1883)

'Knock!'

'Knock, and it shall be opened unto you.' Matthew 7:7
SUGGESTED FURTHER READING: Luke 18:1–27

When the text says, 'knock, and it shall be opened unto you', it teaches us that the way of winning admission to the blessing is simple, and suitable to common people. If I have to enter in by a door, which is well secured, I shall need tools and science. I confess I do not understand the art; you must send for a gentleman who understands picklocks, 'jemmies,' and all sorts of burglarious instruments: but if I am only told to knock, fool as I am at opening doors, I know how to knock. Any uneducated man can knock if that is all which is required of him. Is there a person here who cannot put words together in prayer? Never mind, friend; knocking can be done by one who is no orator. Perhaps another cries, 'I am no scholar.' Never mind, a man can knock though he may be no philosopher. A dumb man can knock. A blind man can knock. With a palsied hand a man may knock. He who knows nothing of his book can still lift a hammer and let it fall. The way to open heaven's gate is wonderfully simplified to those who are lowly enough to follow the Holy Spirit's guidance, and ask, seek, and knock believingly. God has not provided a salvation which can only be understood by learned men; he has not prepared a gospel which requires half-a-dozen folio volumes to describe it: it is intended for the ignorant, the short-witted, and the dying, as well as for others, and hence it must be as plain as knocking at a door. This is it: believe and live. Seek God with all your heart and soul, and strength, through Jesus Christ, and the door of his mercy will certainly open to you. The gate of grace is meant to yield admission to unscientific people since it shall be opened to those who knock. I am sure this door will open to you, because it has been opened to so many before you.

FOR MEDITATION: The gate to life is narrow (Matthew 7:13–14) and the way to the Father is exclusive (John 14:6), but God always lets in those who knock at the door by faith in the Lord Jesus Christ (John 10:9; Acts 14:27). But be warned that one day it will be too late even to knock (Luke 13:24–25).

SERMON NO. 1723

28 MAY (WHITSUN 1882)

The indwelling and outflowing of the Holy Spirit

'He that believeth on me, as the scripture hath said, out of his belly shall flow rivers of living water. (But this spake he of the Spirit, which they that believe on him should receive.)' John 7:38–39
'It is expedient for you that I go away: for if I go not away, the Comforter will not come unto you; but if I depart, I will send him unto you.' John 16:7
SUGGESTED FURTHER READING: Psalm 1:1–6

What a word is this! 'Rivers of living water'!! Oh that all professing Christians were such fountains. See how spontaneous it is: out of the midst of him 'shall flow'. No pumping is required; nothing is said about machinery and hydraulics; the man does not want exciting and stirring up, but, just as he is, influence of the best kind quietly flows away from him. Did you ever hear a great hubbub in the morning, a great outcry, a sounding of trumpets and drums, and did you ever ask, 'What is it?' Did a voice reply, 'The sun is about to rise, and he is making this noise that all may be aware of it'? No, he shines, but he has nothing to say about it; even so the genuine Christian just goes about flooding the world with blessing, and so far from claiming attention for himself, it may be that he himself is unconscious of what he is effecting. God so blesses him that 'his leaf also shall not wither; and whatsoever he doeth shall prosper', for he is 'like a tree planted by the rivers of water, that bringeth forth his fruit in his season': his verdure and fruit are the natural outcome of his vigorous life. Oh, the blessed spontaneity of the work of grace when a man gets into the fullness of it, for then he seems to eat and drink and sleep eternal life, and he spreads a savour of salvation all round. And this is to be perpetual, not like intermittent springs which burst forth and flow in torrents and then cease, but it is to be an everyday outgushing. In summer and winter, by day and by night, wherever the man is, he shall be a blessing. As he breathes, he shall breathe benedictions; as he thinks, his mind shall be devising generous things; and when he acts, his acts shall be as though the hand of God were working by the hand of man.

FOR MEDITATION: (*Our Own Hymn Book* no. 450 v.4—James Montgomery, 1819)
 'The young, the old inspire with wisdom from above;
 And give us hearts and tongues of fire, to pray, and praise, and love.'

SERMON NO. 1662

29 MAY (1881)

The judgment seat of Christ

'But why dost thou judge thy brother? Or why dost thou set at nought thy brother? For we shall all stand before the judgment seat of Christ.'
Romans 14:10
SUGGESTED FURTHER READING: Matthew 7:1–5

Some Christians not only form judgments upon all that are round about them as to the facts that come under their notice, but also, without any facts whatever, conceive notions concerning people whom they have never seen, and are full of obstinate prejudices against them. Many twist words into meanings which they were never intended to mean by the person who used them; others, even without so much as the excuse of misunderstanding words, imagine evil against their brethren. They dream that they are slighted, and hard judgments follow. Once imagine that you are badly treated, and you will think that everything is done out of spite to you, and the next thing is to think spitefully of others. There are people who are liberally gifted in the line of gossip and who by their talk would make you think that you were living in Sodom and Gomorrah. You are made to fear that everyone you have trusted is a vile deceiver, that every man who is zealous is mercenary, that every minister is preaching in public what he secretly disbelieves, that every generous subscriber only gives out of pride, that, in fact, you are living in a place where the race of Judas Iscariot is to be seen, reproduced ten thousand times over. One goes to bed and cannot sleep after talking to these tale-bearers. The consolation is that there is no truth in their wonderful discoveries. These slanderous statements are a base burlesque of judgment, and nothing more. Why are they thought so much of? After you and I have done our best to hold our mimic court and have summoned this and that man before us, what is it at its best but child's play, and at its worst a violent usurpation of the rights of Christ Jesus, who alone reigns as lawgiver in the midst of his church today, and who will sit as judge on the clouds of heaven by-and-by to judge the world in righteousness?

FOR MEDITATION: The Lord Jesus Christ was far less ready to judge others than we are (Luke 12:14; John 12:47). When we judge others we not only condemn God's law (James 4:11–12) but also invite God to rubber-stamp the judgment we are passing upon ourselves (Romans 2:1–3).

SERMON NO. 1601

30 MAY (1880)

The Mediator—Judge and Saviour

'And he commanded us to preach unto the people, and to testify that it is he which was ordained of God to be the Judge of quick and dead. To him give all the prophets witness, that through his name whosoever believeth in him shall receive remission of sins.' Acts 10:42–43
SUGGESTED FURTHER READING: Isaiah 59:12–20

Jesus Christ comes to judge mankind because there are sinners to be judged. If you find me a nation which has no tribunals, no punishments, no courts of justice, no judges, it must either be the scene of utter anarchy or else a nation where all obey the law, and such a thing as a criminal is unknown. The setting up of the last great assize, and the making of that assize to have reference to all men, the living and the dead, and the appointment of the supremest person in existence, even the Son of God, to conduct that assize, all these facts imply guilt somewhere, and abundance of it. If it is not thereby proved that every one of the living and the dead have offended, it at least implies that they are all under suspicion: that they are all actually guilty we learn from other portions of God's word. The judgment held by the Mediator is proof that the mediatorial office has reference to sin, and deals with men as transgressors of the law. The second part of our Lord's mediatorial office implies this most certainly; for he comes as Saviour, and such an office would be needless if there were no sin and ruin; it is idle to talk of saving those who have never fallen. He comes to remit sin, but there can be no remission of sins to those who have never transgressed. The largeness of the promise here used that 'whosoever believeth in him shall receive remission of sins', goes to prove that there is sin in everybody. However wide the 'whosoever' is, so wide, depend upon it, is the guilt: the remedy measures the disease. Remission is promised upon belief in Jesus Christ, because fallen man needs to be pardoned. Putting the two things together, the very fact that there is a Mediator at all regards man as fallen.

FOR MEDITATION: Consider the Lord Jesus Christ as Mediator in the light of God being Judge (Hebrews 12:23–24) and of God being Saviour (1 Timothy 2:3–5). Are you trusting in him as the one who mediates on your behalf?

SERMON NO. 1540

31 MAY (PREACHED 18 MAY 1884)

Two Pauls and a blinded sorcerer

'Then the deputy, when he saw what was done, believed, being astonished at the doctrine of the Lord.' Acts 13:12
SUGGESTED FURTHER READING: Genesis 32:22–28

Sergius Paulus was one of the great ones of the earth, for those days, comparable to a king, and when he believed, it was a noble gain to the cause. A chamberlain of the queen of Ethiopia had believed before him, but as not many great men, 'not many mighty' are chosen, the conversion of the Proconsul of Cyprus was a great triumph for the gospel. It is noteworthy that from this point Saul of Tarsus is called Paul, and we read no more of Barnabas and Saul, but of Paul and Barnabas. If Saul had assumed the name of Paul from this memorable conversion it would not have been an unworthy act, for his joy at the winning of Sergius Paulus might fitly have expressed itself in a fashion suggested by a common custom among Romans. As Scipio after he conquered Africa was called Scipio Africanus, so this man Saul after such a glorious winning of Sergius Paulus for Christ might himself become Paul. It is very singular, but from this moment we do not find him called Saul except when he is telling the story of his conversion and necessarily uses his old name. Luke in the Acts of the Apostles henceforth calls him Paul, and that name must often have cheered the suffering apostle; when he was persecuted he would remember his own namesake, the Roman proconsul, whom he had brought to the feet of Jesus, and he would see him standing in the front as a bright believer, while Elymas in the background, utterly confounded, would serve as a dark figure to bring out the lights of the picture all the more clearly. Courage then, brothers and sisters, whenever you are trying to serve your Lord: if you are assailed, take heart and hope that a great victory is near.

FOR MEDITATION: Not many great men of the world become Christians (1 Corinthians 1:26). The apostle Paul had audiences with other great ones, but could never have celebrated a spiritual victory by adopting the names of Felix (Acts 24:24–27), Festus (Acts 26:24–25) or Agrippa (Acts 26:26–29). Can anyone cherish your name as the result of leading you to the Lord? If so, can you cherish the name of another you have in turn led to the Lord?

SERMON NO. 1781

1 JUNE (WHITSUN 1884)

Pentecost

'The day of Pentecost.' Acts 2:1
SUGGESTED FURTHER READING (Spurgeon): Leviticus 23:4–21

If you will count the days, you will find that it was exactly fifty days after the original Passover that the law was given on Mount Sinai. Many careful readers have observed this, but have feared to attach importance to the fact because the Jews did not connect it with Pentecost. Now we assert that as the inauguration of the law was on Pentecost, so also was the inauguration of the Gospel. At the commencement of the Old Testament dispensation, what manifestation do we get? God gives his people *a law*. At the commencement of the New Testament dispensation, what do we get? A law? No, the Lord gives his people *the Spirit*. That is a very different matter. Under the old covenant the command was given; but under the new covenant the will and the power to obey are bestowed upon us by the Holy Spirit. No more have we the law upon stone, but the Spirit writes the precept upon the fleshy tablets of the heart. Moses on the mount can only tell us what to do, but Jesus ascended on high pours out the power to do it. Now we are not under the law, but under grace, and the Spirit is our guiding force. In the church of God our rule is not according to the letter of a law, but according to the Spirit of the Lord. Some people look for a specific ordinance for every item of procedure on the part of the church, but, so far as I can see, there is a singular absence of written rule and ritual concerning particulars, apart from the two great standing ordinances. I do believe that under this dispensation saints are left to the freedom of the Spirit, and are not specifically commanded in every detail by a written law. Neither this form of church government, nor that is forced upon us, but life is permitted to assume its own necessary form, under the moulding power of the Holy Spirit.

FOR MEDITATION: (*Our Own Hymn Book* no. 449 v.1—Isaac Watts, 1709)
   'Great was the day, the joy was great,
   When the divine disciples met;
   Whilst on their heads the Spirit came,
   And sat like tongues of cloven flame.'

SERMON NO. 1783

2 JUNE (1881)

Jesus knew what he would do

'This he said to prove him: for he himself knew what he would do.' John 6:6

SUGGESTED FURTHER READING: John 6:60–71

Observe, dear friends, how careful the Holy Spirit is that we should not make a mistake about our Lord Jesus Christ. He knew that men are liable to think too little of the ever blessed Son of God, and that some, who call themselves Christians, nevertheless deny Christ's divinity, and are ever ready to forge an argument against the true and real deity of the Saviour out of anything which appears to limit his power or knowledge. Here is an instance of the care of the Spirit to prevent our falling into an erroneous conclusion. Our Lord consults with Philip, asking this poor disciple, 'Whence shall we buy bread, that these may eat?' Some might therefore have inferred that Jesus did not know what to do, but felt embarrassed. From this they would argue that Jesus cannot be Almighty God, for surely embarrassment is inconsistent with Omnipotence. Why should Jesus consult with Philip if he knows all things? Now, the Holy Spirit would have us beware of falling into low thoughts of our great Redeemer and Lord, and especially of ever being so mistaken as to think that he is not God; therefore he plainly tells us, 'this he said to prove him: for he himself knew what he would do.' Jesus was not asking information or taking counsel with Philip because he felt any doubt about his line of procedure, or needed help from his disciple. He did not want Philip to multiply bread, but he desired to multiply Philip's faith. Take heed, therefore, dear friends, that you never think little of the Saviour, or impute any of his acts to motives that would lessen his glory. Learn here, too, that we, being very apt to make mistakes concerning Christ, daily need the Spirit of God to interpret Christ to us.

FOR MEDITATION: As God the Son, the Lord Jesus Christ not only had a unique knowledge of God the Father and his ways (John 7:29; 8:55; 10:15; 13:3), but he also knew what the future held (John 13:1; 18:4) and what was in men (John 2:25), even down to their thoughts (Matthew 9:4; 12:25; Luke 6:8) and loves (John 5:42; 21:15–17). In short, 'Lord, thou knowest all things' (John 21:17).

3 JUNE (1883)

Supposing him to have been in the company

'Supposing him to have been in the company.' Luke 2:44
SUGGESTED FURTHER READING: Song of Solomon 3:1–4

Why was he not with his mother that day? Truly he had to be about the business of his heavenly Father, but why did he permit his human mother to miss him? Was it not because she needed to be taught, as well as the rest of us, the value of his company? Perhaps, if we never missed him, we might not know how sweet he is. I can picture Mary, when she had lost the dear child, weeping floods of tears. Then she began to understand what old Simeon meant when he said, 'Yea, a sword shall pierce through thy own soul also'. The sword was piercing her heart even then to prepare her for three other days in which she would mourn him as dead with still bitterer grief. See how she enquired everywhere, 'Have you seen him?' She reminds me of the spouse in the Song, 'Saw ye him whom my soul loveth?' I think I see her going through the streets, and saying at the close of the day, 'I sought him, but I found him not.' Everywhere the same question, 'Saw ye him whom my soul loveth?' but she gets no tidings of him. Peace is all unknown to her till she finds him. But, oh, how precious he was in her eyes when at last she discovered him in the temple. How careful she was of him afterwards, how happy to think that no harm had come to her dear charge! If you and I ever lose the society of Christ in our service we will go to him, and cry, 'My Lord, do not leave me again. What a fool I am if thou art not my wisdom! How weak I am if thou art not my strength! How worse than silent I am if thou art not mouth to me! How heartless is all my talk, and how flat it falls upon the hearer's ears, if thou art not the spirit and the life of all my speaking!' Oh, if all our preaching and teaching were in the power of the presence of our divine Master, how different it would be!

FOR MEDITATION: (*Our Own Hymn Book* no. 766 vv.3&4—Thomas Shepherd, 1692)
> 'When wilt Thou come unto me, Lord? Until Thou dost appear,
> I count each moment for a day, each minute for a year.
> There's no such thing as pleasure here, my Jesus is my all;
> As Thou dost shine or disappear, my pleasures rise or fall.'

SERMON NO. 1724

4 JUNE (1882)

The true gospel no hidden gospel

'But if our gospel be hid, it is hid to them that are lost: in whom the god of this world hath blinded the minds of them which believe not, lest the light of the glorious gospel of Christ, who is the image of God, should shine unto them.' 2 Corinthians 4:3–4

SUGGESTED FURTHER READING (Spurgeon): 2 Corinthians 3:12–18

Whenever I get a book which puzzles me very much to make out its meaning, I wish I could send it back to the author, and tell him to write it over again, because I am sure he is not very clear about his own meaning, or else he could easily make me know what he meant. A man has never fairly mastered a subject until he is able to communicate his thoughts on that subject, so that people of ordinary intelligence can tell what he is at. Now, the Lord has in his own mind a clearly-defined way of salvation for men, and he has expressed himself without ambiguity. Certain divines like to preach an incomprehensible gospel, for it gives them the air of wisdom in the judgment of the foolish. Certain hearers prefer sermons which they cannot understand. To them the difficult and intricate are as marrow and fatness. I heard of one who said he liked a bit of gristle in the sermons, or a bone to try his teeth upon. We could easily gratify such friends, but we see no authority in Scripture for gratifying this longing. I carefully endeavour to take the stones out of the fruit before preparing the dish. When we are eating it is by no means a good thing to swallow the bones, for our digestion might not master them, and we might be injured by their presence within. Souls want spiritual nutriment, not problems and riddles. So, when a man preaches the gospel so that you cannot make head or tail of it, you need not fret, for what he has to say is not worth your trouble in listening to it. If it be the Lord's own gospel, you who are doers of the Lord's will can understand it; and if you cannot it is not the gospel of the glory of Christ, but a gospel of human inventing. The true gospel is simplicity itself.

FOR MEDITATION: If a preacher is going to be a worthy herald of the gospel, there are several things for him to avoid—feeling ashamed (Romans 1:16), trying to sound clever (1 Corinthians 1:17), being boastful (1 Corinthians 9:16), wrong motives (Philippians 1:15) and flattery (1 Thessalonians 2:4–5). Beware of a man who displays such characteristics.

SERMON NO. 1663

5 JUNE (1881)

Farm labourers

'*Neither is he that planteth any thing, neither he that watereth; but God that giveth the increase. Now he that planteth and he that watereth are one: and every man shall receive his own reward according to his own labour. For we are labourers together with God.*' 1 Corinthians 3:7–9

SUGGESTED FURTHER READING: 1 Corinthians 1:10–17

When a great man has a large farm of his own, what would he think if Hodge the ploughman should say, 'Look here, I plough this farm, and therefore it is mine: I shall call this field Hodge's Acres'? 'No', says Hobbs, 'I reaped that land last harvest, and therefore it is mine, and I shall call it Hobbs's Field.' If all the other labourers became Hodgeites and Hobbsites, and so parcelled out the farm among them, I think the landlord would soon eject the lot of them. The farm belongs to its owner, and let it be called by his name; it is absurd to call it by the names of the bumpkins who labour upon it. Is that a disrespectful title to apply to labourers? Why, I meant it for anybody and everybody whose name is used as the head of a party in the church. I meant Luther, Calvin, Wesley, and other great men, for at their best as compared with their Master they are only farm labourers, and we ought not to call parts of the farm by their names. Remember how Paul put it, 'Who then is Paul, and who is Apollos?' 'Is Christ divided? was Paul crucified for you? or were ye baptized in the name of Paul?' The entire church belongs to him who has chosen it in his sovereignty, bought it with his blood, fenced it by his grace, cultivated it by his wisdom, and preserved it by his power. There is still only one church on the face of the earth, and those who love the Lord should keep this truth in mind. Paul is a labourer, Apollos is a labourer, Cephas is a labourer, but the farm is not Paul's, not so much as an acre of it, nor does a single parcel of land belong to Apollos, or the smallest allotment to Cephas: 'ye are Christ's; and Christ is God's.' The fact is that in this case the labourers belong to the land, and not the land to the labourers.

FOR MEDITATION: Jesus called the church 'my church' (Matthew 16:18). 'Christ, the Son of the living God' is both the rock on which the church is built (Matthew 16:16–18) and its head (Ephesians 5:23; Colossians 1:18). The responsibility and privilege of a church leader is to serve in a caretaker capacity (1 Timothy 3:5), not to usurp power (3 John 9–10).

SERMON NO. 1602

6 JUNE (1880)

Unprofitable servants

'*And cast ye the unprofitable servant into outer darkness: there shall be weeping and gnashing of teeth.*' Matthew 25:30
'*So likewise ye, when ye shall have done all those things which are commanded you, say, We are unprofitable servants: we have done that which was our duty to do.*' Luke 17:10
'*His lord said unto him, Well done, thou good and faithful servant.*' Matthew 25:21
SUGGESTED FURTHER READING: Job 22:1–3; 35:1–7

These texts are graven on my heart, as with an iron pen, by a merciless wound, inflicted when I was too feeble to bear it. When I was exceedingly ill in the South of France, and deeply depressed in spirit, so deeply depressed and so sick and ill that I scarce knew how to live, one of those malicious persons who commonly haunt all public men, and especially ministers, sent me anonymously a letter, openly directed to 'That unprofitable servant C. H. Spurgeon.' This letter contained tracts directed to the enemies of the Lord Jesus, with passages marked and underlined, with notes applying them to myself. How many Rabshakehs have in their day written to me! Ordinarily I read them with the patience which comes of use, and they go to light the fire. I do not look for exemption from this annoyance, nor do I usually feel it hard to bear, but in the hour when my spirits were depressed, and I was in terrible pain, this reviling letter cut me to the quick. I turned upon my bed and asked, 'Am I, then, an unprofitable servant?' I grieved exceedingly, and could not lift up my head or find rest. I reviewed my life, and saw its infirmities and imperfections, but knew not how to put my case till this second text came to my relief, and answered as the verdict of my bruised heart. I said to myself, 'I hope I am not an unprofitable servant in the sense in which this person intends to call me so; but I am assuredly so in the other sense.' I cast myself upon my Lord and Master once again with a deeper sense of the meaning of the text than I had felt before: his atoning sacrifice revived me, and in humble faith I found rest.

FOR MEDITATION: (*Our Own Hymn Book* no. 670 v.4—Isaac Watts, 1709)
 'Then will He own my worthless name before His Father's face;
 And in the New Jerusalem appoint my soul a place.'

7 JUNE (PREACHED 8 JUNE 1879)

Greater things yet. Who shall see them?

'Jesus answered and said unto him, Because I said unto thee, I saw thee under the fig tree, believest thou? thou shalt see greater things than these. And he saith unto him, Verily, verily, I say unto you, Hereafter ye shall see heaven open, and the angels of God ascending and descending upon the Son of man.' John 1:50–51

SUGGESTED FURTHER READING (Spurgeon): Genesis 28:10–22

Let us pray, for as we pray our prayers ascend to heaven, and our praises too. If we lead an angelical life our thoughts will always be going up to heaven, or returning thence. Beloved, have you realised this, that as you have believed in Christ upon the testimony of his word, you have now the right of access to the eternal throne at all times? You have only to speak and God will hear you. Some of God's people do not know much about this. Praying is a religious exercise with them, a very proper exercise, but it is not speaking with God; it is not doing business with God, and obtaining supplies at his hands. It is a ladder without angels, or, if you please, with ascending angels only, but none coming down with heavenly gifts. Beloved, I hope you have not fallen into this error. What, is not prayer real with you? Do you expect nothing from it? Would you send an angel on a fool's errand? Do these ascend to heaven in mere sport, and rush up and down to do nothing? Let us mean business when we pray, or we shall be mockers of the divine majesty. Too many come before God and ask for everything in general but nothing in particular, and they get but scant answers to their pointless prayers. Many more are very slack in prayer, and hence they starve their souls. Many angels must go up if many are to come down. Prayer must be constant and real with us. We should live as if we really had power with God, as if like Elijah we could go the top of Carmel and pray a brazen heaven away and deluge the earth with showers of blessings. Are you unable so to live? Then the fault lies at your own door.

FOR MEDITATION: Answers to prayer are not automatic (2 Chronicles 7:14). Praying must come before answers to prayer (James 4:2). It should be no surprise when the wrong kind of prayer produces the wrong kind of answer (Isaiah 1:15; James 4:3).

8 JUNE (1879)

Our place; at Jesus' feet

'At his feet.' Luke 7:38
SUGGESTED FURTHER READING: Revelation 1:9–20

We are described as being in various positions with regard to our Lord. We are *on his heart*. Just as the priest of old carried the names of the twelve tribes, so Jesus carries all his people on his heart; that is where we are at this time. There are favoured times when, like John, we are *on his bosom*. We feel his heart beating with true affection to us. We not only believe his love, but there is a kind of spiritual sensitiveness which causes us to feel that Jesus loves us. We seem to say, 'God is love, I know, I feel', for in our very hearts 'the love of God is shed abroad' by the Holy Spirit. It is a blessed posture to be in. We are described, also, as being *in the hand* of Christ. All his saints are in his hand. He gives 'unto them eternal life; and they shall never perish,' for he says none shall 'pluck them out of my hand.' See your position in the hollow of his hand, while in the Father's hand the hand of Christ is embraced, and he tells us 'no man is able to pluck them out of my Father's hand.' Then, too, we are described as being *on his shoulders*. Does not the good Shepherd, when he finds the strayed sheep, cast it upon his shoulders and carry it home? When Aaron stood pleading before the Lord he not only carried the names of the tribes upon his breastplate, but he had them in 'ouches of gold' upon his shoulders. Christ carries us on the heart of his love and on the shoulders of his power. Thus we are perfectly safe. You see, then, where we are; and I do not want you to forget this, while I urge you to seek to be 'at his feet'. You can keep all the other positions, and this too; for, though that is impossible for the body, it is quite possible for the spirit. The highest delight and the fullest assurance are perfectly consistent with the lowliest reverence. You may rise even *to the Master's lips*, until you can say with the spouse, 'Let him kiss me with the kisses of his mouth: for thy love is better than wine'; and yet you may still be lying at his feet, conscious of your unworthiness, and bowed into the dust under a sense of his love.

FOR MEDITATION: (*Our Own Hymn Book* no. 578 v.1—Samuel Stennett, 1787)
   'Prostrate, dear Jesus, at Thy feet a guilty rebel lies;
   And upwards to Thy mercy-seat presumes to lift his eyes.'

SERMON NO. 2066

9 JUNE (1881)

The Nazarene and the sect of the Nazarenes

'And he came and dwelt in a city called Nazareth: that it might be fulfilled which was spoken by the prophets, He shall be called a Nazarene.' Matthew 2:23
'We have found this man a pestilent fellow, and a mover of sedition among all the Jews throughout the world, and a ringleader of the sect of the Nazarenes.' Acts 24:5
SUGGESTED FURTHER READING (Spurgeon): John 1:43-46

It was a marvel that Jesus should live on this world at all. He who inhabits all things, whom space is not wide enough to contain, dwells on this poor, dusky planet. If he must dwell in this world, why is he born in Judaea? Though I am grieved it should be so, yet the Jews are a people greatly despised; shame on Christians when they ever join in such despising. But still if Jesus must be a man in this world, why is he not born in Rome, in the capital of the nations? Why must it be in a little miserable country like Judaea? Yet if he shall be born in Judaea, why must he live in Galilee, that most despicable part of Judaea? If he must live in Galilee, why not at Capernaum? Why does he choose Nazareth? Why must he go to the lowest of the low, that most despised place of a despised country? And if he must come to Nazareth (follow him a step lower), why must he be a carpenter's son? Why, if he lives there, can he not be the son of the minister of the synagague, or some respectable scribe? No; he must be reputed to be a poor man's son. And then if he must be a carpenter's son, why can he not so constrain men's hearts that they shall receive him? For the deepest depth of all is that, even as a carpenter's son, his fellow citizens will not endure him, but take him to the brow of the hill to cast him down headlong from the cliff whereon the city stood. Was there ever such condescension as that of the Saviour? If in the lowest depth there be a lower deep, he plunges into it for our sakes. He emptied himself. Our old version says that he 'made himself of no reputation,' but the new one is in this case much better: he 'emptied himself' [Revised Version, 1881].

FOR MEDITATION: (*Our Own Hymn Book* no. 268 v.1—William Robertson, 1751)
'Rejected and despised of men, behold a man of woe!
And grief His close companion still through all His life below!'

SERMON NO. 1632

10 JUNE (1883)

The devil's last throw

'And as he was yet a coming, the devil threw him down, and tare him.'
Luke 9:42
SUGGESTED FURTHER READING (Spurgeon): Mark 9:14–29

I suppose that we have never seen Satanic possession, although I am not quite sure about it, for some men exhibit symptoms which are very like it. The present existence of demons within the bodies of men I shall neither assert nor deny; but certainly, in our Saviour's day it was very common for devils to take possession of men and torment them greatly. It would seem that Satan was let loose while Christ was here below that the serpent might come into personal conflict with the appointed seed of the woman, that the two champions might stand foot to foot in solemn duel, and that the Lord Jesus might win a glorious victory over him. Since his defeat by our Lord and by his apostles, it would seem that Satan's power over human bodies has been greatly limited; but we have still among us the same thing in another and worse shape, namely, the power of sin over men's minds. That this is akin to the power of the devil over the body is clear from holy Scripture: 'the god of this world hath blinded the minds of them which believe not'; 'the spirit that now worketh in the children of disobedience', says the apostle Paul. Satan works in all ungodly men, as a smith at his forge; do you wonder that they sometimes curse and swear? These are only the sparks from the forge below, flying out of the chimney. The evil one is found co-operating with evil natures, finding fire for their tinder, blowing up the flame that is within them, and in every way assisting them, and exciting them to do evil, so that, even if men are not possessed of devils in the sense in which they were so in Christ's day, yet the evil one still has power over them and leads them whithersoever he desires.

FOR MEDITATION: Whether we are considering the possibility of demon-possession or another subject, we cannot be too dogmatic about the spiritual dimension of other people's experiences. Among those who got it wrong were Job's friends (Job 32:3; 42:7–8), the Jews (Luke 13:1–5) and the disciples (John 9:1–3). Even the apostle Paul found it impossible to be dogmatic about a spiritual experience of his own (2 Corinthians 12:1–3).

SERMON NO. 1746

11 JUNE (1882)

'Jehovah-Rophi'

'I am [Jehovah-Rophi] the LORD *that healeth thee.'* Exodus 15:26
SUGGESTED FURTHER READING: Job 19:20–27

Why are diseases and pains left in the bodies of God's people? Our bodies are redeemed, for Christ has redeemed our entire manhood, but 'if Christ be in you, the body is dead because of sin', even though the spirit is alive 'because of righteousness.' It is not till the resurrection that we shall enjoy the full result of the redemption of the body. Resurrection will accomplish for our bodies what regeneration has done for our souls. We were born again, but that divine work was exercised only upon our spiritual nature; our bodies were not born again: hence they still abide under the liability of disease, decay, and death, though even these evils have been turned into blessings. This frail, sensitive and earthly frame, which Paul calls 'our vile body,' grows weary and worn, and by-and-by it will fade away and die, unless the Lord shall come; and even if he should come, this feeble fabric must be totally changed, for 'flesh and blood' as they now are 'cannot inherit the kingdom of God; neither doth corruption inherit incorruption.' Even to this day the body is under death because of sin, and is left so on purpose to remind us of the effects of sin, that we may feel within ourselves what sin has done, and may the better guess at what sin would have done if we had remained under it, for the pains of hell would have been ours for ever. These griefs of body are meant to make us recollect what we owe to the redemption of our Lord Jesus, and so to keep us humble and grateful. Aches and pains are also sent to keep us on the wing for heaven, even as thorns in the nest drive the bird from its sloth. They make us long for the land where the inhabitant shall no more say, 'I am sick.'

FOR MEDITATION: Sickness is as much a fact of life to the godly as to the unbeliever. Asa had foot-trouble (2 Chronicles 16:12), Hezekiah had a life-threatening boil (2 Kings 20:1,7), Job was afflicted with sores (Job 2:7–8), Paul seems to have had eye-problems (Galatians 4:13–15), and Timothy an upset stomach plus other ailments (1 Timothy 5:23). Sickness rather than old age claimed the lives of Elisha (2 Kings 13:14), Lazarus (John 11:1–6,14) and nearly Epaphroditus also (Philippians 2:25–30). The resurrection body of the believer will never suffer (1 Corinthians 15:42–43; Revelation 21:4).

SERMON NO. 1664

12 JUNE (1881)

Christ's word with you

'Come unto me, all ye that labour and are heavy laden, and I will give you rest.' Matthew 11:28
SUGGESTED FURTHER READING: Acts 27:21–44

Here is a ship which cannot get into the haven. The pilot comes on board. The captain says, 'Pilot, can you get her into harbour?' 'Yes, captain, I will guarantee that I will get the ship into harbour if you leave her with me.' The captain goes to the helm, or gives orders as to steering the vessel, and at once the pilot objects that they are not trusting him. 'Yes, I am,' says the captain, 'and I expect you to get me into harbour, for you promised to do so.' 'Of course I promised,' replies the pilot; 'but then it was understood that I should take charge of the ship for the time being.' He orders the helm to be changed, and the captain declares that it shall not be done. Then cries the pilot, 'I cannot get you into the harbour, and I will not pretend to do so. Unless you trust me I can do nothing, and the proof that you trust me is that you obey my orders.' Now, then, trust Jesus, so as to be obedient to him, and he will pilot you safely. Yield yourself up to follow his example, to imitate his spirit, and obey his commands, and you are a saved man. Your ship shall not be driven out to sea while Jesus steers it; but do not go away under the delusion that you have only to say, 'I trust Christ,' and that you are saved directly. Nothing of the kind. You must really trust him, practically trust him, or there is no hope for you. Give yourself up to Jesus, renounce your old sins, forsake your old habits, live as Christ will enable you to live, and immediately you shall find peace to your soul. You cannot enjoy rest, and yet riot in sin. Shall the drunkard have rest, and yet drown his soul in his cups? Shall an adulterer have rest, and wallow in his filthiness? Shall a man blaspheme, and have rest? Shall a man be a rogue and a liar, and have rest? Impossible. These things must be given up by coming to Jesus Christ, who will help you to give them up, and make a new man of you, and then you shall receive rest in your soul.

FOR MEDITATION: (*Our Own Hymn Book* no. 495 v.4—Isaac Watts, 1709)
'Jesus, we come at Thy command;
With faith, and hope, and humble zeal
Resign our spirits to Thy hand,
To mould and guide us at Thy will.'

SERMON NO. 1691

13 JUNE (1880)

Free grace a motive for free giving

'Now our Lord Jesus Christ himself, and God, even our Father, which hath loved us, and hath given us everlasting consolation and good hope through grace, comfort your hearts, and stablish you in every good word and work.' 2 Thessalonians 2:16–17
SUGGESTED FURTHER READING: Titus 2:11–3:7

Observe that as if the apostle feared that we should get away from this doctrine of grace he added that God 'hath given us everlasting consolation and good hope through grace'. Some people do not like the sound of that word 'grace.' It is too Calvinistic. We do not care what you call it, but it is the very best word in the Bible next to the name of God our Saviour. It is from the grace of God that all our hope begins. Man as a rebel can never earn anything but damnation through his own merits: grace must reign, or man must die. Every blessing that can ever come to condemned sinners such as we are must come because God's great love wills it to come, because 'he is gracious, and full of compassion'. All other roads are broken up; grace alone bridges the chasm and makes a way for traffic between heaven and earth. Grace reigns in our spiritual comfort, and grace alone; let us glorify God for it. Everlasting consolation is not a blessing given to us as the result of our own works. This is most clear from the last part of our text, for there it is asked that the Lord may comfort our hearts, not because we are established 'in every good word and work', but that we may be so. All the good works which adorn the Christian character are the result of God's grace, and not the cause of it. Grace is given us in order that we may serve God, not because we do serve God. To make us holy is the object of divine grace, but grace did not wait until it found us holy, or it would never have visited us.

FOR MEDITATION: (*Our Own Hymn Book* no. 728 v.1—Isaac Watts, 1709)
'Behold what wondrous grace
The Father hath bestowed
On sinners of a mortal race
To call them sons of God!'

14 JUNE (1883)

'Beginning at Jerusalem'

'And that repentance and remission of sins should be preached in his name among all nations, beginning at Jerusalem.' Luke 24:47

SUGGESTED FURTHER READING: Romans 11:1–12

The Lord Jesus knew that there would come a time when some of his disciples would despise the Jews, and therefore he said, 'When you preach my gospel, begin with them'. This is a standing commandment, and everywhere we ought to preach the gospel to the Jew as well as to the Gentile; Paul even says, 'to the Jew first'. Some seem to think that there ought to be no mission to the Jews, that there is no hope of converting them, that they are of no use when they are converted, and so on. I have even heard some who call themselves Christians speak slightingly of the Jewish people. What! and your Lord and Master a Jew! There is no race on earth as exalted as they are. They are the seed of Abraham, God's friend. We have nobles and dukes in England, but how far could they trace their pedigree? Why, up to a nobody. But the poorest Jew on earth is descended linearly from Jacob, and Isaac, and Abraham. Instead of treating them with anything like disrespect, the Saviour says, 'beginning at Jerusalem.' Just as we say, 'Ladies first,' so it is 'the Jew first'. They take precedence among races and are to be first waited on at the gospel feast. Jesus would have us entertain a deep regard to that nation which God chose of old, and out of which Christ also came, for he is of the seed of Abraham according to the flesh. He puts those first who knew him first. Let us never sneer at a Jew again, for our Lord teaches us the rule of his house when he says, 'beginning at Jerusalem.' Let the seed of Israel first have the gospel presented to them, and if they reject it we shall be clear of their blood. But we shall not be faithful to our orders unless we have taken note of Jews as well as Gentiles.

FOR MEDITATION: Paul was singled out for harsh treatment by the Jews, who plotted to kill him (Acts 9:23), opposed and expelled him (Acts 13:45,50), stoned him (Acts 14:19) and again tried to kill him (Acts 21:31; 23:12). What he suffered at their hands left a lasting impression on him (2 Corinthians 11:24). If even he could resist the temptation to disown them (Acts 22:3; Romans 9:3–5; 11:1) and instead prayed for their salvation (Romans 10:1), what business have we to write them off?

SERMON NO. 1729

15 JUNE (1879)

The work of grace the warrant for obedience

'He that made me whole, the same said unto me, Take up thy bed and walk.' John 5:11
SUGGESTED FURTHER READING: 1 John 4:19–5:3

Do not love to God and love to man spring up as a sure consequence of the love of God shed abroad in the heart? Does not everyone see the necessity which calls for the one love to follow the other? But love is the mother of obedience: thus everything connected with our Lord lays us under obligation to obey him. There is not a single blessing of the covenant which does not necessarily entail its corresponding duty; and here I scarcely like to say *duty*, for these blessings of the covenant make duty to be our privilege and holiness to be our delight. Henceforth redeemed from sin we would live no longer therein: henceforth made heirs of heaven we endeavour to lead the heavenly life, so that even while we are below 'our conversation is in heaven; from whence also we look for the Saviour, the Lord Jesus Christ'. Brethren, he that made you whole has commanded this and that to be done by you: I counsel you to keep the King's commandment. As Mary said to the waiters at the wedding at Cana so say I to you: 'Whatsoever he saith unto you, do it.' Does he bid you pray? Then 'Pray without ceasing.' Does he bid you watch as well as pray? Then guard every act, and thought, and word. Does he bid you love your brethren? Then love them 'with a pure heart fervently'. Does he bid you serve them and humble yourself for his sake? Then do so, and become the servant of all. Has he said, 'Be ye holy; for I am holy'? Then aim at this by his Holy Spirit. Has he said, 'Be ye therefore perfect, even as your Father which is in heaven is perfect'? Then strive after perfection, for he that made you whole has a right to direct your way, and it will be both your safety and your happiness to submit yourselves to his commands.

FOR MEDITATION: (*Our Own Hymn Book* no. 787 v.5—Edward Caswall, 1849)
    'Thee, Jesu, may our voices bless:
    Thee may we love alone:
    And ever in our lives express
    The image of Thine own.'

SERMON NO. 1479

16 JUNE (PREACHED 15 JUNE 1884)

Our sanctuary

'A glorious high throne from the beginning is the place of our sanctuary.'
'Heal me, O LORD, and I shall be healed; save me, and I shall be saved: for thou art my praise.' Jeremiah 17:12,14
SUGGESTED FURTHER READING: Psalm 146:1–10

This is good argument in prayer: 'I have made my boast in thee, O God; I pray thee, let not my glorying be stopped. Be to me as I have declared thou wilt be.' But suppose you cannot say so much as that, then put it this way: 'Heal me, O Lord, heal me this morning; save me, O Lord, save me at once, and thou shalt be my praise. Lord, I promise that I will never rob thee of the honour of my salvation; if thou wilt but save me thou shalt have all the glory of it.' Oh, how I used to feel when I first sought the Lord, that, if saved, it must be all of grace; I felt that I should never have a word to say in my own praise, but every syllable should be for Jesus. I was ashamed and confounded, and could never open my mouth any more in my own defence, but all must be to my Redeemer's praise. When I get to heaven how I will bless and magnify his name; meanwhile I would practice the holy exercise even here. O troubled ones, come to him just as you are; trust him, and he will save you. Then will your heart say—

> 'Now for the love I bear his name, what was my gain I count my loss;
> My former pride I call my shame, and nail my glory to His cross.'

Henceforth I give myself up wholly to that one work of praising, magnifying and adoring the name of the Most High. After fifty years of life I have no ambition but to glorify my Lord. Beloved, if you get the glorious high throne to be your sanctuary, I am sure you will praise the Lord your King for ever and ever.

FOR MEDITATION: (*Our Own Hymn Book* no. 148 song 1 v.3—Isaac Watts, 1719)
> 'Wide as His vast dominion lies, make the Creator's name be known;
> Loud as His thunder shout His praise, and sound it lofty as His throne.'

N.B. This sermon was preached four days before Spurgeon's 50th birthday on 19 June 1884.

SERMON NO. 1786

17 JUNE (1883)

Buying without money

'He that hath no money; come ye, buy, and eat.' Isaiah 55:1
SUGGESTED FURTHER READING: Psalm 49:1–15

'No money'! Then *he cannot pay his old debts.* His sins rise up before him, but he cannot make amends for them. What a long file is needed to hold the record of his debts; it must be deep as the bottomless pit and high as heaven. He owes ten thousand talents, and has 'nothing to pay': he has not a penny, he has no money whatever! He is reduced to bankruptcy, and cannot pay a farthing in the pound. Moreover, *he cannot meet his present expenses.* Poor man! He must live; he must eat the bread of heaven, and he must drink of the water of life: but he has nothing with which to procure these good things. His soul hungers, even faints after the mercy of God, but he has no price with which to procure it. This day he would pluck his eyes out to be pleasing with God, but he has nothing to offer which the Lord could accept. He is reduced to such beggary that like the prodigal he cries, 'I perish with hunger!' *He cannot face the future.* He hardly dares to think of it, and yet the thought of it will come in. He remembers the needs which will surround him on a dying bed, and the terrible demands of the resurrection morning when the ringing trump shall introduce him to the dread Assize, and he shall stand before his God to render his account. He knows that he cannot answer him for one sin of a thousand. He dreads the thought of the world to come! He has nothing with which to meet the demands of the eternal future. He has 'no money', nothing that will pass current in the Day of Judgment. He is brought to the last stage of spiritual destitution; poverty has come upon him like an armed man. This is a terrible plight to be in, yet I wish that every sinner here might be reduced to it, for when he is so reduced and brought low, grace will come in, and the tide will turn. The only hope for a man who has 'no money' must be outside himself.

FOR MEDITATION: (*Our Own Hymn Book* no. 487 v.5—Charles Wesley, 1750)
'Ye bankrupt debtors know the sovereign grace of heaven;
Though sums immense ye owe, a free discharge is given:
The year of jubilee is come; return, ye ransomed sinners, home.'

SERMON NO. 1726

18 JUNE (1882)

The exceeding riches of grace

'That in the ages to come he might shew the exceeding riches of his grace in his kindness toward us through Christ Jesus.' Ephesians 2:7
SUGGESTED FURTHER READING: Ephesians 3:7–19

This grace is above all measure. Yet we have four measures for it—height, depth, breadth, length—and this mercy of God is so exceeding great that in each of these measures it baffles description. *It is higher* than our sin, though that be exceedingly heinous and proudly threatens the gates of heaven: it is higher than our thoughts, though our imagination sometimes takes a condor's flight. Oh, the height of divine mercy! It rises to the throne of the Eternal. As for *the depths of grace*, the sea has immense depths, but the mercy of God is altogether unfathomable. Great sins sink into it and are lost; but grace is just as deep after it has swallowed up a world's sin as it was before. There are inconceivably deep places in God's mercy where the blackest sins are lost. Out of these come the choicest pearls of grace. Oh the depths! As for *the breadth of mercy*, David says, 'As far as the east is from the west, so far hath he removed our transgressions from us.' What greater breadth can be conceived? As for *the length of it*, it is 'from everlasting to everlasting'. Can anybody tell me the length of that? My sins began less than fifty years ago, but the Lord's mercy began—oh, when did it begin? It was always with him, and his plans of mercy are from everlasting. There is a beginning to man's sin, but there is no beginning to pardoning love. I shall cease to sin, I hope, long before another fifty years are over, and I shall be beyond fear of further fault; but the mercy of the Lord will never end, world without end. Who then can compass a matter which in any one of its measurements far surpasses all human computation? Grace is above all calculation.

FOR MEDITATION: (*Our Own Hymn Book* no. 202 v.4—Samuel Davies, 1769)
  'Oh may this strange, this matchless grace
  This God-like miracle of love,
  Fill the wide earth with grateful praise,
  And all the angelic choirs above:
  Who is a pardoning God like Thee?
  Or who has grace so rich and free?'

SERMON NO. 1665

19 JUNE (1881)

Heart-disease curable

'*He hath sent me to bind up the brokenhearted.*' Isaiah 61:1
SUGGESTED FURTHER READING (Spurgeon): Luke 4:16–30

This physician is fully qualified. He is called Christos, or Christ, which signifies anointed; 'the LORD hath anointed me'. I am sure that Jesus can cure broken hearts, because God has given him the Spirit, even the Comforter, to rest upon him without measure, that his words may drop with the oil of comfort. O, trust him now. He has all the fitness for his work that God can give him. He is complete, and we are complete in him. A broken heart needs oil to be poured into its wounds, and 'Christ' is an oily name: he is christened a Saviour, anointed a healer. The good Samaritan poured in oil and wine, but here is heavenly oil in the hands of one who is himself the health of our countenance. As if this were not enough, notice that our Lord is commissioned: 'he hath sent me', he says. First, 'anointed me', then, 'sent me'. Our Lord said to the blind man, 'Go, wash in the Pool of Siloam, (which is, by interpretation, Sent.)' How I wish that you who are broken-hearted would go and wash in this pool, and find comfort in the blessed fact that the anointed is sent of God to you. The Great Father thought so much of you that he sent a special messenger to heal you; he sent the best one there was in heaven to be a missionary to you. No other was fit to be second to him; but God emptied heaven of its superlative glory and sent his own Son down below that he might bind up broken hearts. I cannot imagine a failure of this Messiah, the sent one. This is the Shiloh for whose salvation Jacob waited, looking for him who should be sent. This is the Apostle, or sent one of our profession, sent on purpose that he might comfort all the heirs of sorrow. Jesus is carrying on a mission, a mission for the desolate. He is a missionary to the forlorn, commissioned to commiserate, appointed to relieve. Observe, then, his qualifications and his commission. He bears a diploma of the highest value. He is the royal physician, surgeon in ordinary to all bleeding hearts. O that you would put your mournful cases into his hands.

FOR MEDITATION: (*Our Own Hymn Book* no. 257 v.5—Philip Doddridge, 1755)
'He comes, the broken heart to bind, the bleeding soul to cure;
And, with the treasures of His grace to enrich the humble poor.'

SERMON NO. 1604

20 JUNE (1880)

Mahanaim, or Hosts of angels

'*And Jacob went on his way, and the angels of God met him. And when Jacob saw them, he said, This is God's host: and he called the name of that place Mahanaim.*' Genesis 32:1-2
SUGGESTED FURTHER READING: Genesis 35:1-15

Jacob 'called the name of that place Mahanaim' [two camps]. I wish we had some way in this western world, in these modern times, of naming places and children more sensibly. We must either borrow some antiquated title, as if we were too short of sense to make one for ourselves, or else our names are sheer nonsense and mean nothing. Why not choose names which should commemorate our mercies? Might not our houses be far more full of interest if around us we saw memorials of the happy events of our lives? Should we not note down remarkable blessings in our diaries, to hand down to our children? Should we not tell our sons and daughters, 'There God helped your father, boy;' 'thus and thus the Lord comforted your mother, girl;' 'there God was very gracious to our family'? Keep records of your race! Preserve the household memoranda! I think it is a great help for a man to know what God did for his father and his grandfather, for he hopes that their God will be his God also. Jacob took care to make notes, for he again and again named places by the facts which there were seen. Jacob named Bethel, Galeed, Peniel, Mahanaim and other places, for he was a great name giver. Nor were his names forgotten, for hundreds of years after good King David came to the same spot as Jacob, and found it still known as Mahanaim, and there the servants of God of another kind met him also [see 2 Samuel 17:27-29].

FOR MEDITATION: Take a Biblical journey through the origins of some other place names—Beersheba (Genesis 21:31), Jehovah-jireh (Genesis 22:14), Bethel (Genesis 28:17-19), Galeed (Genesis 31:46-48), Peniel (Genesis 32:30), Succoth (Genesis 33:17), Marah (Exodus 15:23), Massah and Meribah (Exodus 17:7), Taberah (Numbers 11:3), Kibroth-hattaavah (Numbers 11:34), Eschol (Numbers 13:24), Hormah (Numbers 21:3), Gilgal (Joshua 5:9), Achor (Joshua 7:25-26), Bochim (Judges 2:4-5), Ramath-lehi (Judges 15:17), En-hakkore (Judges 15:19), Baal-perazim (2 Samuel 5:20), Perez-uzzah (2 Samuel 6:6-8), Berachah (2 Chronicles 20:26).

SERMON NO. 1544

21 JUNE (PREACHED 1 JUNE 1884)

Smoking flax

'The smoking flax shall he not quench.' Isaiah 42:3
SUGGESTED FURTHER READING: John 20:24-31

A dear sister came in after service this morning, and told me that she was fifty years old on the same day as myself [19 June 1884], so she came to shake hands with me; she added, 'I am like you in that, but I am the very reverse of you in other things.' I replied, 'Then you must be a good woman.' 'No,' she said, 'that is not what I mean.' 'But are you not a believer?' 'Well,' she said, 'I—I will try to be.' I got hold of her hand, and I said, 'You are not going to tell me that you will try and believe my Lord Jesus Christ, for that means unbelief of him who must be true;' and I held her fast while I added, 'When your mother was about, did you say to her, "Mother, I will try and believe you"? No, you would believe her because she was true; and I must have you believe Jesus Christ.' She said, 'Sir, do pray for me.' 'No,' I said, 'I am not inclined to do that. What should I pray for you about? If you will not believe my Lord, what blessing can he give you? What has he ever done that you should say, "I cannot believe him"?' She again answered, 'I will try.' I was not content till I had reminded her of the word, 'He that believeth on the Son hath everlasting life', and I pressed her to a full faith in the risen Lord. The Holy Spirit enabled her to trust, and then she cried, 'I have been looking to my feelings, sir, and this has been my mistake.' I have no doubt that she had done so, and a great many others are doing the same; their doubts are just that horrible smoke which comes from smoking flax. O, poor doubters, believe the Lord Jesus Christ! To say, 'I cannot believe him,' is to say in other words that he is a liar, and we cannot allow you to say *that*.

FOR MEDITATION: (*Our Own Hymn Book* no. 682 v.1—John Needham, 1768)
    'Kind are the words that Jesus speaks
    To cheer the drooping saint;
    "My grace sufficient is for you,
    Though nature's powers may faint."'

22 JUNE (1884)

Humility the friend of prayer

'*I am not worthy of the least of all the mercies, and of all the truth, which thou hast shewed unto thy servant; for with my staff I passed over this Jordan; and now I am become two bands.*' Genesis 32:10

SUGGESTED FURTHER READING: Nehemiah 1:1–11

It may be truly said that this is the first prayer in the Bible of a man for himself, which is given at full length; and being the first, it may be viewed in some degree as a pattern for succeeding pleaders. If you examine it carefully, you will find that it is a valuable model which may be copied by any child of God in the day of his trouble. Jacob begins by pleading the covenant: 'O God of my father Abraham, and God of my father Isaac': what better plea can we have than the covenant of a faithful God, which he has already fulfilled to our fathers? He next pleads a special promise which had been made to himself. That promise was wrapped up in the folds of a precept which he was obeying: 'Thou saidst unto me, Return unto thy country, and to thy kindred, and I will deal well with thee.' While we plead the general covenant made with all believers in Christ, we may also particularly and especially plead any promise which has been laid home to our own soul by the Spirit of the blessed God. Next, he proceeded to plead his own unworthiness; by faith he turned even his faultiness into an argument: 'I am not worthy of the least of all the mercies'. Furthermore, he went on to plead with God, stating his special danger: 'Deliver me, I pray thee, from the hand of my brother, from the hand of Esau'. He also set the little children and their danger before God, a strong plea with such a God of love as we have: 'lest he will come and smite me, and the mother with the children.' Then he concluded with what must ever remain a potent plea with God: 'thou saidst'. He urged God's promise, and virtually cried, 'Do as thou hast said.' It is wise to spread the promise before him who gave it, and to beg for its fulfilment.

FOR MEDITATION: (*Our Own Hymn Book* no. 214 v.3—Joseph Addison, 1712)
  'To all my weak complaints and cries
  Thy mercy lent an ear,
  Ere yet my feeble thoughts had learnt
  To form themselves in prayer.'

SERMON NO. 1787

23 JUNE (PREACHED 22 JUNE 1879)

Constant, instant, expectant

'Continuing instant in prayer.' Romans 12:12
SUGGESTED FURTHER READING: Matthew 9:35–10:7

If some people looked out for answers to prayer they might soon have them, for their prayers would be answered by themselves. I was reminded of that by a little boy whose father prayed in the family that the Lord would visit the poor and relieve their wants. When he had finished, his little boy said, 'Father, I wish I had your money.' 'Why so?' 'Because,' he said, 'I would answer your prayers for you.' 'Which prayers, John?' 'Why, father, you prayed that the poor might be helped, and you could do it very well with your own money.' I like better still that story of the good man at the prayer-meeting, who, reading the list of prayers, found one for a poor widow that her distress might be relieved, so he began to read it, but stopped and added, 'we won't trouble the Lord with that; I will attend to that myself.' Numbers of prayers are of that kind: we are praying God to do what we ought to do ourselves, and that is sheer impertinence. It we really prayed in earnest, expecting to be heard, our answer would often come in this very way, by our being stirred up to see that the Lord had heard us. The Lord might well say to us, 'You say, "Thy kingdom come"; arise and help to make my kingdom come! You ask that my name may be hallowed; go yourself and hallow my name.' Oh, that we had the expectancy which would teach us practical action, so that we should find the answer to our prayer given before we asked, according to the promise, 'before they call, I will answer; and while they are yet speaking, I will hear.'

FOR MEDITATION: (*Our Own Hymn Book* no. 978 v.4—John Newton, 1779)
    'Beyond thy utmost wants
    His love and power can bless;
    To praying souls He always grants
    More than they can express.'

SERMON NO. 1480

24 JUNE (1883)

The voice from the cloud and the voice of the Beloved

'While he yet spake, behold, a bright cloud overshadowed them: and behold a voice out of the cloud, which said, This is my beloved Son, in whom I am well pleased; hear ye him. And when the disciples heard it, they fell on their face, and were sore afraid. And Jesus came and touched them, and said, Arise, and be not afraid.' Matthew 17:5–7
SUGGESTED FURTHER READING: Galatians 3:23–4:7

Other sons are the Lord's by adoption and regeneration, but none are such in the sense in which the Lord said, 'This is my beloved Son'. Beyond all others and in a special sense he is 'his only begotten Son'. 'Unto which of the angels said he at any time, Thou art my Son, this day have I begotten thee?' We do not understand, we cannot understand the doctrine of the eternal affiliation of the Son of God. I suppose it to be well-nigh profane to endeavour to look into that sublime mystery: a holy delicacy forbids; and besides, the glory is too bright: we lack the eyes which could perceive anything in such a blaze of light. This, however, we may observe: namely, that Jesus is not the Son of God so that the idea exactly tallies with sonship among men, for he is co-equal and co-eternal with the Father, and he is himself called 'The mighty God, The everlasting Father'. He is not of fewer years than the Father, for 'In the beginning was the Word'. Yet doubtless sonship is the nearest approach to the great mystery which could be found among human likenesses, and the word 'Son' is the nearest description that could be given in human language. Hence the Father, looking at Jesus and at none other beside him, says of him and of him only, 'This is my beloved Son'. He says, 'I proceeded forth and came from God'. He is 'the only begotten Son, which is in the bosom of the Father'. Oh, dear friends, how we ought to fix our gaze upon Jesus! His is a most singular personality, the wonder of wonders, for he is Son of God as truly as he is Son of man. Truly he is man, and we err not when we so think of him, for he both suffered and died: yet truly he is God, for he lives for ever and ever, 'upholding all things by the word of his power'.

FOR MEDITATION: (*Our Own Hymn Book* no. 251 v.6—Robert Robinson, 1774)
  'Brightness of the Father's glory, shall Thy praise unuttered lie?
  Fly, my tongue, such guilty silence! Sing the Lord who came to die.'

SERMON NO. 1727

25 JUNE (1882)

The first recorded words of Jesus

'*And when they saw him, they were amazed: and his mother said unto him, Son, why hast thou thus dealt with us? behold thy father and I have sought thee sorrowing. And he said unto them, How is it that ye sought me? Wist ye not that I must be about my Father's business?*' Luke 2:48–49

SUGGESTED FURTHER READING: Luke 11:27–32

I have heard it said that Dissenters do not go to their chapels for worship, but for hearing sermons. It is not true; but if it were, I beg to say that hearing sermons may be one of the divinest forms of worship out of heaven; for in hearing the gospel as it should be heard, every sacred passion is brought into play, and every power of our renewed manhood is made to bow before the Majesty on high. Faith by embracing the promise, love by rejoicing in it, hope by expecting its fulfilment—all is worship when the theme is some gracious word of the Most High. Thought, memory, understanding, emotion, all are exercised. I do not know that I have ever worshipped God better than when I have heard a humble, simple-minded man tell out the story of the cross and of his own conversion. With the tears running down my eyes I have heard the gospel and adored the living God who has sent it among men. I have so seldom the privilege of hearing a sermon that, when I do, it occasions an intense delight which I can scarce describe, and I then draw nearer to God than in any other exercise. I suppose it is so with you: at any rate, it would be so if the preaching were what it ought to be. True hearing begets worship. This holy child was about his Father's business when he was simply asking questions and learning of the appointed teachers. In fact, we want to do more of this kind of business. We are meagre, lean, and weak, because we are frothing at the mouth with talking too much before we have drank in the truth into our inmost souls. Remember, the good matter cannot come out of you if it has never gone into you; and if you have no time for receiving instruction the matter which comes out of you will be of little worth.

FOR MEDITATION: Read Psalm 119:1–3 and meditate on the blessings pronounced upon those who hear God's word (Matthew 13:16) and keep it (Luke 11:28; Revelation 1:3; 22:7).

SERMON NO. 1666

26 JUNE (1881)

Only trust him! Only trust him!

'He said unto them, Go show yourselves unto the priests. And it came to pass, that, as they went, they were cleansed.' Luke 17:14
SUGGESTED FURTHER READING: 1 John 3:19–4:1

Some could believe in Christ if they felt in a mysterious fashion. It is rather difficult to understand people but when I have been talking to some enquirers I have thought that they expected even a physical sensation within their bodies. I remember one saying to me, 'Sir, I was quite sure I was saved, for I felt so light.' Poor simpleton, what does it matter whether you felt light or heavy? What has that to do with it? Perhaps you were light-headed, or half out of your mind with absurd excitement. Beware of such nonsense. To feel light may be interpreted into being weighed in the balances and found wanting; it is a sensation which may frighten as much as console. 'Oh,' says one, 'but I felt so singular.' Many who are now in Bedlam could say the same. What does it matter what you felt? It is not feeling that will save you. Believing on Jesus will bring you the blessings of grace, but strange feelings may be produced by what you have eaten, or by the weather, or by hysteria, or a hundred other things. Do you not know that when politics are being discussed, or when some other subject is under dispute, an earnest orator will often stir men with excitement till their flesh creeps? But what of that? Excitement does not save anybody. Many are melted to tears by a novel or a play, but what is the benefit? You may be moved with religious excitement, and half the emotion may be purely physical, and there may be nothing of the grace of God in it. The wiser way is calmly to sit down and say, 'Here is God's way of salvation through his crucified Son, Jesus Christ; he has promised that if I trust his Son he will save me from sinning, make a new man of me, and heal me of my spiritual diseases. I will trust him, for I am sure that the witness of God is true.' By that simple and deliberate act of faith you are saved.

FOR MEDITATION: (*Our Own Hymn Book* no. 538 v.2—Amelia Matilda Hull, 1860)
  'It is not thy tears of repentance or prayers,
  But the blood that atones for the soul:
  On Him, then, who shed it, believing at once
  Thy weight of iniquities roll.'

SERMON NO. 1635

27 JUNE (1880)

God glorified by children's mouths

'Out of the mouth of babes and sucklings hast thou ordained strength because of thine enemies, that thou mightest still the enemy and the avenger.' Psalm 8:2

SUGGESTED FURTHER READING: Revelation 12:1–17

Our text speaks of 'enemies', and of 'the enemy and the avenger.' The 'enemies' of God are the seed of the serpent, the men of this world, the children of darkness, all men who have not been renewed in the spirit of their minds and have not been turned 'from darkness to light, and from the power of Satan unto God'. God has many enemies; above all, there is 'the enemy', that leading spirit, 'the prince of the power of the air,' who has dominion over 'the children of disobedience' and those apostate angels whom he seduced into mutiny, so that they revolted with him from beneath the standard of God: Satan is the enemy who contends against the cause of truth and love, the cause of God. He is called 'the avenger' because he seeks to revenge himself on God. Through his own sin and folly he was expelled from heaven; the 'son of the morning' became the prince of darkness by his own wilful deed, and he wanders up and down the universe of God, seeking to take revenge upon the just and holy Judge for the sentence which he has passed upon him. Ever there rages a tremendous battle between good and evil, between God and this avenger, and the evil powers associated with him. This battle rages from day to day, and will never cease till the Lord has put all enemies under the feet of his glorious Son, who 'was manifested, that he might destroy the works of the devil.' Victory shall crown the strife between good and evil, and the cry shall be heard, 'Alleluia: for the Lord God omnipotent reigneth.'

FOR MEDITATION: To resist Satan we must be aware of his character and ways (2 Corinthians 2:11). If he cannot deter us from being saved (Acts 13:6–12), he will try to destroy us (1 Peter 5:8–9), distract us (Matthew 16:21–23), deceive us (John 8:44; 2 Corinthians 11:13–15; 2 Thessalonians 2:9–10; Revelation 12:9; 20:10) or discredit us (1 Timothy 3:6–7).

N.B. This sermon was 'In connection with the Centenary of Sabbath Schools' started by Robert Raikes in 1780. Statues of Raikes were erected at the Victoria Embankment, London, and in his birthplace, Gloucester.

SERMON NO. 1545

28 JUNE (PREACHED 29 JUNE 1884)

Ruth's reward; or, Cheer for converts

'The LORD *recompense thy work, and a full reward be given thee of the* LORD *God of Israel, under whose wings thou art come to trust.'* Ruth 2:12

SUGGESTED FURTHER READING: Isaiah 40:1–11

I remember when I first went to the house of God as a Christian youth, who had lately come to know the Lord, that I looked with veneration on every officer and member of the church. I thought them all, if not quite angels, yet very nearly as good; at any rate, I had no disposition to criticise *them,* for I felt myself to be so undeserving. I do not think that I have quite so high an idea of all professed Christians as I had then, for I am afraid that I could not truthfully entertain it; but, for all that, I think far better of them than many are apt to do. I believe that young people, when first brought to Christ, have so deep a sense of their own imperfection, and know so little of the infirmities of others, that they look up to the members of the church with a very high esteem, and this fixes upon such members, officers, and pastors a great responsibility. Since these converts are lowly in their own eyes it is proper and safe to encourage them; moreover, it is kind and needful to do so. Never be critical and severe with them, but deal tenderly with their budding graces; a frosty sentence may nip them; a genial word will develop them. Our Lord bids you feed the lambs; act the shepherd towards them, and never overdrive them, lest they faint by the way. It is a lovely sight to see a matronly Christian cheering on her class of girls, bearing with their waywardness and folly, and fostering everything that is hopeful in them. These are the mothers in Israel, to whom shall be honour. I love to see the advanced man of God giving a hearty grip to a youth, loving him, and advising him, yes, and adding a word of praise when it can be judiciously applied.

FOR MEDITATION: God's people are like sheep who need the care of shepherds (John 21:15–17; Acts 20:28; 1 Peter 5:2) and new converts are like children who need the extra care of nurses and fathers (1 Thessalonians 2:7,11). Even earthly parents are warned not to provoke and discourage their children (Ephesians 6:4; Colossians 3:21).

29 JUNE (1879)

The red heifer

'For if the blood of bulls and of goats, and the ashes of an heifer sprinkling the unclean, sanctifieth to the purifying of the flesh: how much more shall the blood of Christ, who through the eternal Spirit offered himself without spot to God, purge your conscience from dead works to serve the living God?' Hebrews 9:13–14
SUGGESTED FURTHER READING (Spurgeon): Numbers 19:1–22

Recollect that our Lord himself was spotless, pure and perfect, and yet—speak it with bated breath—God 'hath made him to be sin for us,' even him 'who knew no sin'. Whisper it with greater awe still—he was 'made a curse for us'—yes, a curse, 'for it is written, Cursed is every one that hangeth on a tree'. That red heifer, though without spot and never having borne a yoke, was regarded as a polluted thing. Take it out of the camp. It must not live; kill it. It is a polluted thing; burn it right up, for God cannot endure it. Behold, and wonder that God's own ever-blessed, adorable Son, in inconceivable condescension of unutterable love, took the place of sin, the place of the sinner, and 'was numbered with the transgressors'. He must die; hang him up on a cross; he must be forsaken of men, and even deserted of God. 'It pleased the LORD to bruise him; he hath put him to grief'; he shall 'make his soul an offering for sin'. 'All we like sheep have gone astray; we have turned every one to his own way; and the LORD hath laid on him the iniquity of us all'; not only the punishment, but the iniquity, the very sin itself, was laid upon the Ever-Blessed. The wise men of our age say it is impossible that sin should be lawfully imputed to the innocent; that is what the philosophers say, but God declares that it was done: 'he hath made him to be sin ... who knew no sin'. Therefore, it was possible; yes, it is done: 'It is finished'. The sacrifice then is much greater. 'How much more', we may cry exultingly as we think of it, 'shall the blood of Christ, who through the eternal Spirit offered himself without spot to God, purge your conscience from dead works to serve the living God?'

FOR MEDITATION: (*Our Own Hymn Book* no. 303 v.2—Albert Midlane, 1864)
   'No tongue can tell the wrath He bore, the wrath so due to me;
   Sin's just desert; He bore it all, to set the sinner free!'

30 JUNE (PREACHED 29 JUNE 1879)

The philosophy of promise

'New things do I declare: before they spring forth I tell you of them.'
Isaiah 42:9
SUGGESTED FURTHER READING: Ephesians 6:18–20

If God blessed some churches in London in proportion to their prayers, he would not bless them much: for the prayer meetings are held in the vestry, and that is not full, nor one-half full at the best. A prayer meeting in the chapel itself would look like a drop in a bucket, and so they hide the nakedness of the land by holding a hole-and-corner meeting in the vestry. Such things as prayer meetings in the chapel are not expected; a snug little room is quite large enough. Alas, there are not many brethren to pray. Two or three prose so long and so drearily, that they fill up the evening, and then they ask the Lord to forgive their *shortcomings*; they would do better to ask forgiveness for their longcomings, which are the death of all fervency. There is not much prayer in these long sermonizings, and the whole business is far more formal than real. Scant will be the blessing if the Lord is going to bless them in proportion to their prayers. Do you wonder that the minister cannot preach when the people do not pray? I see some of you up from the country; perhaps you are deacons, and yet do not attend the prayer meetings yourselves. I have known such things; and I cry shame upon you. And then you find fault with the minister. Have you never heard of the minister who suddenly seemed to fail, and, when the people complained, he said, 'Ah, I may well fail, for I have lost my prayer-book!' Someone said, 'I did not know you used a prayer-book, sir.' 'Oh!' said he, 'my prayer-book used to be written on the hearts of my people, and while they prayed for me God blessed me and I had success, but they have given up praying for me, and what can I do?'

FOR MEDITATION: To expect the preacher to pray and speak without also praying ourselves is an act of presumption whether we do so as God's gathered people (1 Samuel 12:19–25) or as individuals (Acts 8:22–24). Read Jeremiah 42:1–43:4 to see how a prayerless congregation were totally unprepared to hear God's word because they had failed to support the preacher as he prayed over his sermon.

1 JULY (1883)

The works of the devil destroyed

'For this purpose the Son of God was manifested, that he might destroy the works of the devil.' 1 John 3:8
SUGGESTED FURTHER READING: Genesis 3:1–19

Men have become wonderfully proficient in the science of excuse-making, frequently imputing their own guilt to the devil's guile. Yet sin in a sadly true sense does come from the devil; he first introduced it into the world. How or when he himself first sinned and fell from being an angel of light to become the apostle of darkness we will not conjecture. Many have thought that the pride of his lofty station, or envy of the foreseen glories of the Son of man, may have overthrown him; but, at any rate, he kept not his first estate, but became a rebel against his Lord, and the active promoter of all evil. Being expelled from heaven for his wickedness, he desired to wreak his revenge upon God by alienating the human race from its obedience. He saw what an interest the Creator had taken in man, and therefore judged that he could grieve him greatly by seducing man from obedience. He perceived that the Maker, when he formed the earth, did not rest; when he had made birds and fishes, did not rest; when he had made sun, moon, and stars, did not rest; but when he had fashioned man, he was so well content that then he took a day of rest, and consecrated it for ever to be a Sabbath. Thus was God's unresting care for man made manifest. 'Surely,' said the evil one, 'if I can turn this favoured being into an enemy of God, then I shall bring dishonour upon the name of the Most High, and have my revenge.' Therefore he alighted in the garden, and tempted our first parents, thus opening the gate by which sin entered into the world with all its train of woe. In that sense sin is truthfully described as being the work of the devil. He brought the flame, which has caused so great a burning. Since then he has been in some degree the author of sin by often tempting men.

FOR MEDITATION: Beware of Satan's wicked works—tempting (Matthew 4:1), sowing (Matthew 13:39), stealing (Luke 8:12), murdering and lying (John 8:44), oppressing (Acts 10:38), attacking (Ephesians 6:11,16), hindering (1 Thessalonians 2:18), devouring (1 Peter 5:8), deceiving and accusing (Revelation 12:9–10). Rejoice in the Saviour's wonderful works of destroying the devil and his power (Hebrews 2:14–15,18)!

SERMON NO. 1728

2 JULY (1882)

'Love and I'—a mystery

'I have declared unto them thy name, and will declare it: that the love wherewith thou hast loved me may be in them, and I in them.' John 17:26

SUGGESTED FURTHER READING: 1 John 3:1–18

This indwelling of the Father's love in us has the most blessed results. It has an *expulsive* result. As soon as it gets into the heart it says to all love of sin, 'Get away from here; there remains no room for you here.' When the light enters in, the darkness receives immediate notice of ejectment; the night is gone as soon as the dawn appears. It has also a *repulsive* power by which it repels the assaults of sin. As though a man snatched the sun out of the heaven, made a round shield with it, held it in the very face of the prince of darkness, and blinded him with the light, so does the love of God the Father repel the enemy. It girds the soul with the armour of light. It repels the devil, the love of the world, the love of sin, and all outward temptations. And then what an *impulsive* power it has. Get the love of Christ into you, and it is as when an engine receives fire and steam, and so obtains the force which drives it. Then have you strengthening, then have you motive power, then are you urged on to this and that heroic deed which, apart from this sublime love, you never would have thought of. For Christ you can live, for Christ you can suffer, for Christ you can die, when once the Father's love to him has taken full possession of your spirit. And, oh, how elevating it is. How it lifts a man up above self and sin; how it makes him seek the things that are above! How purifying it is; and how happy it makes the subject of its influence. If you are unhappy you want more of the love of God.

FOR MEDITATION: (*Our Own Hymn Book* no. 797 v.3—Charles Wesley, 1746)
'God only knows the love of God:
Oh that it now were shed abroad
In this poor stony heart:
For love I sigh, for love I pine:
This only portion, Lord, be mine,
Be mine this better part.'

SERMON NO. 1667

3 JULY (1884)

Peter's blunder: a lesson to ourselves

'Put Peter said, Not so, Lord; for I have never eaten any thing that is common or unclean.' Acts 10:14

SUGGESTED FURTHER READING: James 3:1–12

'Not so, Lord'. This is a very curious expression. I do not mind how you turn it into English from the original, but it is a very strange compound. If Peter had said, 'Not so,' there would have been a clear consistency in his language and tone. But 'Not so, *Lord*', is an odd jumble of self-will and reverence, of pride and humility, of contradiction and devotion. Surely, when you say, 'Not so,' it ought not to be said to the Lord; and if you say, 'Lord', you ought not to put side by side with such an ascription the expression, 'Not so'. Peter always was a blunderer in his early days, and he had not grown out of his old habits of honest impetuosity. He meant well, and his expression was not intended to convey all that we might easily make of it. At any rate, it is not for us to condemn him. Who are we that we should sit in judgment on a saint of God? Besides, we are not without fault ourselves in the matter of incorrect speech. You and I have said some very curious compound things in our time. We have uttered exclamations that have been so good that the Lord accepted them: but they have been so bad that he could not have accepted them if it had not been for his infinite mercy. In our utterances there has been faith mixed with unbelief, love defaced with a want of submission, gratitude combined with distrust, humility flavoured with self-conceit, courage undermined with cowardice, fervour mingled with indifference. We are as strange beings as the image which Nebuchadnezzar saw in his dream; and our speech betrays the fact. When we were fashioned by God first of all we were 'fearfully and wonderfully made', but when we fell, and were unmade by sin, we became monstrosities, combinations of contrarieties.

FOR MEDITATION: Spurgeon went on to illustrate how Peter had fallen back into his old habits, recalling times when by Peter's lips his Lord had been rebuked (Matthew 16:22), refused (John 13:6–8) and flatly contradicted (Matthew 26:31–35). Certain obligations are placed upon us if we call Jesus 'Lord' (Luke 6:46; 1 Corinthians 12:3) and God 'Father' (1 Peter 1:17).

SERMON NO. 1823

4 JULY (1880)

Good news for thirsty souls

'I will give unto him that is athirst of the fountain of the water of life freely.' Revelation 21:6
SUGGESTED FURTHER READING (Spurgeon): John 4:1–15

Turn to the first verse of the fifty-fifth chapter of Isaiah, 'Ho, every one that thirsteth, come ye to the waters, and he that hath no money; come ye, buy, and eat; yea, come, buy wine and milk without money and without price.' Grace must be gratis; the word 'freely' in our text makes it clear that salvation is an absolute gift, but here the fact is put in a negative form that there may be no mistake whatever. Mercy is 'without money and without price', without price in any possible sense. We neither purchase, nor procure, nor earn, nor produce salvation by merit, effort, sacrifice, or service. It comes to us, not because we deserve it, but because we need it. We are blessed with it out of the goodwill and pleasure of the Lord, and we do not purchase it by good deeds, good desires, pious resolves, or persevering endeavours. We are empty and he fills us. In order that you may come to Jesus, no preparation is required. You may come just as you are, and come at once: only confess that you need him, desire to have him, and then take him by trusting him. He is like wine and milk, supplying delight and satisfaction, and you are to take him as men would take a drink. How could the invitation be put more broadly than it is? How could it be uttered more earnestly? It has a 'Ho' to give it tongue. Tradesmen in certain parts of London stand outside their shops and cry 'Buy, buy!' or call out 'Ho!' to the passers-by because they are anxious to sell their wares. Jesus is yet more eager to distribute his rich grace, for he longs to see men saved. Ho! you that pass by, stop here awhile: turn your attention this way: here is something worthy of your thoughts. 'Ho, every one that thirsteth, come ye to the waters, and he that hath no money'.

FOR MEDITATION: (*Our Own Hymn Book* no. 488 v.4—Isaac Watts, 1706)
'Ho, ye that pant for living streams,
And pine away and die,
Here you may quench your raging thirst
With springs that never dry.'

SERMON NO. 1549

5 JULY (1883)

A cure for unsavoury meats: or, Salt for the white of an egg

'Can that which is unsavoury be eaten without salt? Or is there any taste in the white of an egg?' Job 6:6
SUGGESTED FURTHER READING: Philippians 1:12–18

You have read Dr Hawker's Morning and Evening Portions, perhaps? I do not suppose that you have learned much of fresh exposition from them, or that you have been struck with any great originality of idea in them, but if you have read them profitably you have said to yourself, 'Well, this one point there is in Hawker: his subject is Christ on the first of January, Christ on the last of December, and Christ all the other days of the year.' He speaks of nothing else but Christ. He seems to bring forth the Lord Jesus in his portions every day as a matter of course, just as your maid always puts the bread on the table, whatever else she does not place there. So it was with Hawker and men like him; Christ crucified was their all in all. Their dear Lord and Master was never long absent from their discoursing. If they preached doctrine, it was 'the truth' as it 'is in Jesus'. If they preached experience, it was to 'know him ... and the fellowship of his sufferings'. And if they went into practice, as they did, their idea of holiness was to be made like Jesus and to follow 'him without the camp, bearing his reproach.' Now, I do not believe a sermon can have savour in it unless it has Christ in it, for he has 'the savour of' all 'good ointments', and there is no sweetness without him. What shall we say of him? 'Thy name is as ointment poured forth, therefore do the virgins love thee.' His name is so fragrant that it perfumes heaven itself: Jehovah smells a savour of rest in the name, person and work of his well-beloved Son. Therefore an essential to savoury meat is that it shall have Christ in it. He has said, 'my flesh is meat indeed, and my blood is drink indeed', and there is no meat and no drink that has such savour in it as this.

FOR MEDITATION: Whether his subject is peace by Jesus Christ (Acts 10:36), the gospel of Christ (Romans 15:19), the cross of Christ (1 Corinthians 1:23), the resurrection of Christ (1 Corinthians 15:12), the lordship of Christ (2 Corinthians 4:5) or the unsearchable riches of Christ (Ephesians 3:8), the Christian minister's privilege, priority and obligation must be to preach Christ.

SERMON NO. 1730

6 JULY (1879)

Our change of masters

'Being then made free from sin, ye became the servants of righteousness.'
Romans 6:18
SUGGESTED FURTHER READING: John 8:31–36

I am made free by omnipotent love! I have escaped from the taskmaster's fetters, and I am the Lord's free man! Let all the angels praise my redeeming Lord. Let all the spirits before the throne praise the Lord, who has led his people out of bondage, 'for he is good: for his mercy endureth for ever.' Now, how came we to be free? We have become free in three ways. First, by *purchase*, for our Saviour has paid the full redemption money for us, and there is not a penny due upon us. Blessed be his name, there is no mortgage on his inheritance; the price is all paid and we are Christ's unencumbered property for ever. Here we stand at this moment free, because we are ransomed, and we know that our 'redeemer liveth'. Our body, soul, and spirit are all bought with a price, and in our complete manhood we are Christ's. Next, we are free by *power* as well as by purchase. Just as the Israelites were the Lord's own people, but he had to bring them 'out of Egypt with a mighty hand, and with an outstretched arm,' so has the Lord by power broken the neck of sin and brought us up from the dominion of the old Pharaoh of evil and set us free. The Spirit's power, the same power which raised Christ from the dead, the same power which made the heavens and the earth, has delivered us, and we are the ransomed of the Lord. And then we are free by *privilege*: 'as many as received him, to them gave he *the privilege* to become the sons of God'. God has declared us free. His own royal, majestic, and divine decree has bidden the prisoners go forth. The Lord himself looses the prisoners, and declares that they shall no more be held in captivity. Price and power and privilege meet together in our liberty.

FOR MEDITATION: (*Our Own Hymn Book* no. 116 song 2 v.5—Isaac Watts, 1719)
 'Now I am Thine, for ever Thine,
 Nor shall my purpose move!
 Thy hand hath loosed my bands of pain,
 And bound me with Thy love.'

SERMON NO. 1482

7 JULY (1881)

My comfort in affliction

'This is my comfort in my affliction: for thy word hath quickened me.'
Psalm 119:50
SUGGESTED FURTHER READING: Romans 15:1–6

Believers have their peculiar comfort under affliction. 'This', says David, 'is my comfort in my affliction'. '*This*'—dwell on the word *'this'*, as different from the consolations of other men. The drunkard takes his cup and he quotes Solomon, 'Give strong drink unto him that is ready to perish, and wine unto those that be of heavy hearts'; and as he drains his cup, he says, 'This is my comfort in my affliction'. The miser hides his gold, takes down his purse, and chinks it. Oh, the music of those golden notes! And he cries, 'This is my comfort in my affliction'. Men mostly have some comfort or other. Some have allowable comforts, though they be but of minor quality; they find comfort in the sympathy of men, in domestic kindness, in philosophic reflection, in homely content; but such comforts generally fail, always fail, when the trial becomes exceedingly severe. Now, just as the wicked man and the worldly man can say of this or that, '*This* is my comfort', the Christian comes forward, and bringing with him the Word of God brimming with rich promises, he says, 'This is my comfort in my affliction'. You put down your comfort, and I put down mine. '*This* is my comfort'—he is evidently not ashamed of it; he is evidently ready to set forth his solace in preference to all others; and while others say, I derive consolation from *this*, and I from *that*, David opens the Holy Scripture, and cheerfully exclaims, '*This* is my comfort'. Can you say the same? '*This*', in opposition to everything else, this promise of God, this covenant of his grace, '*This* is my comfort'.

FOR MEDITATION: (*Our Own Hymn Book* no. 482 v.2—Anne Steele, 1760)
'Here may the wretched sons of want
Exhaustless riches find;
Riches, above what earth can grant,
And lasting as the mind.'

SERMON NO. 1872

8 JULY (PREACHED 3 JULY 1881)

The swiftly running word

'His word runneth very swiftly.' Psalm 147:15
SUGGESTED FURTHER READING: Hebrews 1:1–2:4

The word as it comes from God takes several forms. At first it came forth as a *fiat*: 'Let there be,' 'and there was'. When there were no angels to hear him, when matter did not exist to obey him, when there was nothing but himself, the self-existent One, Jehovah spoke, and the things which are began to be. Since then he has spoken to his creatures by the word of *command*, which should ever be obeyed; even as David said, 'I will delight myself in thy statutes: I will not forget thy word.' The word of the Lord comes forth in the form of a precept from his temple, or a statute from his throne, and we ought most reverently to treasure up every syllable that God speaks to us in that form, for we are his servants. He also speaks by way of *teaching*. He instructs us by revealing himself through his word. All true doctrine is the word of God, and is to be devoutly believed. Our prayer should be, 'give me understanding according to thy word.' His word is also spoken in the form of *promise*, rich, free and gracious, the word on which his children live. In this form it is sweeter than honey or the honeycomb. It flashes forth also like lightning flames in *threatenings*, when God dooms the ungodly or warns them of what shall follow unless they repent. Terrible indeed is the word by which justice takes vengeance upon the wicked. But chief of all, and above all, is THE WORD of whom John speaks: 'In the beginning was the Word, and the Word was with God, and the Word was God. The same was in the beginning with God.' This is he of whom we read in the Revelation, 'he was clothed with a vesture dipped in blood: and his name is called The Word of God.' That Word is the incarnation of God, wherein God has been pleased to manifest himself more fully than by all other words or works.

FOR MEDITATION: (*Our Own Hymn Book* no. 192 v.6—Isaac Watts, 1709)
  'His very word of grace is strong
  As that which built the skies;
  The voice that rolls the stars along
  Speaks all the promises.'

9 JULY (1882)

The still small voice

'*And after the fire a still small voice. And it was so, when Elijah heard it, that he wrapped his face in his mantle, and went out, and stood in the entering in of the cave. And, behold, there came a voice unto him, and said, What doest thou here, Elijah?*' 1 Kings 19:12–13
SUGGESTED FURTHER READING: 1 Samuel 14:24–31

At one time Christian people thought very little of the bodily system: they called their physical frame a vile body, as indeed it is in some sense, but not in every sense. If they had any doubts, fears, and tremblings our good fathers laid them all on the back of the devil, or ascribed them to their own unbelief, when frequently their depressions arose from lack of food or fresh air, or from a torpid liver, or a weak stomach. A thousand things can cast us down, and we ought not to despise the body through which they act upon us. Rather should we attend to natural laws and look to the God of those laws to help us. God, who made the body, and who gave it such a close affinity to the mind, observes how dependent the soul is upon the body, and often begins his restoring work by healing our diseases. We who dwell in houses of clay are often cribbed, cabined, and confined from loftier things by reason of the dust to which our soul cleaves. The Lord who heals his people began in Elijah's case by refreshing his languid frame. He restored him by sleep and by food. If any of you are depressed and in mental trouble, I would invite you to look to your health, and not to blame yourselves till first you have seen whether your sadness arises from sickness or from sin, from a feeble body or a rebellious mind. Do not think it unspiritual to remember that you have a body, for you certainly have one and ought not to ignore its existence. If your heavenly Father thinks of your physical frame, he gives you a hint to do the same. If the Lord in his wisdom began with the high-spirited Elijah by feeding and refreshing his mortal body, we ought to count it wisdom to look to our outward parts: it is of heretics that we read that they promote 'neglecting of the body': wise men value it as 'the temple of the Holy Ghost'.

FOR MEDITATION: Our bodies are not to be dishonoured (Romans 1:24), used for sin (Romans 6:12–13; 1 Corinthians 6:18) or neglected (Colossians 2:23), but should be nourished and cherished (Ephesians 5:29), exercised (1 Timothy 4:8) and given medical treatment (1 Timothy 5:23).

SERMON NO. 1668

10 JULY (1881)

The double 'come'

'And the Spirit and the bride say, Come. And let him that heareth say, Come.' Revelation 22:17
SUGGESTED FURTHER READING: Isaiah 55:1–5

The Old Testament closes with the word 'curse'; let not the New Testament conclude in the same fashion. What, then, shall it be? Shall the last sentences be full of tender invitation and earnest entreaty to the sinner, bidding him come to Christ and live? Yes, let it be so: and yet shall we forget the Lord himself while we are thinking of the sinner? He has told us that he will come; should not the very last word of Scripture have a reference to him and to his glorious advent? Should not the Spirit at the last, as well as at the first, bear witness to Jesus? Shall not the last word that shall linger in the reader's ear speak of the approaching glory of the Lord? Yes, let it be so; but it would be best of all if we could have a word that would combine the four: a promise to the righteous, a threatening to the wicked, an invitation to the poor and needy, and a welcome to the coming One. Who could devise such a verse? The Holy Spirit is equal to the emergency. He can dictate such a verse: he has dictated it. Here it is in the words of our text: 'And the Spirit and the bride say, Come. And let him that heareth say, Come.' That 'Come' is a promise to the righteous, for at the coming of the Lord they shall have their portion and their glory, for his reward is with him. That 'Come' is a word of thunder to the wicked, for when he comes he shall 'break them with a rod of iron;' he shall 'dash them in pieces like a potter's vessel.' That 'Come' is a word of invitation to the sinner: 'let him that is athirst come. And whosoever will, let him take the water of life freely.' And yet it is a welcome to our Well-beloved; for when the Spirit and the bride say 'Come', they invite the coming One, the Messiah whose second advent our heart desires, to whom we cry, 'Even so, come, Lord Jesus.'

FOR MEDITATION: (*Our Own Hymn Book* no. 509 v.2—Albert Midlane, 1865)
'Come, and welcome; start for glory, leave the wretched world behind:
Christ will spread His banner o'er thee, thou in Him a friend shalt find;
Come, and welcome, to a Saviour good and kind.'

11 JULY (PREACHED 17 JUNE 1880)

Two good things

'It is good for me that I have been afflicted; that I might learn thy statutes.' Psalm 119:71
'It is good for me to draw near to God: I have put my trust in the Lord GOD, that I may declare all thy works.' Psalm 73:28
SUGGESTED FURTHER READING: Galatians 1:11–24

I desire to bear my witness in the last words of Psalm 73: 'I have put my trust in the Lord GOD, that I may declare all thy works.' My first text, as far as it relates to a preacher, shows how he is taught in private: 'It is good for me that I have been afflicted; that I might learn thy statutes': my second text, so far as it relates to the preacher, shows how he is helped to preach in public: 'it is good for me to draw near to God: I have put my trust in the Lord GOD, that I may declare all thy works.' To be able to speak of God's works to others is no small gift, and you gain it by trusting in God yourself, finding his promise true, and then bearing witness to others. Draw near to God, and have communion with him, and then come down from the mount and speak with the people, believing what you say, and expecting God to bless it to those who hear it. That is the way to preach; and I pray that every one of us who opens his mouth for God may do it in this fashion. It is not merely what is in the Bible that we have to set before the people, but what we ourselves have tasted and felt of the good word of truth experimentally, declaring Jesus Christ in the power of his resurrection as we know it in our own hearts. We cannot do this except by intimate personal fellowship with God. You, dear friends, who are engaged in teaching, cannot learn the truth without some measure of affliction, and you cannot tell it out in the right spirit without a large measure of drawing near unto God. Then you can say, 'This poor man cried, and the LORD heard him'. You can say, 'one thing I know, that, whereas I was blind, now I see.' You can say, 'I sought the Lord, and he heard me.'

FOR MEDITATION: There is far more to preaching than learning facts and copying from other preachers! Note the importance placed upon personal dealings with God by the apostles Paul (Acts 22:14–15; 26:16; 1 Corinthians 11:23; 15:3), Peter (2 Peter 1:16) and John (1 John 1:1–3) in fulfilment of what the Lord Jesus Christ had said (Matthew 28:19–20).

SERMON NO. 1629

12 JULY (PREACHED 29 JUNE 1884)

The proof of our ministry

'Since ye seek a proof of Christ speaking in me, which to you-ward is not weak, but is mighty in you.' 'Examine yourselves, whether ye be in the faith; prove your own selves. Know ye not your own selves, how that Jesus Christ is in you, except ye be reprobates?' 2 Corinthians 13:3,5
SUGGESTED FURTHER READING (Spurgeon): 2 Corinthians 12:14-21

The general conduct and conversation of members of a church must always be the best recommendation of the ministry which feeds them. My heart sinks within me when I hear of those who have been numbered with us, and have shared our love and esteem, and yet have behaved inconsistently. Is this to be laid at my door? I confess I cannot help blaming myself, and growing sad. Did I not hear of an earnest Temperance man in public, drinking in private? Is this the fruit of my ministry? Did I hear of another professor whose household is a scene of constant strife? Did I observe coldness and indifference creeping over others? Did I find a brother censorious and bitter? Is this the result of my labour? I could weep and break my heart. Do we hear that some are not upright and truthful in their dealings? Do people say, 'These are members of Spurgeon's church'? I do not blame the world for so saying. It is only just that men should estimate our ministry by its results. We cannot help such judgments, nor do we repine at them. You are either our joy and crown, or else our sorrow and dishonour. You must estimate whether a man farms well by the crops which he raises. You cannot condemn him if a few thorns and thistles spring up in the hedgerows, because those things are so natural to the soil that they are there in no time, but if the acres are covered with thistles, if there is a preponderance of weeds, everybody says, 'This is wretched farming.' Farmers may make a great outcry about new machinery and artificial manures, but if there is no harvest it is poor work. Oh, dear sirs, by the love you bear to us, who labour for Christ among you, 'let your conversation be as it becometh the gospel of Christ'.

FOR MEDITATION: The faithful pastor will desire fruit from his ministry (Romans 1:13; Philippians 4:17). When he sees it, he will be glad (Colossians 1:3-6), but the absence of fruit won't do anybody any good (Hebrews 13:15-17).

SERMON NO. 1788

13 JULY (1879)

The present crisis

'*I will go and return to my place, till they acknowledge their offence, and seek my face: in their affliction they will seek me early.*' Hosea 5:15
SUGGESTED FURTHER READING: Daniel 9:1–21

All hope for a country lies in the true believers who dwell in it. Remember Sodom, and how it would have been spared had there been ten righteous men found there, and know that you also 'are the salt of the earth', by whom it is to be conserved. Loathe the spirit of those who say that, because we are citizens of heaven we are to have nothing to do with the concerns of men below. A more un-Christianlike sentiment, a more selfish sentiment, never degraded spiritual minds. Wherever the Jews dwelt in the days of their scattering they were commanded to care for the good of the people among whom they dwelt. Here are the words of the Lord by Jeremiah: 'seek the peace of the city whither I have caused you to be carried away captives, and pray unto the LORD for it: for in the peace thereof shall ye have peace.' Surely Christians are not to be less generous than Jews. Happily we are not under a despot; in England we are our own governors, and the man who in this land does nothing to secure the good government of the country is, by his silence, on the side of wrong. You cannot shirk your responsibility anyhow except by clearing out of the land altogether, and then if it suffers by your absence you will still be found guilty. You are part and parcel of the nation, for you share in its protection and privileges, and it is yours as Christian men to feel that you are bound in return to do all you can in the midst of it to promote truth and righteousness. What then? What course should we now pursue? Let us make confession of sin on behalf of the people as Moses, Jeremiah and Daniel did. You may not consider that to be sin which I judge to be so, but, my brother, you see sin enough all around you of one sort or another. Take it to yourself, and as the high priest went in to the holy place to plead for the people, so act as a priest before God, in your quiet personal devotions. Confess the sin of this nation before God.

FOR MEDITATION: Consider the words and prayers of some other godly men who identified themselves with the sinful condition of their nation (2 Chronicles 34:19–21; Ezra 9:5–15; Nehemiah 1:4–11; Isaiah 6:5). We also are to practise good prayerful citizenship (1 Timothy 2:1–4).

SERMON NO. 1483

14 JULY (PREACHED 13 JULY 1884)

Receiving the Holy Ghost

'He said unto them, have ye received the Holy Ghost since ye believed?'
Acts 19:2
SUGGESTED FURTHER READING: 1 Corinthians 14:1–25

When the Holy Spirit was given in the earliest ages he showed his presence by certain miraculous signs. Some of those who received the Holy Spirit spoke with tongues; others began to prophesy, and a third class received the gifts of healing, so that wherever they laid their hands disease fled before them. I am sure that if these powers were given now in connection with the reception of the Holy Spirit and your believing, you would all be anxious to possess them. I can hardly imagine a single Christian who would not put to himself the enquiry, 'Have I received the Holy Spirit in that fashion?' You would want to be healing, or to be speaking with tongues, or to be working miracles, by which you could benefit your fellow-men and glorify God, would you not? Now, be it never forgotten that those works of the Holy Spirit which are permanent must assuredly be of greater value than those which were transitory. We cannot suppose that the Holy Spirit brought forth the best wine at first, and that his operations gradually deteriorated. It is a rule of the kingdom to keep the best wine to the last, and therefore I conclude that you and I are not left to partake of the dregs, but that those works of the Holy Spirit which are at this time granted to the Church of God are every way as valuable as those earlier miraculous gifts which have departed from us. The work of the Holy Spirit, by which men are quickened from their death in sin, is not inferior to the power which made men speak with tongues. The work of the Holy Spirit, when he comforts men and makes them glad in Christ, is by no means second to the opening of the eyes of the blind. Why, sirs, men might have the gifts of the Spirit as to miracles, and yet might perish after all; but he that has the spiritual gifts of the Holy Spirit shall never perish: they are saving blessings, and where they come they lift the man out of his sinful estate, and make him to be a child of God.

FOR MEDITATION: (*Our Own Hymn Book* no. 464 v.7—Andrew Reed, 1842)
 'Spirit divine! attend our prayers, make a lost world Thy home;
 Descend with all Thy gracious powers! oh come, great Spirit, come.'

SERMON NO. 1790

15 JULY (1883)

Accepted of the great Father

'He hath made us accepted in the beloved.' Ephesians 1:6
SUGGESTED FURTHER READING: Romans 14:7–18

If we be indeed 'accepted in the beloved', does it not show how close, how real our union with the Beloved must be? Do we even share in Christ's acceptance with God? Then we are one with him in everything. Here is a father who has no particular interest in such and such a woman, but his son takes to himself that woman to be his wife, and now the loving father says, 'That woman is my daughter,' and so she is received into his love for his son's sake. He says to her; 'You are my dear son's wife; therefore you are my daughter, and dear to me, and welcome to my house at any time.' Thus it is with the great God. He says to us, whom Christ has espoused unto himself, that we may be his bride in blessed conjugal union for ever and ever, 'Come to my heart, my children, for he is my Son, and I love you for his sake; I accept you in him.' Is not that a wonderful union, closer than the marriage bond, which causes us to share in Christ's righteousness, so that the holy God can say to us who are sinful by nature, 'You are acceptable to me because of your connection with my Son'? If a woman of base character were married to the best of men it would not make her acceptable. A father would scarcely know what to do with such a daughter-in-law: we should try and carry out our relationship as far as we could with all kindness, but we could hardly say that such a person brought into our family by marriage would be acceptable to us; but, oh, the Lord sees his people so wrapped up in Christ that he must accept them in him. If I accept a man, I cannot quarrel with his little finger; if I accept a man, I accept his whole body and so, since the Father accepts Christ, he accepts every member of his mystical body.

FOR MEDITATION: (*Our Own Hymn Book* no. 397 v.2—Count Zinzendorf, 1739; tr. by John Wesley, 1740)
    'When from the dust of death I rise,
    To take my mansion in the skies,
    E'en then shall this be all my plea,
    "Jesus hath lived and died for me."'

SERMON NO. 1731

16 JULY (1882)

Teaching for the outer and inner circles

'And with many such parables spake he the word unto them, as they were able to hear it. But without a parable spake he not unto them: and when they were alone, he expounded all things to his disciples.' Mark 4:33–34
SUGGESTED FURTHER READING: Matthew 28:16–20

Our Lord had two great objects before him in his ministry. The first was to preach the word to the outlying masses, that out of them he might gather a people to himself who should be his disciples. This part of his work he carried on with great perseverance, traversing the Holy Land from end to end and finding here one and there another, but never ceasing to preach the gospel to the crowds that flocked to him. His second object was to train those who became his disciples, that having gathered them to himself he might educate them in the truth. He taught them concerning the Father and his love, concerning himself, his work, his death and his resurrection, concerning the divine Comforter and his indwelling, and all else that would make for their progress and profit. While our Lord was here he gathered the men together who should carry on the work after he was gone. He did not think it enough to make converts: he wished to make disciples. He did not think it enough even to make beginners in discipleship, but he would have them advance in knowledge and holiness, learning till they were 'able to teach others also.' To this day this same double work is carried on by the divine Spirit through the ministers and servants of God. We are to preach to the multitude who make up the outer ring; for our Lord said, 'Go ye into all the world, and preach the gospel to every creature.' We are to evangelize all, making no distinction of rank or character: to every person with whom we come in contact we are to proclaim the kingdom of God. That being done, however, the minister's work is only begun; he is now to expound the mystery, open up the higher doctrine and lead the discipled ones into the deep things of God, that there may be in the church fathers, instructors, and leaders.

FOR MEDITATION: Examine Timothy's ministerial training and progress in 2 Timothy. He had learned the way of salvation in the Scriptures (3:14–15), had come to faith in the Lord Jesus Christ himself (1:5) and had observed the apostle Paul in action (3:10). Now he was to be active in preaching, teaching and evangelism (4:2–5) and in extending training to others (2:2).

SERMON NO. 1669

17 JULY (1884)

The history of sundry fools

'Fools because of their transgression, and because of their iniquities, are afflicted. Their soul abhorreth all manner of meat; and they draw near unto the gates of death. Then they cry unto the LORD in their trouble, and he saveth them out of their distresses. He sent his word, and healed them, and delivered them from their destructions.' Psalm 107:17–20
SUGGESTED FURTHER READING: Matthew 7:13–27

In the twentieth verse we read, 'and delivered them from their destructions.' What! Are there many destructions to a man? Oh, yes, a great many! I have known one man destroyed by his shop, another by his wife, another by his children. Many a woman is destroyed by her clothes; many a man is destroyed by his eating; millions are destroyed by their drinking. Everything about us will destroy us unless God saves us. There are a thousand gates to hell, though there is only one road to heaven. One man may perish by debauchery, another by respectability. One man may be lost in the ale-house, another through his teetotalism, if he makes a god of it. One man may go down to hell by his want of common decency, and another by his pride, prudery and self-righteousness. Do not deceive yourself; the way to ruin is easy, and many crowd it. If you want to go to heaven, we shall have to tell you a great deal about what is to be believed; but if you want to go to hell, I have no need to tell you anything: 'How shall we escape, if we neglect so great salvation?' A little matter of neglect will land you in hell. But it is not a little matter of thought that will bring you to heaven; there must be a stirring up of the entire soul, an awakening of the whole man to seek after God in Christ Jesus, or else you shall perish. Surrounded, then, with destructions, snares about your bed, snares about your table, snares in your solitude, snares in the street, snares in your shop, snares at dawn of day and snares at set of sun, you are in terrible danger; yet people surrounded with destructions have been saved. They have cried to God in their trouble, and he has delivered them out of their destructions; will he not do the same at your cry?

FOR MEDITATION: (*Our Own Hymn Book* no. 30 v.3—Charles H. Spurgeon, 1866)
  'In answer to my piteous cries, from hell's dark brink I'm brought;
  My Jesus saw me from the skies, and swift salvation wrought.'

SERMON NO. 1824

18 JULY (PREACHED 17 JULY 1881)

Faith: what is it? How can it be obtained?

'By grace are ye saved through faith.' Ephesians 2:8
SUGGESTED FURTHER READING: Acts 3:1–16

Faith occupies the position of a channel or conduit-pipe. Grace is the fountain and the stream: faith is the aqueduct along which the flood of mercy flows down to refresh the thirsty sons of men. It is a great pity when the aqueduct is broken. It is a sad sight to see around Rome the many noble aqueducts which no longer convey water into the city, because the arches are broken and the marvellous structures are in ruins. The aqueduct must be kept entire to convey the current; and, even so, faith must be true and sound, leading right up to God and coming right down to ourselves, that it may become a serviceable channel of mercy to our souls. Still, I again remind you that faith is the channel or aqueduct, and not the fountain head, and we must not look so much to it that we exalt it above the divine source of all blessing which lies in the grace of God. Never make a Christ out of your faith, nor think of it as if it were the independent source of your salvation. Our life is found in 'Looking unto Jesus', not in looking to our own faith. By faith all things become possible to us; yet the power is not in the faith, but in the God upon whom faith relies. Grace is the locomotive, and faith is the chain by which the carriage of the soul is attached to the great motive power. The righteousness of faith is not the moral excellence of faith, but the righteousness of Jesus Christ which faith grasps and appropriates. The peace within the soul is not derived from the contemplation of our own faith, but it comes to us from him who is our peace, the hem of whose garment faith touches, and virtue comes out of him into the soul.

FOR MEDITATION: God's people have achieved great things through faith in the living God (Hebrews 11:33–34). Consider the undeserved blessings of God's favour which can come to us through the channel of faith in the Lord Jesus Christ (Romans 3:25)—justification (Romans 3:30), the promise of the Spirit (Galatians 3:14), righteousness (Philippians 3:9), resurrection (Colossians 2:12), salvation (2 Timothy 3:15), God's promises (Hebrews 6:12) and God's keeping power (1 Peter 1:5).

19 JULY (PREACHED 20 JULY 1884)

Helps to full assurance

'These things have I written unto you that believe on the name of the Son of God; that ye may know that ye have eternal life, and that ye may believe on the name of the Son of God.' 1 John 5:13
SUGGESTED FURTHER READING: 2 Thessalonians 1:1–12

To unbelievers this text is not written: it is for all who trust in Jesus, but it is for none besides. If you enquire why it is not addressed to unbelievers, I answer, simply because it would be preposterous to wish men to be assured of that which is not true. John never wished that a man who had not believed in Jesus Christ should even think that he had eternal life, for it would be a fatal error. 'He that believeth not the Son shall not see life'; how, then, could he have an assurance of possessing it? Faith is a necessary preliminary to assurance; you must have the blade of faith before you can have the ripe corn of assurance. Dear friends, do not dream of being sure that you are saved apart from making sure that you have trusted yourselves with the crucified Saviour. The atonement presented by Jesus Christ, the Son of God, gives assurance of salvation to all who trust in it, but to none besides. It would be taking things out of their due order, and it would be doing you real and perhaps fatal mischief if we should lead you to presume that you have eternal life before you have unreservedly believed in the Lord Jesus Christ. 'He that believeth on the Son hath everlasting life: and he that believeth not the Son shall not see life; but the wrath of God abideth on him.' I speak, therefore, to all of you who have come to Christ, however imperfect and undeveloped your spiritual life may as yet be, but I invite none beside to the banquet of joyous confidence. As with a drawn sword of fire, John's words guard the way like the cherub at the gate of Paradise: his words, 'These things have I written unto you that believe on the name of the Son of God', keep back every man who has not believed in Jesus from dreaming that he has eternal life.

FOR MEDITATION: Those who are not in a right relationship to God ought to experience the wrong kind of assurance, that they face death (Romans 1:32), judgment (Romans 2:2), disinheritance (1 Corinthians 6:9–10) and wrath (Ephesians 5:5–6). Only those who heed the gospel and trust in the Lord Jesus Christ can be assured of deliverance from all this (John 5:24).

SERMON NO. 1791

20 JULY (1879)

Our motto

'With good will doing service, as to the Lord, and not to men.' Ephesians 6:7

SUGGESTED FURTHER READING: Luke 22:24–30

When we come to serve Christ, is anything good enough for him? Could our zeal know no respite, could our prayers know no pause, could our efforts know no relaxation, could we give all we have of time, wealth, talent, and opportunity, could we die a martyr's death a thousand times, would not he, the Best Beloved of our souls, deserve far more? Ah, that he would. Therefore self-congratulation is banished for ever. When you have done all, you will feel that it is not worthy of the matchless merit of Jesus, and you will be humbled at the thought. Thus, while doing all for Jesus stimulates zeal, it fosters humility, a happy blending of useful effects. The resolve to do all as unto the Lord will elevate you above that craving for recognition which is a disease with many. It is a sad fault in many Christians that they cannot do anything unless the entire world is told of it. The hen in the farm-yard has laid an egg, and feels so proud of the achievement that she must cackle about it: everybody must know of that one poor egg till all the country round resounds with the news. It is so with some professors: their work must be published, or they can do no more. 'Here have I,' said one, 'been teaching in the school for years, and nobody ever thanked me for it; I believe that some of us who do the most are the least noticed, and what a shame it is.' But if you have done your service unto the Lord you should not talk so, or we shall suspect you of having other aims. The servant of Jesus will say, 'I do not want human notice. I did it for the Master; he noticed me, and I am content. I tried to please him, and I did please him, and therefore I ask no more, for I have gained my end. I seek no praise of men, for I fear lest the breath of human praise should tarnish the pure silver of my service.'

FOR MEDITATION: The realisation that we are unprofitable servants (Luke 17:10), serving the Lord Christ (Colossians 3:23–24), who took upon himself the form of a servant (Philippians 2:7), ought to be enough to cure us of the vain desire for the praise of men.

'Men heed thee, love thee, praise thee not;
The Master praises. What are men?' (Horatius Bonar)

SERMON NO. 1484

21 JULY (PROBABLY PREACHED 11 JUNE 1882)

The marvellous magnet

'I, if I be lifted up from the earth, will draw all men unto me. This he said, signifying what death he should die.' John 12:32–33
SUGGESTED FURTHER READING: 1 Thessalonians 2:1–13

I dare say that you have heard the oft-recounted story of the missionaries among the Greenlanders. Our Moravian brethren, full of fire and zeal and self-denial, went right away among the ignorant folk of Greenland, as those people then were, longing to convert them. Using large prudence, they thought, 'These people are so benighted that it cannot be of any use to preach Jesus Christ to them at first. They do not even know that there is a God, so let us begin by teaching them the nature of the Deity, showing them right and wrong, proving to them the need of atonement for sin, and setting before them the rewards of the righteous and the penalties of the wicked.' This was judged to be most fit preparatory work. Watch for the result! They went on for years, but had no converts. What was there in all that fine preparatory teaching that could convert anybody? Jesus was being locked out of the Greenlanders' hearts by those who wanted him to enter. But one day one of the missionaries happened to read to a poor Greenlander the story of Jesus bleeding on the cross, and how God had sent his Son to die, 'that whosoever believeth in him should not perish, but have everlasting life', and the Greenlander said, 'Would you read me that again? What wonderful words! Did the Son of God die for us poor Greenlanders that we may live?' The missionary answered that it was even so; and, clapping his hands, the simple native cried, 'Why did you not tell us that before?' Ah, just so! Why not tell them this at once, and leave it to clear its own path? That is the point to begin with. Let us start with 'the Lamb of God, which taketh away the sin of the world.' 'God so loved the world, that he gave his only begotten Son, that whosoever believeth in him should not perish, but have everlasting life.' To my mind that is the point to begin with and the point to go on with; yes, that is the truth to conclude with.

FOR MEDITATION: Desiring to be teachers of the law is a mistake (1 Timothy 1:7). Preaching the good news of the gospel involves preaching Jesus (Acts 8:35), the cross (1 Corinthians 1:17–18,23), the resurrection (1 Corinthians 15:1–4,12), deliverance (Luke 4:18) and peace (Acts 10:36).

SERMON NO. 1717

22 JULY (PREACHED 26 JUNE 1881)

Ziklag; or, David encouraging himself in God

'*And David was greatly distressed; for the people spake of stoning him, because the soul of all the people was grieved, every man for his sons and for his daughters: but David encouraged himself in the* LORD *his God.*' '*And David enquired at the* LORD, *saying, Shall I pursue after this troop? Shall I overtake them? And he answered him, Pursue: for thou shalt surely overtake them, and without fail recover all.*' 1 Samuel 30:6,8
SUGGESTED FURTHER READING: Psalm 73:1–28

Even when your trouble has been brought upon you by your own fault, faith is still available. When your affliction is evidently a chastisement for grievous transgression, still trust in the Lord. The Lord Jesus prayed for erring Peter that his faith might not fail him: his hope of recovery lay there. Faith under a sense of guilt is one of those noble kinds of faith at which some are staggered. To my mind the faith of a saint is comparatively easy; it is the faith of a sinner that is hard. When you know that you have walked uprightly before God, and have not stained your garments, then you can trust him without difficulty: but, oh, when you have stepped aside, and when at last the heavenly Father makes you smart under his rod, to cast yourself upon him then is faith indeed. Do not fail to exercise it, for this is the faith which saves. What faith is that which first of all brings men into possession of a good hope but the faith of a sinner? Often in life, when our sinnership becomes more manifest to us than usual, we shall be driven to that first sort of faith, in which, being unworthy, we trust entirely in pardoning grace. It would be wise always to live by this same faith. If any of you at this time are in great distress, and are conscious that you richly deserve all your troubles because of your folly, still trust in the mercy of the Lord. Do not doubt the Lord your Saviour, for he invites his backsliding children to return unto him. Though you have fallen by your iniquity, yet take with you words and return unto the Lord. May the Holy Spirit give you renewed trust in the Lord, who forgives 'iniquity and transgression and sin,' and 'retaineth not his anger for ever, because he delighteth in mercy.'

FOR MEDITATION: (*Our Own Hymn Book* no. 130 v.2—John Ryland, 1775)
'Thy gracious ears, O Saviour, bow to my distressful cries,
For who shall stand, O Lord, if Thou shouldst mark iniquities?'

23 JULY (1882)

The voice behind thee

'*And thine ears shall hear a word behind thee, saying, This is the way, walk ye in it, when ye turn to the right hand, and when ye turn to the left.*' Isaiah 30:21

SUGGESTED FURTHER READING: Romans 10:14–21

Some of you will be pestered and worried as long as you live if you will not come to Christ. Omnipotence has servants everywhere, and these are all charged to warn you of your peril. I knew one who would not go to a place of worship, and turned every Bible out of his house; but he found a copy of the holy Book in his house, and as he cursed and swore he learned that it was the property of a daughter whom he loved too much to scold, and he was obliged to let the sacred volume rest where she had placed it. A Bible in a house where it is forbidden to be read is a splendid power for good, as he soon discovered. In a house where it is outwardly honoured the Bible may have little influence, but if it gets where it must not be allowed, everybody reads it. If you can make God's Word to be forbidden fruit, Eve will feed on it, and Adam will follow her. Thus the grace of God came into the house, and it would never be expelled. Down by Mitcham, when the lavender is growing, if you take a house there you will discern a smell of lavender; you may shut the windows and close the doors, but when any people enter a whiff of lavender enters with them; you cannot help it; and if you live where the gospel is preached at all you will be sure to hear it, and made to know of it. It is God's intention that you should. It is a voice that comes unasked and undesired, but come it does, 'a word behind thee'; it is the voice of an unseen caller whose existence has been almost forgotten. It is not the teachers that speak in this powerful way. The teachers you have seen with your eyes, and they have done you no good; but someone calls whom you never saw and never will see till he sits on the throne of judgment at the last great day.

FOR MEDITATION: (*Our Own Hymn Book* no. 497 v.3—Albert Midlane, 1865)

'Soon that voice will cease its calling, now it speaks, and speaks to thee;
Sinner, heed the gracious message, to the blood for refuge flee;
Take salvation, take it *now*, and happy be.'

24 JULY (1881)

A miniature portrait of Joseph

'The LORD *was with Joseph.*' Genesis 39:2
SUGGESTED FURTHER READING: Colossians 4:7–17

Scripture frequently sums up a man's life in a single sentence. Here is the biography of Joseph sketched by inspiration: 'God was with him', as Stephen testified in his famous speech recorded in Acts 7:9. Here is the life-story of Abraham: 'Abraham believed God'. Of Moses we read, 'the man Moses was very meek'. Take a New Testament life, such as that of John the Baptist, and you have it in a line: 'John did no miracle: but all things that John spake concerning this man were true.' The mere name of John, 'that disciple whom Jesus loved', would serve for an epitaph of him: it pictures both the man and his history. Holy Scripture excels in this kind of full-length miniature painting. As Michelangelo is said to have drawn a portrait with a single stroke of his crayon, so the Spirit of God sketches a man to the life in a single sentence. 'The LORD was with Joseph'. Observe, however, that the portraits of Scripture give us not only the outer, but the inner life of the man. 'Man looketh on the outward appearance, but the LORD looketh on the heart'; and so the Scriptural descriptions of men are not of their visible life alone, but of their spiritual life. Here we have Joseph as God saw him, the real Joseph. Externally it did not always appear that God was with him, for he did not always seem to be a prosperous man, but when you come to look into the inmost soul of this servant of God, you see his true likeness—he lived in communion with the Most High, and God blessed him: 'the LORD was with Joseph, and he was a prosperous man'. Dear friends, how would you like to have your inner biography sketched? How would your soul appear if set out in detail before the entire world as to its desires, affections, and thoughts?

FOR MEDITATION: Consider some of the other miniature portraits to be found in Scripture—Noah (Genesis 6:9), Hanani (Nehemiah 7:2), Job (Job 1:1), Joseph of Arimathaea (Luke 23:50), Stephen (Acts 6:5), Barnabas (Acts 11:24), Apollos (Acts 18:24) and Elijah (James 5:16–17). However, some are not so complimentary—Jonadab (2 Samuel 13:3) and Athaliah (2 Chronicles 24:7)!

SERMON NO. 1610

25 JULY (1880)

The gift unspeakable

'Thanks be unto God for his unspeakable gift.' 2 Corinthians 9:15
SUGGESTED FURTHER READING: Ephesians 1:15–23

Hold a theology which magnifies Christ, a divinity which teaches that Christ is God's unspeakable gift. When a man gets cutting down sin, paring down depravity, and making little of future punishment, let him no longer preach to you. Some modern divines whittle away the gospel to the small end of nothing. They make our divine Lord to be a sort of blessed nobody; they bring down salvation to mere salvability, make certainties into probabilities, and treat verities as mere opinions. When you see a preacher making the gospel small by degrees and miserably less, till there is not enough of it left to make soup for a sick grasshopper, get you gone. Such diminution and adulteration will not do for me: my heart cries, 'Thanks be unto God for his unspeakable gift.' These gentlemen, you know, are highly cultivated and can tell us all about it: they have a theology which is suited to their educated reason: to them grace can be weighed in scales and atonement in balances, unless indeed both are as the drop of a bucket, not worthy of being mentioned at all. Every grand truth with them is dwarfed and dwindled down into utter insignificance. The thought of the nineteenth century makes men the heirs of apes, while it declares their souls to be mortal, and their sins to be trifles. Our Bibles are made to be mere human records, and our hopes are treated as childish dreams. These pygmy thinkers shorten all things to their pygmy scale. As for me, I believe in the colossal, a need deep as hell and grace as high as heaven. I believe in a pit that is bottomless, and in mercy above the heavens. I believe in an infinite God and an infinite atonement, infinite love and infinite mercy, 'an everlasting covenant, ordered in all things, and sure', of which the substance and the seal is an infinite Christ. Christ is all; Christ is unspeakable, the unspeakable gift of God. Hold to that.

FOR MEDITATION: (*Our Own Hymn Book* no. 438 v.1—Samuel Medley, 1789)
    'Oh, could I speak the matchless worth,
    Oh, could I sound the glories forth which in my Saviour shine!
    I'd soar and touch the heavenly strings,
    And vie with Gabriel while he sings in notes almost divine.'

SERMON NO. 1550

26 JULY (PREACHED 6 JULY 1884)

Joseph of Arimathaea

'Joseph of Arimathaea, an honourable counsellor, which also waited for the kingdom of God, came, and went in boldly unto Pilate, and craved the body of Jesus.' 'And he bought fine linen ... and laid him in a sepulchre which was hewn out of a rock, and rolled a stone unto the door of the sepulchre.' Mark 15:43,46
SUGGESTED FURTHER READING: Jude 1–4

Years ago, when they talked of the French invading England, an old lady grew very indignant and threatened deadly resistance. When she was asked what the women of England could do, she said they would rise to a man. I have no doubt whatever that they would do their best in any such emergency. Every iron in the fire-place, whether it be poker or shovel, would be grasped to defend our hearths and homes, and just so now, when error knows no bounds, we must stand up for the defence of the truth. Since they push error to extremes, it becomes us to hold by every particle of the faith. I will not, for my own part, give up a corner of my creed for any man. Even if we might have been prepared to modify expressions had the age been different, we are not in that mood now. A generation of vipers shall have a naked file to bite at. We will modify nothing. If truth bears a stern aspect we will not veil it. If there be an offence in the cross we will not conceal it. This shall be my answer to those who would have us attune ourselves to the spirit of the age: I know no Spirit but one, and he is unchanging in every age. Your extravagance of doubt shall have no influence over us except to make us bind the gospel more closely to our hearts. If we gave you an inch you would take a mile, and so no inch shall be given you. Our resolve is to live for the Book as we read it, for the gospel as we rest in it, for the Lord as he made atonement, for the kingdom as it rules over all. I beg every trembling Christian to take heart, put on his Lord's livery, and advance to the fray. Come out now, if you never did before! Come out, if there is any manliness in you, in these days of blasphemy and rebuke.

FOR MEDITATION: (*Our Own Hymn Book* no. 670 v.1—Isaac Watts, 1709)
  'I'm not ashamed to own my Lord, or to defend His cause;
  Maintain the honour of His word, the glory of His cross.'

SERMON NO. 1789

27 JULY (1879)

The shame and spitting

'I gave my back to the smiters, and my cheeks to them that plucked off the hair: I hid not my face from shame and spitting.' Isaiah 50:6
SUGGESTED FURTHER READING (Spurgeon): Matthew 26:62–68; 27:27–30

Is not this one of the prophecies to which our Lord himself referred in the incident recorded in Luke 18:31–33? 'Then he took unto him the twelve, and said unto them, Behold, we go up to Jerusalem, and all things that are written by the prophets concerning the Son of man shall be accomplished. For he shall be delivered unto the Gentiles, and shall be mocked, and spitefully entreated, and spitted on: and they shall scourge him, and put him to death'. Such a remarkable prophecy of scourging and spitting as this which is now before us must surely refer to the Lord Jesus; its highest fulfilment is assuredly found in him alone. Of whom else, let me ask, could you conceive the prophet to have spoken if you read the whole chapter? Of whom else could he say in the same breath, 'I clothe the heavens with blackness, and I make sackcloth their covering.' 'I gave my back to the smiters, and my cheeks to them that plucked off the hair' (Isaiah 50:3,6)? What a descent from the omnipotence which veils the heavens with clouds to the gracious condescension which does not veil its own face, but permits it to be spat upon! No other could thus have spoken of himself but he who is both God and man. He must be divine: how else could he say, 'behold, at my rebuke I dry up the sea, I make the rivers a wilderness' (Isaiah 50:2)? And yet he must at the same time be 'a man of sorrows, and acquainted with grief', for there is a strange depth of pathos in the words, 'I gave my back to the smiters, and my cheeks to them that plucked off the hair: I hid not my face from shame and spitting.' Whatever others may say, we believe that the speaker in this verse is Jesus of Nazareth, the King of the Jews, the Son of God and the Son of man, our Redeemer.

FOR MEDITATION: (*Our Own Hymn Book* no. 937 vv.3&4—Joseph Stennett, 1709)
> 'Hurried from bar to bar, with blows and scoffs abused;
> Reviled by Herod's men of war, with Pilate's scourges bruised.
> His sweet and reverend face with spittle all profaned;
> That visage, full of heavenly grace, with His own blood distained.'

SERMON NO. 1486

28 JULY (PREACHED 10 AUGUST 1879)

More and more, or less and less

'For whosoever hath, to him shall be given, and he shall have more abundance: but whosoever hath not, from him shall be taken away even that he hath.' Matthew 13:12

SUGGESTED FURTHER READING: 1 John 2:15–17

In these days such a garden is projected on a large scale by some of our public writers and speakers. The church and the world are to become one, and saints and sinners are to blend together in one universal round of play-going. We are actually urged by persons who suppose themselves to be Christians to renew the old league which was established in the days of Noah, and brought on the Flood, when 'the sons of God' and 'the daughters of men' joined in alliance, because the sons of God thought that they should greatly improve the world by uniting with it. At this time we are told that it is wrong on our part to forsake the debasing amusements of the ungodly, for if we would join in them we might improve their tone and quality. If heaven would go down to hell, hell would be greatly improved. See how benevolent Satan has turned, and how anxious to be reformed. Hear the voice of God, which runs in another manner: 'come out from among them, and be ye separate ... and touch not the unclean thing'. 'If any man love the world, the love of the Father is not in him.' Beware of religious play-going and pious theatricals, for they are a snare into which only the vain and foolish will fall. Let thorns be thorns, and let not wheat attempt to grow among them. See that plot of ground, how charming is its aspect, wheat springing up with its green blades among the thorns and thistles! Is it not a delightful compromise? What was the end of this conglomeration? Why, the wheat died; it was choked, and could not grow in such uncongenial society. Know this, that if you receive Christ you must cast out the love of the world. Christ will be either king or nobody. He will have the whole of our heart or none of it.

FOR MEDITATION: Worldliness does not come from God (1 John 2:16), but is in direct opposition to him (James 4:4) and leads us away from him (2 Timothy 4:10). Christ died to 'deliver us from this present evil world' (Galatians 1:4).

SERMON NO. 1488

29 JULY (PREACHED 10 AUGUST 1879)

The plague of the heart

'What prayer and supplication soever be made by any man, or by all thy people Israel, which shall know every man the plague of his own heart, and spread forth his hands toward this house: then hear thou in heaven thy dwelling place, and forgive, and do, and give to every man according to his ways, whose heart thou knowest; (for thou, even thou only, knowest the hearts of all the children of men;) that they may fear thee.'
1 Kings 8:38–40
SUGGESTED FURTHER READING: 1 Peter 1:22–2:2

Did you notice in my text a little word, which follows 'forgive':—'and *do*'? Now, when the Lord forgives a man's sins he then begins to do for him many wonderful things. For instance, that hardness of the heart he melts down; that uneasiness he quiets; that tendency to sin he destroys by imparting a new tendency to holiness. The Lord can make the old sinner become a babe in grace, so that he shall be just as if he were born again; no, he *shall* be born again. An old man who had lived a vicious life sat down in his cottage a sad remnant of humanity, a worn-out waster of life, and when his little grandchild came with curly locks, and clambered up his knee, he patted his cheeks, and murmured to himself, 'O God, if I could be a little child again and begin anew!' That wish of many shall be fulfilled to all who look to Jesus. 'Except ye be converted, and become as little children, ye shall not enter into the kingdom of heaven.' 'Ye must be born again.' The mercy is that you *may* be born again. New life shall enter old hearts, or old hearts shall be made new and filled with the life eternal, which forever has the dew of its youth. Turning your eye to the great sacrifice, altar, temple, priest, even Jesus Christ, and crying to him the prayer of faith, his Spirit will come upon you, and working miracles upon you, will make you a new creature in Christ Jesus. Old things shall pass away, and all things shall become new. After that the Lord will continue to do great things for you. He will keep you to the end; he will lead you from strength to strength and from joy to joy. He will make you useful.

FOR MEDITATION: (*Our Own Hymn Book* no. 531 v.3—Thomas Gibbons, 1769)
   'Transgressors of the deepest stain in Him salvation find:
   His blood removes the foulest guilt, His Spirit heals the mind.'

SERMON NO. 1489

30 JULY (PREACHED 31 JULY 1881)

The word of the cross

'For the preaching of the cross is to them that perish foolishness; but unto us which are saved it is the power of God.' 1 Corinthians 1:18
SUGGESTED FURTHER READING: Galatians 6:11–18

The power with which God created the world was no greater than the power with which he made us new men in Christ Jesus. The power with which he sustains the world is not greater than the power by which he sustains his people under trial and temptation; and even the raising of the dead at the end of the world will be no greater display of divine power than the raising of dead souls out of their spiritual graves. These wonders of power are being performed in our own experience every day of the week, entirely through the cross. I appeal to you who are truly converted; were you converted through the wisdom of man? I appeal to you that are kept from sinning; are you led towards holiness by the power of elocution, of rhetoric, or of logic? I appeal to you who are despairing; are you ever revived by musical words and rhythmical sentences? Or do you owe all to Jesus crucified? What is your life, my brethren, but the cross? Whence comes the bread of your soul but from the cross? What is your joy but the cross? What is your delight, what is your heaven, but the Blessed One, once crucified for you, who 'ever liveth to make intercession for' you? Cling to the cross, then. Put both arms around it! Hold to the Crucified, and never let him go. Come afresh to the cross at this moment, and rest there now and for ever! Then, with the power of God resting upon you, go forth and preach the cross! Tell out the story of the bleeding Lamb. Repeat the wondrous tale, and nothing else. Never mind how you do it, only proclaim that Jesus died for sinners. The cross held up by a babe's hand is just as powerful as if a giant held it up. The power lies in the word itself, or rather in the Holy Spirit who works by it and with it.

FOR MEDITATION: Read 1 Corinthians 1:18–24. Paul gives one declaration (v.23—notice the conveyance, 'we preach', and the content, 'Christ crucified', of his message), three descriptions (vv.23–24—this message was a stumbling-block to Jews, stupidity to Gentiles, but strength to Christians) and two deductions (v.18). Read v.18 again—which of these two deductions describes you?

SERMON NO. 1611

31 JULY (1884)

How to meet the doctrine of election

'But he answered and said, I am not sent but unto the lost sheep of the house of Israel. Then came she and worshipped him, saying, Lord, help me.' Matthew 15:24–25
SUGGESTED FURTHER READING: John 6:35–47

There is such a thing as *the choice of God*. The Lord has a people who are 'redeemed from among men'. The Lord Jesus has a people of whom he has said, 'thine they were, and thou gavest them me'. Some are 'ordained to eternal life', and therefore believe in the Lord Jesus Christ. Does this fact discourage you? I do not see why it should. Why should you not be among that number? 'But suppose that I am not?' says one. Why do you not suppose that you are? You do not know anything about it: therefore why suppose at all? To give up supposing would be a far more sensible thing than to brew for yourself a deadly potion of despair out of the worthless husks of mere supposition. I have enough to do to bear up under facts, without overloading myself with conjectures. What God has not revealed we are not bound to know. Indeed, it would seem better for us to be in ignorance where the Lord grants no information. The Lord has chosen a people to be saved, and I feel glad to think that he has done so, for none can prove that I am not of the number. If there are some whom God will save, then I know also who they are, for he tells me that they are such as repent of sin, confess it, forsake it, and believe in the Lord Jesus Christ unto eternal life. These same things would my soul desire to do, and when I do so, I know that I am of the chosen number, and shall be saved. What is there in this to discourage a soul? Yet it does discourage some. When people are in the dark they are afraid of anything, everything! nothing!! 'There were they in great fear, where no fear was'.

FOR MEDITATION: (*Our Own Hymn Book* no. 499 v.4—Hewett, 1850)
   'Try the freeness of My grace
   Sure, 'twill suit thy trying case,
   Mourning souls will ne'er complain,
   Having sought My face in vain.'

SERMON NO. 1797

1 AUGUST (1880)

Today! Today! Today!

'To day if ye will hear his voice, harden not your heart.' Psalm 95:7–8
SUGGESTED FURTHER READING: Acts 24:22–27

'To day if ye will hear his voice'. This is the uniform time and tense of the Holy Spirit's exhortations. He says nothing about tomorrow, except to forbid our boasting of it, since we know 'not what a day may bring forth.' All his instructions are set to the time and tune of 'Today, today, today.' He speaks of pressing and immediate necessities requiring to be supplied 'today', and of urgent duties which must be fulfilled 'today'. He says, 'Consecrate yourselves to day to the LORD'. 'I command thee this thing to day.' 'Son, go work to day in my vineyard.' Therefore, 'To day if ye will hear his voice, harden not your heart'. 'Today' is a time of obligation. Every man is under a present necessity as a subject of God to obey his Lord today, and having rebelled against his God, every sinner is under law to repent of sin today. 'Repent ye therefore, and be converted, that your sins may be blotted out,' is the cry of Scripture to everyone who has sinned against the Most High (Acts 3:19). If I should repent tomorrow, yet it will be a sin to remain impenitent today. If I should believe in Christ next year, yet it will be a heinous offence to have been an unbeliever this year. I have no more right to continue to disobey than I ever had to disobey at all. When the law has been broken it is still binding, and every fresh offence against it is reckoned to our charge. We are bound to confess and forsake sin now, and delay increases our sin. I met with a striking sentence in the works of William Mason which is well worthy to be written among your memoranda: 'Every day of delay leaves a day more to repent of, and a day less to repent in.'

FOR MEDITATION: Never leave till tomorrow what you can do today (Proverbs 3:28; 27:1). For a sample of the possible kinds of reversals that tomorrow may bring see Exodus 16:19–20, Joshua 22:18, Isaiah 22:13, Matthew 6:30, Luke 12:19–20, James 4:13–14. It is no more than commonsense to avoid the presumption of Isaiah 56:12.

SERMON NO. 1551

2 AUGUST (PREACHED 3 AUGUST 1879)

The Prophet like unto Moses

'*The* LORD *thy God will raise up unto thee a Prophet from the midst of thee, of thy brethren, like unto me; unto him ye shall hearken.*' '*I will raise them up a Prophet from among their brethren, like unto thee, and will put my words in his mouth; and he shall speak unto them all that I shall command him. And it shall come to pass, that whosoever will not hearken unto my words which he shall speak in my name, I will require it of him.*' Deuteronomy 18:15,18–19
SUGGESTED FURTHER READING: Acts 10:34–43

Moses is described as a prophet 'mighty in words and in deeds', and it is singular that there never was another prophet mighty in word and deed till Jesus came. Moses not only spoke with matchless power, but wrought miracles. You shall find no other prophet who did both. Other prophets who spoke well wrought no miracles, or only 'here and there' whilst those who wrought miracles, such as Elijah and Elisha, have left us few words that they spoke: indeed, their prophecies were but lightning flashes, and not as the bright shining of a sun. When you come to our Lord Jesus you find lip and heart working together, with equal perfectness of witness. You cannot tell in which he is the more marvellous, in his speech or in his act. 'Never man spake like this man', but certainly never man wrought such marvels of mercy as Jesus did. He far exceeds Moses and all the prophets put together in the variety, multitude and wonderful character of the miracles which he did. If men bow before prophets who can cast down their rods, and they become serpents, if they yield homage to prophets who call fire from heaven, how much more should they accept him whose words are matchless music, and whose miracles of love were felt even beyond the boundaries of this visible world; for the angels of God flew from heaven to minister to him, the devils of the pit fled before his voice, and the caverns of death heard his call and yielded up their prey. Who would not accept this prophet like unto Moses, to whom the Holy Spirit bare witness by mighty signs and wonders?

FOR MEDITATION: The Lord Jesus Christ was indeed 'a prophet mighty in deed and word' (Luke 24:19). His words and his deeds both give us ample evidence for trusting in him (John 14:10–11), but also both stand in condemnation against all who reject him (John 15:22–24).

SERMON NO. 1487

3 AUGUST (1884)

The glory in the rear

'And the angel of God, which went before the camp of Israel, removed and went behind them; and the pillar of the cloud went from before their face, and stood behind them: and it came between the camp of the Egyptians and the camp of Israel.' Exodus 14:19–20
'The glory of the LORD shall be thy rearward.' Isaiah 58:8
'For the LORD will go before you; and the God of Israel will be your rearward.' Isaiah 52:12
SUGGESTED FURTHER READING: Jonah 1:1–17

What have you and I to guide us but the word of the Lord? 'Well,' says one, 'I guide myself by outward providences.' Do you? You will get into a terrible maze one of these days. Jonah wanted to flee from the presence of the Lord, and therefore he went down to the seaside, and lo, he found a ship going to Tarshish. Might he not have said, 'I must be in the way of duty in going to Tarshish, for no sooner did I go down to the wharf than I found a ship starting immediately, and a cabin vacant for a passenger. I paid my fare, and walked on board at once. I did not need to go off to the shipping-agent's, and wait for the next liner, but all was prepared for me. Was not that a providence!' Yes, but if you get following providence, and turning aside from the word, you may soon find yourself in the sea, and no great fish prepared for you. Our way is clearly set before us in the word of God, and that most sure word of testimony should be followed. I have known a brother wanting to go abroad to preach the gospel to the heathen, but a great many difficulties have been thrown in his way, and therefore he has said, 'I can see that I am not called to go.' Why not? Is no man called unless his way is easy? I should think myself all the more called to a service if I found obstacles in my way. The course of true service never did run smooth. I should say, 'The devil is trying to hinder me, but I will do it in spite of all the devils in hell.' Will you always be wanting to have your bread buttered for you on both sides?

FOR MEDITATION: (*Our Own Hymn Book* no. 212 v.3—Isaac Watts, 1709)
   'Through seas and storms of deep distress
   We sail by faith and not by sight;
   Faith guides us in the wilderness
   Through all the briars and the night.'

SERMON NO. 1793

4 AUGUST (1881)

The bride and her ornaments: the sin of forgetting God

'Can a maid forget her ornaments, or a bride her attire? yet my people have forgotten me days without number.' Jeremiah 2:32

SUGGESTED FURTHER READING: Revelation 3:14–22

It is a clear proof of the great love of God to his people that he will not lose their love without earnest expostulation. When you do not care at all for a person, he may love you or hate you, it is all the same to you; but when you have great love for him, then you earnestly desire to possess his heart in return. This, then, is clear proof that God greatly loves his people, since, whenever their hearts wander from him, he is greatly grieved, and he rebukes them, and earnestly pleads with them, setting the coldness of their hearts in a true light, and striving to bring them back to warm affection towards himself. Not only are God's rebukes proofs of his love, but when he goes farther, and deals out blows as well as words, there is love in every stroke of his hand. Most truly does he say, 'As many as I love I rebuke and chasten', since rebukes and chastenings are proofs that he will not lose our hearts without a struggle for them. Do not look, therefore, upon a sermon that rebukes as something to be avoided. Far from it. Hear it and accept it as a token of love from God to your souls. That man is very foolish who will not bear the warning of a friend. Few prize a friend's rebukes, and yet a wise man knows that there is no greater token of the affection of a friend than when he will undertake the unpleasant duty of pointing out our faults. Many parents are like Eli: they cannot endure the task of chastening their children; and so, when their sons grow up to be their plague, they must not wonder, for they have procured this evil to themselves by their unworthy love of ease. Our heavenly Father is never an Eli: he will not 'spare the rod and spoil the child.' He loves us too well to suffer us to go on in our iniquity. He will not stay his hand, and leave us to perish. He will scourge rather than abandon; he will chide rather than lose. Today he speaks in tones of severity that he may not be compelled to utter tomorrow words of doom.

FOR MEDITATION: (*Our Own Hymn Book* no. 639 v.1—Philip Doddridge, 1755)

    'Do not I love Thee, O my Lord? Behold my heart and see;
    And turn each odious idol out that dares to rival Thee.'

SERMON NO. 1634(A)

5 AUGUST (PREACHED 12 AUGUST 1880)

The valley of the shadow of death

'Yea, though I walk through the valley of the shadow of death, I will fear no evil: for thou art with me; thy rod and thy staff they comfort me.'
Psalm 23:4
SUGGESTED FURTHER READING: 2 Corinthians 1:3–11

I sucked the honey out of this verse some days ago when a tempest howled around me, but its sweetness is there still. I shall enjoy it, I doubt not, when I come near death's gate; but I have had it already sealed to my own soul with richness and fullness of comfort by the blessed Spirit of our God. Would to God that every believer who is burdened and cast down might find it as precious to his own heart as I have found it to mine. This verse is no doubt very applicable to the experience of a believer when he comes to die, but, for certain, that is not its only intent. It has an inexpressibly delightful application to the dying, but it is for the living, too; and at this time if, through any peculiar trials, your soul is cast down within you, and you are walking through the death-shade, I pray you to repeat the words of the text, and may the Lord help you to feel that they are true: 'Yea, though I walk through the valley of the shadow of death, I will fear no evil: for thou art with me; thy rod and thy staff they comfort me.' The words are not in the future tense, and therefore are not reserved for a distant moment. Do not postpone to the future that which you so greatly need in the present. 'Though I walk', even at this hour, through the dark valley, thou, O Lord, 'art with me; thy rod and thy staff they comfort me.' David was not dying; the psalm is fall of happy, peaceful life. He is lying down 'in green pastures', and following his Lord 'beside the still waters'; if a cloud has descended upon him, and he feels himself like one threatened with death, he nevertheless expects 'goodness and mercy' to follow him through all his days. The song is not to lie upon the shelf till our last day, but it is to be sung upon our stringed instruments all the days of our lives.

FOR MEDITATION: (*Our Own Hymn Book* no. 23 version 1 v.3—Isaac Watts, 1719)
   'When I walk through the shades of death, thy presence is my stay;
   A word of Thy supporting breath drives all my fears away.'

Who is this?

'*For who is this that engaged his heart to approach unto me? saith the* LORD.' Jeremiah 30:21
SUGGESTED FURTHER READING: Romans 5:12–19

I seem to see in my spirit that old legend of Rome worked out in very deed. So says the story: in the Roman Forum there gaped a vast chasm which threatened the destruction of the Forum, if not of Rome. The wise men declared that the gulf would never close unless the most precious thing in Rome was cast into it. See how it yawns and cracks every moment more horribly. Hasten to bring this noblest thing! For love of Rome sacrifice your best! But what, or who is this? Where is a treasure fit for sacrifice? Then Curtius, a belted knight, mounted his charger, and rightly judging that valour and love of country were the noblest treasures of Rome, he leaped into the gulf. The yawning earth closed upon a greathearted Roman, for her hunger was appeased. Perhaps it is only an idle tale: but what I have declared is truth. There gaped between God and man a dread abyss, deep as hell, wide as eternity, and only the best thing that heaven contained could fill it. That best thing was he, the peerless Son of God, the matchless, perfect man, and he came, laying aside his glory, making himself of no reputation, and he sprang into the gulf, which there and then closed, once for all. One great result of Christ's having died is to leave us a way of access, which is freely opened to every poor, penitent sinner. Come. Are you using that way of access? Do you use it every day? Having used it, and thus having drawn near to God, do you dwell near to God? Do you abide in God? Is God the main thought of your life, the chief delight and object of your being? If it is not so, I earnestly invite you by the Spirit's help to make it so. You must engage your heart to come to God in Christ.

FOR MEDITATION: (*Our Own Hymn Book* no. 296 v.6—Horatius Bonar, 1856)
    'Jesus, whose dwelling is the skies,
    Went down into the grave for me;
    There overcame my enemies,
    There won the glorious victory.'

7 AUGUST (1881)

The minstrel

'*But now bring me a minstrel. And it came to pass, when the minstrel played, that the hand of the LORD came upon him.*' 2 Kings 3:15
SUGGESTED FURTHER READING: Psalm 96:1–13

'Bring me a minstrel', said the prophet, for his mind was easily moved by that charming art. Music and song soothed, calmed and cheered him. '*Through every pulse the music stole, and held high converse with his soul.*' On the wings of melody his mind rose above the noisy camp, and floated far away from the loathed presence of Jehoram; the melting mystic strain laid all his passions asleep, and his soul was left in silence to hear the voice of the Lord. Well did Luther say, 'Music is the art of the prophets, the only art that can calm the agitations of the soul; it is one of the most magnificent and delightful presents God has given us.' Among our own helps singing holds a chief place, as says the apostle, 'Speaking to yourselves in psalms and hymns and spiritual songs, singing and making melody in your heart to the Lord'. Note how he connects it with peace in his epistle to the Colossians: 'Let the peace of God rule in your hearts … teaching and admonishing one another in psalms and hymns and spiritual songs, singing with grace in your hearts to the Lord.' 'I cannot sing,' says one. You need not sing as sweetly as Asaph and Heman, and other sweet birds of paradise whose names we read in Scripture, but we should all sing better if we sang more. Those with cracked voices would be kind if they would not sing quite so loudly in the congregation, for they grievously disturb other people, but they might get alone and have good times with themselves, where nobody could complain of their strong voices and lusty tones. It is good to sing praises unto the Lord, and a part of its goodness lies in the comfort which it brings. It is not without significance, that after supper, before our Lord went to his great sacrifice, he sang a hymn. Did not even he find refreshment in that holy exercise?

FOR MEDITATION: (*Our Own Hymn Book* no. 136 song 2 v.1—Isaac Watts, 1719)
   'Give to our God immortal praise;
   Mercy and truth are all His ways:
   Wonders of grace to God belong,
   Repeat His mercies in your song.'

SERMON NO. 1612

8 AUGUST (1880)

The friends of Jesus

'Ye are my friends, if ye do whatsoever I command you.' John 15:14
SUGGESTED FURTHER READING: Song of Solomon 5:9–16

It is the highest honour in the world to be called the friend of Christ. There is no title surely that excels in dignity that which was worn by Abraham, who 'was called the Friend of God.' Lord Brooke was so delighted with the friendship of Sir Philip Sydney that he ordered to be engraved upon his tomb nothing but this, 'Here lies the friend of Sir Philip Sydney.' There is beauty in such a feeling, but yet it is a small matter compared with being able to say, 'Here lives a friend of Christ.' O wondrous condescension that he should call me 'friend.' If I am indeed a true believer, not only is he my friend, without which I could have no hope here or hereafter, but he has in the aboundings of his grace been pleased to regard me as his friend, and write me down in the honoured list of intimates who are permitted to speak familiarly with him, as those do between whom there are no secrets, for their hearts are told out to him while he hides nothing from them, but says, 'If it were not so, I would have told you.' Beloved, in what a light this sets obedience to Christ's commandments. The doctrine of our text transfigures obedience, and makes it the joy and glory of life. How precious it is, for it is a better seal to friendship than the possession of the largest gifts and influence. Christ does not say, 'Ye are my friends, if ye rise to a position of respectability among men, or honour in the church.' No, however poor you may be, and those to whom he spoke these words were very poor, he says, 'Ye are my friends, if ye do whatsoever I command you.' Obedience is better than wealth and better than rank. Jesus values his friends, not by what they have, or what they wear, but by what they do.

FOR MEDITATION: The true believer is privileged to share with 'father Abraham' not only a saving faith (Romans 4:16; Galatians 3:7–9), but also the Saviour-Friend (Isaiah 41:8; James 2:21–23). 'What a Friend we have in Jesus' (Joseph Medlicott Scriven).

9 AUGUST (PREACHED 10 AUGUST 1884)

'Return, return, O Shulamite; return, return!'

'Return, return, O Shulamite; return, return, that we may look upon thee. What will ye see in the Shulamite? As it were the company of two armies.' Song of Solomon 6:13
SUGGESTED FURTHER READING (Spurgeon): John 21:15–19

Notice that in the text that word 'return' is put four times over. Is it not because it is of the highest importance that every child of God should keep returning, and coming nearer to the Father's house? Is it not because it is our highest joy, our strongest security, our best enrichment, to be always coming to Christ 'as unto a living stone,' and getting into closer fellowship with him? As he calls four times, is it not a hint that we are slow to come? We ought to come to Jesus not only at his first call, but even at the glances of his eyes, when he looks as though he longed for our love: it ought to be our rapture to think only of him, and live wholly to him; but as we fail to answer to first pleas, he cries four times, 'Return, return; return, return. Come to your own Husband, your own loving Lord.' He ceases not to entreat until we do return. Do not the reduplications of this call hint at his strong desire after us, his condescending love for us? It does seem so wonderful to me that Christ should want our fellowship, but he does: he cannot be happy without us. Still he sits down upon the well when he is thirsty, and looking across to Samaria's fallen daughter he says to her, 'Give me to drink.' His people are his fullness; he cannot be filled if they are away: I dared not have said this if the Holy Spirit had not declared it, but it is true. Without his people Jesus would be a Head without a body, and that is a ghastly object, a King without subjects, and that would have been a wretched parody of royalty, a Shepherd without sheep, and that would have been a sorrowful office, having many pains but no reward. Jesus must have us, or he is a Bridegroom without a bride, bereaved and barren. Oh, how he loves us! How he longs for communion with us! Shall he stand and cry, 'Return, return,' and will we not come to him at once?

FOR MEDITATION: (*Our Own Hymn Book* no. 853 v.2—Isaac Watts, 1709)
   'Here I behold Thy distant face, and 'tis a pleasing sight;
   But to abide in Thine embrace is infinite delight.'

Bochim; or, The weepers

'*And it came to pass, when the angel of the* LORD *spake these words unto all the children of Israel, that the people lifted up their voice, and wept. And they called the name of that place Bochim: and they sacrificed there unto the* LORD.' Judges 2:4–5
SUGGESTED FURTHER READING: Deuteronomy 4:1–31

When repentance is hearty it is practical. When a man truly turns to God, he turns away from sin. If Satan be effectually driven out of a man, the emancipated one sweeps his house out, and purges himself of the filth which he formerly harboured; he plucks out right-eye lusts and cuts off right-arm sins, for he feels that he cannot longer transgress against his God. Next, these people had not repented, for they did not bring their children up rightly. The next generation, it is said, 'knew not the LORD,' neither the mighty works of the Lord. That was because their parents did not teach them. Not that parents can teach children so that they know the Lord in their hearts, but God has so put it, 'Train up a child in the way he should go: and when he is old, he will not depart from it.' That is the great general rule of God's moral government. If parents make known the things of God to their children, it cannot be said that the children do not know the works of God. If parents teach with affectionate earnestness, their children learn at least the letter of the truth. I do not believe in your repentance for sin if you tolerate your child's living in it. I cannot believe that you know the Lord unless you long for your offspring to know him. A man says, 'Oh, it is an evil thing, but, you know, young people will have their own way, and we must not be too strict.' Sorrowfully do we foresee what will become of young people who have parents that do not love them enough to restrain them from doing evil. Well may you weep, for you are murdering the souls of your own flesh and blood. Woe unto you, with all your tears, if you have no regard for your household, and no care to bring up your children in the fear of God.

FOR MEDITATION: (*Our own Hymn Book* no. 542 v.2—Albert Midlane, 1865)

'Tears, though flowing like a river, never can one sin efface;
Jesus' tears would not avail thee—blood alone can meet thy case;
Fly to Jesus! Life is found in His embrace.'

SERMON NO. 1680

11 AUGUST (1881)

Singing in the ways of the Lord

'Yea, they shall sing in the ways of the LORD: for great is the glory of the LORD.' Psalm 138:5
SUGGESTED FURTHER READING: Isaiah 58:6–14

I do see some on a Sunday who look dreadfully solemn, and they walk to their places of worship as if they were going to the gallows and never expected to come back alive; but that is not the spirit in which I would have you go up to the house of God. Go with lightly tripping feet, saying,

> 'I have been there and still will go:
> 'Tis like a little heaven below.'

I would not be kept away, or bought out of the house of God by all that could be offered me. I believe that Sunday should be spent in recreation. You are dreadfully shocked, and well you may be; but what do I mean by 'recreation'? It means creating us over anew. Oh, that everybody who talks about spending the Sunday in recreation would know the meaning of the word 'recreation', and would come to be recreated, regenerated, renewed, refreshed, invigorated, strengthened, revived, and made to rejoice in God. The Lord's day is the highest hill of the week. On that day we stand on tiptoe on Pisgah, and look to the rest which 'remaineth … to the people of God.' It is the type of that everlasting Sabbath which 'remaineth … to the people of God.' Now, as it is with Sabbath-keeping and going up to the house of God, that there we sing in God's ways, so it is with all God's ways: they are all full of delight to his people. Those who heartily enter into them are happy people. Blessed are the people in whose heart are God's ways; their heart shall be full of joy, and overflowing with delight.

FOR MEDITATION: The early Christians were busy about the Lord's work on the first day of the week both in the morning (Matthew 28:1; Mark 16:2,9–10; Luke 24:1; John 20:1–2) and in the evening (Luke 24:13,28–33; John 20:19; Acts 20:7). Note how their trials and sorrows turned to joy in the Lord (Matthew 28:8; Luke 24:36–41; John 20:19–20; Acts 20:9–12).

SERMON NO. 1615

12 AUGUST (1883)

A gospel worth dying for

'*To testify the gospel of the grace of God.*' Acts 20:24
SUGGESTED FURTHER READING (Spurgeon): Romans 3:19–26

This is a gospel so well worth the preaching that I can understand Paul saying, 'neither count I my life dear unto myself, so that I might finish my course with joy, and the ministry, which I have received of the Lord Jesus, to testify the gospel of the grace of God.' I read in an old book a dream of one who was under concern of soul. He fell asleep and dreamed that he was out in the wilds in a terrible storm. The lightnings flamed around him, and the voice of the thunder made the earth to rock beneath him. He looked eagerly around for a shelter. He ran to the first house before him, but he was denied admittance. He that dwelt there was named Justice, and he said in angry tones, 'Go away; I cannot shelter a criminal, a traitor to his King and God!' He fled to the next house, and it turned out to be the mansion of Truth. Truth came to the door with calm but stern countenance, and said, 'You are full of falsehood, you cannot sojourn here.' He fled to the home of Peace, which stood near, and hoped that there perhaps he might be housed from the storm, but Peace said, 'Begone! There is no peace, saith my God, to the wicked.' He could not then tell what to do, for the storm waxed yet more furious, when he saw a portal over which was written 'Mercy.' 'Yes,' said he, 'this is the place for me, for I am guilty.' The door was open and he was welcomed there. To that house I invite you. Come in and be at rest. You who cannot as yet be harboured by justice, or peace, or truth, may come to mercy, and receive abundant grace. Do you seem inclined to accept the way and method of grace?

FOR MEDITATION: (*Our Own Hymn Book* no. 546 v.3—Charlotte Elliott, 1836)
    'Just as I am—though tossed about
    With many a conflict, many a doubt,
    Fightings within, and fears without,
    O Lamb of God, I come.'

SERMON NO. 1734

13 AUGUST (1882)

Brought up from the horrible pit

'He brought me up also out of an horrible pit, out of the miry clay, and set my feet upon a rock, and established my goings. And he hath put a new song in my mouth, even praise unto our God: many shall see it, and fear, and shall trust in the LORD.' Psalm 40:2–3
SUGGESTED FURTHER READING: Matthew 27:45–54

What shall the 'many' do? They shall *'see'*. Their eyes shall be opened, and they shall see their Lord in the horrible pit, and in the miry clay; and as they look they shall see that he was there for them. What joy this will create in their spirits! If they do not see the Lord Jesus as their Substitute they shall, at any rate, be made to see the exceeding sinfulness of sin. If when Jesus only takes imputed sin, and has no sin of his own, yet he must be cast into the horrible pit and sink in the miry clay, then what will become of men who have their own sins about them, provoking the fierce anger of the Lord? If God thus smites his well-beloved, oh sinner, how will he smite you! Beware, 'ye that forget God, lest' he 'tear you in pieces, and there be none to deliver' you. By the suffering Surety all covered with his own blood, I beseech you, provoke not God; for if his Only-Begotten must suffer so, you must suffer yet more if you break his law and next reject his gospel. 'Many shall see'. Do you wonder that it is added, 'and *fear*'? It makes men fear to see a bleeding Christ, and to know that they crucified him. It makes men fear, however, with a sweet filial fear that is akin to hope, when they see that Jesus died for sinners, 'the just for the unjust' to bring them to God. When they see the Lord of love acting as a scapegoat, and bearing their sins away into the wilderness of forgetfulness, they begin to hate their evil ways, and to have a reverent fear of God; for so says the Scripture, 'there is forgiveness with thee, that thou mayest be feared.' But best of all they come to *'trust* in the LORD.' They build their hope of salvation upon the righteousness of God as manifested in Christ Jesus. Oh, I would to God that some of you would trust him at once.

FOR MEDITATION: Observe some of the characters around the cross. For the thief fearing was believing (Luke 23:40–42), for the centurion seeing was believing (Matthew 27:54; Mark 15:39; Luke 23:47), but for the religious mockers only seeing Christ delivered would have made them believe (Mark 15:31–32). With which of these can you identify?

SERMON NO. 1674

14 AUGUST (1884)

Sight for those who see not

'And Jesus said, For judgment I am come into this world, that they which see not might see; and that they which see might be made blind.' John 9:39
SUGGESTED FURTHER READING: 2 Corinthians 2:12–17

Whoever you may be, if you hear the gospel at any time it must have some effect upon you. It will either be to your soul 'a savour of life unto life', or else 'a savour of death unto death'. It will be antidote or poison, curing or killing, softening the conscience or searing it. It will either make you see, or else, because you fancy that you see, its very brightness will make you blind, like Saul of Tarsus, who cried, 'I could not see for the glory of that light'. You cannot be indifferent to the gospel if you become a hearer of it. 'I am come', said Christ—that fact none of you can escape: 'For judgment I am come', and that judgment must take place in your mind and conscience whether you like it or not. This coming and judgment have a wonderfully marked and decided effect. It is not that of a little improvement or of slight alteration; it is the turning of things upside down, so 'that they which see not might see; and that they which see might be made blind'. It is a very violent change from light to darkness or darkness to light. In either case it is absolute reversion of condition. Now, the gospel will do just that for you: if you live without it, it will make you die; if you feel that you are dead without it, it will make you live. 'He hath put down the mighty from their seats, and exalted them of low degree. He hath filled the hungry with good things, and the rich he hath sent empty away.' Learn hence that there will always be some effect upon the human mind wherever Christ comes, and that this effect will be a very decided one, changing all their conditions as much as if the laws of nature were reversed. The Lord's approach to a soul will lift it into the light more and more gloriously; or else it will plunge it into deeper darkness, deeper responsibility, deeper guilt, and consequently deeper woe.

FOR MEDITATION: (*Our Own Hymn Book* no. 602 v.3—Anna Shipton, 1855)
'Jesus! Master! as of yore
Thou didst bid the blind man see,
Light upon my soul restore;
Jesus! Master! heal Thou me.'

SERMON NO. 1798

15 AUGUST (1880)

Faith working by love

'Faith which worketh by love.' Galatians 5:6
SUGGESTED FURTHER READING: 1 Peter 1:3–9

Faith creates love in the soul wherever it really dwells. Do not, I pray you, begin to say, 'I am afraid I do not love the Lord as I ought', and so on. Take it for granted that you do not love him to the full of his infinite deserts, and instead of raising questions about the degree of your love, ask yourself whether you believe in him? Are you trusting in the Lord Jesus? Are you confiding in him? If the root is there, the flower will appear before long. 'Whosoever believeth that Jesus is the Christ is born of God', and all who are born of the God of love must themselves love God. Do not talk of trying to love God. You cannot force yourself to love anybody: who in his senses would ever dream of such a thing? Such attempts would be utter folly. Love must be free-born; it cannot be bought or forced. We cannot tell what love is though we feel it. It is a mysterious something, not to be described by the cold maker of definitions, but it is always a product of something else which goes before it. If you believe you will love; if you do not believe you will never love till you do believe. Go to the root of the matter. Do not try to grow the hyacinth of love without the bulb of faith. Do you trust Jesus with all your heart, and are you confiding your soul's eternal interests with him? Then I know that you love him, though you may for a while be occupied with other pursuits. Love slumbers in you like fire in a flint, or rather, it smoulders like fire in smouldering turf, but before long it will burn vehemently, like coals of juniper. Look well to your faith and your love will not fail.

FOR MEDITATION: (*Our Own Hymn Book* no. 195 vv.2&3—Frederick William Faber, 1852)
'Oh, how I fear Thee, living God, with deepest, tenderest fears,
And worship Thee with trembling hope, and penitential tears.
Yet I may love Thee too, O Lord, almighty as Thou art,
For Thou hast stooped to ask of me the love of my poor heart.'

16 AUGUST (PREACHED 14 AUGUST 1881)

Shut in or shut out

'The LORD shut him in.' Genesis 7:16
SUGGESTED FURTHER READING: John 10:7–30

The Lord shut Noah in. Take notice that this was very close shutting, so as to keep out the water. I fancy that if you saw a huge vessel lying upon the dry land where the floods would come to float it, you would be very anxious about that great opening in its side. It was evidently a huge doorway, for a pair of elephants had passed through it, so that it was a gaping leak which would take in enough water in an hour to sink the ark to the bottom. How could the great door be closed? All the timbers are watertight, and the ship is well calked, and pitched inside and outside with pitch; but all will go for nothing unless we can secure the big door. Merely to shut the door will be of no use. When the rain begins to fall in torrents from above, and the waters leap up from below, and the ship commences to rise, she will take in any quantity of water at the points where the door fits into the wood. Shipwrights will be wanted, and the calkers must come, and the men with the pitch. No shipwright could manage to shut so huge a door close enough for safety unless you gave him time, and called in the help of other workers. Hence 'the LORD shut him in' because nobody else could safely be trusted to shut such a door, against which a forty days' tempest was to beat most furiously. What a mercy it is that when we get into Christ by faith, and are shut in from the world with him, we are perfectly safe, because the Lord himself has shut us in. We are not only brought to Christ Jesus by divine power, but we are preserved in Christ Jesus unto eternal life by the same divine might.

FOR MEDITATION: (*Our Own Hymn Book* no. 501 v.4—John Coleman's Collection, 1846)
   'Come to the ark, ere yet the flood
   Your lingering steps oppose:
   Come, for the door which open stood
   Is now about to close.'

SERMON NO. 1613

17 AUGUST (1879)

Contention ended and grace reigning

'For the iniquity of his covetousness was I wroth, and smote him: I hid me, and was wroth, and he went on frowardly in the way of his heart. I have seen his ways, and will heal him: I will lead him also, and restore comforts unto him and to his mourners.' Isaiah 57:17–18
SUGGESTED FURTHER READING: James 4:1–10

It is wonderful how the pity of God has in some cases been excited, even by a temporary repentance. When wicked Ahab 'rent his clothes, and put sackcloth upon' himself, the Lord took note of it and said, 'Seest thou how Ahab humbleth himself before me? because he humbleth himself before me, I will not bring the evil in his days'. When the Ninevites repented, though probably there was very little spiritual about their humbling, yet it was sincere as far as it went, the Lord turned from his fierce anger and there was a reprieve for the wicked city. This plainly shows that the Lord is speedily moved by true humiliation, and if any soul will but lie before him in self-abasement and lowliness, he will no longer contend, but will put away his anger. Besides he has given a promise of grace which runs thus, 'Humble yourselves in the sight of the Lord, and he shall lift you up' (James 4:10). He cannot spurn those who submit themselves before him, for it is written, 'Though the LORD be high, yet hath he respect unto the lowly'. He is full of grace, and that grace is for the poor and needy. Condescension to the lowly is his glory, as Mary sang of old, and as many fainting ones may sing at this moment if they will: 'He hath put down the mighty from their seats, and exalted them of low degree. He hath filled the hungry with good things; and the rich he hath sent empty away.' The Lord delights in mercy, and his mercy delights to come to those who are most abased in their own esteem, and judge themselves to be least worthy of it. We are quite sure that the divine contention will come to an end with the humble and contrite, because the promise is 'I dwell in the high and holy place, with him also that is of a contrite and humble spirit'.

FOR MEDITATION: (*Our Own Hymn Book* no. 586 v.1—John Newton, 1779)
  'Approach, my soul, the mercy-seat where Jesus answers prayer;
  There humbly fall before His feet, for none can perish there.'

18 AUGUST (PREACHED 17 AUGUST 1884)

Pleading and encouragement

'Have I any pleasure at all that the wicked should die? saith the Lord GOD': and not that he should return from his ways, and live?' 'For I have no pleasure in the death of him that dieth, saith the Lord GOD: wherefore turn yourselves, and live ye.' Ezekiel 18:23,32
SUGGESTED FURTHER READING: Romans 2:1–11

Remember the perfection of the character of God as the moral Ruler of the Universe. He is the Judge of all, and must do right. If a judge upon the bench were known to take delight in the punishment of offenders, he ought to be removed at once, for it would be clear that he was thoroughly unfit for his office. A man who would take pleasure in hanging or imprisoning, would be of the foul breed of Judge Jeffreys and other monsters, from whom I trust our bench is for ever purged. But if I heard it said that a judge never pronounced the sentence of death without tears, that when he came home from the court and remembered that some had been banished for life by the sentences which he had been bound to deliver, he sat in a moody, unhappy state all the evening, I should say, 'Yes, that is the kind of person to be a judge.' Aversion to punishment is necessary to justice in a judge. Such a one is God, who takes no pleasure either in sin or in the punishment which is the consequence of sin; he hates both sin and its consequence, and only comes at last to heavy blows with men when everything else has failed. When the sinner must be condemned, or else the foundations of society would be out of course, then he delivers the terrible sentence, but even then it is with unfeigned reluctance, and he cries, 'How shall I give thee up?' The Great Judge of all seems to descend from the glory of his judgment-seat, and show his more familiar face to you in the text, as in effect he cries, 'I have judged, I have condemned and I have punished, but, as I live, I find no pleasure in all this; my pleasure comes when men turn to me and live.'

FOR MEDITATION: (*Our Own Hymn Book* no. 202 v.3—Samuel Davies, 1769)
'In wonder lost, with trembling joy we take the pardon of our God;
Pardon for crimes of deepest dye; a pardon bought with Jesus' blood:
Who is a pardoning God like Thee? Or who has grace so rich and free?'

SERMON NO. 1795

19 AUGUST (1883)

The doctrines of grace do not lead to sin

'For sin shall not have dominion over you: for ye are not under the law, but under grace. What then? Shall we sin, because we are not under the law, but under grace? God forbid.' Romans 6:14–15
SUGGESTED FURTHER READING: Romans 2:17–3:8

Who dares to suggest that the men who believed in the grace of God have been sinners above other sinners? With all their faults, those who throw stones at them will be few if they first prove themselves to be their superiors in character. When have they been the patrons of vice, or the defenders of injustice? Pitch upon the point in English history when this doctrine was very strong in the land; who were the men that held these doctrines most firmly? Men like Owen, Charnock, Manton, Howe, and I hesitate not to add Oliver Cromwell. What kind of men were these? Did they pander to the licentiousness of a court? Did they invent a Book of Sports for Sabbath diversion? Did they haunt ale-houses and places of revelry? Every historian will tell you, the greatest fault of these men in the eyes of their enemies was that they were too precise for the generation in which they lived, so that they called them Puritans, and condemned them as holding a gloomy theology. If there was iniquity in the land in that day, it was to be found with the theological party which preached up salvation by works. The gentlemen with their womanish locks and essenced hair, whose speech savoured of profanity, were the advocates of salvation by works, and all bedabbled with lust they pleaded for human merit; but the men who believed in grace alone were of another style. They were not in the chambers of rioting and wantonness; where were they? They might be found on their knees crying to God for help in temptation; in persecuting times they might be found in prison, cheerfully suffering the loss of all things for the truth's sake. The Puritans were the godliest men on the face of the earth. Are men so inconsistent as to nickname them for their purity, and yet say that their doctrines lead to sin?

FOR MEDITATION: (*Our Own Hymn Book* no. 980 v.3—John Newton, 1779)
   'With my burden I begin, Lord, remove this load of sin;
   Let Thy blood, for sinners spilt, set my conscience free from guilt.'

SERMON NO. 1735

20 AUGUST (PROBABLY PREACHED 19 OR 26 AUGUST 1883)

High doctrine and broad doctrine

'All that the Father giveth me shall come to me; and him that cometh to me I will in no wise cast out.' John 6:37
SUGGESTED FURTHER READING: Hebrews 6:13–20

I want you to notice in my text the blessed certainty of this salvation: 'him that cometh to me I will in no wise cast out.' Two or three negatives in the Greek language make a negation stronger, though they would have no such effect in the English tongue. It is a very strong negative here: 'him that cometh to me I will not not cast out', or, 'I will never never cast out.' As much as to say, 'On no account, or for no reason, or on no pretence, or from no motive whatever, will I ever in time or in eternity cast out the soul that comes to me.' That is how it stands, a declaration of absolute certainty from which there can be no escaping. What a blessed thing it is to get your foot on certainties! Certain preachers, who are much cried up nowadays, are very uncertain preachers, for they do not themselves know what they will be propounding tomorrow. They make their creed as they go along, and a very poor one it is when they make it. I believe in something sure and certain, namely, in infallible Scripture, and that which the Lord has written therein, never to be altered while the world stands. My text is certain as the truth of Christ Jesus, and if we had ever seen that beautiful face of his we could not distrust him. Can your imagination picture for a minute the ever-blessed face of the Son of God? Could you look into that face, and suspect him of a lie? And when he says, 'Verily, verily, I say unto you, He that believeth on me hath everlasting life', the saying must be true. If you believe in him, you have everlasting life. When he says, 'him that cometh to me I will never never cast out', the declaration must be true. He never, never, can cast you out, whoever you may be, however long you may live, or whatever else may happen, if you come to him.

FOR MEDITATION: If you are a Christian, rejoice in some of the other multiple negatives in the Greek, which strongly deny the possibility of the believer thirsting (John 6:35), perishing (John 10:28), having sin remembered (Hebrews 8:12) or being blotted out of the book of life (Revelation 3:5). In Hebrews 13:5 five Greek negatives combine to emphasise that God will never leave you nor forsake you!

SERMON NO. 1762

21 AUGUST (1881)

Dressing in the morning

'*The night is far spent, the day is at hand: let us therefore cast off the works of darkness, and let us put on the armour of light. Let us walk honestly, as in the day; not in rioting and drunkenness, not in chambering and wantonness, not in strife and envying. But put ye on the Lord Jesus Christ, and make not provision for the flesh, to fulfil the lusts thereof.*' Romans 13:12–14
SUGGESTED FURTHER READING: Colossians 3:5–17

The text says, 'put ye on the Lord Jesus Christ'. What made him use the three names there? Because he meant to point out the three senses in which we clothe ourselves from head to foot with Christ. 'Put ye on the Lord', become his servant, wear his livery, let him be your Rabbi, your Master, your King, your Lord. 'Put ye on … Jesus' the Saviour, acknowledge yourself as a saved one, saved by him whose name is called Jesus 'for he shall save his people from their sins.' 'Put ye on … Christ', that is the Anointed: take an anointing from God the Holy Spirit through Jesus Christ to whom he is given without measure. As Christ is anointed to be prophet, priest, and king, put him on in all these three offices and rejoice to do so. 'Put ye on the Lord Jesus Christ'. Do not put on Jesus only as your Saviour; put him on as your Commander. Do not only put him on as your Master and Saviour, but as your Christ, anointed for you. Take a whole Christ to yourself that you may be wholly in him, and so may be spiritual, gracious, holy. Henceforth may those around you see nothing of you, but much of your Lord. May your outward character be so Christlike that men may see Christ displayed upon you, as a new garment is displayed by the act of wearing it. May the spirit of glory and of Christ rest upon you. May you be clothed with power. Our Lord said to his disciples, 'tarry ye in the city of Jerusalem, until ye be endued with power from on high'—the word signifies 'clothed'. If we are clothed with Christ we shall be 'clothed with power from on high'; even as he has said, 'the works that I do shall he do also.' Therefore 'put ye on the Lord Jesus Christ'.

FOR MEDITATION: Putting on the likeness of God (Ephesians 4:24) and the armour of God (Ephesians 6:11,14; 1 Thessalonians 5:8) should be far more important to us than fussing about what clothes to put on (Matthew 6:25,31–33; 1 Peter 3:3–4).

SERMON NO. 1614

22 AUGUST (1880)

Redemption by price

'Ye are not your own: for ye are bought with a price.' 1 Corinthians 6:19–20
SUGGESTED FURTHER READING: Romans 6:12–19

'Ye were not redeemed with corruptible things, as silver and gold, from your vain conversation ... but with the precious blood of Christ, as of a lamb without blemish and without spot'. There is a sanctity about a blood-bought man or woman of the highest degree: the Lord has purchased him with his life. A sanctity surrounds even these frail bodies, for the apostle is speaking about them in the text now before us. Let me read what he says upon them: 'What? know ye not that your body is the temple of the Holy Ghost which is in you, which ye have of God, and ye are not your own?' Never, therefore, give up your body to idleness, drunkenness, or any form of uncleanness. Paul speaks especially of fornication as a thing not to be thought of among the saints, because the body has been valued by God at a great price, and purchased accordingly, and must not therefore be defiled by impure behaviour. Though Paul in another sense called it a 'vile body', yet it cannot be vile in all respects, for even now it is a sacred thing, the shrine of the eternal Spirit. We ought to value the very dust of the departed saint. It little matters what becomes of a dead body, yet would I have it laid reverently in its last resting-place, and let its bones be undisturbed until the trump of the archangel shall sound, for every atom of a believer's body has been redeemed with the blood of Jesus Christ, as well as his soul and spirit; his entire manhood has been purchased by Christ Jesus. I want you, then, to think of yourselves, you believers, as precious things. The Lord says to each one of his own beloved, 'Since thou wast precious in my sight, thou hast been honourable, and I have loved thee'.

FOR MEDITATION: (*Our Own Hymn Book* no. 282 v.5—Isaac Watts, 1709)
   'Were the whole realm of nature mine,
   That were a present far too small;
   Love so amazing, so divine,
   Demands my soul, my life, my all!'

SERMON NO. 1554

23 AUGUST (PREACHED 12 AUGUST 1883)

The blind man's eyes opened; or, Practical Christianity

'Jesus answered, Neither hath this man sinned, nor his parents: but that the works of God should be made manifest in him. I must work the works of him that sent me, while it is day: the night cometh, when no man can work.' John 9:3–4
SUGGESTED FURTHER READING: Job 22:3–11

The world will still stick to its unfounded belief that if the Tower of Siloam falls upon any men they must be sinners above all sinners upon the face of the earth. A cruel doctrine, a vile doctrine, fit for savages, but not to be mentioned by Christians, who know that 'whom the Lord loveth he chasteneth,' and even his best beloved have been taken away on a sudden. Yet I do see a good deal of this cruel notion about, and if men are in trouble, I hear it muttered, 'Well, of course they brought it on themselves.' Is this your way of cheering them? Cheap moral observations steeped in vinegar make a poor dish for an invalid. Such censures are a sorry way of helping a lame dog over a stile; no, it is putting up another stile for him so that he cannot get over it at all. Now I mark this of my Lord, that it is written of him that he 'giveth to all men liberally, and upbraideth not'. When he fed those thousands in the wilderness it would have been most just if he had said to them, 'Why did you all come out into the wilderness, and not bring your provision with you? What have you to do out here without something to eat? You are unthrifty, and deserve to hunger.' No, no, he never said a word of the sort, but he fed them, fed them all, and sent them home filled. You and I are not sent into the world to thunder out commandments from the top of Sinai: we 'are come unto mount Sion'. We are not to go on circuit as if we were judge and hangman rolled into one, to meet all the sorrow and misery in the world with bitter words of censure and condemnation. If we do so, how different we are from that blessed Master of ours who says not a word by way of rebuke to those who seek him.

FOR MEDITATION: (*Our Own Hymn Book* no. 607 v.2—Elizabeth Codner, 1860)
'Pass me not, O gracious Father! Sinful though my heart may be;
Thou might'st curse me, but the rather let Thy mercy light on me,
Even me.'

24 AUGUST (1879)

Remember Lot's wife

'Remember Lot's wife.' Luke 17:32
SUGGESTED FURTHER READING (Spurgeon): Genesis 19:12–26

I do not suppose Lot's wife to be standing there now, as some travellers have imagined: the pillar was not even there in Christ's day, for if it had been, as Bengel very properly remarks, our Lord would have said, 'See Lot's wife', but as she was not there he said, 'Remember' her. Her doom came on a sudden, without a further warning or a moment's time to consider. What if sudden death should strike some of you down at this moment? You professors who still love the world, what if you now fell dead? You professed Christians who sneak in among the ungodly to have a suck at their pleasures, suppose you should be struck down in the theatre one of these days! You that pretend to be Christians and frequent the dancing saloon, suppose you should fall dead there! It would not be a new thing under the sun, for God deals severely with those who profess to come under his covenant; he has jealous laws for those who join his church and yet have not the grace of God in their hearts. These men die not the death of common men, but are often overtaken by strange punishments, that the world may see that the Lord has set a wall of fire around his church, which none may break through on peril of their lives. Ananias and Sapphira entered the church, but they could not live there; a glance of Peter's eye and they fell dead before him. Such judgments still purge the ranks of the professing church, as all that observe must know, for the Lord will be sanctified of them that come near to him. 'For this cause', said the apostle, 'many are weak and sickly among you, and many sleep', because the discipline of God goes on in the midst of his visible church. He lets the world alone till the fire-shower comes, but to those that profess to be his people he is always a jealous God. I speak strong things; strong things are wanted in these compromising days. May the Holy Spirit impress these weighty facts on all your hearts.

FOR MEDITATION: The Christian is assured of deliverance from eternal death and judgment (John 5:24), but should take care not to provoke God to carry out bodily judgment now (Acts 5:1–11; 1 Corinthians 5:3–5; 11:27–31; 1 Peter 4:17; Revelation 2:21–23).

25 AUGUST (1881)

The principal wheat

'The principal wheat.' Isaiah 28:25
SUGGESTED FURTHER READING: 1 Timothy 1:1–7

The farmer was right in having a principal crop, and in selecting the right seed to be his principal care. I do not suppose that he ever entered into any dispute upon the matter. He felt sure that wheat must be his principal produce, and he gave his thoughts to it. I cannot bear to hear people disputing as to whether it is worthwhile to give their hearts to Christ. The people who question the value of faith have never tried it. Whenever you observe some conceited creature writing an essay against true religion, and putting it into one of our precious 'reviews', do not be carried away by hearing people say that it is mightily clever. If you read it, say to yourselves, 'Certainly, this is a clever thing, for here is a blind man writing upon the harmony of colours; see what learned observations he makes upon scarlet and blue, which, he says, are precisely the same, only some narrow-minded folks insist upon their being different.' You may regard the wise remarks of an unregenerate philosopher as a very fine essay by a deaf man upon music. Can a horse write upon angels? He does not know anything about the subject, nor does the unrenewed man understand the regenerate man. He has not the powers and faculties that would enable him to know, for the carnal man knows not the things that are of God: 'they are spiritually discerned', and as he has no spirit he cannot discern them. Until he is born again he has no spiritual knowledge or judgment. 'That which is born of the flesh is flesh; and that which is born of the Spirit is spirit.' 'Ye must be born again.' We are willing to take the evidence of scientific men upon the science that they have mastered, but we care nothing for their opinion upon a matter which is quite out of their range.

FOR MEDITATION: Spiritual ignorance promotes self (Romans 10:3), prolongs separation from God (Ephesians 4:18), produces scoffing (2 Peter 3:3–5) and perverts the Scriptures (2 Peter 3:16). Far from being taken in by it, the Christian should by godly behaviour shun it (1 Peter 1:14) and silence it (1 Peter 2:15).

SERMON NO. 1626

26 AUGUST (1883)

The King's weighings

'Talk no more so exceeding proudly; let not arrogancy come out of your mouth: for the LORD *is a God of knowledge, and by him actions are weighed.'* 1 Samuel 2:3

SUGGESTED FURTHER READING: Proverbs 16:1–11

It is not the result of the action but the action itself which God weighs. He who swindles and prospers is just as vile as he whose theft lodged him in prison. He who acts uprightly, and becomes a loser thereby, is just as honoured before God as if his honesty had led on to wealth. If we seek to do good and fail in our endeavour, we shall be accepted for the attempt, and not condemned for the failure. You have all admired Grace Darling because of her gallant act in rescuing mariners from a wreck [on 7 September 1838]; but suppose she had not saved a single sailor, and had been herself drowned, would she not have been equally a heroine? Of course she would. Her success had nothing to do with the excellence of her design; the moral weight of her conduct lay in the self-sacrificing courage, which led her on such a howling, murky night to risk her life upon the cruel waters for her unknown fellow-men. Had she been swallowed up by the remorseless deep, her action would have weighed as much before the throne of God as when she landed the saved ones at the lighthouse. If a man gives his life to convert the heathen, and he does not succeed, he shall have as much reward of God as he who turns a nation to the faith. Two ministers have laboured in the same field: the first preached the gospel faithfully, but saw scant results; the second, following him, found the rough work done, and reaped full sheaves from the field. The thoughtless are apt to think the second man greatly superior to the first, but it is not so: 'One soweth, and another reapeth.' When God comes to weigh the actions of men, he may give greater praise to the sower than to the reaper.

FOR MEDITATION: Success is not down to us (Ecclesiastes 11:6), but God knows the secrets and intentions of our hearts (Hebrews 4:12) and it is he who will eventually reveal who has been faithful as required (1 Corinthians 4:1–5). However successful they may be, the ungodly will be weighed in the balances and found wanting (Psalm 62:9; Daniel 5:27).

SERMON NO. 1736

27 AUGUST (1882)

Stand fast

'Be not moved away from the hope of the gospel.' Colossians 1:23
SUGGESTED FURTHER READING: Proverbs 1:1–19

We are like the little coney, of whom Agur speaks. He hid himself among the rocks, and the sportsman, I have no doubt, said, 'Why don't you come out, little coney? Come, and let me be your friend.' But the coney, though he was feeble, was wise, and he hid himself in the rocks all the more, because a stranger invited him out. Do the same when Satan cries, 'Come away and be free. Be a man. Do not be always trusting in authority.' Say, 'No, I shall keep where I am.' As I was riding along in the south of France one day I saw a pair of fine birds overhead. The driver called out in the French tongue, 'Eagles!' Yes; and there was a man below with a gun, who was wishful to get a nearer acquaintance with the eagles, but they did not come down to oblige him. He pointed his rifle at them, but his shots did not reach half way, for the royal birds kept above. The higher air is the fit dominion for eagles. Up there is the eagle's playground, where he plays with the callow lightnings. Up above the smoke and clouds he dwells. Keep there, eagles! Keep there! If men can get you within range, they mean no good to you. Keep up, Christians. Keep up in the higher element, resting in Jesus Christ, and do not come down to find a perch for yourself among the trees of philosophy. Whatever we do, let us never leave the way of truth, of peace, of safety. We are going along the king's highway, and the thieves on the side of the road say, 'Come off the highway: it is so dull and monotonous. Come into the woods; we will show you fair flowers, and ferny dells, and quiet caves. Come, listen to the birds that sing all day and all night too. Come quick with us.' We heed you not: he that travels along the king's highway is under the king's protection, but he that wanders into the dark mountains and lonesome woods may take care of himself. We shall do as we have done, following the way that leads from the banishment, the way of trusting in the Saviour and in him alone.

FOR MEDITATION: 'Stand fast'—in the faith (1 Corinthians 16:13), in liberty (Galatians 5:1), in one spirit (Philippians 1:27), in the Lord (Philippians 4:1; 1 Thessalonians 3:8) and in what you have been taught (2 Thessalonians 2:15).

SERMON NO. 1688

28 AUGUST (1881)

Saved in hope

'*For we are saved by hope: but hope that is seen is not hope: for what a man seeth, why doth he yet hope for? But if we hope for that we see not, then do we with patience wait for it.*' Romans 8:24–25
SUGGESTED FURTHER READING: 1 Corinthians 15:35–57

When we die we shall leave our body behind us for a while: we shall not, therefore, as to our entire manhood, be perfect in heaven till the resurrection: we shall be morally perfect, but as a complete man is made up of body as well as soul, we shall not be physically perfect, while one part of our person shall remain in the tomb. When the resurrection trumpet shall sound, this body will rise, but it will rise redeemed; and as our soul regenerated is very different from our soul under the bondage of sin, so the body when it is risen will be widely different from the body as it now is. The infirmities caused by sickness and age will be unknown among the glorified, for they 'are as the angels of God'. None shall enter into glory halt or maimed, decrepit or malformed. You will have no blind eye there, my sister, no deaf ear there, my brother; there shall be no quivering of paralysis or wasting of consumption. There we shall possess everlasting youth; the body which 'is sown in weakness' shall be 'raised in power', and shall at once fly upon the errands of its Lord. Paul says, 'It is sown a natural (or soulish) body', fit for the soul; 'it is raised a spiritual body', fit for the spirit, the highest nature of man. I suppose we shall inhabit such a body as cherubs wear when they fly upon the wings of the wind, or such as may be fit for a seraph when like a flame of fire he flashes at Jehovah's bidding. Whatever it is, poor frame of mine, you shall be very much changed from what you are now. You are the shrivelled bulb, which shall be put into the earth, but you shall arise a glorious flower, a golden cup to hold the sunlight of Jehovah's face. The greatness of your glory you know not as yet, except that you shall be fashioned like the glorious body of the Lord Jesus.

FOR MEDITATION: In heaven the resurrection body of the Christian will completely lose the ability to suffer and sorrow (Revelation 7:16–17; 21:4), but will gain a wonderful new ability to see (1 John 3:2; Revelation 22:4–5). The rich man in Hades provides us with a glimpse of what the unsaved in hell will experience (Luke 16:23–24).

SERMON NO. 1616

29 AUGUST (1880)

The glories of forgiving grace

'In whom we have redemption through his blood, the forgiveness of sins, according to the riches of his grace.' Ephesians 1:7
SUGGESTED FURTHER READING: Numbers 14:11–20

The measure of forgiveness is the riches of God's grace, and this statement leads us to observe that it is not the character or person of the offender which is the measure of mercy, but the character of the offended One. Is there not rich consolation in this undoubted fact? The pardon to be hoped for is not to be measured by you and what you are, but by God and what he is. In matters of offence and forgiveness the rule almost always holds good, that pardon becomes likely or unlikely, easy or difficult, not so much according to the offence as according to the character of the person offended. One man will forgive a grievous wrong while another will not overlook a wry word. Take an instance from English history: John had most villainously treated his brother Richard in his absence. Was it likely that when he of the lion's heart came home he would pass over his brother's grievous offence? If you look at John, villain that he was, it was most unlikely that he should be forgiven; but then, if you consider the brave, high-souled Richard, the very flower of chivalry, you expect a generous deed. Base as John was he was likely to be forgiven, because Richard was so free of heart, and accordingly pardon was right royally given by the great-hearted monarch. Had John been only half as guilty, if his brother Richard had been like himself, he would have made him lay his neck on the block. If John had been Richard and Richard had been John, no matter how small the offence, there would have been no likelihood of pardon at all. So is it in all matters of transgression and pardon. You must take the offence somewhat into account, it is true, but not one-half as much as the character of the person who has been offended.

FOR MEDITATION: (*Our Own Hymn Book* no. 231 v.3—John Kent, 1803)
   'The basis of eternal love
   Shall mercy's frame sustain;
   Earth, hell, or sin, the same to move,
   Shall all conspire in vain.'

SERMON NO. 1555

Despair denounced and grace glorified

'Then he said unto me, Son of man, these bones are the whole house of Israel: behold, they say, Our bones are dried, and our hope is lost: we are cut off for our parts. Therefore prophesy and say unto them, Thus saith the Lord GOD; behold, O my people, I will open your graves, and cause you to come up out of your graves, and bring you into the land of Israel.'
Ezekiel 37:11–12
SUGGESTED FURTHER READING: Ephesians 2:1–10

They said, 'We are as dried bones.' 'Yes,' says God, 'and I will quicken you'; but the Lord even goes beyond anything which they have felt or said, for they did not say they were buried. No, they were as bones scattered in the open valley, unburied; but the Lord knows they are worse than they think they are, and so he goes further in mercy than they thought they had gone in misery. He says, 'I will open your graves,' and that looks as if they were finally laid in the sepulchre; but the Lord adds, 'and cause you to come up out of your graves'. Sinner, you have described yourself in a very distressing manner, but God accepts it as true and deals with you as being such as you describe, or even worse. He regards men not only as dead, but as entombed, in as hopeless a case as corpses pent up in the sepulchre and forgotten as dead men out of mind. O the mercy of the Lord! There is no bound to it. Observe how the word brings comfort by introducing another actor upon the scene. You are like a dried bone, good for nothing and able for nothing, but the Lord comes in himself, and says, 'I will.' 'I will open your graves, and cause you to come up out of your graves.' If God will save you, cannot you be saved? If it is all of grace from top to bottom, cannot you be saved? If there is no merit wanted of you, no previous goodness to qualify you, cannot salvation come to you? If 'Christ died for the ungodly', cannot you have a share in his death? If he 'came into the world to save sinners', then why not you? If the gospel is not another shape of law requiring something of us, but if it be all free sovereign grace, why should not you have it as well as I?

FOR MEDITATION: (*Our Own Hymn Book* no. 612 v.4—Samuel Stennett, 1787)
   'Darkness fills my trembling soul; floods of sorrow o'er me roll;
   Pity, Father, pity me; all my hope's alone in Thee.'

31 AUGUST (1879)

The first note of my song

'*Who forgiveth all thine iniquities.*' Psalm 103:3
SUGGESTED FURTHER READING: Isaiah 59:1–13

Notice the word which in our text expresses sin: 'iniquities'. Pull it to pieces: it is in-equities, the matters in which we are not according to equity. Sometimes we fall short, sometimes we go beyond, sometimes we do not act in equity towards our friends, our relatives, or strangers; constantly we do not act in strict equity towards God. Now, he says, all our in-equities, everything in which we fall short of the perfect rule of equity, or go beyond that rule, all these he forgives. What a blessed, comprehensive word this is. I was reading the other day in a very delightful little book [by S.G.Prout], entitled, 'Never say "die"', which is admirably calculated to comfort a seeking soul, these few words, which struck me forcibly. The writer says, 'All our righteousness are as filthy rags. If you will bring your good living and your precious righteousness to Christ *you must make sin of the whole lot*—there is nothing else you can do with it—and ask to have it all forgiven: the man who will be saved by his own righteousness says hopelessly, "Die" to his own soul. You must cast all this splendid rubbish of yours *on the heap* along with the oaths and the lies, the drinkings and Sabbath breakings, and the foul living, and let the ever-flowing stream that keeps eddying round wash it all away.' As I read it I thought, That is what I will do with mine: I will put my sermons, my prayers, my almsgivings, everything, on the same heap as my sins, and let them go together. Lord, be pleased to forgive all mine in-equities, my good works and my bad works. I might have tried to sort them a little, but one is so much like the other that I fling them all overboard, and swim to glory on the cross. We have no hope but in our Lord Jesus: we need pardoning mercy for all we have ever done, for sin has been mixed with it all.

FOR MEDITATION: (*Our Own Hymn Book* no. 545 v.4—Russell Sturgis Cook, 1850)
'Come, leave thy burden at the cross;
Count all thy gains but empty dross:
My grace repays all earthly loss:
O needy sinner, come!'

SERMON NO. 1492

1 SEPTEMBER (PREACHED 2 SEPTEMBER 1883)

John's first doxology

'Unto him that loved us, and washed us from our sins in his own blood, and hath made us kings and priests unto God and his Father; to him be glory and dominion for ever and ever. Amen.' Revelation 1:5–6
SUGGESTED FURTHER READING: 1 Chronicles 29:10–13

In this first outburst only two things are ascribed to our Lord: 'to him be glory and dominion for ever and ever.' Now turn to chapter 4:9 and read, 'those beasts give glory and honour and thanks to him that sat on the throne'. Here we have three words of honour. Run on to verse eleven, and read the same: 'saying, Thou art worthy, O Lord, to receive glory and honour and power'. The doxology has grown from two to three in each of these verses. Now turn to chapter 5:13—'And every creature which is in heaven, and on the earth, and under the earth, and such as are in the sea, and all that are in them, heard I saying, Blessing, and honour, and glory, and power, be unto him that sitteth upon the throne, and unto the Lamb for ever and ever.' Here we have four praise-notes. Steadily but surely there is an advance. By the time we get to chapter 7:12, we have reached the number of perfection, and may not look for more: 'Blessing, and glory, and wisdom, and thanksgiving, and honour, and power, and might, be unto our God for ever and ever. Amen.' If you begin praising God you are bound to go on. The work engrosses the heart. It deepens and broadens like a rolling river. Praise is somewhat like an avalanche, which may begin with a snow-flake on the mountain moved by the wing of a bird, but that flake binds others to itself and becomes a rolling ball: this rolling ball gathers more snow about it till it is huge, immense; it crashes through a forest; it thunders down into the valley; it buries a village under its stupendous mass. Thus praise may begin with the tear of gratitude; anon the heart swells with love; thankfulness rises to a song; it breaks forth into a shout; it mounts up to join the everlasting hallelujahs which surround the throne of the Eternal.

FOR MEDITATION: (*Our Own Hymn Book* no. 317 v.5—John S. B. Monsell, 1863)
> 'Sing, O heavens! O earth, rejoice! Angel harp, and human voice,
> Round Him, in His glory, raise your ascended Saviour's praise.
> Alleluia!'

SERMON NO. 1737

2 SEPTEMBER (1883)

The Exeter-Hall sermon to young men

'O LORD, *truly I am thy servant; I am thy servant, and the son of thine handmaid: thou hast loosed my bonds.*' Psalm 116:16
SUGGESTED FURTHER READING: Ecclesiastes 11:9–12:14

I remember young men that began life when I began, that are now—I will not say what. Ah! I remember hearing their names mentioned as models; they were such fine young men, and had just gone up to London. Yes, and they are tonight, if not in jail, in the workhouse. It all came about in this way: the young man sent word home to his mother what the text was on the Sunday, yet he had not been to hear a sermon at all. He had been to some amusement, to spend a happy day: wherever he went he had neglected the house of God; and by-and-by there was a little wrong in his small accounts, just a little matter; but that man could not pick himself up again, once having lost his character. There was another. There was nothing wrong in his accounts, but his habits were loose. By-and-by he was ill. Who could wonder? When a man plays with edged tools he is very likely to cut himself. It was not long before he was so sickly that he could not attend to business, and before long he died; and they said—I fear it was true—that he killed himself by vice. And that is how thousands do in London. Oh, if you become the servant of God this will not happen to you! You may not be rich; you may not be famous; you may not be great: you need not want these things. They are gilded vanities full often. But to be a man, to the fullness of your manhood, to be free and dare to look every other man in the world in the face, speak the truth and do the right, to be a man that can look God in the face because Christ has covered him with his glorious righteousness, this is the ambition with which I would fire the spirit of every young man before me; and I pray God that the flame may burn in his life by the power of the divine Spirit.

FOR MEDITATION: Young men can shun youthful passions (2 Timothy 2:22) and overcome the wicked one (1 John 2:13), but only if God's word is known by them (2 Timothy 3:14–17), abides in them (1 John 2:14) and is applied by them (Psalm 119:9).

SERMON NO. 1740

3 SEPTEMBER (1882)

A great mistake and the way to rectify it

'Thou sayest, I am rich, and increased with goods, and have need of nothing; and knowest not that thou art wretched, and miserable, and poor, and blind, and naked.' Revelation 3:17
SUGGESTED FURTHER READING: Psalm 10:1–18

Remember the Tay Bridge disaster. Without doubt it was not fitted for its position; its ordinary strain was all it could bear, but nobody thought so. Undoubtedly the engineers reckoned it would stand any test to which it might be put; therefore no attention was given to it to make it stronger and to provide against sudden disaster; consequently a specially fierce hurricane one night swept it all away. That is the picture of many a church and many a man; because he is thought to be pious, and the church is thought to be correct and vigorous, no attempt is made for improvement, no special prayer, no cries to heaven, no repentance because of backsliding; so when there comes an unusual pressure, a night of terrible temptation, the whole fabric falls in ruin. How much better is the condition of the man who feels that he is weak, and goes to the strong for strength! I know another railway-bridge which is showing signs of danger; there are cracks in the brickwork and other problems: in all probability it would soon have come down if let alone: but it has been noticed by the railway people, who are as busy as possible trying to repair it and prevent an accident. Is not this much better than a delusive belief that all is safe? If there is a crack in the substantial part of your religious structure, what a mercy to see it! If the supporting pillars begin to give way, what a blessing to perceive the fact! 'Oh,' says one, 'you make us feel uneasy.' Yes, it is often a great blessing to be uneasy, and that blessing I pray the Holy Spirit to confer upon you. It is infinitely better to be uneasy and to get right than to be perfectly serene and all the while to be wrong.

FOR MEDITATION: Thinking we stand may lead to a fall (Proverbs 16:18; 1 Corinthians 10:12; 1 Timothy 3:6) and a rude awakening (Psalm 30:6–7; Daniel 4:28–33; Matthew 26:31–35). Psalm 119:116–117 is the proper way to address God, not *'For ever I'll love you; for ever I'll stand.'*
N.B. The original Tay Bridge collapsed on 28 December 1879 with the loss of a train and all 80 of its passengers and crew.

SERMON NO. 1677

4 SEPTEMBER (1879)

Among lions

'*My soul is among lions.*' Psalm 57:4
SUGGESTED FURTHER READING: Psalm 7:1–8

The text speaks of a soul among lions. Why did the psalmist call them lions? 'Dogs' is about as good a name as they deserve. Why call them lions? Because at times the Christian man is exposed to enemies who are very *strong*, perhaps strong in the jaw, very strong in biting, rending, and tearing. Sometimes the Christian man is exposed to those who loudly roar out their infidelities and their blasphemies against Christ, and it is an awful thing to be among such lions as those. The lion is not only strong but also *cruel*; and it is real cruelty, which subjects well-meaning men to reproach and misrepresentation. The enemies of Christ and his people are often as cruel as lions, and would slay *us* if the law permitted them. The lion is a creature of great *craftiness*, creeping along stealthily, and then making a sudden spring; and so will the ungodly creep up to the Christian, and, if possible, spring upon him when they can catch him in an unguarded moment. If they fancy they spy a fault in him they come down upon him with all their weight! The ungodly watch the righteous, and if they can catch him in his speech, or if they can make him angry and cause him to speak an unguarded word, how eagerly they pounce upon him. They magnify his fault, put it under a microscope of ten thousand power, and make a great thing of it. 'Report it! Report it!' they say, 'So would we have it!' Anything against a trueborn child of God is a sweet nut for them. Such as are daily watched, daily carped at, daily abused, daily hindered in everything that is good and gracious, go with their tears before the God they serve and cry to him, 'My soul is among lions'.

FOR MEDITATION: Consider the personal testimonies of those who conquered real lions (1 Samuel 17:34–37; Daniel 6:19–23). The Lord Jesus Christ conquered greater enemies who behaved like lions (Psalm 22:13,21); from such God can also deliver us (2 Timothy 4:17–18), even if the 'lion' involved is the devil himself (1 Peter 5:8–10).

5 SEPTEMBER (PREACHED 4 SEPTEMBER 1881)

Love's labours

'*[Charity] beareth all things, believeth all things, hopeth all things, endureth all things.*' 1 Corinthians 13:7
SUGGESTED FURTHER READING: Ephesians 4:25–5:2

A horrid blight falls upon some communities through suspicion and mistrust. Though everything may be pure and right, yet certain weak minds are suddenly fevered with anxiety through the notion that all is wrong and rotten. This unholy mistrust is in the air, a blight upon all peace: it is a sort of fusty mildew of the soul by which all sweet perfume of confidence is killed. The best man is suspected of being a designing knave, though he is honest as the day, and the smallest fault or error is frightfully exaggerated, till we seem to dwell among criminals and to be all villains together. If I did not believe in my brethren I would not profess to be one of them. I believe that with all their faults they are the best people in the world, and that, although the church of God is not perfect, yet she is the bride of One who is. I have the utmost respect for her, for her Lord's sake. The Roman matron said 'Where my husband is Caias I am Caia'; where Christ is King, she who stands at his right hand is 'the queen in gold of Ophir.' God forbid that I should rail at her of whom her Lord says, 'Since thou wast precious in my sight, thou hast been honourable, and I have loved thee'. True love believes good of others as long as ever it can, and when it is forced to fear that wrong has been done, love will not readily yield to evidence, but gives the accused brother the benefit of many a doubt. When the thing is too clear, love says, 'Yes, but the friend must have been under very strong temptation, and if I had been there I dare say I should have done worse', or else love hopes that the erring one may have offended from a good though mistaken motive; she believes that the good man must have been mistaken, or he would not have acted so. Love, as far as she can, believes in her fellows.

FOR MEDITATION: Loving forbearance of others in respect of their real or supposed faults should not prove a great problem to us (Ephesians 4:1–3; Colossians 3:12–14), especially in the light of God's loving forbearance towards us despite his thorough knowledge of our sinfulness (Romans 2:4; 3:25).

SERMON NO. 1617

6 SEPTEMBER (PREACHED 4 SEPTEMBER 1881)

Love's transformations: a Communion meditation

'If ye loved me, ye would rejoice, because I said, I go unto the Father.'
John 14:28
SUGGESTED FURTHER READING: Matthew 10:32–40

The chiefest love that we have should go to Jesus Christ himself: not so much to his salvation, as to himself, should our hearts fly. 'If ye loved *me*, ye would rejoice'. We do well to love Christ's house, his day, his book, his church, his service, his blood and his throne, but we must, above all these things, love his person. That is the tender point; 'We love *him*,' and other things in him. We love his church for his sake, his truth because it is his truth, his cross because he bore it for us, and his salvation because it was purchased by his blood. I counsel you to pull up the sluices of your love, and let the full tide flow towards Jesus. LOVE HIM. For, first, he is the source of all benefits; therefore, in loving him you value the benefits, but you trace them to their fountain-head. Should we love the gift better than the giver? Should the wife love her jewels better than the beloved one who gave them? It must not be so. Love the very person of Jesus, the God, the man, Emmanuel, God with us. Realize him as a distinct existence. Let him stand before you now 'with scars of honour in his flesh, and triumph in his eyes' as we sang just now. Love him as the source of your hope, your pardon, your life, your future glory. Loving him we learn to prize all his gifts the more, for he that loves the giver values the smallest gift for the giver's sake. Your love to the person of Jesus will not make you think less of the benefits which he bestows, but infinitely more. Shoot at the centre of the target. Love him, and, loving him, you will value all that he gives. Loving Jesus we have him for our own, and that is a great blessing.

FOR MEDITATION: (*Our Own Hymn Book* no. 786 v.5—Bernard of Clairvaux, 1153; tr. by Edward Caswall, 1849)
'Jesus, our only joy be Thou,
As Thou our crown wilt be;
Jesus, be Thou our glory now,
And through eternity.'

7 SEPTEMBER (1879)

The glory of God in the face of Jesus Christ

'For God, who commanded the light to shine out of darkness, hath shined in our hearts, to give the light of the knowledge of the glory of God in the face of Jesus Christ.' 2 Corinthians 4:6
SUGGESTED FURTHER READING: John 12:35–46

Why did not everybody see the glory of God in Jesus Christ when he was here? It was conspicuous enough. Answer: it matters not how brightly the sun shines among blind men. Now, the human heart is blind; it refuses to see God in creation except after a dim fashion, but it utterly refuses to discern God in Christ, and therefore he is the 'despised and rejected of men'. Moreover, there is a 'god of this world', the prince of darkness, and since he hates the light, he deepens and confirms the natural darkness of the human mind, lest the light should reach the heart. He blinds men's minds with error and falsehood and foul imaginations, blocking up the windows of the soul either with unclean desires, or with dense ignorance, or with pride. The reason why we did not at one time perceive the glory of God in Christ was because we were blind by nature and darkened by the evil one. As only the pure in heart can see God, we, being impure in heart, could not see God in Christ. What, then, has happened to us? To eternal grace be endless praise, God himself 'hath shined in our hearts': that same God who said 'Light be' and light was, 'hath shined in our hearts'. You know creation's story, how all things lay in black darkness. God might have gone on to make a world in darkness if he had pleased, but if he had done so it would have been to us as though it had never been, for we could not have perceived it; therefore he early said, 'Let there be light'. Now, God's glory in the face of Jesus Christ might have been all there, and we should never have discerned it, and as far as we are concerned it would have been as though it had never been, if the Lord had not entered into us amid the thick darkness and said, 'Let there be light'. Then burst in the everlasting morning, the light shined in the darkness, and the darkness fled before it. Do you recollect the incoming of that illumination?

FOR MEDITATION: (*Our Own Hymn Book* no. 425 v.2—Isaac Watts, 1709)
   'See where it shines in Jesus' face, the brightest image of His grace;
   God, in the person of His Son, has all His mightiest works outdone.'

SERMON NO. 1493

8 SEPTEMBER (PREACHED 11 SEPTEMBER 1881)

Holiness, the law of God's house

'This is the law of the house; Upon the top of the mountain the whole limit thereof round about shall be most holy. Behold, this is the law of the house.' Ezekiel 43:12
SUGGESTED FURTHER READING: Romans 12:1–13

Do I so live as to be *separated*? Is there in my business a difference between me and those with whom I trade? Are my thoughts different? Does the current of my desire run in a different direction? Am I at home with the ungodly, or does their sin vex me? Am I one of them, or am I 'as a speckled bird' among them? Search and see whether you are holy in that sense or not. Next, let each one ask, am I *consecrated*? Am I living to God with my body, my soul, my spirit? Am I using my substance, my talents, my time, my voice, my thoughts for God's glory? What am I living for? Am I making a pretence to live to God, and am I after all really living to self? Am I like Ananias and Sapphira, pretending to give all, and yet keeping back a part of the price? The preacher would search his own heart, and he begs you all to search yours. Next ask the question, am I living in *conformity* to the mind of the holy God? Am I living as Christ would have lived in my place? Do I as a master, as a servant, as a husband, as a wife, or as a child, act as God himself would have me act so that he could say to me, 'Well done, thou good and faithful servant'? He is a jealous God: am I obeying him with care? If I am not walking in obedience to God I am behaving disorderly; I am breaking the law of the house, and that the house of the living God. Ought we not to take heed lest we insult the king in his own palace, and 'perish from the way, when his wrath is kindled but a little.' Then, again, do I live in *communion* with God? I cannot be holy and yet have a wall of division between me and God. Is there a great gulf of separation between me and the Lord? Then I am a stranger to holiness.

FOR MEDITATION: (*Our Own Hymn Book* no. 653 vv.1&2—Charitie Lees Smith, 1861)
'Lord, I desire to live as one who bears a blood-bought name,
As one who fears but grieving Thee, and knows no other shame.
As one by whom Thy walk below should never be forgot;
As one who fain would keep apart from all Thou lovest not.'

SERMON NO. 1618

9 SEPTEMBER (1883)

'Glory be unto the Father'

'Blessed be the God and Father of our Lord Jesus Christ, who hath blessed us with all spiritual blessings in heavenly places in Christ: according as he hath chosen us in him before the foundation of the world, that we should be holy and without blame before him in love.' Ephesians 1:3–4
SUGGESTED FURTHER READING: Mark 12:28–34

We are to 'be holy and without blame before him in love'. Love is the anointing oil, which is to be poured on all the Lord's priests; when he has robed them in their spotless garments, they shall partake of the unction of love. When he has delivered us from all sin, one choice thing shall be seen in us, and that is love, abounding love. 'God is love; and he that dwelleth in love dwelleth in God, and God in him.' As we love we live unto God. Perfect life will be perfect love. Judge of your sanctification by this: do you grow in love to God? Do you also increase in love to the brethren? If your heart grows hard with the proud notion that you are somebody by reason of your high attainments, and that the poor little saints around you are unworthy even to unloose the latchets of your shoes, you are not growing in holiness. Do you love poor sinners more? If your heart does not grow tender you are not growing holy. What a blessed thing it would be to be saturated with love! They said of Basil, that he was a pillar of fire because of his zeal. I wish it could be said of us that we were flames of fire because of our love. Oh, to love our neighbour as ourselves, thinking no evil! 'Oh,' says one, 'we should be imposed upon!' That would be no harm compared with being hardened by selfishness. 'But we should be ill-treated and defrauded.' Suppose we were; it would be better than being miserly and cruel. The worst of ills is hate; the best of blessings is love. When we become incapable of selfishness, and get right away from unkindness of heart and uncharitableness of thought, Christ will be living in us and we in him, and then we shall be fulfilling the purpose of electing love and the design of the innumerable spiritual blessings which are already given us in Christ Jesus. To this let us all aspire.

FOR MEDITATION: Continue and abide in love (John 15:9–10); when love is confirmed (2 Corinthians 2:8), proved (2 Corinthians 8:8,24) and increased (Philippians 1:9; 1 Thessalonians 4:9–10), spiritual progress will follow (2 Peter 1:7–8); otherwise we may lose our first love (Revelation 2:4).

SERMON NO. 1738

10 SEPTEMBER (1882)

The Samaritan woman and her mission

'Upon this came his disciples, and marvelled that he talked with the woman ... The woman ... went her way into the city, and saith to the men, Come, see a man, which told me all things that ever I did.' John 4:27–29

SUGGESTED FURTHER READING: Amos 7:10–17

Although the conference was thus broken up, the consequence was the Lord's glory, even as often out of evil he works good. Since the woman cannot sit and gaze upon the divine face of her Lord, nor hear the strange music which flowed from his blessed lips, she will give herself to holy activity: she goes her way to the city and speaks to the men. This is well: there is little to deplore when men's hearts are so right that you cannot take them off from glorifying Christ, and when, if you disturb their private communion, they are ready at once for public service. Driven away from sitting, like Mary, at the Master's feet, let us rise to play the Martha, by preparing a table for the Lord. Always reckon, whenever you are taken off from your usual course of life, as it were by a jerk, that the Lord has some special work for you to do. Do not fret, or try to buck the engine to get on the old lines again. No, if the switch is turned by the divine hand, go on; he that has the management of all the railroads of your life knows better which way your soul should go than you yourself can know. I have observed Christian people jerked out of a pious family where they were extremely happy, and placed in the midst of ungodliness, a situation not of their own choosing or seeking, but appointed of the Lord, that they may bring godliness into that house, and shed light in the midst of the darkness. You may be taken away from a church where your soul has flourished, and may feel like one banished and bereaved. Never mind. If you are sent to a church where everything is dreary and dead, go there like a firebrand to set them on flame. Your Lord would not have permitted the breaking up of your peace unless he had some high service for you.

FOR MEDITATION: Christians should live the life to which God has led them (1 Corinthians 7:7); change is not wrong, but should not be sought for change's sake (1 Corinthians 7:8–9,20–21). Major changes should only be pursued if we are sure that it is God's will (Luke 5:8–11,27–28), but at such times obedience can bring great confidence. Most of Paul's epistles begin with the assurance that God called him to be an apostle.

SERMON NO. 1678

11 SEPTEMBER (1881)

Is it nothing to you?

'Is it nothing to you, all ye that pass by? behold, and see if there be any sorrow like unto my sorrow, which is done unto me, wherewith the LORD *hath afflicted me in the day of his fierce anger.'* Lamentations 1:12
SUGGESTED FURTHER READING (Spurgeon): Psalm 22:14–31

What power the cross has had on other men's minds to gird them to heroic deeds. I shall never forget when I shook the hand of Livingstone. I count it one of the great honours of my life to have known him, and even men of the world will join in doing homage to his name. But it was the love of Christ that made him tread pathless Africa and die among the heathen. He was not the first by many a thousand who counted it all joy to succumb to climate and to perish among strangers for the cross of Christ. Moffat still lives, and what a life! There was John Williams, who laid down his life at Erromanga for Christ's sake. These are but the later ranks of a mighty host that counted not life dear to them for Jesus' sake. Look at the first centuries, how men marched to the rack to be tortured, to the stake to be burned, to the amphitheatre to be devoured of beasts for Christ's sake. The lifting up of the little finger of Christ was enough to move hosts of men and women to court death and defy the flames. The Roman empire, with all its legions and cruelties, could not stand against the insignificant, unlettered, humble, but earnest and intense followers of Jesus. The sufferings of Christ made them strong to suffer. Later ages tell the same story. Our own land has seen the heroes of the cross enduring unto the end. Over there at Smithfield there were men and women, who early in the morning, while the sun was scarcely up, were summoned to stand at fiery stakes and burn; they were seen to clap their hands, when every finger was a candle, and cry, 'None but Christ! None but Christ!'

FOR MEDITATION: (Frances Ridley Havergal, who had died 3 June 1879)
   'I could not do without Him! Jesus is more to me
   Than all the richest treasures of earth could ever be.
   The more I find Him precious—the more I find Him true—
   The more I long to witness the self-same bliss in you.'

N.B. David Livingstone marked his copy of Spurgeon's sermon no. 418 (10 November 1861) 'Very good—D.L.'; it is preserved at Spurgeon's College.

SERMON NO. 1620

12 SEPTEMBER (1880)

Walking humbly with God

'*He hath shewed thee, O man, what is good; and what doth the* LORD *require of thee, but to do justly, and to love mercy, and to walk humbly with thy God?*' Micah 6:8
SUGGESTED FURTHER READING: 1 Peter 5:1–7

If a man once really comes to live and act as in the sight of God, his life must be one of eminent holiness, and if, under a sense of God's glory, he abides in deep humility of spirit, we may expect to see about him all that is tender and quiet. Like his Lord, he will be 'meek and lowly in heart'. He will not domineer over his fellow-men; he will not be hard, cruel, unkind; he cannot be. He who feels that he must walk with great softness and tenderness before his God, cannot trample on others as if they were only fit to be the dust of his feet. You will not see him supremely disdainful, carrying his head among the stars as though he were some great one; no, he has learned to walk humbly with God, and he thinks of himself soberly, as he ought to think. For a man to put on humility before God and throw it off before men would be hypocrisy of the vilest kind. Alas, it is too often seen, but it is base to the utmost; flee from it as you would from forgery and counterfeit, and in very truth 'walk humbly with thy God'. I cannot tell you all that my text means, nor if you know it yourself can you make others understand it; still they will know that it is something very admirable which makes you to be a good neighbour and a considerate friend, the comfort of the sorrowful, the helper of all. They may not understand whence the quiet spirit derives its gentle dew, but they will perceive its freshness, its sparkling purity, and its goodness, and wonder at its cause. True humility begets a suavity, a gentleness, a tenderness, a Christ-likeness, which men may mock at for a while, but which for the most part wins their hearts. The more instructed soon take knowledge of a meek-spirited man that he must have been with Jesus and have learned of him.

FOR MEDITATION: (*Our Own Hymn Book* no. 704 v.1—Charles Wesley, 1741)
'Lord, if Thou Thy grace impart, poor in spirit, meek in heart,
I shall as my Master be, rooted in humility.'

13 SEPTEMBER (PREACHED 14 SEPTEMBER 1884)

'Though he were dead'

'Martha saith unto him, I know that he shall rise again in the resurrection at the last day. Jesus said unto her, I am the resurrection, and the life: he that believeth in me, though he were dead, yet shall he live: and whosoever liveth and believeth in me shall never die.' John 11:24–26
SUGGESTED FURTHER READING: Luke 16:19–31

There is an essential difference between the decease of the godly and the death of the ungodly. Death comes to the ungodly as a penal infliction, but to the righteous as a summons to his Father's palace: to the sinner it is an execution, to the saint an undressing. Death to the wicked is the King of terrors: death to the saint is the end of terrors, the commencement of glory. To die in the Lord is a covenant blessing. Death is ours; it is set down in the list of our possessions among the 'all things', and it follows 'life' in the list as if it were an equal favour. No longer is it death to die. The name remains, but the thing itself is changed. Why, then, are we in bondage through fear of death? Why do we dread the process which gives us liberty? I am told that people who in the cruel ages had lain in prison for years suffered much more in the moment of the knocking off of their fetters than they had endured for months in wearing the hard iron; and yet I suppose that no man languishing in a dungeon would have been unwilling to stretch out his arm or leg, that the heavy chains might be beaten off by the smith. We should all be content to endure that little inconvenience to obtain lasting liberty. Now, such is death, the knocking off of the fetters; yet the iron may never seem to be so truly iron as when that last liberating blow of grace is about to fall. Let us not mind the harsh grating of the key as it turns in the lock; if we understand it aright it will be as music to our ears. Imagine that your last hour is come! The key turns with pain for a moment, but, lo, the bolt is shot! The iron gate is open! The spirit is free! Glory be unto the Lord for ever and ever!

FOR MEDITATION: (*Our Own Hymn Book* no. 839 v.4—John Williams, 1801)
    'Though perished all my cold remains,
    Though all consumed my heart and reins
    Yet for myself, my wondering eyes
    God shall behold, with glad surprise.'

14 SEPTEMBER (1879)

The one foundation

'For other foundation can no man lay than that is laid, which is Jesus Christ.' 1 Corinthians 3:11

SUGGESTED FURTHER READING: 1 Peter 2:4–10

A foundation has the shaping of the building, and the true church shapes and forms itself upon the Lord Jesus as its ground plan and outline. The shape of a building must, to a very large extent, be determined by its foundation. If you have ever traced the foundations of an ancient abbey or castle, as they have appeared on a level with the soil, you have proceeded to infer the form of the building from the run of the ground line. Here was a sharp angle, there was a circular tower; there was a buttress, and there was a recess. The building must have followed the ground line, and so must every true church be built upon Christ, in the sense of following his word and ordinances to the best of its knowledge and understanding. The law of Christ is the law of the church. All the decrees of popes and councils, all the resolutions of assemblies, synods, presbyteries, and associations, and all the ordinances of men as individuals, however great they be, when they are all put together, if they at all differ from the law of Christ, are mere wind and waste paper; worse, they are treasonable insults to the majesty of King Jesus. Those who build apart from the authority of Christ build off of the foundation, and their fabric will fall. There is no law and no authority in a true church but that of Christ himself; we who are his ministers are his servants and the servants of the church, and not lords or lawmakers. To his law a faithful church brings all things as to the sure test. As churches we are not legislators, but subjects; it is not for us to frame constitutions, invent offices, and decree rites and ceremonies, but we are to take everything out of the mouth of Christ, and to do what he bids us, as he bids us, and when he bids us.

FOR MEDITATION: (*Our Own Hymn Book* no. 549 v.1—Edward Mote, 1825)
'My hope is built on nothing less than Jesus' blood and righteousness;
I dare not trust the sweetest frame; but wholly lean on Jesus' name:
On Christ the solid rock I stand, all other ground is sinking sand.'

SERMON NO. 1494

15 SEPTEMBER (PREACHED 17 SEPTEMBER 1882)

Filling the empty vessels

'But my God shall supply all your need according to his riches in glory by Christ Jesus.' Philippians 4:19
SUGGESTED FURTHER READING: Colossians 1:24–2:10

Does God supply all his people's needs by Christ Jesus? Yes, first, by giving them Christ Jesus, for there is everything in Christ Jesus. Christ is all. The man who has Christ has all things, as says the apostle, 'all are yours; and ye are Christ's; and Christ is God's.' You will never have a spiritual want which is not supplied in Christ. If you need courage, he can create it. If you need patience, he can teach it. If you need love, he can inspire it. You want washing, but there is the fountain. You require a garment, but there is the robe of righteousness. You would have great wants if you went to heaven without Christ, but you shall not go there without him: even there he shall supply you with everything. He it is that prepares your mansion, provides your wedding-dress, leads you to his throne, and bids you sit there with him for ever. God will supply your eternal needs by giving you Christ. Moreover, all things shall come to you by virtue of Christ's merit. You deserve no good thing, but he deserves it and he says, 'Set it to my poor servant's account.' You may use Christ's name at the Bank of Heaven freely, for though God might not give his favour to you, he will always give it to his dear, dying, risen, pleading Son. When Jesus' name is quoted all things are yielded by the Father. God will give you all things by Christ: therefore do not go to anybody else after those things. If you have begun in the Spirit do not attempt to be perfected by the flesh. If your only hope is in what Christ has done, stick to that, and add nothing to it. Be this your motto, *'None but Jesus! None but Jesus!'* Jesus is our all. We are complete in him. We need no *addenda* to the volume of his love.

FOR MEDITATION: (*Our Own Hymn Book* no. 84 song 2 v.4—Isaac Watts, 1719)
   'All needful grace will God bestow,
   And crown that grace with glory too;
   He gives us all things, and withholds
   No real good from upright souls.'

16 SEPTEMBER (1883)

Bankrupt debtors discharged

'And when they had nothing to pay, he frankly forgave them both.' Luke 7:42
SUGGESTED FURTHER READING: Romans 3:27–4:8

I do believe that the Lord will give us our quittance when we have got to our last penny, and not till then, because only then do we look to the Lord Jesus Christ. Ah, my dear friends, as long as we have anything else to look to, we never will look to Christ. That blessed port into which no ship did ever run in a storm without finding a sure haven is shunned by all your gallant vessels: they will rather put into any port along the coast of self-deceit than make for the harbour which is marked out by the two lighthouses of free grace and dying love. As long as a man can scrape the meal-barrel and find a little in it, as long as he can hold up the oil-cruse, and it drips, if it only yields a drop in a week, he will never come to Christ for heavenly provision. As long as he has one rusty counterfeit penny hidden away in the corner of his till, the sinner will never accept the riches of redeeming love; but when it is all up with him, when he has nothing in the parlour, nothing in the kitchen, nothing in the cellar, when there is neither stick nor stock left, then he prizes Jesus and his salvation. We break to make. We are emptied to be filled. When we cannot give, God can forgive. If any of you have any goodness of your own, you will perish for ever. If you have anything you can trust to of your own, you will be lost as sure as you are living men and women; but if you are reduced to sore extremity, and God's fierce wrath seems to burn against you, then not only may you have mercy, but mercy is yours already.

FOR MEDITATION: (*Our Own Hymn Book* no. 546 v.4—Charlotte Elliott, 1836)
  'Just as I am—poor, wretched, blind,
  Sight, riches, healing of the mind,
  Yea, all I need, in Thee to find,
  O Lamb of God, I come.'

17 SEPTEMBER (1882)

One war over and another begun

'And when Gideon perceived that he was an angel of the LORD, *Gideon said, Alas, O Lord GOD! For because I have seen an angel of the* LORD *face to face. And the* LORD *said unto him, Peace be unto thee; fear not; thou shalt not die. Then Gideon built an altar there unto the* LORD, *and called it Jehovah-shalom.'* Judges 6:22–24
SUGGESTED FURTHER READING: John 16:25–33

'The LORD said unto him, Peace [*Shalom*] be unto thee; fear not; thou shalt not die.' The Lord would not have his Gideons disturbed in mind. If we are to trouble the enemy we must not be troubled ourselves. 'Comfort ye, comfort ye my people, saith your God. Speak ye comfortably to Jerusalem, and cry unto her, that her warfare is accomplished, that her iniquity is pardoned'. This is how God would have his prophets speak, and this is how he speaks himself. He wants his workers to be full of comfort while they labour. Notice, brethren, the great power of God in speaking home the truth. Suppose I salute you with, 'Brethren, peace be to you.' That would be a sweet word; but when the Lord says it, you feel the peace itself. Suppose Peter had stood up in that boat which was tossed upon the Galilean lake, and had said to the waves, 'be still', the waves would not have taken much notice of him, and the whistling blast would have defied him; but when Jesus said, 'Peace, be still', the rampant lions of the sea crouched at his feet, and there was a great calm. Oh, that the great Master's voice would sound the requiem of trouble in every tempest-driven heart by saying, 'Peace be unto you', so that you may become perfectly restful in your God. 'Peace!': the word is *shalom*, the word which Gideon borrowed and applied to the altar which he raised in obedience to the Lord's bidding. It signifies not only quiet, but prosperity, success, 'good fortune', as the multitude say. When God spoke that word home to his dear servant's heart, a great joy was born within him to prepare him for his great warfare.

FOR MEDITATION: (*Our Own Hymn Book* no. 733 v.2—James Grant, 1784)
'Loud roaring the billows now nigh overwhelm,
But skilful's the Pilot who sits at the helm,
His wisdom conducts thee, His power thee defends,
In safety and quiet thy warfare He ends.'

SERMON NO. 1679

18 SEPTEMBER (1881)

The Pentecostal wind and fire

'And suddenly there came a sound from heaven as of a rushing mighty wind, and it filled all the house where they were sitting. And there appeared unto them cloven tongues like as of fire, and it sat upon each of them. And they were filled with the Holy Ghost, and began to speak with other tongues, as the Spirit gave them utterance.' Acts 2:2–4
SUGGESTED FURTHER READING: Psalm 83:1–18

Wind and fire together! Rushing mighty wind alone how terrible! Who shall stand against it? See how the gallant ships dash together, and the monarchs of the forest bow their heads. And fire alone! Who shall stand against it when it devours its prey? But set wind and fire to work in hearty union! Remember the old city of London. When first the flames began it was utterly impossible to quench them because the wind fanned the flame, and the buildings gave way before the fire-torrent. Set the prairie on fire. If a rain-shower falls, and the air is still, the grass may perhaps cease to burn, but let the wind encourage the flame, and see how the devourer sweeps along while the tall grass is licked up by tongues of fire. We have lately read of forests on fire. What a sight! Hear how the mighty trees are crashing in the flame! What can stand against it! The fire sets the mountains on a blaze. What a smoke blackens the skies; it grows dark at noon. As hill after hill offers up its sacrifice, the timid imagine that the great day of the Lord has come. If we could see a spiritual conflagration of equal grandeur it would be a consummation devoutly to be wished. O God, send us the Holy Spirit in this fashion: give us both the breath of spiritual life and the fire of unconquerable zeal, till nation after nation shall yield to the sway of Jesus. O thou who art our God, answer us by fire, we pray thee. Answer us both by wind and fire, and then shall we see thee to be God indeed. The kingdom comes not, and the work is flagging. O that thou wouldest send the wind and the fire! Thou wilt do this when we are all of one accord, all believing, all expecting, all prepared by prayer. Lord, bring us to this waiting state.

FOR MEDITATION: (*Our Own Hymn Book* no. 451 v.5—Charles H. Spurgeon, 1866)
  'Obedient to Thy will, we wait to feel Thy power,
  O Lord of life, our hopes fulfil, and bless this hallowed hour.'

SERMON NO. 1619

19 SEPTEMBER (PREACHED 18 SEPTEMBER 1884)

Strength and recovery

'And I will strengthen them in the LORD: *and they shall walk up and down in his name, saith the* LORD.*'* Zechariah 10:12

SUGGESTED FURTHER READING (Spurgeon): Psalm 23:1–6

This kind of strength is exceedingly useful in all manner of ways. It is useful for our daily *walk*, work, and warfare. A man that is strong in the Lord is quiet and calm; he is not afraid of evil tidings, for 'his heart is fixed, trusting in the LORD', and in this quietude lies his deliverance from fret and faint. He is not amazed when he is troubled on every side, for he knows that he will have to bear his share of affliction, and he accepts the will of God. He has bowed his heart by the grace of God to bear all that the Lord decrees. He feels that God is with him, that his strength will be equal to his day, that the all-sufficient God will supply all his 'need according to his riches in glory by Christ Jesus'; and so he travels on serenely through this vale of tears. Half our fretting and quarrelling comes from our weakness. When a man is well he is not half so likely to be discontented with himself or to fall out with everybody else as he is when he is sickening or weak. God give you strength, dear friends, for your daily walk at home and abroad, for this will be to the comfort of those around you. And then, besides our walk, we have our *work*, and we want strength for that. Whatsoever the Lord has called you to do, the power with which to do it must come from himself. He renders 'to every man according to his work', giving double power for double labour. You will not find the power in your natural abilities, neither can you attain it by imitating some successful man, but God himself will grant you strength for every service to which he calls you. Then, besides our walk and our work, there is a *warfare* going on. Alas! We have to fight with the world, the flesh, and the devil, foes without and foes within, but we shall be more than a match for all adversaries if we do but realize this text: 'I will strengthen them in the LORD'. For all the battles which shall disturb us between here and heaven our strength is found in God himself.

FOR MEDITATION: (*Our Own Hymn Book* no. 119 song 2 v.6—Isaac Watts, 1719)
  'Make me to walk in Thy commands, 'tis a delightful road;
  Nor let my head, or heart, or hands, offend against my God.'

20 SEPTEMBER (PREACHED 21 SEPTEMBER 1884)

Heaven below

'They shall hunger no more, neither thirst any more; neither shall the sun light on them, nor any heat. For the Lamb which is in the midst of the throne shall feed them, and shall lead them unto living fountains of waters.' Revelation 7:16–17
SUGGESTED FURTHER READING: Psalm 112:1–10

If you are being daily fed by Jesus and are dwelling in God, the light of the sun, as to temporal prosperity, will do you no harm. You may be rich, but you will not trust in uncertain riches; you may be famous, but you will be as humble as if you were obscure; you may be learned, but you will sit at Jesus' feet; you may be indulged with all kinds of worldly prosperity, and yet these things will not prove a snare unto you. 'Neither shall the sun light on them, nor any heat.' Those who dwell in God are not now parched with inward heat. We notice people of God who are anxious and fretful, and cause a great deal of misery for people round about them by always worrying, fidgeting, and being in a state of nervous excitement. But holy souls, who abide in Christ, take everything calmly. You can remember such people, both men and women; whatever happened they remained unmoved, patient and cheerful. Great losses came in the course of business, but the brother did not lose his balance; sad bereavements came, but the sister did not repine. If the believer endured a sharp affliction, his chief concern was that the Lord would sanctify it to him: if people persecuted or slandered him, he was not surprised, for he expected to be hated by the world when he became a follower of Jesus. If he prospered, he did not get into a heat of pride, and begin to crow over everybody else like a cock on his dunghill. In patience he possessed his soul. God's good gift of the Holy Spirit comforted and strengthened him. He could say, 'My heart is fixed, O God, my heart is fixed: I will sing and give praise.' 'Neither shall the sun light on them, nor any heat.'

FOR MEDITATION: (*Our Own Hymn Book* no. 775 v.5—John Mason, 1683)
   'Down from above the blessed Dove
   Is come into my breast,
   To witness Thine eternal love,
   And give my spirit rest.'

SERMON NO. 1800

21 SEPTEMBER (1879)

The King-Priest

'He ... shall sit and rule upon his throne; and he shall be a priest upon his throne: and the counsel of peace shall be between them both.' Zechariah 6:13

SUGGESTED FURTHER READING (Spurgeon): Psalm 110:1–7

Remember that this same Jesus which was crucified God has proclaimed to be both Lord and King. Trust in the man of the thorn-crown must foster and nourish reverence for the Lord who wears many crowns. We must not only trust but worship. We must never dissever from that shame and spitting the fact that the four living creatures and the elders prostrate themselves before the Lamb, and sing unto his praise, 'Thou art worthy to take the book, and to open the seals thereof: for thou wast slain, and hast redeemed us to God by thy blood'.

'Salvation to God, who sits on the throne,
Let all cry aloud, and honour the Son;
The praises of Jesus the angels proclaim,
Fall down on their faces and worship the Lamb.'

O you that come to him today laden with guilt and full of fears, to wash yourselves in the fountain which he filled from his own veins, you must also come to obey him, and to walk in his statutes. You may not come to him merely that you may get your sins forgiven; you must come to be cleansed from the power of evil, and to yield yourselves to God. Jesus was given that he might be a leader and a commander to the people, as well as their deliverer and Saviour. A true disciple looks to his Master for ruling as well as for teaching, and he expects to render obedience as well as to receive instruction. There may be no separation between these two points: our priest to save must ever be regarded as our king to rule. He puts away sin, but he expects to reign over the forgiven spirit; he washes our feet, but he looks that we also practice his precepts and example of love, for he says, 'ye also ought to wash one another's feet.'

FOR MEDITATION: (*Our Own Hymn Book* no. 395 v.7—Isaac Watts, 1709)
'Jesus, the King of Glory, reigns on Sion's heavenly hill;
Looks like a lamb that has been slain, and wears His priesthood still.'

SERMON NO. 1495

22 SEPTEMBER (PREACHED 25 SEPTEMBER 1881)

The ark of the covenant

'When ye be multiplied and increased in the land, in those days, saith the LORD, *they shall say no more, The ark of the covenant of the* LORD: *neither shall it come to mind: neither shall they remember it; neither shall they visit it; neither shall that be done any more.'* Jeremiah 3:16
'And the temple of God was opened in heaven, and there was seen in his temple the ark of his testament [or covenant].' Revelation 11:19
SUGGESTED FURTHER READING (Spurgeon): Hebrews 8:6–9:5

The ark was called 'the ark of the covenant'. It represented a covenant of works, as it was a part of a visible sanctuary; how soon was that covenant broken! There is no wonder that in the breaking of that covenant the golden pot of manna was lost, and that 'Aaron's rod that budded' was no more seen, for we are told in the Chronicles that when they opened the ark, in the days of Solomon, there was nothing found in it 'save the two tables which Moses put therein at Horeb, when the LORD made a covenant with the children of Israel, when they came out of Egypt.' Hebrews 9:4 tells us that they were there originally, and so it is probable that they were taken away by the Philistines. How soon we should lose the sweet things of God if we were under the covenant of works, and how soon we should miss the gentle sovereignty of his shepherd rod! I thank and bless God that in Christ Jesus we have a covenant of grace which can never fail, and never can be broken, and in him we have all that our souls desire: pot of manna and rod of Aaron, covenant provision and covenant rule we find in him. Have you ever seen Christ as your covenant? It is not every believer that has seen him in that light. When we first come to Christ we look to him as our Saviour, and we are lightened, and a very blessed look it is. It may not be till years later that we come to understand that God has entered into covenant with us in Christ, that he will bless us, sanctify us and keep us to the end. But, mark you, while a knowledge of Christ as a Saviour gives you the bread of life yet the 'wines on the lees well refined' and the 'fat things full of marrow' are unknown to you till you can spell that word 'covenant'.

FOR MEDITATION: (*Our Own Hymn Book* no. 132 v.2—Isaac Watts, 1719)
   'Enter with all Thy glorious train, Thy Spirit and Thy word;
   All that the ark did once contain could no such grace afford.'

23 SEPTEMBER (1883)

'Let not your heart be troubled'

'Let not your heart be troubled: ye believe in God, believe also in me. In my father's house are many mansions: if it were not so, I would have told you. I go to prepare a place for you. And if I go and prepare a place for you, I will come again, and receive you unto myself; that where I am, there ye may be also. And whither I go ye know, and the way ye know.' John 14:1–4
SUGGESTED FURTHER READING: 2 Corinthians 5:1–10

Mark that word, 'a place'. We are too apt to entertain cloudy ideas of the ultimate inheritance of those who 'attain unto the resurrection of the dead.' 'Heaven is a state,' says somebody. Yes, certainly it is a state, but it is a place too, and in the future it will be more distinctly a place. Observe that our blessed Lord went away in body, not as a disembodied spirit, but as one who had eaten with his disciples, and whose body had been handled by them. His body needed a 'place', and he has gone 'to prepare a place' for us, not only as we shall be for a while, pure spirits, but as we are to be ultimately, body, soul and spirit. When a child of God dies, where does his spirit go? There is no question about that matter we are informed by the inspired apostle: 'absent from the body ... present with the Lord.' But that is a spiritual matter, and something yet remains. My spirit is not the whole of myself, for I am taught so to respect my body as to regard it as a precious portion of my complete self, 'the temple of God'. The Lord Jesus Christ did not redeem my spirit alone, but my body too, and consequently he means to have a 'place' where I, this person who is here, in the wholeness of my individuality, may rest forever. Jesus means to have a place made for the entire manhood of his chosen, that they may be where he is and as he is. Our ultimate abode will be a state of blessedness, but it must also be a place suited for our risen bodies. It is not, therefore, a cloudland, an airy something, impalpable and dreamy. No, it will be as really a place as this earth is a place. Our glorious Lord has gone for the ultimate purpose of preparing a suitable place for his people.

FOR MEDITATION: The Christian's eternal home is spoken of in terms of places: as a house (Psalm 23:6; 2 Corinthians 5:1–2) with many mansions, as a city (Hebrews 11:16; 12:22; 13:14; Revelation 21:2,10) and as a country (Hebrews 11:14,16), but Judas went to another 'place' (Acts 1:25).

24 SEPTEMBER (1882)

Shutting, sealing, and covering; or, Messiah's glorious work

'Seventy weeks are determined upon thy people and upon thy holy city, to finish the transgression, and to make an end of sins, and to make reconciliation for iniquity, and to bring in everlasting righteousness, and to seal up the vision and prophecy, and to anoint the most Holy.' Daniel 9:24

SUGGESTED FURTHER READING: 2 Corinthians 5:11–21

Observe that the terms for sin are left in an absolute form. It is said, 'to finish the transgression,' 'to make an end of sins,' 'to make reconciliation for iniquity'. Whose transgression is this? Whose sins are these? Whose iniquity is it? It is not said. No word is employed to set out the people for whom atonement is made, as is done in verses like, 'Christ also loved the church, and gave himself for it'; 'I lay down my life for the sheep.' The mass of evil is left unlabelled, that any penitent sinner may look to the Messiah and find in him the remover of sin. What transgression is finished? Transgression of every kind. What sins are made an end of? Sins of every sort, against law, against gospel, against God, against men, sins past, sins present, sins to come. And what iniquity is expiated? Every form of iniquity, whatever falls short by omission, whatever goes beyond by commission. Christ in this passage is spoken of in general terms as removing sins, transgressions, and iniquities in the mass. In other places we read of the objects of his substitution, but here all is left indefinite to encourage all. He gives us no catalogue of offences, for where should he write it? The very heavens could not hold the enumeration; but he just takes the whole unformed, horrible, black, disgusting mass, and this is what he does with it: he encloses it, fastens it up and buries it for ever. He finishes it, makes an end of it, and makes expiation for it. The Messiah came to wipe out and destroy sin, and this is and will be the effect of his work. Put all the three sentences into one and this is the sum of them.

FOR MEDITATION: (*Our Own Hymn Book* no. 564 vv.1&2—Charles Wesley, 1762; Augustus M. Toplady, 1776)
'Charged with the complicated load of our enormous debt,
By faith, I see the Lamb of God expire beneath its weight!
My numerous sins transferred to Him, shall never more be found,
Lost in His blood's atoning stream where every crime is drowned!'

SERMON NO. 1681

25 SEPTEMBER (1884)

The lion and the bear: trophies hung up

'Thy servant slew both the lion and the bear: and this uncircumcised Philistine shall be as one of them, seeing he hath defied the armies of the living God. David said moreover, The LORD *that delivered me out of the paw of the lion, and out of the paw of the bear, he will deliver me out of the hand of this Philistine.'* 1 Samuel 17:36–37
SUGGESTED FURTHER READING: Philippians 2:12–18

In God's word the car of truth runs on two rails of parallel statement. A great many people want to pull up one of the rails. They will not accept two sets of truth. 'Predestination and free agency do not agree,' the modern Solomons assert. Who said, 'they do not agree'? They do agree as fully as two rails on the tram line, but some narrow spirits must set aside either the one or the other; they cannot accept *both*. This has long been a puzzle on paper, but in practice it is ease itself. So here the practical action of the believer, throwing his whole might into his Master's service, perfectly well agrees with his falling back upon the working of God, and knowing that it is God that works all things for him. David's slaying of the lion, the bear and the Philistine is clear, but God's delivering him 'out of the paw of the lion, and out of the paw of the bear,' and the hand of the Philistine, is equally clear. Make it plain to your own self. I believe that, when I preach, I ought to prepare and study my sermon as if its success altogether depended upon me, but that, when I am thus thoroughly furnished, I am to trust in God as much as if I had done nothing at all. The same view should be taken of your life and of your service for God. Work as if you were to be saved by your works, and then trust Christ only, since it is only by faith in him that you are capable of a single good work. Work for God with all your might, as if you did it all, but then always remember that 'it is God which worketh in you both to will and to do of his good pleasure.' How is that Philistine to be killed? 'By God,' says one. True; but not without David. 'By David,' says another. Yes, but not without God.

FOR MEDITATION: Christians are God's fellow workers (1 Corinthians 3:9; 2 Corinthians 6:1). We serve him, but he alone grants success (1 Corinthians 3:5–7), as he lives in us (Galatians 2:20), speaks through us (2 Corinthians 5:20) and gives us strength to be victorious in the Christian life (Romans 8:37; Ephesians 6:10; Philippians 4:13; Colossians 1:29).

SERMON NO. 1810

26 SEPTEMBER (PREACHED 28 SEPTEMBER 1879)

Questions which ought to be asked

'But none saith, Where is God my Maker, who giveth songs in the night; who teacheth us more than the beasts of the earth, and maketh us wiser than the fowls of heaven?' Job 35:10–11
SUGGESTED FURTHER READING (Spurgeon): Psalm 42:1–11

If any seek an answer to the grave enquiries of the text, and do sincerely ask, 'Where is God my Maker?' let us give the answers. Where is *God*? He is everywhere. He is all around you now. If you want him, here he is. He waits to be gracious to you. Where is God your *Maker*? He is within eye-sight of you. You cannot see him, but he sees you. He reads each thought and every motion of your spirit, and records it too. He is within ear-shot of you. Speak, and he will hear you. Whisper; you need not even form the words with the lips, but let the thought be in the soul, and he is so near you, for in him you 'live, and move, and have' your being, that he will know your heart before you know it yourself. Where is your *Comforter*? He is ready with his 'songs in the night'. Where is your *Instructor*? He waits to make you wise unto salvation. 'Where, then, may I meet him?' says one. You cannot meet him; you must not attempt it, except through the Mediator; 'there is one God, and one mediator between God and men, the man Christ Jesus'. If you come to Jesus you have come to God. 'God was in Christ, reconciling the world unto himself, not imputing their trespasses unto them; and hath committed unto us the word of reconciliation', which word we preach. Believe in Jesus Christ, and your God is with you. Trust your soul with Jesus Christ, and you have found your Creator, and you shall never again have to say, 'Where is God my Maker?' for you shall live in him, and he shall live in you. You have found your Comforter and you shall joy in him, while he shall joy in you. You have also in Christ Jesus found your Instructor, who shall guide you through life, and bring you to perfection in the bright world above.

FOR MEDITATION: (*Our Own Hymn Book* no. 550 v.1—Ray Palmer, 1831)
   'My faith looks up to Thee, Thou Lamb of Calvary, Saviour divine:
   Now hear me while I pray; take all my guilt away;
   Oh let me from this day be wholly Thine.'

27 SEPTEMBER (PREACHED 28 SEPTEMBER 1879)

Self-righteousness, a smouldering heap of rubbish

'Which say, Stand by thyself, come not near to me; for I am holier than thou. These are a smoke in my nose, a fire that burneth all the day.'
Isaiah 65:5
SUGGESTED FURTHER READING: 1 John 1:5–10

For a man to be self-righteous is in itself a sin of sins. First, it is *blasphemy*. Perhaps you do not see that. Follow me, then. God is holy. Here comes this base imposter and boasts, 'And I am holy too.' Is that not a ludicrous and contemptible form of blasphemy? It is profanity in its very essence. The cherubim are crying 'Holy, holy, holy, is the LORD God of hosts: the whole earth is full of his glory' and amid it all there is heard this squeaking pretender, whining, 'And I am holy too.' O wretched egotist, you at once lie and blaspheme! 'The stars are not pure in his sight', 'and his angels he charged with folly', and do you, that are born of woman, and defiled from head to foot, dare to talk about righteousness, when you are a mass of sin? More, this self-righteousness is *idolatry*, for the man who counts himself to be righteous by his own works worships himself. Practically, the object of his adoration is his own dear, delectable, excellent self; all his confidence is in himself, his boasting is in himself, and, though he may sing psalms to God with his voice, yet his heart is really singing hymns to himself, and he is saying to himself, 'You have done well, my soul; there is something great and bright in you; you deserve much of your Creator; you shall surely enter heaven on your own terms. At your worst you have never been so bad as your fellow-men; at your best you are a right noble being, and a brilliant reward is your due.' What is this but idolatry in its worst form? Then, again, it is *profanity*, for it gives God the distinct lie. The Lord declares that no man is righteous. He says that he looked from heaven and surveyed the sons of men, and he saw that 'there is none that doeth good, no, not one.' To this divine assertion self-righteousness gives a flat contradiction, for it claims to be itself holy.

FOR MEDITATION: (*Our Own Hymn Book* no. 530 v.1—Isaac Watts, 1709)
  'Vain are the hopes the sons of men
  On their own works have built;
  Their hearts by nature are unclean,
  And all their actions guilt.'

SERMON NO. 1497

28 SEPTEMBER (1882)

Chariots of iron

'And the LORD *was with Judah; and he drave out the inhabitants of the mountain; but could not drive out the inhabitants of the valley, because they had chariots of iron. And they gave Hebron unto Caleb, as Moses said: and he expelled thence the three sons of Anak.'* Judges 1:19–20
SUGGESTED FURTHER READING (Spurgeon): Psalm 78:10–59

There was no excuse for this on the part of Judah, as there is really no excuse for us when we think any part of God's work to be too difficult for us, for, recollect, there was a special promise made about this very case. Kindly look at Deuteronomy 20:1 and you will see how the Lord says, 'When thou goest out to battle against thine enemies, and seest horses, and chariots ... be not afraid of them: for the LORD thy God is with thee'. If there is a special promise made to meet an emergency, who are we that we should be cast down by the difficulty? Besides that, they received a special commission. Read the second verse of the chapter from which our text is taken: 'the LORD said, Judah shall go up: behold, I have delivered the land into his hand.' Iron chariots or no chariots, God had delivered the country into their hand. Besides that, their God had done greater deeds than this: he had divided the Red Sea, and drowned the chivalry of Egypt; he had divided the Jordan into halves and led his people through the river dryshod; he had made the walls of Jericho to fall flat to the ground. Why then was he distrusted because of those wretched chariots of iron? Come then, brothers and sisters, have you got into a cleft stick in the matter of your personal affairs, and are you saying, 'I cannot pray about it: I cannot trust God about it'? Is that right? Look your Bibles up, and see whether there is not a promise exactly suited to your singular condition. Look back upon your own experience and see whether God has not done already for you and others of his people a greater thing than your present trial requires. Why will you say that you cannot drive out the chariots of iron? Be of good courage, and go forward. God is able to deliver you; therefore fear not; he will supply your need; be not dismayed.

FOR MEDITATION: (*Our Own Hymn Book* no. 106 part 2 v.1—Isaac Watts, 1719)
'God of eternal love, how fickle are our ways!
And yet how oft did Israel prove Thy constancy of grace!'

SERMON NO. 1690

29 SEPTEMBER (PREACHED 28 SEPTEMBER 1884)

The parable of the lost sheep

'*And when he cometh home, he calleth together his friends and neighbours, saying unto them, Rejoice with me; for I have found my sheep which was lost. I say unto you, that likewise joy shall be in heaven over one sinner that repenteth, more than over ninety and nine just persons, which need no repentance.*' Luke 15:6–7
SUGGESTED FURTHER READING: Genesis 45:16–28

The text tells us there was more joy over that one lost sheep than over the ninety-and-nine that went not astray. Who are these 'just persons, which need no repentance'? Well, you should never explain a parable so as to make it run on four legs if it was only meant to go on two. There may not be such persons at all, and yet the parable may be strictly accurate. If all of us had been such persons, and had never needed repentance, we should not have given as much joy to the heart of Christ as one sinner does when he repents. But suppose it to mean you and me who have long ago repented, who have, in a certain sense, now no need of repentance, because we are justified men and women; we do not give so much joy to the heart of God, for the time being, as a sinner does when he first returns to God. It is not that it is a good thing to go astray, or a bad thing to be kept from it. You understand how that is: there are seven children in a family, and six of them are all well, but one dear child is taken seriously ill, and is brought near to the gates of death. It has recovered, its life is spared, and do you wonder that for the time being it gives more joy to the household than all the healthy ones? There is a great deal more delight expressed about it than over all those that have not been ill at all. This does not show it is a good thing to be ill; we are only speaking of the joy which comes of recovery from sickness. Take another case: you have a son who has been long away in a far country, and another son at home. You love them both equally, but when the absent son comes home he is for a season most upon your thoughts. Is it not natural that it should be so?

FOR MEDITATION: The Lord Jesus Christ spoke about the joy of sowing and reaping just after he found a lost sheep by a well (John 4:6–7,36). Other lost sheep have joined in the rejoicing after being discovered up a tree (Luke 19:4–6,10), in a desert (Acts 8:26–27,39) and in a prison (Acts 16:23–24,34). Where did the good shepherd find you?

30 SEPTEMBER (1883)

Spiritual knowledge and its practical results

'For this cause we also, since the day we heard it, do not cease to pray for you, and to desire that ye might be filled with the knowledge of his will in all wisdom and spiritual understanding; that ye might walk worthy of the Lord unto all pleasing, being fruitful in every good work, and increasing in the knowledge of God.' Colossians 1:9–10
SUGGESTED FURTHER READING: Daniel 2:1–23

Intercessory prayer is increased in value when it is not from one person alone, but is offered in intimate union with other saints. Paul says, 'we also', not 'I only', but 'we also, since the day we heard it, do not cease'. 'If two of you shall agree on earth as touching any thing' concerning the kingdom, you have the blessing secured to you by a special promise of God. Remember how Abraham prayed for the cities of the plain, but succeeded not until Lot also added his supplication for Zoar. Then the little city was spared. I compare Abraham's intercession to a ton weight of prayer, and poor Lot's I can hardly reckon to have been more than half an ounce, but still that half-ounce turned the scale. So here is Paul, and with him is youthful Timothy, who, compared with Paul, is inconsiderable, yet Paul's prayer is all the more effectual because Timothy's prayer is joined with it. Our Lord sent out his servants 'by two and two', and it is well when they come back to him in prayer two and two. I commend to you the habit of frequent prayer together. When a Christian friend drops in, his visit will perhaps end in mere talk unless you secure its spiritual profit by at least a few minutes spent in united prayer. I frequently during the day, when a friend comes in upon the Master's business, say, 'Let us pray before you go,' and I always find the request is welcomed. Such prayers do not occupy much time, and if they did, it might be well spent; but such united supplications oil the wheels of life's heavy wagon, and cause it to move with less of that creaking which we too often hear. 'I alone' is certainly a good word in prayer; but 'we also' is a better one.

FOR MEDITATION: If the Lord Jesus Christ asked his disciples to watch and pray with him and was disappointed when they failed (Matthew 26:38,40), and if Paul asked others to strive together with him in prayer on his behalf (Romans 15:30), Christians must need mutual support and fellowship in prayer. How much scope for this does your prayer-life allow?

SERMON NO. 1742

1 OCTOBER (1882)

Ask and have

'Ye lust, and have not: ye kill, and desire to have, and cannot obtain: ye fight and war, yet ye have not, because ye ask not. Ye ask, and receive not, because ye ask amiss, that ye may consume it upon your lusts.'
James 4:2–3
SUGGESTED FURTHER READING (Spurgeon): Luke 10:38–11:13

The promises of God are rich and inexhaustible, and their fulfilment is to be had by prayer. Jesus says, 'All things are delivered unto me of my Father', and Paul says, 'all things are yours … and ye are Christ's'. Who would not pray when all things are thus handed over to us? And promises that were first made to individuals, are all made to us if we know how to plead them in prayer. Israel went through the Red Sea ages ago, and yet we read in the sixty-sixth Psalm, 'there did we rejoice in him.' Only Jacob was present at Peniel, and yet Hosea says 'there he spake with us'. Paul wants to give us a great promise for times of need, and he quotes from the Old Testament; 'for he hath said, I will never leave thee, nor forsake thee.' Where did Paul get that? That is the assurance which the Lord gave to Joshua: 'I will not fail thee nor forsake thee.' Surely the promise was for Joshua only. No; it is for us; 'no … scripture is of any private interpretation'; all Scripture is ours. See how God appears to Solomon at night, and he says, 'Ask what I shall give thee.' Solomon asks for wisdom. 'Oh, that is Solomon,' say you. Listen: 'If any of you lack wisdom, let him ask of God'. God gave Solomon wealth and fame into the bargain. Is that not peculiar to Solomon? No, for it is said of the true wisdom, 'Length of days is in her right hand; and in her left hand riches and honour', and is not this much like our Saviour's word, 'seek ye first the kingdom of God, and his righteousness; and all these things shall be added unto you'? Thus you see the Lord's promises have many fulfilments, and they are waiting now to pour their treasures into the lap of prayer.

FOR MEDITATION: (*Our Own Hymn Book* no. 958 v.1—Albert Midlane, 1865)

'Father, for Thy promised blessing,
Still we plead before Thy throne;
For the times of sweet refreshing,
Which can come from Thee alone.'

SERMON NO. 1682

2 OCTOBER (1881)

Mongrel religion

'So these nations feared the LORD, *and served their graven images, both their children, and their children's children: as did their fathers, so do they unto this day.'* 2 Kings 17:41
SUGGESTED FURTHER READING: 1 Corinthians 10:14–22

The greatest curse, perhaps, that ever visited the world came upon it in this way. Certain vain-glorious preachers desired to convert the world at a stroke, and to make converts without the work of the Spirit. They saw the people worshipping their gods, and thought that if they could call these by the names of saints and martyrs, the people would not mind the change, and so they would be converted. The idea was to Christianize heathenism. They virtually said to idolaters, 'Now, good people, you may keep on with your worship, and yet you can be Christians at the same time. This image of the Queen of heaven at your door need not be moved. Light the lamp still; only call the image "our Lady," and "the Blessed Virgin." Here is another image; don't pull it down, but change its name from Jupiter to Peter.' Thus with a mere change of names they perpetuated idolatry: they set up their altars in the groves, and upon every high hill, and the people were converted, without knowing it, to a baser heathenism than their own. They wanted priests, and, lo, there they were, robed like those who served at the altars of Jupiter. The people saw the same altars, sniffed the same incense, kept the same holy days and observed the same carnivals as before, and called everything by Christian names. Hence came what is now called the Roman Catholic religion, which is simply fearing God and serving other gods. Every village has its own peculiar saint, and often its own particular black or white image of the Virgin, with miracles and wonders to sanctify the shrine. This evil spread so universally that Christianity seemed in danger of extinction from the prevalence of idolatry, and it would have utterly expired had it not been of God, and had he not once more put forth his hand and raised up reformers, who cried out, 'there is one God, and one mediator between God and men'.

FOR MEDITATION: (*Our Own Hymn Book* no. 655 v.2—Jane Taylor, 1812)
 'Ye tempting sweets, forbear; ye dearest idols, fall;
 My love ye must not share, Jesus shall have it all:
 Though painful and acute the smart, His love can heal the bleeding heart!'

SERMON NO. 1622

3 OCTOBER (PREACHED 5 OCTOBER 1879)

Mistrust of God deplored and denounced

'How long will it be ere they believe me?' Numbers 14:11
SUGGESTED FURTHER READING (Spurgeon): Hebrews 3:7–19

Why are men lost? All their sins which they have done cannot destroy them if they believe in Jesus, but the damning point is that they will not believe in him. Thus says the Scripture 'he that believeth not is condemned already'. Why? 'Because he hath not believed in the ... Son of God.' God himself hangs on a tree in human form and bleeds to death bearing the sin of man, and yet men turn their backs on this infinite display of love and refuse to believe it, and therefore they sink to death and hell. I look upon the myriads now in outer darkness and I ask, 'who slew all these?' The answer is, 'they could not enter' into heaven 'because of unbelief.' They perished because they would not believe in the testimony of God concerning reconciliation by the blood of his Son. May we not well hate this murderous unbelief? We may hate it, again, because it brings so much misery and weakness upon the children of God. My brethren, if we believed God's promises we should no longer be bowed down with sorrow, for our sorrow would be turned into joy. We should glory in our infirmities; we should 'glory in tribulations also', seeing the good result which the Lord brings forth from them. The man who steadily believes his God is calm, quiet, and strong. If men fail him, his God supports him. Suppose his business fails him, his chief business is to serve his God, and that has not failed. If he is himself sick and racked with pain, he resigns himself to the great Father's chastening hand and patience is given. If health is utterly failing, he leaves himself with God, that he may take down his tabernacle curtain by curtain, confident that he will build it again in nobler form. When death approaches, he so fully believes in God that he feels it will be gain to him to pass out of this state of trial into everlasting blessedness at the Lord's right hand; and so he is always happy. How strong such a man becomes.

FOR MEDITATION: (*Our Own Hymn Book* no. 670 v.3—Isaac Watts, 1709)
'Firm as His throne His promise stands,
And He can well secure
What I've committed to His hands,
Till the decisive hour.'

4 OCTOBER (1883)

The Lord with two or three

'Where two or three are gathered together in my name, there am I in the midst of them.' Matthew 18:20
SUGGESTED FURTHER READING: 2 Peter 1:1–11

When Sir Thomas Abney was Lord Mayor of London, in the middle of the banquet which takes place on the first night, he disappeared for a quarter-of-an-hour, and when he came back, he said to the friends around him that he had been keeping a particular engagement with a most intimate friend, and so he had retired for a while. That appointment was to have family prayer with his household in the Mansion House, and that gathering for prayer he would not have given up on any account whatever. Say to all other things, 'You must stand back; I have a particular appointment; I must meet the Lord Jesus Christ with two or three of his people. He says that he will be there, and I should not like him to say, "Where is my servant? Where is my son? Where is my daughter? Are they absent when I am here?"' It is such a blessing to get to know the Lord Jesus personally. I heard the other day of a famous infidel, an agnostic, (that is, an ignoramus, a person who knows nothing), and he went to a certain house to meet an elderly lady of considerable literary renown. He was told that she believed in the Word of God, and was a faithful follower of the Lord Jesus, so he thought that he would have a word with her before he went away. 'Madam,' said he, 'I have been astonished to hear one thing of you. I hear that you believe in the Bible.' 'Yes, sir,' she said, 'every word of it.' 'And pray, Madam,' he said, 'however came you to believe in that book?' She replied, 'One of the principal reasons that I have for believing in the Book is that I am intimately acquainted with the Author of it.' That was a blessed answer. Faith gets to know Christ; and so, knowing Christ, and meeting him in the midst of his people, it becomes armed against all unbelief.

FOR MEDITATION: (*Our Own Hymn Book* no. 988 v.3—Samuel Stennett, 1787)
'We meet at Thy command, dear Lord,
Relying on Thy faithful word:
Now send Thy Spirit from above,
Now fill our hearts with heavenly love.'

SERMON NO. 1761

5 OCTOBER (1884)

Thought-reading extraordinary

'LORD, *thou hast heard the desire of the humble: thou wilt prepare their heart, thou wilt cause thine ear to hear.*' Psalm 10:17
SUGGESTED FURTHER READING: 1 Samuel 1:1–20

We have heard a good deal lately about thought-reading. I give no opinion of that matter among men, but here is a wonderful instance of it with the Lord: 'thou hast heard the desire of the humble'. This kind of desire-reading is the prerogative of God alone. He knows our desires even when we do not know them ourselves. It is quite impossible for the person sitting next to you to know your wishes, and it is quite as well, perhaps, that it is so. Certain it is that the servant of God, Eli himself, fresh from the shrine of the Most High, could not read Hannah's desire. Her lips were moving, and one would think if anything would be learned it might be from the moving of the lips, but Eli thought her drunken and therefore chattering to herself, and so he rebuked her. Was it not a mercy for Hannah that God heard her humble desire, and knew all about it? Beloved, the Lord is reading your thought now: my dear sister, your groaning out of the very deeps has ascended to the heights. You would not like to tell your inward feelings: perhaps your secret is too painful to be told: never mind, God's ear is so quick that he can hear your desires. Wonderful art! We should be very glad if the Lord had promised to hear us when we speak, but he has gone far beyond that, and he hears the unspeakable and unutterable. Was there ever power and pity like this? Be comforted, you that are full of desires, with hearts ready to break, crying in your spirit, 'Oh that the Lord would hear me! Oh that he would give me peace! Oh that the days of my mourning were ended! "Oh that I knew where I might find him! that I might come even to his seat!"' Do not sink in despair; there is no reason for fear; your case is among the most hopeful, for it is the way of the Lord to hear 'the desire of the humble'.

FOR MEDITATION: (*Our Own Hymn Book* no. 998 v.1—Benjamin Beddome, 1818)

'When God inclines the heart to pray,
He hath an ear to hear;
To Him there's music in a groan,
And beauty in a tear.'

SERMON NO. 1802

6 OCTOBER (1881)

With the disciples on the lake of Galilee

'And they feared exceedingly, and said one to another, What manner of man is this, that even the wind and the sea obey him.' Mark 4:41 *(see also* Matthew 8:27*)*

SUGGESTED FURTHER READING: John 13:1–17

Our loving Lord is still God over all. He is to be honoured and reverenced, worshipped and adored, by all who draw near to him. However much he is our brother, he says, 'Ye call me Master and Lord: and ye say well; for so I am.' He is all the greater because of his condescension to us, and we are bound to recognize this. Whenever Jesus is near, the feeling of holy awe and solemn dread will steal over true disciples. I am afraid of that way of being so familiar with Christ as to talk of him as 'dear Jesus,' and 'dear Lord,' as if he were some Jack or Harry that we might pat on the back whenever we liked. No, no. This will never do. It is not such language as men would use to their prince: let them not thus address the King of kings. However favoured we may be, we are but dust and ashes, and our spirit must be chastened with reverence. When Jesus is near us we ought to fear exceedingly because we have doubted him. If you had been suspicious of a dear friend, and had indulged hard thoughts about him, and on a sudden you found yourself sitting in the same room with him, you would feel awkward, especially if you understood that he knew what you had said and thought. Oh, you will feel ashamed of yourself, my brother, if Jesus shall draw near to you. The wisest thing you can do in such a case is to say, 'My Master, my Lord, since thou dost favour me with thy presence I will first fall at thy feet, and confess that I did doubt thee, that I did think that the stormy wind would swallow up the vessel, and that the waves would devour both thee and me. Forgive me, Master; forgive me for having thought so ill of thee.' Whenever we are near to Christ, one of the first feelings should be that of great humiliation. Let us fall at his feet, and confess how ill we have thought of him.

FOR MEDITATION: Sometimes the forwardness of the disciples when addressing Jesus as 'Lord' brought them rebukes (Matthew 16:22–23; 17:4–5; Luke 9:54–55; 10:40–42; John 13:6–8). Contrast these occasions with the glorious confessions of his lordship which resulted from his words or actions (Luke 5:4–8; John 11:25–27; 20:27–28).

SERMON NO. 1686

7 OCTOBER (1883)

A loving entreaty

'Put me in remembrance: let us plead together: declare thou, that thou mayest be justified.' Isaiah 43:26
SUGGESTED FURTHER READING: Malachi 1:6–14

The Lord charged it upon Israel that they had not delighted in him: 'thou hast been weary of me, O Israel.' Is not this a charge which cannot be denied? You men and women who are not regenerate and have never received the pardon of your sin, is it not true that you are weary of God? You readily enough grow tired of a sermon in which we try to speak of him, though you would listen for hours to a silly tale. You become tired of the Sabbath-day. What a weariness it is! You are weary of the Bible; how little do you read it! A foolish novel suits you better. If you hear Christians talking wisely and seriously of the things of Christ, you have no liking for their words; you would rather listen to a comic song. To you the house of God is the temple of dullness, and the worship of God is bondage. As for God himself, you will not allow yourself to remember him; he is not in all your thoughts. You sometimes think that even heaven itself would be a weary place for you if it were full of the praising and adoring of God, and communion with him. Can you deny this? If you can, you are invited to state your innocence before the Lord. But I know that in truth you cannot raise the question; for there is within your mind an unquestionable aversion to the service of God; in fact, you would feel happier if there were no God, and if thoughts of eternity never intruded themselves. Take heed lest your aversion become mutual, and God should say, 'my soul lothed them, and their soul also abhorred me.'

FOR MEDITATION: Those who are weary of God are justly required to give a reason for this (Micah 6:3). After all God can give plenty of reasons why he should be weary of us (Isaiah 1:14; 7:13; 43:24; Jeremiah 15:6). How perverse it must be for sinners to demand an explanation of this from God (Malachi 2:17)!

SERMON NO. 1743

8 OCTOBER (1882)

The great cross-bearer and his followers

'And when they had mocked him, they took off the purple from him, and put his own clothes on him, and led him out to crucify him. And they compel one Simon a Cyrenian, who passed by, coming out of the country, the father of Alexander and Rufus, to bear his cross.' Mark 15:20–21
SUGGESTED FURTHER READING: Acts 13:26–41

He wore his own clothes that there might be a fulfilment of prophecy. It may not strike you at first, but you will soon see it. Our Lord must not go to die in the purple: he must march to the cross in that vestment which 'was without seam, woven from the top throughout', or else the word could not have been fulfilled, 'They parted my garments among them, and upon my vesture did they cast lots.' Other raiment could readily have been rent and divided, but this garment, which was peculiar to the Saviour, could not have been so rent without destroying it, and therefore the soldiers cast lots for it. Little did they who put it on him dream that they were thus accessory to the fulfilment of a prophecy. Does it not strike you as strange that the Pharisees, who were so full of hatred to Christ, did not carefully draw back from the fulfilment of so many types and prophecies? Their rabbis and teachers knew the prophecy of Zechariah, that the Messiah should be sold for 'thirty pieces of silver': why did it not occur to them to make their bribe to Judas twenty-nine or thirty-one silver pieces? Why, again, did they cast the price unto the potter by buying of him the field of blood? Could they not, so to speak, have baulked the prophecy thereby? Here were voluntarily fulfilled by themselves prophecies which condemned them. If it had been their object to fulfil type and prophecy, they could not have acted more carefully than they did. So they put his own garments on him, and unwittingly they furnished the possibility for the fulfilment of the prophet's word, 'They part my garments among them, and cast lots upon my vesture.'

FOR MEDITATION: The events around the cross were planned by God, yet carried out by wicked men (Acts 2:23; 4:27–28). Some prophecies were deliberately fulfilled by the Lord Jesus Christ (Luke 22:37; John 19:28), while others were ignorantly fulfilled by his friends (Matthew 26:31) and enemies (Matthew 27:9–10,39–43 (c.f. Psalm 22:7–8); John 19:24,36–37) even though he told them exactly what was going on (Matthew 26:53–56).

SERMON NO. 1683

9 OCTOBER (1881)

Whole-hearted religion

'*And I will give them one heart, and one way, that they may fear me for ever, for the good of them, and of their children after them.*' Jeremiah 32:39

SUGGESTED FURTHER READING (Spurgeon): Psalm 86:1–17

God has given us to fear him for ever. *Persecution* comes; Christians are ridiculed in the workshop, they are pointed out in the street, and an opprobrious name is hooted at them; now we shall know who are God's elect and who are not. Persecution acts as a winnowing fan, and those who are light as chaff are driven away by its blast, but those who are true corn remain and are purified. Careless of man's esteem, the truly God-fearing man with one heart holds on his one way and fears the Lord for ever. Then, perhaps, comes a more serious test, the trial of *prosperity*. A man grows rich and rises into another class of society. If he is not a real Christian, he will forsake the Lord, but if he is a true-born heir of the kingdom, he will fear the Lord for ever, and consecrate his substance to him. A heart wholly given to God will stand the wear and tear of life in all conditions, whether in honour or in contempt. *Poverty* is a severe test to many, and I have known numbers of professors forsake the house of God because, as they said, their clothes were not fit to come in; but that is a poor excuse; I fear their hearts were not fit to come in. The fear of God would make the godly man swallow his pride and follow Christ in rags: he will bear a famine of bread and a famine of water, but he cannot endure a famine of the word of God. His soul must be fed, and so he must and will be found where the Lord's table is spread with the bread of heaven. When God stripped Job of all his riches, it was then that his integrity was seen and proved.

FOR MEDITATION: (*Our Own Hymn Book* no. 116 song 2 v.6—Isaac Watts, 1719)
  'Here in Thy courts I leave my vow,
  And Thy rich grace record:
  Witness, ye saints, who hear me now,
  If I forsake the Lord.'

SERMON NO. 1623

10 OCTOBER (1880)

Asleep and yet awake—a riddle

'I sleep, but my heart waketh: it is the voice of my beloved that knocketh.' Song of Solomon 5:2
SUGGESTED FURTHER READING: Proverbs 26:13–16

You cannot walk the road to heaven asleep, nor preach the gospel as you should, nor serve God and your generation aright, if you are in a spiritual slumber. I know a great many who are so, alive, I hope, but very sleepy. They do very little; they are too sluggish to attempt much. 'The slothful man saith, There is a lion in the way; a lion is in the streets.' This was his argument for keeping in the chimney-corner. In truth, the lion is about as real as the monster which has been described of late as prowling over this county of Surrey and devouring women and children all the way from Banstead Downs to Clapham Common. Solomon seems to have been very familiar with this fable of the sluggard's lion, for in another proverb he makes the idler cry, 'There is a lion without, I shall be slain in the streets.' These poor creatures are so dreamy in spirit that they see a lion everywhere, threatening them if they try to do good in any form; they must sit quiet and still, and try to enjoy themselves as best their sleep will allow them to do, for they cannot venture out to work because of the lion. They cannot teach a little Sunday-school class, for there is a lion there, nor go out to speak to a dozen people in a village: a furious lion is roaring there! In fact, they will be devoured if they leave their easy retirement and put their heads out of doors. God help us to escape this lazy condition. May we live while we live. Let not our souls merely act as salt to keep our carcasses from rottenness, but let them be the seed-plot and hotbed of holy actions out of which shall yet spring glory to God and blessing to our fellow men. If you do not feel active and energetic, make it a matter of self-complaint, and utter the shame-faced confession, 'I sleep'.

FOR MEDITATION: In his care for his people God neither slumbers nor sleeps (Psalm 121:3–4). He expects his people to take notice of his warnings about spiritual sleep, slothfulness, sluggishness and slumber (Proverbs 6:4–11; 24:30–34). Note David's resolve in his service for God (Psalm 132:1–5) and resolve to do likewise (1 Thessalonians 5:6).

SERMON NO. 1561

11 OCTOBER (PREACHED 12 OCTOBER 1884)

The road to honour

'Them that honour me I will honour, and they that despise me shall be lightly esteemed.' 1 Samuel 2:30
SUGGESTED FURTHER READING: John 5:39–47

If we do not honour God, we shall not make God our guiding star and his glory to be our chart and compass; we may live to get *money*, by fair means or foul, cost what it may. What a Gradgrind a man becomes when he forgets God and only remembers gold. Oh, the wretches there are who do not care how many poor people are starved so long as they can make a larger profit: into their little miserable souls it never enters that it is a shame to starve the workers, by putting them to a killing toil in order to earn the scantiest of food. Some make *ambition* their guiding star, and do not care what they say in the House of Commons or elsewhere, so long as they can keep themselves before the public. They make a speech today which they contradict tomorrow; they blurt out of their mouths the first thing that comes into their heads, whether it is mischievous or beneficial. Be it false or true, it is no odds to them so long as their speech will catch the ear. Only for themselves do many politicians live. And so with other men besides. The poet will sing that he may show what a poet he is, but he does not dedicate his magic of language to the God who is only to be praised. All gifts should be used for God, all art of genius, science of mind and skill of hand. These talents come from him, and to him should they be devoted, but, alas, in most cases they are used for meaner ends. There are men whose guiding star is *licentiousness*: they live to please themselves and to gratify the flesh. Wretched, dung-hill breed as they are, they will go back to the oblivion whence they came, after having, I fear, polluted many who else might have escaped from these corruptions. God save men of this corrupt kind, while yet forgiveness can be found; and may we all come to this resolve, that we will honour God.

FOR MEDITATION: (*Our Own Hymn Book* no. 34 version 1 v.5—Tate and Brady, 1696)
  'Fear Him, ye saints, and you will then have nothing else to fear;
  Make you His service your delight, He'll make your wants His care.'

N.B. Thomas Gradgrind—a character in *Hard Times* by Charles Dickens.

12 OCTOBER (1879)

The teaching of the foot-washing

'Jesus knowing that the Father had given all things into his hands, and that he was come from God, and went to God; he riseth from supper, and laid aside his garments; and took a towel, and girded himself. After that he poureth water into a basin, and began to wash the disciples' feet, and to wipe them with the towel wherewith he was girded.' John 13:3–5
SUGGESTED FURTHER READING: Galatians 5:13–26

Christianity says, 'I am willing that others should help me to be holy, and I am also willing to help others to the same end. I am so imperfect that I am willing that anybody should point out my faults and rebuke me for them, and I am so anxious that my brother should be holy that I will lovingly help him to conquer sin.' Sometimes it is more humbling to have your own feet washed than to wash other people's, and hence sometimes our naughty pride says, 'Thou shalt never wash my feet.' Yet it must be so, and pride must sit still like a child, and be both washed and wiped. Again, I perceive that for many it is easy to stoop to the poor, but hard to yield to their equals in estate or ability. I know those who will do a thousand things for a poor man, but they would not do the like service to those of their own rank. You say, 'As for that poor soul, I do not mind conceding many points to him, but this other man will crow over me if I yield to his weakness, and he will expect me to do it again, and so I may be thought to be a person of no spirit, who can easily be put upon.' That also is the speech of anti-Christianity. True Christianity impels us to render and to accept that service which is mutual among true saints. He who kindly reminds me of my faults helps me to be better; let me not be angry with him, but value him for his faithfulness. On the other hand, I must never hint at a failing in a brother unless I believe that he will be the better for it, and even then I must do it gently, for I am not to scald my brethren's feet, but to use cool, sparkling, living water in the washing of them. Refining by fire is God's work: refreshing with water is ours. We are to rebuke in love, not in wrath; we are to wipe as well as wet,to comfort as well as correct.

FOR MEDITATION: (*Our Own Hymn Book* no. 263 v.3—John Hampden Gurney, 1851)
　'Let grace our selfishness expel, our earthliness refine;
　And kindness in our bosoms dwell, as free and true as Thine.'

SERMON NO. 1499

13 OCTOBER (PREACHED 12 OCTOBER 1884)

Jehovah-jireh

'And Abraham called the name of that place Jehovah-jireh: as it is said to this day, In the mount of the LORD *it shall be seen.'* Genesis 22:14
SUGGESTED FURTHER READING: Hebrews 9:6–14

Jesus must pour 'out his soul unto death' that we might live. He must be 'numbered with the transgressors', that we might be numbered with his saints in glory everlasting. Was not this a glorious provision? What greater gift could be bestowed than one in whom God and man are blended in one? When Abraham on the mount offered a sacrifice it was called a 'burnt offering', but when the Lord Jesus Christ on Calvary died, it was not only a burnt offering, but a sin offering, a meat offering, a peace offering and every other kind of sacrifice in one. Under the oldest of all dispensations, before the Mosaic economy, God had not taught to men the distinctions of sacrifice, but an offering unto the Lord meant all that was afterwards set forth by many types. When the venerable patriarch offered a sacrifice, it was an offering for sin, and a sweet smelling savour besides. So was it with our Lord Jesus Christ. When he died he made 'his soul an offering for sin,' and 'put away sin by the sacrifice of himself.' When he died, he also offered unto God a burnt offering, for we read, 'And walk in love, as Christ also hath loved us, and hath given himself for us an offering and a sacrifice to God for a sweetsmelling savour.' When Jesus died he gave to us a peace offering; for we come to feast upon him with God, and to us his 'flesh is meat indeed,' and his 'blood is drink indeed.' One would need many a day in which to speak upon the infinite virtues and excellencies of Christ, in whom all perfections are sweetly hived. Blessed be his name, God has most gloriously provided for us in the day of our need. Jehovah-jireh!

FOR MEDITATION: Consider further the multi-purpose single offering of the Lord Jesus Christ (Daniel 9:24). The shedding of his blood served as a sin offering (Isaiah 53:10; Hebrews 10:5–10), a burnt offering (Hebrews 10:5–10), a peace offering (Ephesians 2:13–17) and a drink offering (Isaiah 53:12; Matthew 26:27–28). The offering of himself was so complete that it needed to be made once and once only (Hebrews 7:27; 9:12,26–28; 10:10; 1 Peter 3:18).

14 OCTOBER (1883)

Where the 'if' lies

'Jesus said unto him, If thou canst believe, all things are possible to him that believeth.' Mark 9:23
SUGGESTED FURTHER READING: Mark 5:25–34

A boy was awakened in a house, which had taken fire. He could be seen from the street, poor child, and his danger was great indeed. He rushed to the window: his father stood below and called to him to drop into his arms; but it was a long way down, and the child was afraid. He clung to the window, but dared not drop. Do you know what made him let go his hold and fall into his father's arms? There came a burst of fire out of the window and scorched him and then he dropped directly. I wish some of you would get just such a touch of the fires of despair as to compel you to say:

> 'I can but perish if I go; I am resolved to try,
> For if I stay away I know I must for ever die.'

Years ago one of our students was greatly emaciated with what seemed to be consumption. He had heard of a certain medicine, which was said to be useful in such cases, but he had no faith in it. When he was growing worse and worse I said, 'Brother, you are at death's door; try that man's stuff. There may be something in it. At any rate, nothing else does you any good.' He took the medicine through sheer despair of all other prescriptions, and God blessed it to him so that he is alive at this day. He would never have tried the remedy if he had not felt that there was no other hope. Even so, it will be well for you to be driven into a corner as to your soul's estate, that you may believe in Christ Jesus and say with his disciples in old time, 'to whom shall we go? thou hast the words of eternal life.'

FOR MEDITATION: (*Our Own Hymn Book* no. 551 v.2—Charles Wesley, 1740)
> 'Other refuge have I none, hangs my helpless soul on Thee!
> Leave, ah! Leave me not alone, still support and comfort me!
> All my trust on Thee is stayed, all my help from Thee I bring;
> Cover my defenceless head with the shadow of Thy wing.'

SERMON NO. 1744

15 OCTOBER (1882)

'Feed my lambs:' a Sabbath-school sermon

'So when they had dined, Jesus saith to Simon Peter, Simon, son of Jonas, lovest thou me more than these? He saith unto him, Yea, Lord; thou knowest that I love thee. He saith unto him, Feed my lambs.' John 21:15
SUGGESTED FURTHER READING: 2 Timothy 3:10–17

Christian children mainly need to be taught the doctrine, precept, and life of the gospel: they require to have divine truth put before them clearly and forcibly. Why should the higher doctrines, the doctrines of grace, be kept back from them? They are not, as some say, bones; or if they be bones, they are full of marrow, and covered with fatness. If there is any doctrine too difficult for a child, it is rather the fault of the teacher's conception of it than of the child's power to receive it, provided that child is really converted to God. It is ours to make doctrine simple; this is to be a main part of our work. Teach the little ones the whole truth and nothing but the truth, for instruction is the great want of the child's nature. A child has not only to live as you and I have, but also to grow; hence he has double need of food. When fathers say of their boys, 'What appetites they have!' they should remember that we also would have great appetites if we had not only to keep the machinery going, but to enlarge it at the same time. Children in grace have to grow, rising to greater capacity in knowing, being, doing, and feeling, and to greater power from God; above all they must be well fed or instructed, because they are in danger of having their cravings perversely satisfied with error. Youth is susceptible to evil doctrine. Whether we teach young Christians truth or not, the devil will be sure to teach them error. They will hear of it somehow, even if they are watched by the most careful guardians. The only way to keep chaff out of the child's little measure is to fill it brimful with good wheat. Oh that the Spirit of God may help us to do this! The more the young are taught the better; it will keep them from being misled.

FOR MEDITATION: (*Our Own Hymn Book* no. 104 v.5—Sir Robert Grant, 1839)
    'Frail children of dust, and feeble as frail,
    In Thee do we trust, nor find Thee to fail;
    Thy mercies how tender, how firm to the end,
    Our Maker, Defender, Redeemer, and Friend!'

SERMON NO. 1684

16 OCTOBER (1881)

Welcome! Welcome!

'And the people, when they knew it, followed him: and he received them, and spake unto them of the kingdom of God, and healed them that had need of healing.' Luke 9:11

SUGGESTED FURTHER READING: Mark 10:13–16

Our Master welcomed the young, saying, 'Suffer the little children to come unto me, and forbid them not: for of such is the kingdom of God.' Dear boys and girls, Jesus will not put you by to wait till you are older, but he will welcome you just as you are. How sweetly Jesus is doing this to my knowledge with many little folks. I heard last week of a poor boy who lived near my house. A meeting is held by some of our friends in a cottage, and this boy came one night and said, 'Please, sir, may I come in?' The good man of the house answered, 'You may if you will wash your face and hands.' 'That I will do, sir,' he said; and he soon returned and took his seat. He was an attentive hearer and a devout worshipper. Though only twelve years old he loved the prayer-meeting, and was always there. One evening he said to the leader, 'Please, sir, may I pray?' and this poor child then poured out his heart before God with such sweetness that he impressed all who listened to him. One night as he went out of the room he shook hands with the good man of the house and said, 'Good-bye, sir, perhaps we may not meet again till we meet in heaven.' His words seem prophetic now, for before the next meeting a brewer's dray passed over him, and his sweet young spirit ascended to Jesus whom he loved so well. What a joy to know that this poor child is now beholding the face of our Father who is in heaven. I am glad to say that we are continually receiving boys and girls into the church. Child-piety is no rarity among us; we find it no cause of difficulty, but a well-spring of delight. Dear children, do not be afraid to come because you are so little, for Jesus has told the big people that unless they receive him as little children they shall in no wise enter into the kingdom of heaven. 'Those that seek me early shall find me.'

FOR MEDITATION: (*Our Own Hymn Book* no. 509 v.1—Albert Midlane, 1865)
'Come, and welcome, to the Saviour, He in mercy bids thee come:
Come, be happy in His favour, longer from Him do not roam;
Come, and welcome, come to Jesus, sinner, come!'

17 OCTOBER (1880)

Harvest past, summer ended, and men unsaved

'The harvest is past, the summer is ended, and we are not saved.'
Jeremiah 8:20
SUGGESTED FURTHER READING: Hebrews 12:12–17

Many make a great mistake about salvation; they mistake the meaning of the term, and to them salvation means being delivered from going down into the pit of hell, just as to these Jews it meant rescue from Nebuchadnezzar. Now, the right meaning of salvation is purification from evil. These people never thought of this: they never said, 'We are not cleansed, we are not made holy,' but 'we are not saved.' If their cry had been, 'The harvest is past, the summer is ended, and we have not yet conquered sin', that would have been a mark of something good and true, but they showed no trace of it. There is not much in a man's desiring to be saved if he means by that an escape from the punishment of his offences. Was there ever a murderer yet who did not wish to be saved from the gallows? When a man is tied up to be flogged for a deed of brutal violence, and his back is bared for the lash, depend upon it he repents of what he did, that is to say, he repents that he has to suffer for it; but that is all, and a sorry all too. He has no sorrow for the agony which he inflicted on his innocent victim, no regret for maiming him for life. What is the value of such a repentance? Here is the point, my hearers; do you wish to have new hearts? If you do you shall have them. Do you wish to leave the sins you have loved? Do you desire to live as Christ lived? Do you wish to keep the commandments of God? Do you sigh for purity of life? Do you wish henceforth to be as God would have you to be, just, loving, kind, chaste, after the example of the great Redeemer? If so, then truly the desire you have comes from God.

FOR MEDITATION: (*Our Own Hymn Book* no. 585 v.3—Joseph Hart, 1759)

'Let us trust Thee evermore;
Every moment on Thee call
For new life, new will, new power:
Let us trust Thee, Lord, for all!
May we nothing know beside
Jesus, and Him crucified!'

SERMON NO. 1562

18 OCTOBER (PREACHED 16 OCTOBER 1884)

A proclamation from the King of kings

'*Go and proclaim these words toward the north, and say, Return, thou backsliding Israel, saith the* LORD*; and I will not cause mine anger to fall upon you: for I am merciful, saith the* LORD*, and I will not keep anger for ever. Only acknowledge thine iniquity, that thou hast transgressed against the* LORD *thy God, and hast scattered thy ways to the strangers under every green tree, and ye have not obeyed my voice, saith the* LORD.' Jeremiah 3:12–13
SUGGESTED FURTHER READING: Hosea 5:15–6:6

Notice the advice that God here gives as to how we are to return. He says, '*Only acknowledge thine iniquity*'. 'Oh,' you have said, 'I cannot get back to God: it is such a long way back to him. I feel that I have to set myself right, and in that process to pass through a world of sorrow.' Yet the Lord says, 'Only acknowledge'. I rejoice in those blessed '*onlys*' of the Bible! 'Only acknowledge thine iniquity'. 'Alas, I have so wandered!' Acknowledge it. 'But I have done it so many times!' Acknowledge it. 'But I have wandered against light and knowledge!' Acknowledge it. It is not a hard thing to do, to get to your chamber, and before God to confess your faults. You have, first of all, to have a knowledge of it, and then to ac-knowledge it. Feel your sin, and then confess it. Be convinced of it, and then plead guilty at the judgment-seat. Do not attempt to excuse it, or to make apologies for it. As long as you do so, you will never get peace; but let this perilous stuff be purged from off your soul by a clear, plain acknowledgment, such as David made when he said, 'Deliver me from bloodguiltiness'. He had tried to call his crime by other names, but his forgiveness came when he owned that it was murder. When we know our sin, God will make us know his grace, but if we are self-righteous, our pride will be our ruin.

FOR MEDITATION: (*Our Own Hymn Book* no. 521 v.3—William Bengo Collyer, 1812)
    'Return, O wanderer! return!
    He heard thy deep repentant sigh!
    He saw thy softened spirit mourn,
    When no intruding ear was nigh.'

SERMON NO. 1833

19 OCTOBER (1879)

Number 1,500, or, Lifting up the brazen serpent

'And Moses made a serpent of brass, and put it upon a pole, and it came to pass, that if a serpent had bitten any man, when he beheld the serpent of brass, he lived.' Numbers 21:9
SUGGESTED FURTHER READING (Spurgeon): John 3:1–18

This particular remedy of a serpent lifted on a pole was exceedingly instructive, though I do not suppose that Israel understood it. We have been taught by our Lord and know the meaning. It was a serpent impaled upon a pole. As you would take a sharp pole and drive it through a serpent's head to kill it, so this brazen serpent was exhibited as killed, and hung up as dead before all eyes. It was the image of a dead snake. Wonder of wonders that our Lord Jesus should condescend to be symbolized by a dead serpent. The instruction to us after reading John's gospel is this: our Lord Jesus Christ, in infinite humiliation, deigned to come into the world, and to be made a curse for us. The brazen serpent had no venom of itself, but it took the form of a fiery serpent. Christ is no sinner, and in him is no sin. But the brazen serpent was in the form of a serpent; and so was Jesus sent forth by God 'in the likeness of sinful flesh'. He came under the law, and sin was imputed to him, and therefore he came under the wrath and curse of God for our sakes. In Christ Jesus, if you will look at him upon the cross, you will see that sin is slain and hung up as a dead serpent: there too is death put to death, for he 'hath abolished death and hath brought life and immortality to light': and there also is the curse for ever ended because he has endured it, 'being made a curse for us: for it is written, Cursed is every one that hangeth on a tree'. Thus are these serpents hung up upon the cross as a spectacle to all beholders, all slain by our dying Lord. Sin, death, and the curse are as dead serpents now. Oh, what a sight! If you can see it what joy it will give you. Had the Hebrews understood it, that dead serpent, dangling from a pole, would have prophesied to them the glorious sight which this day our faith gazes upon—Jesus slain, and sin, death, and hell slain in him.

FOR MEDITATION: (*Our Own Hymn Book* no. 539 v.3—Isaac Watts, 1709)
'High on the cross the Saviour hung, high in the heavens He reigns;
Here sinners, by the old serpent stung, look, and forget their pains.'

20 OCTOBER (PREACHED 19 OCTOBER 1884)

Obadiah; or, Early piety eminent piety

'I thy servant fear the LORD *from my youth.'* 1 Kings 18:12
SUGGESTED FURTHER READING (Spurgeon): Psalm 71:1–18

To be a believer in God early in life is to be saved from a thousand regrets. Such a man shall never have to say that he carries in his bones the sins of his youth. Early piety helps us to form associations for the rest of life which will prove helpful, and it saves us from those which are harmful. The Christian young man will not fall into the common sins of young men, and injure his constitution by excesses. He will be likely to be married to a Christian woman, and so to have a holy companion in his march towards heaven. He will select as his associates those who will be his friends in the church and not in the tavern, his helpers in virtue, and not his tempters to vice. Depend upon it, a great deal depends upon whom we choose for our companions when we begin life. If we start in bad company, it is very hard to break away from it. The man brought to Christ early in life has this further advantage, that he is helped to form holy habits, and he is saved from being the slave of their opposites. Habits soon become a second nature; to form new ones is hard work, but those formed in youth remain in old age. There is something in that verse,

> ''Tis easier work if we begin to serve the Lord betimes
> But sinners who grow old in sin are hardened in their crimes.'

Moreover, I notice that, very frequently, those who are brought to Christ whilst young grow in grace more rapidly and readily than others do. They have not so much to unlearn, and not such a heavy weight of old memories to carry. The scars and bleeding sores which come of having spent years in the service of the devil are missed by those whom the Lord brings into his church before they have wandered far into the world.

FOR MEDITATION: (*Our Own Hymn Book* no. 1015 v.1—Thomas Hastings, 1834—see also v.2 tomorrow)
> 'God of mercy, hear our prayer
> For the children Thou hast given;
> Let them all Thy blessings share,
> Grace on earth, and bliss in heaven!'

SERMON NO. 1804

21 OCTOBER (1883)

Abijah, or Some good thing towards the Lord

'And all Israel shall mourn for him, and bury him: for he only of Jeroboam shall come to the grave, because in him there is found some good thing toward the LORD *God of Israel in the house of Jeroboam.'* 1 Kings 14:13
SUGGESTED FURTHER READING: Philemon 1–7

This 'good thing' is described to us in the text in a certain measure. It was a 'good thing towards the LORD God of Israel'. The good thing looked towards the living God. In children there often will be found good things towards their parents: let these be cultivated, but these are not sufficient evidences of grace. In children there will sometimes be found good things towards amiability and moral excellence: let all good things be commended and fostered, but they are not sure fruits of grace. It is towards God that the good thing must be that saves the soul. Remember how we read in the New Testament of 'repentance toward God, and faith toward our Lord Jesus Christ.' The way the face of the good thing looks is a main point about it. There is life in a look. If a man is travelling away from God every step he takes increases his distance from him, but if his face is toward the Lord he may be only capable of a child's tottering step, but yet he is moving nearer and nearer every moment. There was 'some good thing' in this child towards God, and that is the most distinguishing mark of a truly good thing. The child had love, and there was in it love to Jehovah. He had faith, but it was faith in Jehovah. His religious fear was the fear of the living God; his childlike thoughts, desires, prayers and hymns went towards the true God. This is what we desire to see not only in children, but in adults: we wish to see their hearts turned to the Lord, and their minds and wills moving towards the Most High. Strange that it should be wonderful for the creature man to look towards his Creator and yet it is so. Indeed there is no surer sign of a renewed heart than when a man exclaims, 'I will arise and go to my father'.

FOR MEDITATION: (*Our Own Hymn Book* no. 1015 v.2—Thomas Hastings, 1834—see also v.1 yesterday)
'In the morning of their days
May their hearts be drawn to Thee;
Let them learn to lisp Thy praise
In their earliest infancy.'

SERMON NO. 1745

22 OCTOBER (1882)

God's non-remembrance of sin

'I, even I, am he that blotteth out thy transgressions for mine own sake, and will not remember thy sins.' Isaiah 43:25
'For I will forgive their iniquity, and I will remember their sin no more.' Jeremiah 31:34
'For I will be merciful to their unrighteousness, and their sins and their iniquities will I remember no more.' Hebrews 8:12
'And their sins and iniquities will I remember no more.' Hebrews 10:17
SUGGESTED FURTHER READING: Isaiah 44:21–28

We may not speak, except after the manner of men, of the Lord God as having memory; and yet how blessed it is that he should himself use the speech which is current among ourselves, and represent himself after the manner of a man, and then say, 'their sins and their iniquities will I remember no more.' He wishes us to know that his pardon is so true and deep that it amounts to an absolute oblivion, a total forgetting of all the wrong-doing of the pardoned ones. You know what we do when we exercise memory. To speak popularly, a man lays up a thing in his mind: but when sin is forgiven it is not laid up in God's mind. A certain matter has happened, and we remember it, storing it away in our memory. We read that 'Mary kept all these things, and pondered them in her heart.' We make a kind of storeroom of our memory, and there things are preserved, like fruits in autumn, stored up to be used by and by. We reckon a man to be fortunate who has a good memory, so that he can lay by things in his brain where he can get at them in time of need. The Lord will not do this with our sins. He will not store them in his archives: he will not give them house-room. The record of our sin shall not be laid up in the divine treasury: we shall not cry with Job, 'My transgression is sealed up in a bag, and thou sewest up mine iniquity.' As for the ungodly, their sins are written with an iron pen, and the measure of their iniquity is daily filling, till it be poured out upon their own head: their sins have gone before them to the judgment seat, and are crying aloud for vengeance.

FOR MEDITATION: Because God promises not to remember our sins, we can confidently approach him and seek this mercy (Psalm 25:6–7; 79:8–9; Isaiah 64:9). But those who refuse to repent are assured that God will remember and punish their sins (Jeremiah 14:10; Hosea 7:1–2; 8:13; 9:9).

SERMON NO. 1685

23 OCTOBER (1881)

Without Christ—nothing

'Without me ye can do nothing.' John 15:5
SUGGESTED FURTHER READING: 2 Timothy 3:1–9

'Without me ye can do nothing.' As I listened to the song within these words I began to laugh: I wonder if you will laugh too. It was to myself I laughed, like Abraham of old. I thought of those who are going to destroy the orthodox doctrine from off the face of the earth. How they boast of the decline and death of old-fashioned evangelism. I have read once or twice that I am the last of the Puritans; the race is all dying out. To this I object: I am willing to be esteemed last in merit, but not last as ending the race. There are many others who are steadfast in the faith. They say our old theology is decaying, and that nobody believes it. It is all a lie; but wise men say so, and therefore we are bound to consider ourselves obsolete and extinct. We are, in their esteem, as much out of date as antediluvians would be could they walk down our streets. Yes, they are going to quench our coal and blot us out from Israel. Newspapers and reviews and the general intelligence of the age all join to dance upon our graves. Put on your nightcaps, you good people of the evangelical order, and go home to bed and sleep the sleep of the righteous, for the end of you is come. Thus say the Philistines, but the armies of the Lord think not so. The adversaries exult exceedingly, but Christ is not with them. They know very little about him, they do not work in his spirit, nor cry him up, nor extol the gospel of his precious blood, and so I believe that when they have done their little best it will come to nothing. 'Without me ye can do nothing'; if this is true of apostles, much more of opposers! If his friends can do nothing without him, I am sure his foes can do nothing against him.

FOR MEDITATION: (*Our Own Hymn Book* no. 677 v.3—Isaac Watts, 1709)
    'Treasures of everlasting might
    In our Jehovah dwell;
    He gives the conquest to the weak,
    And treads their foes to hell.'

24 OCTOBER (1880)

Desires towards God: a sermon for the weak

'Lord, all my desire is before thee; and my groaning is not hid from thee.'
Psalm 38:9
SUGGESTED FURTHER READING: 2 Corinthians 8:1–17

If you desire to be holy, where did that desire come from? From your own corrupt nature? Impossible. Certain believers in free will may think so, but we are not agreed with them. We believe that none 'can bring a clean thing out of an unclean', neither can thorns bring forth figs. If there is in you a desiring and a groaning of the heart after God, depend upon it human nature never originated it. Can sin desire holiness, or death pant for life? Holy desires are plants which are by no means native to the soil of human nature: their seed comes from a far country. Did the devil work these holy desires, think you? Hearken, brother, does the devil make you thirst after God? Does he make you sigh and cry after the light of your Father's countenance? Does he make you pray to be delivered from temptation? Does he make you sigh to be conformed to the image of Christ? Then the devil has very greatly altered since I met him last, and since he was described in holy scripture, or seen in the conflicts of good men. Who, then, has kindled these heavenly flames of desire? I earnestly avow my belief that every pure desire is as much the work of God as the grace which it desires. He who sincerely longs to be right with God has already somewhat of a work of divine grace within his soul creating those aspirations. Now, as God can say of all that he creates, 'It is very good', I come to the conclusion that these groaning desires after God are very good. They are not great, nor strong, but they are gracious. There is water in a drop as well as in the sea, there is life in a gnat as well as in an elephant, there is light in a beam as well as in the sun, and so is there grace in a desire as truly as in complete sanctification.

FOR MEDITATION: The Christian's good works and spiritual desires are the outworking of God's work within us (2 Corinthians 8:16; Ephesians 2:10; Philippians 2:13). This fact should have a humbling and sobering effect upon our attitudes (1 Corinthians 4:7).

SERMON NO. 1564

25 OCTOBER (1883)

The top of the ladder

'And to know the love of Christ, which passeth knowledge, that ye might be filled with all the fulness of God.' Ephesians 3:19
SUGGESTED FURTHER READING: Romans 15:13–29

If you are full, your speech will be worth hearing, but if you are empty, your communications will be empty also. Sometimes when we preach we are conscious of unfitness for the work because our soul is poverty-stricken. There cannot be much in our mouths if there is little in our hearts. Out of an empty sack you cannot shake a bushel of wheat, even if you shake it very hard. I have heard a brother pray a wearisome while, and I believe he was long because he had nothing to say. A horse can run many miles if he has nothing to carry. Long prayers often mean wind and emptiness. If you are full with a divine fulness, your lips scatter gems more precious than pearls and diamonds; 'filled with all the fulness of God', your paths, like God's paths, 'drop fatness.' Do you not know Christian men of that sort? They are millionaire Christians who make others rich. I know saints whom I rejoice to visit because I always learn from them. It is a privilege to be in the company of full saints, just as it is a misery to hear the clatter of empty professors. It is said that we English people feel delighted if we sit by the side of a lord: this I know, that if I get into the company of one of God's aristocracy, and have a quarter of an hour's talk with him, and a little prayer as well, I feel quite lifted up. My heart is glad within me when I see the grace of God abundant in a brother. I want you, brethren, to be full of sympathy, full of pity, full of mercy, full of wisdom, and when your brethren hear you speak they will be as men who have found running springs and filled up their vessels.

FOR MEDITATION: (*Our Own Hymn Book* no. 457 v.2—Isaac Watts, 1709)
  'Come fill our hearts with inward strength,
  Make our enlarged souls possess,
  And learn the height, and breadth, and length
  Of Thine unmeasurable grace.'

26 OCTOBER (1879)

Refuges of lies and what will become of them

'Judgment also will I lay to the line, and righteousness to the plummet: and the hail shall sweep away the refuge of lies, and the waters shall overflow the hiding place.' Isaiah 28:17
SUGGESTED FURTHER READING: Revelation 6:12–17

'The waters shall overflow the hiding place.' Imagine one who, in the time of Noah's flood, does not choose to enter into the ark, for he does not care to be tied down to God's way of deliverance. Salvation by an ark is too simple, too childish; he wants a more philosophic way. Besides, he does not care to be cooped up with Noah and a handful of narrow-minded people, who shut themselves in and shut everybody else out. He has broader views, and therefore he has found a shelter on the side of the hill, in a great cave where thousands can assemble and enjoy a liberty denied them within the limits of the ark. It is utterly preposterous to suppose the flood will ever reach so high as this elevated cave. It is hundreds of feet above the plain, and in the judgment of the wisest men it is more than safe. After a day or two of extraordinary rain the man would look down from his hiding-place and see the waters covering all the lower area, and creeping up the valleys foot by foot, and he would remark upon the abundance of rain, but scoff at the idea of a general deluge. He would be easy, hoping that the rain would cease, but as it continued he would begin to think, 'I may not be quite so safe after all.' Imagine his horror when the flood at last fills up the ravine, and creeps up the rocky steep. With cruel lip, seeking his destruction, the water threatens the cave wherein he thought to dwell so safely. At last it penetrates his hiding-place, it climbs to the very roof, it sweeps over his head, and his false confidence has proved his ruin. Such will be the end of all that hide themselves, but hide not in Christ.

FOR MEDITATION: (*Our Own Hymn Book* no. 381 v.3—Henry Kirke White, 1807)
   "'Tis He—the Lamb—to Him we fly,
   While the dread tempest passes by:
   God sees His well-beloved's face,
   And spares us in our hiding-place.'

SERMON NO. 1501

27 OCTOBER (PREACHED 26 OCTOBER 1884)

A summary of experience and a body of divinity

'For they themselves shew of us what manner of entering in we had unto you, and how ye turned to God from idols to serve the living and true God; and to wait for his Son from heaven, whom he raised from the dead, even Jesus, which delivered us from the wrath to come.'
1 Thessalonians 1:9–10
SUGGESTED FURTHER READING: Ezekiel 14:1–11

These Thessalonians turned from their idols. Do you tell me that you have no idols? Think again, and you will not be quite so sure. The streets of London are full of fetish worship, and almost every dwelling is a joss-house crammed with idols. Why, multitudes of men are worshipping not calves of gold, but gold in a more portable shape. Small circular idols of gold and silver are much sought after. They are very devoutly worshipped by some, and great things are said concerning their power. I have heard the epithet of 'almighty' ascribed to an American form of these idols. Those who do not worship gold may yet worship rank, name, pleasure, or honour. Most worship self, and I do not know that there is a more degrading form of worship than for a man to put himself upon a pedestal and bow down thereto and worship it. You might just as well adore cats and crocodiles with the ancient Egyptians as pay your life's homage to yourselves. No wooden image set up by the most savage tribe can be more ugly or degrading than our idol when we adore ourselves. Men worship Bacchus still. Do not tell me they do not: why, there is a temple to him at every street corner. While every other trade is content with a shop or a warehouse, this fiend has his palaces, in which plentiful libations are poured forth in his honour. The gods of unchastity and vice are yet among us. It would be 'a shame even to speak of those things which are done of them in secret.' The lusts of the flesh are served even by many who would not like to have it known. We have gods many and lords many in this land. God grant that we may see, through the preaching of the gospel, many turning from such idols.

FOR MEDITATION: Idolatry is not confined to religion, but also pervades secular life. Scripture warns against those who express their idolatry in eating, drinking and playing (1 Corinthians 10:7) and in covetousness (Ephesians 5:5; Colossians 3:5). Do you need to turn from any idolatry?

SERMON NO. 1806

28 OCTOBER (1883)

Marvellous! Marvellous!

'Thus saith the LORD *of hosts; If it be marvellous in the eyes of the remnant of this people in these days, should it also be marvellous in mine eyes? saith the* LORD *of hosts.'* Zechariah 8:6
SUGGESTED FURTHER READING (Spurgeon): Numbers 11:1–23

You who carry Bibles with you which have the marginal readings, will notice that in the margin there is the word 'difficult', and the text may be read thus, 'Thus saith the LORD of hosts; If it be difficult in' your eyes, 'should it also be difficult in mine eyes?' This is the only instance in which the word 'difficult' occurs in our version of the Bible, and in this case it is only to be found in the margin. There is too much of God in the Bible for difficulties to live in it. I should be very glad if I could always put the word 'difficult' into the margin of my life, and never let it stand in the substance of it. I wish my faith would banish it. Difficulty does crop up now and then through unbelief, but where God manifests himself, difficulty vanishes. Leave it in the margin, brother! Leave it in the margin; let it not be read in the annals of your actual life. A brave self-reliance blots the word 'difficult' out of its dictionary, and a full God-reliance may much more safely do so. 'If God be for us,' all things can be accomplished. Things impossible with men are possible with God. The remnant of Israel said. 'It will be difficult'; and then they softened the words a little, and said, 'It will be marvellous in our eyes'; still it came to this at the bottom, that they did not believe the word of the Lord. They could not conceive how the promise could be fulfilled, and therefore because it surpassed their conception, they supposed that the Lord was equally nonplussed and perplexed. Because the restored prosperity of Jerusalem would be a great wonder, they doubted if it could ever be accomplished. Yet, blessed be the name of the Lord, it was accomplished; for 'if we believe not, yet he abideth faithful: he cannot deny himself.'

FOR MEDITATION: (*Our Own Hymn Book* no. 686 v.4—Paul Gerhardt, 1659; tr. by John Wesley, 1739)
'When He makes bare His arm,
What shall His work withstand?
When He His people's cause defends,
Who, who shall stay His hand?'

SERMON NO. 1747

29 OCTOBER (1882)

The law written on the heart

'After those days, saith the LORD, *I will put my law in their inward parts, and write it in their hearts.'* Jeremiah 31:33
SUGGESTED FURTHER READING: Romans 7:12–25

Are there not men who in their anger wish that killing were no murder? Are there not others who do not steal, and yet wish they might take their neighbours' goods? Are there not many who wish that fornication and adultery were not vices? This proves that their hearts are depraved, but it is not so with the regenerate; they would not have the law altered on any account. Their vote is with the law; they regard it as the guardian of society, the basis on which the peace of the universe can alone be built, for only by righteousness can any order of things be established. If we could possess the wisdom of God, we should make just that law which God has made, for the law is 'holy, and just, and good', and promotes man's highest advantage. It is a great thing when a man gets as far as that. But, furthermore, there is wrought in the heart by God a love to the law as well as a consent to it, such a love that the man thanks God that he has given him such a fair and lovely representation of what perfect holiness would be and that he has given such measuring lines, by which he knows how a house is to be built in which God can dwell. Thus thanking the Lord, his prayer, desire, longing, hungering and thirsting are after righteousness, that he may in all things be according to the mind of God. It is a glorious thing when the heart delights itself in the law of the Lord, and finds therein its solace and pleasure. The law is fully written on the heart when a man takes pleasure in holiness, and feels a deep pain whenever sin approaches him. Oh, my dear friend, the Lord has done great things for you when every evil thing is obnoxious to you. Even though you fall into sin through the infirmity of your flesh, yet if it causes you intense agony and sorrow it is because God has written his law in your heart.

FOR MEDITATION: God's word written on the heart by the Holy Spirit has a power unknown to the law written merely on stone (2 Corinthians 3:2–8). Heart-knowledge brings great blessings (Psalm 37:31; 40:8; Isaiah 51:7; Hebrews 8:10–12) which are totally foreign to mere head-knowledge (Isaiah 29:13–14; Mark 7:6–7).

SERMON NO. 1687

30 OCTOBER (1884)

Certain curious calculations about loaves and fishes

'When I brake the five loaves among five thousand, how many baskets full of fragments took ye up? They say unto him, Twelve. And when the seven among four thousand, how many baskets full of fragments took ye up? And they said, Seven. And he said unto them, How is it that ye do not understand?' Mark 8:19–21
SUGGESTED FURTHER READING (Spurgeon): Mark 6:34–44

Care is always taken by Christ of all the broken pieces. The Lord All-sufficient is yet the God of economy. Since Jesus could create as much food as he pleased, you might have thought that it was hardly worth his while to gather up the fragments; and yet he did so. Waste is of Satan, not of God. God is not lavish of creation, nor prodigal of miracles. Though the Lord can raise up in this place, if he pleases, fifty ministers in an instant, he may not do so; but what he would have us do is to make use of such powers as we have. If we are only fragments, our place is not the ground, but the basket. We must not allow ourselves to be thrown away, or to be consumed by an animal passion, or to be left to decay; but we must be in the Lord's store, ready to be used when the time comes. We shall be of some use one of these days, if we are willing to be used. If you, my friend, are not a whole loaf, you are a crust, and no crust may be wasted. If you are not a slice of bread, you are a crumb, and even crumbs are dear to hungry men. If you are not a big fish, yet you may be a little fish, and you must not waste yourself, nor must the church of God allow you to be wasted, but use must be found for you somewhere. But what a wonderful thing this is—Omnipotence picking up crumbs! God All-sufficient, to whom the cattle on a thousand hills are as nothing, who could make a whole sea of fishes, or ten thousand worlds of bread, by his bare will and nothing else—and yet he sets his disciples to gather up broken pieces that nothing may be lost! Surely it ill becomes us to waste a penny, an hour, or an opportunity. Let us be severely economical for the Lord our God.

FOR MEDITATION: Being 'a great waster' (Proverbs 18:9) is nothing to be proud of. Jesus told parables about men who wasted (Luke 15:12–13; 16:1) or failed to use properly (Luke 19:20–26) what had been entrusted to them. If God can be economical with what belongs to him, his people should be careful with all he has entrusted to them (1 Corinthians 4:2).

SERMON NO. 1822

31 OCTOBER (PREACHED 30 OCTOBER 1881)

Baptism—a burial

'Know ye not, that so many of us as were baptized into Jesus Christ were baptized into his death? Therefore we are buried with him by baptism into death: that like as Christ was raised up from the dead by the glory of the Father, even so we also should walk in newness of life.' Romans 6:3–4
SUGGESTED FURTHER READING: 1 Peter 3:18–4:6

Our text must have had a very forcible meaning among the Romans in Paul's time, for they were sunk in all manner of odious vices. Take an average Roman of that period, and you would have found in him a man accustomed to spend a large part of his time in the amphitheatre, hardened by the brutal sight of shows, in which gladiators slew each other to amuse a holiday crowd. Taught in such a school, the Roman was cruel to the last degree, and ferocious in the indulgence of his passions. A depraved man was not regarded as being at all degraded; not only nobles and emperors were monsters of vice, but the public teachers were impure. When those who were regarded as moral were corrupt, you may imagine what the immoral were. 'Enjoy yourself; follow after the pleasures of the flesh,' was the rule of the age. Christianity was the introduction of a new element. See here a Roman converted by the grace of God! What a change is in him! His neighbours say, 'You were not at the amphitheatre this morning. How could you miss the sight of the hundred Germans who tore out each other's bowels?' 'No,' he says, 'I could not bear to be there. I am totally dead to it. If you were to force me to be there, I must shut my eyes, for I could not look on murder committed in sport!' The Christian did not resort to places of licentiousness; he was as good as dead to such filthiness. The fashions and customs of the age were such that Christians could not consent to them, and so they became dead to society. It was not merely that Christians did not go into open sin, but they spoke of it with horror, and their lives rebuked it. Things which the multitude counted a joy, and talked of exultingly, gave no comfort to the follower of Jesus, for he was dead to such evils. This is our solemn avowal when we come forward to be baptized.

FOR MEDITATION: (*Our Own Hymn Book* no. 775 v.4—John Mason, 1683)
  'I need not go abroad for joys, I have a feast at home;
  My sighs are turned into songs, my heart has ceased to roam.'

1 NOVEMBER (PREACHED 2 NOVEMBER 1879)

Satan in a rage

'*Woe to the inhabiters of the earth and of the sea! For the devil is come down unto you, having great wrath, because he knoweth that he hath but a short time.*' Revelation 12:12
SUGGESTED FURTHER READING: Luke 21:5–33

Oftentimes the development of evil is an indication that there is an equal or a greater development of good, and the climax of ill is frequently its end. Do you not know that in the world of nature the darkest time of the night is that which precedes the dawning of the day? May it not be the same in the spiritual and moral world? Does not the old proverb tell us concerning the year, that 'as the day lengthens the cold strengthens'? As the spring comes with lengthened days the frosts often grow more sharp and hard. Is it not also plain to the simplest mind that the turning of the tide happens when the ebb has reached its utmost? Even so when evil is at its height it is nearest to its fall. Look for confirmation to the page of history. When the tale of bricks was doubled Moses came to deliver the oppressed. When Pharaoh would by no means let the people go, and his yoke seemed riveted upon the neck of Israel, then the right arm of God was made bare, and the Red Sea beheld his vengeance. When despots grow most tyrannical, liberty's hour is coming. When the lie becomes exceeding bold, and wears a brazen forehead, then it is that truth confounds her. When Goliath stalks abroad and defies the armies of Israel, then is the stone already in the sling, and the David hard at hand, to lay the giant low. Do not, therefore, dread the advent of greater opposition, nor the apparent increase in strength of those oppositions which already exist, for it has ever been so in the history of events that the hour of the triumph of evil is the hour of its doom. When Belshazzar profanes the holy vessels, the handwriting blazes on the wall, and when Haman is at the king's banquet of wine seeking the blood of the whole race of the Jews, the gallows are prepared for him upon his own roof.

FOR MEDITATION: (*Our Own Hymn Book* no. 335 v.3—John Ryland, 1792)
   'The baffled prince of hell in vain new efforts tries,
   Truth's empire to repel by cruelty and lies;
   The infernal gates shall rage in vain,
   Conquest awaits the lamb once slain.'

2 NOVEMBER (1884)

A call to the Lord's own flock

'Thus shall they know that I the LORD *their God am with them, and that they, even the house of Israel, are my people, saith the Lord* GOD. *And ye my flock, the flock of my pasture, are men, and I am your God, saith the Lord* GOD.*'* Ezekiel 34:30–31
SUGGESTED FURTHER READING: 2 Corinthians 12:1–10

'Ye ... are men': then God knows what kind of persons we are, whom he has loved 'with an everlasting love'. We are Adams, not angels. If you come into the church of God and expect to get among angels, you will be mightily mistaken; and if the brethren should receive you, and hope that they are receiving angels unawares, they will be mistaken, too. We make absurd mistakes through foolish expectations. We shall not find that our brethren and sisters are male and female cherubim, for they are men and women, and nothing more. They are fallen men, too, bearing about them traces of the ruin of their nature; they went astray like lost sheep, even the best of them. They are men, only men, for the best of men are but men at the best. Somebody once wrote to me a letter of denunciation for using that sentence, and, as far as I could make out from his letter, the friend thought himself to be something more than a man. I did not coincide with his judgment, but fancied that he was rather less than a man: from the bitter spirit of his letter I thought him more human than humane. The best men I have ever seen are but men, and, generally, the better men are, the more ready they are to confess their imperfection. Some are tall by the measurement of conceit, but short when brought to the standard of wisdom. God's people are but men; yet they are men and not animals. There are in human form many who are hardly as good as animals, but the saints are gentle, compassionate and gracious. God's people are true men: when the Spirit of God is in them they quit themselves like men; they come to the front and bear the brunt of the battle. 'Men' is a bad word in one sense, but a good one in another.

FOR MEDITATION: As our Creator, God knows what we are made of (Psalm 139:13–14) and remembers that we are only flesh (Psalm 78:39). The apostles quickly corrected those who treated them as supermen or gods (Acts 10:25–26; 14:11–15). See 1 Corinthians 16:13–14 for the balance between the toughness and tenderness desired in the true man of God.

SERMON NO. 1807

3 NOVEMBER (PREACHED 2 NOVEMBER 1884)

To lovers of Jesus: an example

'She hath wrought a good work on me.' Mark 14:6

SUGGESTED FURTHER READING (Spurgeon): John 12:1–19

I believe that Mary had in this anointing of the Saviour some glimpse of his resurrection from the dead and after-existence. For, why do nations at all embalm their dead? Why not consume them in the fire? A mysterious something makes the ordinary Christian shudder at the thought of cremation. That must surely be an acquired taste: unsophisticated nature does not court the furnace or covet the flame; we prefer to lie beneath the green hillock with our fathers. Many nations of antiquity, especially the Egyptians, took great care to anoint the bodies of the departed with precious perfumes, and to lay them asleep in gums and fine linen. Why? Because there darkly shone upon their minds some thought of the hereafter. There remained with man, long after the fall, a glimmering, undefined belief in immortality. That truth was so universally received that the Old Testament takes it for granted. The existence of God and the immortality of the soul lie at the basis of Old Testament teaching. The after-life of the body was accepted also. Immortality was not brought to light, but there it was, and they who reject that doctrine go back into a darkness denser than that in which the heathens themselves dwelt. Why did the Egyptian king embalm his father and lay him in spices, but that he thought that somehow or other there was another life, and he would, therefore, take care of the body? They would not have wasted precious linen, gems and spices, if they had thought that the body was mere rottenness for worms to consume. Mary had deeper and clearer thoughts than that, for she expected that something would happen to that blessed body after Christ had died; she must, therefore, anoint it and bring the most precious spices that she could procure for his burial.

FOR MEDITATION: The Jews had their own burial customs (John 19:40), but the modernising Sadducees did not believe in the resurrection of the dead (Acts 23:8). They were shown up even by Job (Job 19:25–26), corrected by the Lord Jesus Christ (Matthew 22:23,29) and contradicted after the crucifixion by the bodily resurrection of many saints (Matthew 27:51–53) and the Saviour himself (Luke 24:36–39). 'How say some among you that there is no resurrection of the dead?' (1 Corinthians 15:12).

4 NOVEMBER (1883)

Jehovah hath spoken: will ye not hear?

'Hear ye, and give ear; be not proud: for the LORD *hath spoken. Give glory to the* LORD *your God, before he cause darkness, and before your feet stumble upon the dark mountains, and, while ye look for light, he turn it into the shadow of death, and make it gross darkness.'* Jeremiah 13:15–16
SUGGESTED FURTHER READING: Psalm 31:1–24

I do not know what may happen to me in this life; I may be visited with severe physical infirmities, which may cause me mental depression and anguish; but one thing I know—I have committed my mind, my heart, my whole intellectual nature to his keeping who has promised to preserve his own. I desire to believe nothing but what he tells me, to do nothing but what he bids me, and to yield myself to no influence but that which he ordains for my direction; having done this for many a day I believe I can with unstaggering confidence say at the last, 'Father, into thy hand I commit my spirit.' I may confidently hope to cast anchor for ever in that haven which is no new refuge to me, but the daily roadstead of my soul. Can a man be safer as to his soul's condition than when he has ceased depending upon himself and has taken the great Lord to be the Shepherd at whose heel he follows? What shield can so well protect you as the divine faithfulness? Under what rock can you find such shelter as under the truthfulness of God? I am at a pass with all new ideas in religion: I will have none of them. If that grand old Book fails me, I am content to fail; if the Lord deserts me, I resign myself to be deserted: if God lies, there is an end of all things, and we all alike flounder in chaos. We tolerate no such fears. Believing in God I am not fearful of the future. Neither dark mountains nor dark death can cause the believer to stumble, for he cries, 'I know whom I have believed, and I am persuaded that he is able to keep that which I have committed unto him against that day.' But if God is true, what will become of you who will not hear him? If the Bible is true, what must be your portion who pretend to be wiser than the Holy Spirit?

FOR MEDITATION: (*Our Own Hymn Book* no. 97 v.3—Harriett Auber, 1829)
   'Yes, Jesus reigns! The gospel's light beams with mild radiance on our sight;
   And fallen man, redeemed, forgiven, may lift his heart, his hopes to heaven.'

5 NOVEMBER (1882)

The general convocation around mount Zion

'But ye are come unto mount Sion, and unto the city of the living God, the heavenly Jerusalem, and to an innumerable company of angels, to the general assembly and church of the firstborn, which are written in heaven.' Hebrews 12:22–23
SUGGESTED FURTHER READING: Deuteronomy 21:15–17

Note the individuals who compose the company. They are all high born, for they are all *firstborn*. There is but one emphatically firstborn, namely, Jesus Christ himself, 'the firstborn of every creature', but being one with him we become the firstborn of God through the new birth. By our union to Christ, and by the blessed processes of grace, we are made and known to be the firstborn of God. Now the firstborn among men had the *ascendency* and sway in the household, even as the meek 'shall inherit the earth.' The day comes when righteousness shall be to the fore. The firstborn had the *excellency*. 'Reuben, thou art my firstborn, my might, and the beginning of my strength, the excellency of dignity, and the excellency of power'. 'The saints that are in the earth' are 'the excellent, in whom is all my delight.' The firstborn were *consecrated* to God; we, too, are dedicated, set apart unto God; 'ye are not your own'; 'ye are bought with a price'. The firstborn were *redeemed*: so have we been purchased with the precious blood of Christ. The firstborn had the *estate*, the throne, and the priesthood. Vast is the inheritance of the firstborn of God; all things are theirs; they are 'heirs of God, and joint-heirs with Christ'. To the firstborn belonged *honour*: 'this honour have all his saints.' There are younger brothers in every family who receive comparatively little if they happen to be descended from great lords, but there are no younger brethren in the family of God. They are all firstborn, all heirs, and each one of them has all the estate, for so infinite is it, that, even if I have all, you can have all too: an innumerable company of this blessed firstborn race can have the whole of God to be their portion for ever and ever.

FOR MEDITATION: (*Our Own Hymn Book* no. 889 v.1—Charles Wesley, 1745)
'Happy the souls to Jesus joined and saved by grace alone:
Walking in all His ways, they find their heaven on earth begun.'

SERMON NO. 1689

6 NOVEMBER (1881)

The main matter

'Many other signs truly did Jesus in the presence of his disciples, which are not written in this book: but these are written, that ye might believe that Jesus is the Christ, the Son of God; and that, believing, ye might have life through his name.' John 20:30–31
SUGGESTED FURTHER READING: 1 John 5:1–12

The faith which brings life to the soul is faith in the person, offices, nature, and work of Jesus; and though you may be in the dark about a thousand things and may make mistakes about ten thousand more, yet if you believe in the Messiah, the Son of God, you have eternal life. First, I am to believe in Jesus that *he is the Christ*, that he is the promised Messiah, anointed of God to deliver the human race. I must believe that this is he whom God promised at the gate of Eden, when he said that the seed of the woman would bruise the serpent's head. This is the sent One, who 'is come to seek and to save that which was lost': in him we are to believe, for it is written, 'Whosoever believeth that Jesus is the Christ is born of God'. Next we are to believe that *he is the Son of God*, not in the sense in which men are sons of God, but in that higher sense in which he is the only-begotten Son of God, one with the Father, eternally and indissolubly one. 'The Word was with God', but more than that, 'the Word was God.' Now, this is to be believed if we would live unto God. 'Whosoever shall confess that Jesus is the Son of God, God dwelleth in him, and he in God.' 'Who is he that overcometh the world, but he that believeth that Jesus is the Son of God?' A Jesus who is not divine could give us no power to overcome the world, but in his Godhead we find our strength. Put the two together, that he, the divine One, became man, and was sent into the world to redeem us, and we have the right idea of Immanuel, God with us. Will this belief save us? Assuredly it will.

FOR MEDITATION: (*Our Own Hymn Book* no. 435 v.1—Horatius Bonar, 1863)
    'I bless the Christ of God;
    I rest on love divine;
    And with unfaltering lip and heart,
    I call this Saviour mine.'

SERMON NO. 1631

7 NOVEMBER (PREACHED 6 NOVEMBER 1884)

May I?

'If I may.' Matthew 9:21
SUGGESTED FURTHER READING: Matthew 11:16–30

Surely, if any one were to paint the Lord Jesus Christ as an ascetic, repelling with lofty pride the humbler folk who had never reached his dignity of consecration, or if any were to paint him as a Pharisee driving off publicans and sinners, or as an iceberg of righteousness chilling the sinful, it would be a foul slander upon his divine character. If any one were to say that Jesus Christ is exacting, that he will not receive to himself the guilty just as they are, but requires a great deal of them, and will only welcome to himself those who are, like himself, good, true and excellent, that would not be truth but the direct opposite of it; for, 'This man receiveth sinners, and eateth with them', was thrown in his face when he lived here below; and what the prophet said of him was most certainly true, if anything was ever true. 'A bruised reed shall he not break, and the smoking flax shall he not quench'. Little children are wonderful judges of character; they know intuitively who is kind. And so are loving women. They do not go through the processes of reasoning, but they come to a conclusion very soon as to a man's personal character. Now, the children came and clambered our Redeemer's knee, and the mothers brought their infants for his blessing. How can you dream that he will repel you? The women wept and bewailed him; whoever might refuse him they pitied him, and therefore I am sure that he is not hard to move. Therefore I want you to feel sure of this, that there is nothing in the Saviour's character which can for a moment lead him to discard you and to drive you from his presence. Those who know him best will say that it is impossible for him ever to refuse the poor and needy.

FOR MEDITATION: (*Our Own Hymn Book* no. 612 v.7—Samuel Stennett, 1787)
'Yes, I may; for I espy
Pity trickling from Thine eye:
'Tis a father's bowels move,
Move with pardon and with love.'

8 NOVEMBER (PREACHED 9 NOVEMBER 1879)

Prayer to God in trouble an acceptable sacrifice

'And call upon me in the day of trouble; I will deliver thee, and thou shalt glorify me.' Psalm 50:15
SUGGESTED FURTHER READING: Psalm 107:1–32

The man who calls upon God in the day of trouble, evidently possesses a real and sincere belief in the existence of God, in his personality, in his power, in his condescension, and in his continual active intervention in the affairs of men; otherwise he would not call upon him. Many of your beliefs in God are a sort of religious parade, and not the actual walk of faith. Many have a holiday faith which enables them to repeat the creed, and say with the congregation, 'I believe in God the Father Almighty', but in very deed they have no such belief. Do you, my hearer, believe in God the Father Almighty when you are in trouble? Do you go to the great Father at such times and expect help from him? This is real work and not hypocritical play. There is solid metal about the faith, which follows the Lord in the dark, cries to him when the rod is in his hand, and looks to him not for sentimental comforts in prosperity, but for substantial help in bitter adversities. What we want is facts, and trial is the test of fact. Sharp furnace work does away with mere pretence, and this is one of its great uses, for that grace which, like the salamander, lives in the fire is grace indeed. I say, again, that very many publicly declared creed-faiths are mere shams, which like the leaves of autumn's trees would wither and fall if one sharp winter's frost should pass over them. It is not so when a man in the dire hour of his distress casts himself upon God, and believes that he is able to succour and to help him. Then there is evidence of true reliance and real confidence in a real God, whom the mind's eye sees and rejoices in. It is this actuality, this making God real to the soul, which makes our calling upon God in the day of trouble so acceptable to him.

FOR MEDITATION: (*Our Own Hymn Book* no. 194 v.5—Isaac Watts, 1709)
   'Our sorrows and our tears we pour
   Into the bosom of our God;
   He hears us in the mournful hour,
   And helps us bear the heavy load.'

9 NOVEMBER (1884)

The threshing-floor of Ornan

'At that time when David saw that the LORD *had answered him in the threshingfloor of Ornan the Jebusite, then he sacrificed there.' 'Then David said, This is the house of the* LORD *God, and this is the altar of the burnt offering for Israel.'* 1 Chronicles 21:28; 22:1

SUGGESTED FURTHER READING: 1 Corinthians 3:10–17

Begin to build a temple. You say, 'Do you want us to build a new place of worship?' No, I speak only of a spiritual house. Of course, build as many meeting-places as you can where people may come together to hear the word, for many are needed in this growing city, but the peculiar sort of building which I urge upon you is of the heart and spirit. Make your entire being a living temple for the living God. Begin now: the foundations are laid; you would not dream of building on any other, 'For other foundation can no man lay than that is laid, which is Jesus Christ.' The Divine Moriah [see 2 Chronicles 3:1] of Christ's person, the sacred place of his sacrifice, is the mount wherein God shall be seen. Jesus Christ has himself become the foundation of your hope; go and build on him. Set up the pillars of earnest supplication, and arch them over with lofty praises. Remember, your God inhabits 'the praises of Israel.' Build him a house of praise, that he may dwell in you; make your bodies to be the temples of the Holy Spirit, and your spirits the priests that sacrifice therein. In acts of holiness, piety, charity and love spend all your days. Let your houses be churches dedicated to his fear and love; let their chambers be holy as the courts of the tabernacle in the wilderness. Let each morning and evening have its sacrifice. Be yourself a priest at the altar. Let the garments of your daily toil be as vestments, your meals as sacraments; let your thoughts be psalms, your prayers incense, and your breath praise. Let every action be a priestly function, bringing glory unto the Lord from this day forth and for ever.

FOR MEDITATION: The Lord Jesus Christ is temple (John 2:19–21; Revelation 21:22), altar (Hebrews 13:10–12), high priest (Hebrews 4:14–15) and sacrifice (1 Corinthians 5:7; Ephesians 5:2). With him as our only foundation, Christians are also to be a temple (Ephesians 2:19–22), and a priesthood offering spiritual sacrifices (1 Peter 2:5–6).

SERMON NO. 1808

10 NOVEMBER (PREACHED 9 NOVEMBER 1884)

Elijah's plea

'Let it be known ... that I have done all these things at thy word.' 1 Kings 18:36

SUGGESTED FURTHER READING: 1 Timothy 4:6–16

Let every *worker* who has not been successful answer this question: have you done all these things at God's word? Come. *Have you preached the gospel?* Was it the gospel? Was it Christ you preached, or merely something about Christ? Come. Did you give the people bread, or did you give them plates to put the bread on, and knives to cut the bread with? Did you give them drink, or did you give them the cup that had been near the water? Some preaching is not gospel; it is a knife that smells of the cheese, but it is not cheese. See to that matter. If you preached the gospel, *did you preach it rightly?* That is to say, did you state it affectionately, earnestly, clearly, plainly? If you preach the gospel in Latinized language, the common people will not know what it means, and if you use great big academy words and dictionary words, the market people will be lost while they are trying to find out what you are at. You cannot expect God to bless you unless the gospel is preached in a very simple way. Have you preached the truth lovingly, with all your heart, throwing your very self into it, as if beyond everything you desired the conversion of those you taught? Has prayer been mixed with it? Have you gone into the pulpit without prayer? Have you come out of it without prayer? Have you been to the Sabbath-school without prayer? Have you come away from it without prayer? If so, since you failed to ask for the blessing, you must not wonder if you do not get it. And another question: h*as there been an example to back your teaching?* Brethren, have we lived as we have preached? Sisters, have you lived as you have taught in your classes? These are questions we ought to answer, because perhaps God can reply to us, 'No, you have not done according to my word'.

FOR MEDITATION: Paul's charge to Timothy applies to all who are involved in gospel ministry: 'preach the word' (2 Timothy 4:2), 'rightly dividing the word of truth' (2 Timothy 2:15); 'be thou an example of the believers, in word, in conversation, in charity, in spirit, in faith, in purity' (1 Timothy 4:12). Titus received similar instructions (Titus 2:7–8).

11 NOVEMBER (1883)

A Luther sermon at the Tabernacle

'But the just shall live by his faith.' Habakkuk 2:4
SUGGESTED FURTHER READING (Spurgeon): Galatians 3:6–14

Yesterday, four hundred years ago, there came into this wicked world the son of a miner, or refiner of metals, who was to do no little towards undermining the Papacy and refining the church. The name of that babe was Martin Luther, a hero and saint. Blessed was that day, for it bestowed a blessing on all succeeding ages, through 'the monk that shook the world.' His brave spirit overturned the tyranny of error, which had so long held nations in bondage. All human history since then has been more or less affected by the birth of that marvellous boy. He was not an absolutely perfect man; we neither endorse all that he said nor admire all that he did, but he was a man upon whose like men's eyes shall seldom rest, a mighty judge in Israel, a kingly servant of the Lord. We ought oftener to pray to God to send us men of God, men of power. We should pray that, according to the Lord's infinite goodness, his ascension gifts may be continued and multiplied for the perfecting of his church, for 'When he ascended up on high, he led captivity captive, and gave gifts unto men', 'and he gave some, apostles; and some, prophets; and some, evangelists; and some, pastors and teachers'. He continues to bestow these choice gifts according to the church's necessity, and he would scatter them more plentifully, perhaps, if our prayers more earnestly ascended to 'the Lord of the harvest' to thrust 'forth labourers into his harvest.' Even as we believe in the crucified Saviour for our personal salvation, we ought to believe in the ascended Saviour for the perpetual enriching of the church with confessors and evangelists who shall declare the truth of God. I wish to take my little share in commemorating Luther's birthday.

FOR MEDITATION: (*Our Own Hymn Book* no. 690 v.2—Isaac Watts, 1719)
'Trust Him, ye saints, in all your ways,
Pour out your hearts before His face;
When helpers fail, and foes invade,
God is our all-sufficient aid.'

N.B. The sermons on 11 November 1883 commemorated the 400th anniversary of Luther's birth on 10 November 1483 (see also tomorrow).

SERMON NO. 1749

12 NOVEMBER (PREACHED 11 NOVEMBER 1883)

The Luther sermon at Exeter Hall

'For in Jesus Christ neither circumcision availeth any thing, nor uncircumcision; but faith which worketh by love.' Galatians 5:6
SUGGESTED FURTHER READING: Hebrews 13:7–16

In Luther's day superstitious confidence in external observances had overlaid faith in the gospel; ceremonies had multiplied excessively under the authority of the Pope, masses were said for souls in purgatory, and men were actually selling indulgences for sin in the light of day. When God raised up Martin Luther, who was born four centuries ago, he bore emphatic testimony against salvation by outward forms and by the power of priestcraft, affirming that salvation is by faith alone, and that the whole church of God is a company of priests, every believer being a priest unto God. If Luther had not affirmed it, the doctrine would have been just as true, for the distinction between clergy and laity has no excuse in Scripture, which calls the saints, 'God's *kleros*', God's clergy or heritage. Again we read, 'ye are ... a royal priesthood'. Every man that believes in the Lord Jesus Christ is anointed to exercise the Christian priesthood, and therefore he need not put his trust in another, seeing the supposed priest is no more than any other man. Each man must be accountable for himself before God. Each one must read and search the Scriptures for himself, and must believe for himself, and when saved, he must offer up himself as a living sacrifice unto God by Jesus Christ, who is the only 'High Priest of our profession'. So much for the negative side of the text, which is full of warning to this Ritualistic age. The chief testimony of our great Reformer was to the justification of a sinner in the sight of God by faith in Jesus Christ and by that alone. He could fitly have taken this as his motto: 'in Jesus Christ neither circumcision availeth any thing, nor uncircumcision; but faith which worketh by love.'

FOR MEDITATION: (*Our Own Hymn Book* no. 554 v.4—Isaac Watts, 1709)

'The best obedience of my hands
Dares not appear before Thy throne;
But faith can answer Thy demands,
By pleading what my Lord has done.'

SERMON NO. 1750

13 NOVEMBER (UNDATED SERMON)

Certain singular subjects

'And I gave unto Isaac Jacob and Esau: and I gave unto Esau mount Seir, to possess it; but Jacob and his children went down into Egypt.' Joshua 24:4
SUGGESTED FURTHER READING: Ephesians 4:7–14

The Lord says, 'I gave unto Isaac Jacob and Esau'; children are the gift of God. This is true not only of Isaac but of all mortal men. God gave to a worthy couple George Washington, to another pair John Howard, and to a third George Whitefield. Each of these, in his own special way, was a divine gift to men. Children are born with differing talents and varied capacities, but all about them which will make them blessings is the gift of God. I shall not tarry to mention great men whose names mark epochs in history from which men date an increase of light and happiness, but let no man think of these friends and leaders of mankind without admitting the hand of God in their birth, training, disposition and ability. The greatest blessing which God ever gave to man was the man Christ Jesus, and, under him, the next best blessings are men. You remember the passage, 'When he ascended up on high, he led captivity captive, and gave gifts unto men … And he gave some, apostles', and so forth. Ascension gifts are sure to be worthy of the occasion, and therefore eminently precious, and these are all men. Within a man, poor, lowly, humble, and even sinful though that man may be in himself, there may lie concealed an almost infinite blessing from the Most High, even as within an acorn sleeps a forest, or within a flint lies light for a nation's watch-fires. When the negro slave had borne long years of bondage, and hope of deliverance seemed far away, it was God that gave an Abraham Lincoln, who led the nation onward till 'Emancipation' flamed upon its banners. Long before, when England, free in every corner of it, yet held slaves in its colonies, it was God that gave Wilberforce, and raised him up to plead in Parliament the rights of men. In all such acts of righteousness the coming forth of the man at the hour must be attributed to God's own hand.

FOR MEDITATION: God's promise to raise up a special prophet (Deuteronomy 18:15,18) was fulfilled in the coming of the Saviour (Acts 3:18–24). Meanwhile he raised up others—judges (Judges 2:16,18; 3:9,15), priests (1 Samuel 2:35), kings (1 Kings 14:14; Isaiah 44:28; 45:1,13) and prophets (Jeremiah 29:15; Amos 2:11). The Saviour holds all four offices.

SERMON NO. 1718

14 NOVEMBER (1880)

The blood of the testament

'This is the blood of the testament which God hath enjoined unto you.'
Hebrews 9:20
SUGGESTED FURTHER READING (Spurgeon): Exodus 24:1–10

On the day when Moses sprinkled the blood of the covenant on the people and on the book, it was meant to signify that they were a chosen people set apart unto God's service. The blood made them holiness unto the Lord. Moses stood upon an elevated place, and took the scarlet wool and hyssop and sprinkled the blood on all sides. Try and realize a part of the scene. A man just beneath him is wearing a white robe, and a spot of blood has fallen upon it. He sees it. There it is! Will he not prize the crimson sign? I would have preserved that robe as long as I lived, and the blood-spot too. But what would it mean? To the Israelite it meant consecration to God. He would say, 'The blood of the covenant has fallen upon me, and I am henceforth a consecrated man, dedicated to God.' Now, unless the blood is upon you, my brother, you are not saved; but if you are saved you are by that very fact set apart to be God's servant. 'Ye are not your own'; 'ye are bought with a price'. 'Ye were not redeemed with corruptible things, as silver and gold … but with the precious blood of Christ'. A saved man is a bought man, the property of Jesus. Believer, not a hair on your head belongs to you now; you belong to Jesus Christ as his servant as surely as you are redeemed by his blood. Now you are set apart; God's own mark is put upon you. You have believed: that believing has applied the blood to you, and you are Christ's. Cannot you see the private token which the Lord has set on you? Do you not feel it? Oh, then, own its claims in your daily life.

FOR MEDITATION: (*Our Own Hymn Book* no. 412 v.7—Isaac Watts, 1709)
  'Thou hast redeemed our souls with blood,
  Hast set the prisoners free;
  Hast made us kings and priests to God,
  And we shall reign with Thee.'

15 NOVEMBER (PREACHED 28 OCTOBER 1880)

Cheer for the worker, and hope for London

'Then spake the Lord to Paul in the night by a vision, Be not afraid, but speak, and hold not thy peace: for I am with thee, and no man shall set on thee to hurt thee: for I have much people in this city.' Acts 18:9–10
SUGGESTED FURTHER READING: Acts 12:1–24

I believe in London. God means to bless it largely. You will say, 'Why?' Well, I look back upon its past history, and I have hope. The martyrs' blood lies here. When all the country was yielding its martyrs, London furnished its full share. On this very spot where we now are three were burnt for the truth's sake; old Chronicles say, 'At the Butts at Newington, three Anabaptists were burnt.' These were among the earliest of martyrs, before Protestants were known or thought of. Always were Anabaptists a prey, and they who killed them thought they did God service. Members of our ancient persecuted church were often in London burnt for the truth's sake and for Christ's sake, and from the ground their blood is calling still. All over this London of ours, the preaching of the gospel was precious in the old times. You hear the name of 'Gospel Oak,' as you travel in the North of London, and the tree was so called because there the gospel was preached, and crowds gathered beneath its shade to listen to the joyful sound. All about the city secret bands met to worship God after the gospel way. Now, the Lord will never let the blood of the martyrs die out; it will for ever be the seed of the church. See, again, how London kindled with holy fire in the days of Whitefield and Wesley. Go but a mile from this place, and notice Kennington Park, once Kennington Common. What thousands used to gather there to hear the gospel preached! The men of the south of London loved the gospel, multitudes of them, and they do still. I feel sure that God will bless London yet.

FOR MEDITATION: The blood of the martyrs has never been spilt in vain. For evidence that God sees and takes careful note even of the places of martyrdom read Genesis 4:8–10; 2 Chronicles 24:21–22; Matthew 23:34–35; Acts 7:54–58 and Revelation 2:13. Sometimes the persecutor cannot forget the scene either (Acts 22:20).

SERMON NO. 1566

16 NOVEMBER (PREACHED 9 OCTOBER 1884)

How 'the unspeakable' is spoken of

'And men shall speak of the might of thy terrible acts: and I will declare thy greatness. They shall abundantly utter the memory of thy great goodness, and shall sing of thy righteousness.' Psalm 145:6–7

SUGGESTED FURTHER READING: Psalm 99:1–9

Observe how the one follows the other: 'men shall speak of the might of thy terrible acts: *and I will declare thy greatness.*' After the many have spoken in awe, I will deliver my soul with courage. Come in, single testifier for God, for now you will be welcomed! When they have advanced so far as to tremble at God because he has begun to smite them, you stand forward and declare his greatness. The might of his terrible acts has made them see the greatness of his power; they perceive what plagues are in his quiver, and how easily he can draw them forth like arrows, and shoot them from his bow, and never miss the mark. They are obliged to confess all this, and thus a good groundwork is prepared for something more. Tell them of the greatness of his justice, and how he will by no means spare the guilty. Tell them of the greatness of his grace, and how in the person of Jesus Christ he passes by iniquity, transgression, and sin. Tell them of the greatness of his fatherly love, and how he presses returning prodigals to himself, and kisses away their tears. Tell them of the greatness of his saving power to lift up men from the dunghill, and set them among princes, even the princes of his people. Speak exceeding bravely concerning the greatness of his sovereignty, how he can create or can destroy. Tell them that he 'will have mercy on whom' he 'will have mercy, and' he 'will have compassion on whom' he 'will have compassion.' Point to the greatness and splendour of his love, how he receives sinners, how he gives grace to the graceless, and how his Son 'in due time ... died for the ungodly.'

FOR MEDITATION: (*Our Own Hymn Book* no. 179 v.6—Isaac Watts, 1709)
   'Now to my soul, immortal King!
   Speak some forgiving word;
   Then 'twill be double joy to sing
   The glories of my Lord.'

SERMON NO. 1828

17 NOVEMBER (UNDATED SERMON)

The cast-off girdle

'Thus saith the LORD *unto me, Go and get thee a linen girdle, and put it upon thy loins, and put it not in water.'* Jeremiah 13:1
SUGGESTED FURTHER READING: Isaiah 1:16–20

Oh the terror of that sentence, 'put it not in water.' Surely, this is what Satan desires; his malice cannot exceed the wish that we may never be cleansed from our iniquities! How accursed are those of whom Agur says, 'There is a generation that are pure in their own eyes, and yet is not washed from their filthiness.' If that one, first, perfect washing has never exercised its purifying influence upon you, my brother, it is all in vain for you to bear the vessels of the Lord, and to be thought to be great and to be eminent in his house, for you must be put away. On the spot let each one of us pray, 'wash me, and I shall be whiter than snow.' God loves purity, and will not keep unholy men in nearness to himself. Here is the alternative for all professors: you must be washed in the blood of Christ, or be laid aside; which shall it be? The prophet was bidden not to put it in water, which shows that there was not only an absence of the first washing, but there was *no daily cleansing*. Take heed, beloved, that you omit not those after-washings which must follow the washing in the blood of the Lamb. When our blessed Lord took a towel and a basin and went to wash the disciples' feet, he did not perform a superfluous action: Peter was misguided when he said, 'Thou shalt never wash my feet.' It is necessary that we be washed every day. Even 'if we walk in the light, as he is in the light, we have fellowship one with another, and the blood of Jesus Christ his Son cleanseth us from all sin.' We are constantly defiling our feet by marching through this dusty world, and every night we need to be washed. There is sin within us as well as sin without us; and even if we do not leave our chamber, but have to lie upon a sick-bed all day long, impatience is quite enough to defile our feet, and we greatly need to be cleansed.

FOR MEDITATION: (*Our Own Hymn Book* no. 79 v.3—William Goode, 1811)
   'Save us from guilt and shame, Thy glory to display;
   And for the great Redeemer's name, wash all our sins away.'

18 NOVEMBER (1883)

Fathers in Christ

'I write unto you, fathers, because ye have known him that is from the beginning ... I have written unto you, fathers, because ye have known him that is from the beginning.' 1 John 2:13–14
SUGGESTED FURTHER READING: 1 Corinthians 2:14–3:4

If any Christian man might love the world, and I hope none will do so, certainly the fathers may not. You know so much of Christ that you may well despise the world, and you are so soon going home that you ought to set little store by these fleeting things. You have all the marks of what they call declining years—I call them ascending years: you will soon be gone from the world and its changing vanities; therefore do not set your love on earthly treasures. Hold wealth with a loose hand; be ready to depart, for depart you soon will. Before the morning watch you may be gone to your Father's house on high. 'Love not the world'. Another duty of fathers is also mentioned here. While they are not to love the world they must take care that they do not fall victims to any of the lusts of this present evil world, such as 'the lust of the flesh'. Can fathers ever fall that way? Ah me; we have to speak very solemnly and admit that the most advanced saint still needs to be warned against 'the lust of the flesh', the indulgence of appetites which so readily lead men to sin. Then there is 'the lust of the eyes'. Asaph fell into that when he repined because of 'the prosperity of the wicked', and was obliged to confess, 'So foolish was I, and ignorant'. He looked at the prosperous wicked till he began to fret himself about them. That lust of the eye, in desiring more for yourself and envying those that have more—never let it happen to a father. And 'the pride of life,' that thirsting to be thought respectable, that emulation of others, that struggling after honour and such like, this must not be in a father. You are men, and must put away childish things.

FOR MEDITATION: Becoming a man involves giving up childish ways (1 Corinthians 13:11). Becoming an elderly Christian man involves taking on many godly responsibilities (Titus 2:2). Even then exhortation is still needed (1 Timothy 5:1).

SERMON NO. 1751

19 NOVEMBER (UNDATED, PROBABLY LATE 1879)

Sin subdued

'He will subdue our iniquities.' Micah 7:19
SUGGESTED FURTHER READING: Genesis 4:1–7

If there is any sin that gets the mastery over you, you will be lost: you are bound to conquer every sin, mind that. You may call it a besetting sin or not, but it must be either overcome by you, or it will be your ruin. A man may plead that a certain fault is his besetting sin, but I am not so sure of it. A sin that you wilfully indulge, is that a besetting sin? Certainly not. If I had to cross Clapham Common tonight and three stout fellows beset me to take away whatever I had got, I would do my little best in self-defence. That is what I call besetting a man. A besetting sin is a sin that sometimes surprises a man; and then he ought to show fight and drive the besetting sin away. If I were to walk over the common every night, arm-in-arm with a fellow who picked my pocket, I should not say that the man 'beset' me. No, he and I are friends, evidently, and the robbery is only a little dodge of our own. If you go wilfully into sin, or tolerate it, and say you cannot help it, well, you have to help it or you will be lost. One thing is certain: either you must conquer sin or sin will conquer you, and to be conquered by sin is everlasting death. Well, what is to be done? Fall back upon this gracious promise: 'he will subdue our iniquities'. They have to be subdued: Jesus will do the deed, and in his name we will overcome. If we are slothful, we will, in God's strength, do ten times as much as we should have done had we been naturally of an active turn. If we are angry, we will school ourselves till we become meek. Some of the most angry men that I have ever known have come to be the meekest of men. Remember Moses, how he slew the Egyptian in his heat, and yet the man Moses became very meek by the grace of God. You must overcome your sin.

FOR MEDITATION: (*Our Own Hymn Book* no. 652 v.1—John Fawcett, 1782)
    'Oh may my heart by grace renewed,
    Be my Redeemer's throne:
    And be my stubborn will subdued,
    His government to own!'

SERMON NO. 1577

20 NOVEMBER (UNDATED, PROBABLY EARLY NOVEMBER 1880)

I was before

'*Who was before a blasphemer, and a persecutor, and injurious.*'
1 Timothy 1:13
SUGGESTED FURTHER READING (Spurgeon): Acts 26:1–29

Look at Paul. He says, 'I was before a blasphemer, and a persecutor, and injurious'. What then? Why, now that he has become a follower of Christ, he cannot do too much. He put many saints in prison: now he goes into many prisons himself. He hunted them even to strange cities: and now he goes into all manner of strange cities himself. He dragged them before tribunals: and now he himself goes and stands before Roman proconsuls, and before the Roman emperor himself. Paul can never do too much for Christ, because he has done so much for the devil. I remember one who lived four or five miles away from a place of worship, who used to say, 'You old legs, it is no use being tired, for you have got to carry me. You used to take me to the place of amusement when I served the devil, and you shall carry me now to the house of God, that I may worship and serve him.' When sometimes he had an uneasy seat, he used to say, 'It is no use grumbling, old bones; you will have to sit here, or else you will have to stand. Years ago you put up with all kinds of inconveniences when I went to the theatre or some other evil place, when I served Satan; you must be content to do the same now for a better Master and a nobler service.' I think some of us might take a lesson from that old man, and say to ourselves, 'Come, covetousness, you are not going to hinder me from serving the Lord. I used to be liberal to the devil, and I do not intend now to be stingy to God.' If ever I am tempted in that fashion, I will give twice as much as I had thought of doing, so as to spite the devil, for he shall not have his way with me.

FOR MEDITATION: *Our Own Hymn Book* no. 30 v.1—Charles H. Spurgeon, 1866)

'I will exalt Thee, Lord of hosts,
For Thou'st exalted me;
Since Thou hast silenced Satan's boasts,
I'll therefore boast in Thee.'

SERMON NO. 1574

21 NOVEMBER (1880)

The believer catechized

'Believest thou this?' John 11:26
SUGGESTED FURTHER READING: Psalm 126:1–6

Martha says she believes in Jesus as 'the resurrection, and the life'; yet what is her action? Christ commands the bystanders to take away the stone from the sepulchre, and she intervenes with her cry, 'Lord, by this time he stinketh'! She fears the obnoxious consequences of uncovering such a mass of corruption, though he who is 'the resurrection, and the life' stands at the grave's mouth. Ah! Martha, where is your faith in him? Dear heart, she says that she believes in Jesus as 'the resurrection, and the life', and yet she is afraid that her brother will not rise though the Mighty One stands there to raise him. Is she not just like you and me? We believe that God hears prayer, and therefore we pray, but if the Lord desires to surprise us he has only to answer our requests. I have seen God's children running with vast astonishment to tell their friends, 'Here is a wonderful thing! Oh, such a marvellous event has happened to me! I offered a prayer and God has heard me.' An amazing thing that God should do as he said he would! They put these things in books as marvels, and call the volume 'Remarkable Answers to Prayer'. Dear me, is it remarkable that it is cold when it freezes? Do we speak of the remarkable warmth of the sun's beams at midsummer? Is it remarkable that the fires in our houses should warm us when we put our hands to them? Is he a remarkable God because he says he will hear prayer and does it? An answer to prayer should be remembered with gratitude, and yet it should be regarded as the most natural thing in all the world that our heavenly Father should fulfil his promises to his children. It is a great wonder that God should promise, but not a wonder that he should perform.

FOR MEDITATION: Even the members of the early church were totally amazed when Peter was delivered from certain death in accordance with their earnest prayers for him (Acts 12:1–5,12–16). See Mark 11:20–24 for an earlier occasion when Peter, himself amazed, had been taught the importance of faith as one of the conditions of answered prayer.

SERMON NO. 1568

22 NOVEMBER (UNDATED SERMON)

Truthfulness

'*O LORD, are not thine eyes upon the truth?*' Jeremiah 5:3
SUGGESTED FURTHER READING: Ephesians 4:15–25

Our souls require sincerity. Our eternal welfare demands it. Oh, there must be no mistake about our being true before God, for when it comes to dying work, nothing will stand us then but sincerity. When he comes to the light of the judgment-bar, where will the hypocrite appear? Ah, Judas, come and kiss your Master again! Betray him again if you dare! See how the traitor flies! He cannot bear the light, nor can men who are like him. May you never have one drop of Judas-blood within your veins. God take it away if it is there. It is an awful thing to live untruthfully. It is a sort of minor hell to go about and feel that you have not spoken the straight thing in every company. You spoke against a certain person very bitterly when he was not present to defend himself, and now you have to meet him, and to feign admiration of him in the presence of those who heard your former tirade. You are in an awkward position; a worm in a ring of fire could not wriggle more painfully. I thank God that I have learned always to say to a man what I think of him, and I do not find that I make enemies thereby; no, those to whom I have said the hardest things are some of my best friends this day. I am sure that there is no plain path, no easy path, like that of downright truthfulness towards our fellow men, and there is no right path for eternity like that of downright honesty before the living God. May his Spirit work this excellence in us, for he is the great author of 'truth in the inward parts'.

FOR MEDITATION: In terms of gospel-ministry the apostle Peter was senior to the apostle Paul (Galatians 1:18–22; 2:9–10), but it was Paul who took the lead in taking a clear stand for the truth against Peter's glaring inconsistencies (Galatians 2:11–14). Note how graciously Peter was to speak about Paul as he penned his final recorded words (2 Peter 3:15–16).

SERMON NO. 1585

23 NOVEMBER (UNDATED SERMON)

Loyal to the core

'And Ittai answered the king, and said, As the LORD *liveth, and as my lord the king liveth, surely in what place my lord the king shall be, whether in death or life, even there also will thy servant be.'* 2 Samuel 15:21

SUGGESTED FURTHER READING: Proverbs 18:24–19:7

Some men have great expectations: they live upon their friends, and yet complain that charity is cold. These people expect more from their friends than they ought to give. A man's best friends on earth ought to be his own strong arms. Loafers are parasitical plants; they have no root of their own, but like the mistletoe they strike root into some other tree, and suck the very soul out of it for their own nourishment. Sad that men should ever degrade themselves to such despicable meanness! While you can help yourselves, do so, and while you have a right to expect help in times of dire necessity, do not be everlastingly expecting everybody else to be waiting upon you. Feel as David did towards Ittai, that you would by no means wish for services to which you have no claim. Independence of spirit used to be characteristic of Englishmen. I hope it will always continue to be so, and especially among children of God. On the other hand, look at Ittai, perfectly free to go, but in order to end the controversy once for all, and to make David know that he does not mean to leave him, he takes a solemn oath before Jehovah his God, and he doubles it by swearing by the life of David that he will never leave him; in life and in death, he will be with him. He has cast in his lot with him for better and for worse, and he means to be faithful to the end. Old Master Trapp says, 'All faithful friends went on a pilgrimage years ago, and none of them have ever come back.' I scarcely credit that, but I am afraid that friends quite so faithful as Ittai are as scarce as two moons in the sky at once, and you might travel over the edge of the world before you found them. I think, however, that one reason why faithful Ittais have become so scarce may be because large-hearted Davids are so rare.

FOR MEDITATION: Consider some of the marks of a good friend (Proverbs 17:17; 18:24; 27:6). 'The best friend to have is Jesus', who was not only called 'a friend of ... sinners' (Luke 7:34), but who also went on to 'lay down his life for his friends' (John 15:13).

SERMON NO. 1512

24 NOVEMBER (UNDATED SERMON)

The orphan's father

'For in thee the fatherless findeth mercy.' Hosea 14:3
SUGGESTED FURTHER READING: Matthew 18:1–14

I always like to see how a man treats children. You learn a great deal about a man when you see that. Some men abhor children, and almost wish that they could exterminate them. As to the fatherless children they say, 'Let them go to the workhouse: we cannot be troubled with them.' The gentle-hearted one never sees a little child in want without feeling the utmost pity. I feel more sorry for a suffering child than even for a man or a woman. Adults have a measure of a power to help themselves, but if there is poverty in the house, the little one may pine away, but cannot get relief. Little boys and girls have suffered much in this great city when their parents' home has been desolated by poverty, frequently caused by drink and other sins. Who knows the sufferings of the little ones when father dies? I confess it touches my heart that little children should suffer as they do. When men are wicked, one is almost thankful that there should be poverty following their sin to whip them out of it, but these lambs, 'what have they done?' Any tender heart feels this. Is this not a wonderful text which lets us gaze into the heart of God: 'in thee the fatherless findeth mercy'? Great God, the seraphim adore thee. Angels, day without night, stand waiting to do thy bidding. Thy voice is the thunder, and the glance of thine eye is the lightning. At thy bidding kings die, dynasties decay, and empires are blotted out, yet thou carest for little children and widows. It is very beautiful to me. I feel as if I could trust him all the better for that, and come with my daily burdens and cares, and my sins too, and feel sure that he will not refuse me. This is the Father of Jesus, I am sure. How like the Son is to the Father, for if the Father is thus the children's Patron, what think you of the Son and of his likeness to his Father, when he said, 'Suffer the little children to come unto me, and forbid them not: for of such is the kingdom of God.' Does this not encourage you to come, as you see the heart of God laid bare in the blessed statement of the text?

FOR MEDITATION: (*Our Own Hymn Book* no. 195 v.4—Frederick William Faber, 1852)
   'No earthly father loves like Thee, or mother, half so mild,
   Bears and forbears, as Thou hast done with me Thy sinful child.'

SERMON NO. 1695

25 NOVEMBER (1883)

All or none: or, Compromise refused: a sermon with five texts

'*Pharaoh called for Moses and for Aaron, and said, Go ye, sacrifice to your God in the land.*' '*Only ye shall not go very far away.*' '*But who are they that shall go? ... go now, ye that are men, and serve the* LORD.' '*Only let your flocks and your herds be stayed.*' '*There shall not an hoof be left behind.*' Exodus 8:25; 8:28; 10:8, 11; 10:24, 10:26

SUGGESTED FURTHER READING: 2 Chronicles 21:1–20

There are many professing Christians who seem to be determined to be the Lord's, but their children can belong to Pharaoh and to the devil. For instance, the boy is getting of a certain age. Let him be sent to a foreign school, and, preferably, a Roman Catholic school. Will that be useful to his religion? Yet if he should turn out a Papist, his foolish father will almost break his heart. It was all his own doing, was it not? Well, the girls, of course, they must 'go into society.' And so everything is done to put them into places of danger, where they will not be likely to be converted, and where, in all probability, they will become light-hearted and vain. Then a situation is looked out for the boy. How often there is no question about the master being a Christian! Is it a business that the lad can follow without injury to his morals? No, 'it is a fine roaring trade, and a cutting house, where he will pick it up in a smart way. Let him go there.' Yes, and if he goes to perdition? Alas, there are Christians who do not think of that! The children of some professors are offered up to the Moloch [see Jeremiah 32:35] of this world. We think it horrible that heathens offer their children in sacrifice to idols, yet many professors put their children where, according to all likelihood, they will be ruined. Do not let it be so. Do not let the devil entangle you in that compromise, but say, 'No; my house, God helping me, shall be so conducted that I will not put temptation in my children's way. I will not lead them into the paths of sin.'

FOR MEDITATION: Jehoram's disastrous reign was largely due to his marriage into a wicked family (2 Chronicles 21:6), all arranged by his godly father Jehoshaphat (2 Chronicles 18:1)—'the LORD was with' him, he 'sought to the LORD ... and walked in his commandments', 'his heart was lifted up in the ways of the LORD' (2 Chronicles 17:3,4,6) and he did 'right in the sight of the LORD' (2 Chronicles 20:32), yet he ruined his own son.

SERMON NO. 1830

26 NOVEMBER (PREACHED 25 NOVEMBER 1883)

Mourners, inquirers, covenanters

'The children of Israel shall come, they and the children of Judah together, going and weeping: they shall go, and seek the LORD *their God. They shall ask the way to Zion with their faces thitherward, saying, Come, and let us join ourselves to the* LORD *in a perpetual covenant that shall not be forgotten.'* Jeremiah 50:4–5
SUGGESTED FURTHER READING: Psalm 34:1–22

What is it you are seeking? 'I am seeking peace,' says one. May you soon obtain it, and may it be real peace, but I am not sure of you. 'I am seeking,' says another, 'the pardon of sin.' Again, I pray that you may find it, but I am not sure of you. If another shall reply, 'I am seeking the Lord, for I desire above all things to have him for a friend, though to him I have been an enemy', then I have good hope of him. I rejoice over the heart which is crying, 'I want to see my Father's face, and hear him say, "I have blotted out thy sins"; I want to dwell with God, to serve him, to obey him, to grow like him. There has been a quarrel between him and me, and other lords have had dominion over me, but now I desire that he shall be my Lord and King, and myself his loyal humble servant and his beloved child. I hunger and thirst after God!' You see, brethren and sisters, we require a great many things in order to be saved, and yet one thing is needful. I would represent it in this form: here is a little child, picked up from the gutter, diseased and filthy, unclad, unfed; and if you ask me to make out a catalogue of what the child wants, you must give me a sheet of foolscap paper to write it all down, and then I fear I shall leave out many things. I will tell you in one word what that poor infant requires; it wants its mother. If it gets its mother it has all it needs. So to tell what a poor sinner wants might be a long task, but when you say that he wants his heavenly Father you have said it all. This was what the prodigal needed, was it not? He needed his Father, and when he came to his Father, all his necessities were supplied. Oh, souls, you are seeking aright if you are seeking your God.

FOR MEDITATION: (*Our Own Hymn Book* no. 605 v.4—John Morrison, 1781)
   'Our hearts, if God we seek to know, shall know Him and rejoice;
   His coming like the morn shall be, like morning songs His voice.'

SERMON NO. 1752

27 NOVEMBER (UNDATED SERMON)

Choice food for pilgrims to Canaan

'And he said, My presence shall go with thee, and I will give thee rest.'
Exodus 33:14
SUGGESTED FURTHER READING: 2 Chronicles 20:1–30

I have noticed (and I often have to bless God for it) that when I have felt myself to be quite done over and nonplussed, I have simply asked guidance, and something has occurred to me which I had never thought of before, or something which I had thought of and rejected, but which was the best, has occurred strongly to my mind again, or somebody else has come in, taken the leadership and put me aside; but somehow or other God has been glorified, and I have been happy when I have had his presence. I am sure that every believer will find it so in daily life; the first thing is not to have common sense and to be wise, as some say, but to have a sense of God's presence, which is better than common sense, and to trust in him for guidance, which is better than being shrewd. He will make the young men wise and prudent; he will give to babes knowledge and discretion, if they are willing to be led by his divine instruction. You will find it so if you have his presence with you, but if you have not, you will do just as the Israelites did about the matter of the Gibeonites, which seemed too simple to pray about. You will be taken in with those mouldy crusts and patched shoes, and those crafty rascals that say, 'We be come from a far country,' and without taking counsel with God, you will find yourself in fellowship with a brood of scheming Canaanites, who will entangle you and do you no end of harm. You will say 'Oh, but they are such nice old people, and it is wonderful how religiously they talk, and how nicely they persuade me to their side.' Yes, when Satan would deceive, his traps are very simple ones, such as you would never think to be traps at all. When you are quite clear about a thing, pray about it: when you are in difficulty, do as you like. I believe in that fine piece of advice: 'When it is a fine day in this country, carry an umbrella with you. When it is raining hard, do just as you like.'

FOR MEDITATION: (*Our Own Hymn Book* no. 1028 v.1—John Keble, 1827)
   'Sun of my soul, Thou Saviour dear, it is not night if Thou be near:
   Oh! may no earth-born cloud arise to hide Thee from Thy servant's eyes.'

SERMON NO. 1583

28 NOVEMBER (1880)

The lamentations of Jesus

'*When he was come near, he beheld the city, and wept over it.*' Luke 19:41
SUGGESTED FURTHER READING: John 11:32–44

On three occasions we are told that Jesus wept. You know them well, but it may be worthwhile to refresh your memories. Our Saviour wept in *sympathy with domestic sorrow*, and sanctified the tears of the bereaved. We, too, may weep when brothers and friends lie dead, for 'Jesus wept.' There need not be rebellion in our mourning, for Jesus fully consented to the divine will, and yet he wept. We may weep at the graves of those we love, and yet be guiltless of unbelief as to their resurrection, for Jesus knew that Lazarus would rise again, and yet he wept. Our Lord, in weeping over Jerusalem, showed his *sympathy with national troubles*, his distress at the evils which awaited his countrymen. Men should not cease to be patriots when they become believers; saints should bemoan the ills which come upon the guilty people among whom they are numbered, and do so all the more because they are saints. Our Lord's third weeping was induced by *the great burden of human guilt* which pressed upon him. This shows us how we, too, should look upon the guilt of men and mourn over it before God, yet in this special weeping Jesus is alone; there was something in the tears of Gethsemane to which we cannot reach, for he who shed them was then beginning to suffer as our substitute, and in that case he must tread 'the winepress alone; and of the people there was none with' him. Behold beneath the olive trees a solitary weeper, enduring a grief which, blessed be his name, is now impossible to us, seeing he has taken away the transgressions which called for it.

FOR MEDITATION: (*Our Own Hymn Book* no. 265 v.1—Benjamin Beddome, 1818)
    'Did Christ o'er sinners weep,
    And shall our cheeks be dry?
    Let floods of penitential grief
    Burst forth from every eye.'

29 NOVEMBER (UNDATED SERMON)

A delusion dispelled

'Though Noah, Daniel, and Job, were in it, as I live, saith the Lord GOD, they shall deliver neither son nor daughter; they shall but deliver their own souls by their righteousness.' Ezekiel 14:20
SUGGESTED FURTHER READING: Genesis 18:22–33 & 19:24–29

Remember that all the prayers of godly men cannot alter the nature of sin, and if they cannot alter the nature of sin, then they that continue in it must perish. If we were to hold a prayer-meeting to prevent a person from being burnt who would put his hand into the fire, would that be of any use? If a man who cannot swim will persist in leaping into the river, what is the use of my asking you all to pray God to preserve his life? If a man puts a bottle of prussic acid to his lips and drinks it, what is the use of our coming together to pray that his life may be spared, when the deadly poison is destroying it? If he drives a dagger into his heart he must die, unless God is pleased to reverse that order, which, according to the poet, 'is heaven's first law.' There is a way of salvation. Believe in Jesus Christ and live; if you will not have that, where are you, my friend? Are you such a fool as to sit there and say, 'I shall be saved by my wife's prayers'? Your wife's prayers will rather seal your doom. They will rise up in judgment against you. That you were so much prayed for implies that you were admonished and entreated at a most loving rate. You will not be able to say, 'no man cared for my soul.' A mother's prayers will ring in your ears, and excite remorse when repentance is no more possible. The cries of the lost will not be more terrible than the recollection of her tears and agony for you. Oh, do remember this. Sin is fire, and it must burn. Sin is hell, and it must torment the man who continues in it. There is no help for it. Pray as much as we like, if you do not get out of sin, you cannot get out of destruction. If you do not find pardon through our Lord Jesus you must be punished.

FOR MEDITATION: (*Our Own Hymn Book* no. 607 v.5—Elizabeth Codner, 1860)
'Have I long in sin been sleeping,
Long been slighting, grieving Thee?
Has the world my heart been keeping?
Oh forgive and rescue me, even me.'

SERMON NO. 1651

30 NOVEMBER (UNDATED SERMON)

An indictment with four counts

'She obeyed not the voice; she received not correction; she trusted not in the LORD*; she drew not near to her God.'* Zephaniah 3:2
SUGGESTED FURTHER READING: Luke 11:37–52

Putting the four sentences together, 'She obeyed not the voice; she received not correction; she trusted not in the LORD; she drew not near to her God', what then? Why, 'Woe to her'. Read the first verse of the chapter, and there you have it. As I was coming here that word 'woe, woe, woe' seemed to ring in my ears, and I wondered where it came from. I will tell you. It is a word that goes to be made into a worse word. Let me pronounce it for you—woe; that leads to something woe-erse—worse, and to the woe-erst, the worst of all. It is bad, lamentable, destructive, ruinous, painful, wretched, miserable woe, worse, worst. I wish I could pronounce the word as my Master did when he said, 'Woe unto thee, Chorazin! woe unto thee, Bethsaida!' I should hardly like to say as he did, for he had a light to judge which I have not, 'Woe unto you, scribes and Pharisees, hypocrites!' and so on. But that 'woe' as he pronounced it must have sounded terribly, softly, sadly, sternly piercing to the heart. How will the angels sound it at the last? Hear it now, lest you hear it at the last. 'One woe is past; and, behold, there come two woes more', when the Judge of all the earth shall break the seals and pour out the vials, and the ungodly sons of men shall see the star Wormwood, and shall drink of the bitterness of the wrath of God. Woe. It means sorrow here! No rest! No satisfaction! Woe even this day to the man that trusts not in God. But in the next world it means to be driven from the face of Christ, to be followed with a 'woe' which shall have eternal echoes, Woe, woe, woe! I could cry with Mr Whitefield, 'The wrath to come! The wrath to come!' Escape from it while life lasts and Jesus pleads with you, for otherwise this shall fall like a thunderbolt from the hand of the angry Judge, 'Woe to her ... She obeyed not the voice; she received not correction; she trusted not in the LORD; she drew not near to her God.'

FOR MEDITATION: (*Our Own Hymn Book* no. 515 v.5—Joseph Grigg, 1765)
   'Admit Him, ere His anger burn, His feet depart, and ne'er return:
   Admit Him, or the hour's at hand when at His door denied you'll stand.'

1 DECEMBER (UNDATED SERMON)

Soul saving our one business

'I am made all things to all men, that I might by all means save some.'
1 Corinthians 9:22
SUGGESTED FURTHER READING: Jude 14–23

The Christian has reasons for seeking to save some, chiefly because of the terrible future of impenitent souls. That veil which hangs before me is not penetrated by every glance, but he who has his eye touched with heavenly eye-salve sees through it, and what does he see? Myriads upon myriads of spirits in dread procession passing from their bodies, and passing *whither*? Unsaved, unregenerate, unwashed in precious blood, we see them go up to the solemn bar whence in silence the sentence comes forth, and they are banished from the presence of God, banished to horrors which are not to be described nor even to be imagined. This alone is enough to cause us distress day and night. This decision of destiny has about it a terrible solemnity. But the resurrection trumpet sounds. Those spirits come forth from their prison-house. I see them returning to earth, rising from the pit to the bodies in which they lived: and now I see them stand, multitudes in the Valley of Decision. And HE comes, with the crown upon his head and the books before him, sitting on a great white throne. And there they stand as prisoners at the bar. My vision now perceives them; how they tremble! How they quiver like aspen leaves in the gale! Whither can they flee? Rocks cannot hide them; mountains will not open their bowels to conceal them! What shall become of them? The dread angel takes the sickle, reaps them as the reaper cuts up the tares for the oven, and as he gathers he casts them down where despair shall be their everlasting torment! Woe is me; my heart sinks as I see their doom and hear the terrible cries of their too late awakening. Save some, O Christians! By all means save some. By yonder flames, and outer darkness, and the weeping, 'wailing and gnashing of teeth', seek to save some. Let this, as in the case of the apostle, be your great, your ruling object in life, that by all means you may save some.

FOR MEDITATION: (*Our Own Hymn Book* no. 365 v.3—Philip Doddridge, 1755)
  'Ye sinners, seek His grace, Whose wrath ye cannot bear;
  Fly to the shelter of His cross, and find salvation there.'

2 DECEMBER (1883)

Blessed promises for dying outcasts

'For I will restore health unto thee, and I will heal thee of thy wounds, saith the LORD; *because they called thee an Outcast, saying, This is Zion, whom no man seeketh after.'* Jeremiah 30:17
SUGGESTED FURTHER READING: Genesis 21:8–21

God's tastes and man's differ very much. Whom man despises God delights in, and whom man delights in God despises. It often happens that when a transgressor has been put out of the synagogue Jesus finds him directly. When certain offenders happen to transgress in a particular way, which is rejected and denounced by the bulk of ungodly people, then like so many hounds they unite to hunt the wretched being to death, but the Lord Jehovah interposes to save, as if he would say, 'Why do you this, you hypocrites? Why do you denounce those whose sins are no viler than your own?' I believe the Lord Jesus often stands as he did with the woman taken in adultery, and cries, 'He that is without sin among you, let him first cast a stone at her.' Still he convicts men in their consciences and still in sweetness of mercy turns to the poor, condemned one, and says, 'Neither do I condemn thee: go, and sin no more.' Where are you, poor hunted sinner? You are somewhere or other in the crowd, I know. They told you yesterday that they would never associate with you any more. You do not deny your wickedness: still, it is not for your fellow-sinners to be hard with you, for they are not your judges. By faith take this promise to yourself: 'I will restore health unto thee ... because they called thee an Outcast'. You may get a good deal out of it if you have faith to do so. Now that the world has cast you out, the church shall take you in: now that the devil seems tired of you, Christ shall begin with you: now that the door is shut against you by those who once delighted in you, Christ's door is open to receive you. 'Because they called thee an Outcast', he calls you to approach him.

FOR MEDITATION: The Lord Jesus Christ promised never to cast out those who come to him (John 6:37). Rather he was soon on the scene when others cast out those who had been associated with him (John 9:34–35; Acts 7:55–59). He knows exactly what it feels like (Isaiah 53:3).

SERMON NO. 1753

3 DECEMBER (UNDATED SERMON)

Praying and pleading

'O LORD, *though our iniquities testify against us, do thou it for thy name's sake: for our backslidings are many; we have sinned against thee ... yet thou, O* LORD, *art in the midst of us, and we are called by thy name; leave us not.'* Jeremiah 14:7,9

SUGGESTED FURTHER READING: Jeremiah 3:1–14

There are some parts of the book of Jeremiah that I should not like to read to you. I can hardly think that they were meant to be read in public; they are intended rather for our private meditations. There is, however, one picture of infamy which I will only hint at, though it has often excited my profound astonishment. It runs like this: 'They say, If a man put away his wife, and she go from him, and become another man's, shall he return unto her again? shall not that land be greatly polluted? But thou hast played the harlot with many lovers; yet return unto me, saith the LORD.' Do you see the drift of this striking illustration? Here is a woman kindly treated in every way who wilfully leaves her husband. She has not been led astray by a profligate, but has wantonly left her husband of her own wicked self. She has defiled her name and honour, and to crown her infamy she has then even left her paramour, gone on the streets and become utterly vile. Shall her first husband take her back again after her multiplied and manifest impurities? Would it not pollute the land? Everybody will say, 'This is an offence against morality. She has dishonoured herself, her husband and her country.' 'Yet,' says God, 'return unto me'. Is this not beyond the manner of man? So does the mercy of the Lord transcend even the statutes of the law which he gave to Israel. You will see the force of this if you compare Jeremiah chapter 3 with Deuteronomy chapter 24. The parable is startling. God is represented as dealing with an idolatrous nation as it would be an abomination before his own eyes for any man to deal with an unchaste wife. Such delight has Jehovah in mercy that he dispenses it at the risk of public odium.

FOR MEDITATION: (*Our Own Hymn Book* no. 202 v.2—Samuel Davies, 1769)

'Crimes of such horror to forgive, such guilty, daring worms to spare;
This is Thy grand prerogative, and none shall in the honour share:
Who is a pardoning God like Thee? Or who has grace so rich and free?'

SERMON NO. 1661

4 DECEMBER (UNDATED SERMON)

Maschil of Ethan. A majestic song

'I will sing of the mercies of the LORD *for ever: with my mouth will I make known thy faithfulness to all generations. For I have said, Mercy shall be built up for ever: thy faithfulness shalt thou establish in the very heavens.'* Psalm 89:1–2

SUGGESTED FURTHER READING: Lamentations 3:22–33

'Mercy shall be built up'. My expectations are awakened. I am waiting eagerly for the next scene. The designs of mercy are not exhausted; the deeds of mercy are not all told; the display of mercy must reach higher than has ever yet dawned upon my imagination. Its foundations were laid low. In great mercy he gave me a broken heart. That was pure mercy, for God accepts broken hearts; they are very precious in his sight; but it was a higher mercy when he gave me a new heart, which was bound up and united in his fear and filled with his joy. Oh, brethren, let us remember how he showed us the evil of sin, and caused us to feel a sense of shame. That was a choice mercy, but it was a clearer mercy when he gave us a sense of pardon. Oh, it was a blessed day when he gave us the little faith that tremblingly touched his garment's hem. It was better when he gave us faith as a grain of mustard seed that grew. It has been better still when by faith we have been able to do many mighty works for him. We do not know what we shall do yet when he gives us more faith. Far less can we imagine how our powers shall develop in heaven, where faith will come to its full perfection. It will not die, as some idly pretend. There we shall implicitly believe in God. With the place of his throne as the point of our survey, we shall see nothing but his sovereign will to shape events; so with joyful assurance of hope we shall look onward to the advent of our Lord Jesus Christ and the glory that is to follow. We shall sit in heaven, and sing that the Lord reigns.

FOR MEDITATION: (*Our Own Hymn Book* no. 214 v.1—Joseph Addison, 1712)
   'When all Thy mercies, O my God,
   My rising soul surveys,
   Transported with the view, I'm lost
   In wonder, love, and praise.'

SERMON NO. 1565

5 DECEMBER (1880)

The joy of Jesus

'In that hour Jesus rejoiced in spirit, and said, I thank thee, O Father, Lord of heaven and earth, that thou hast hid these things from the wise and prudent, and hast revealed them unto babes: even so, Father; for so it seemed good in thy sight.' Luke 10:21

SUGGESTED FURTHER READING: 1 Corinthians 1:17–2:5

If those who are reckoned to be learned profess to come to Christ they are generally a trial to the church. All the merely human learning that has ever come unto the church has, as a rule, been mischievous to it: and it always needs great grace to keep it in its right place. At first came the Gnostics with their philosophy, and into what perils they dragged the church of God I cannot stay to tell you: then arose others out of whose wisdom grew Arianism, and the church was well-nigh withered to her very heart by that deadly form of heresy. The schoolmen did for her much the same, and to this day whenever any of the would-be-thought-wise men meddle with religion, they tell us that the plain word of God, as we read it, must be interpreted by modern thought, and that it bears another meaning which only the cultured can possibly comprehend. When philosophy invades the domain of revelation, it ends in perverting the gospel, and in bringing in 'another gospel: which is not another'. It is with human wisdom as it is with human riches; 'How hardly shall they that have' it 'enter into the kingdom of God!' True wisdom is another thing; that is a gift which comes from above, and causes no puffing up of the heart, for it adores the God from whom it came. The wisdom which is true and real the Lord is prepared to give to those who confess their lack of wisdom, to those who will be babes in his sight. It is not ignorance which God loves, but conceit that he hates. Knowledge is good, but the affectation of it is evil. O for more true wisdom! May God give us much of it, and may those who are babes as yet come to be men of full stature in Christ Jesus.

FOR MEDITATION: (*Our Own Hymn Book* no. 219 v.4—George Keith, 1787)
  'What was there in you that could merit esteem,
  Or give the Creator delight?
  "'Twas even so, Father," you ever must sing,
  "Because it seemed good in Thy sight."'

SERMON NO. 1571

6 DECEMBER (UNDATED SERMON)

How to read the Bible

'Have ye not read? ... have ye not read? ... If ye had known what this meaneth.' Matthew 12:3,5,7
SUGGESTED FURTHER READING: Luke 24:25–47

That sermon which does not lead to Christ, or of which Jesus Christ is not the top and the bottom, is a sort of sermon that will make the devils in hell to laugh, but might make the angels of God to weep, if they were capable of such emotion. You remember the story I told you of the Welshman who heard a young man preach a very fine sermon, a grand sermon, a highfalutin, spread-eagle sermon; and when he had done, he asked the Welshman what he thought of it. The man replied that he did not think anything of it. 'And why not?' 'Because there was no Jesus Christ in it.' 'Well,' said he, 'but my text did not seem to run that way.' 'Never mind,' said the Welshman, 'your sermon ought to run that way.' 'I do not see that, however,' said the young man. 'No,' said the other, 'you do not see how to preach yet. This is the way to preach. From every little village in England—it does not matter where it is—there is sure to be a road to London. Though there may not be a road to certain other places, there is certain to be a road to London. Now, from every text in the Bible there is a road to Jesus Christ, and the way to preach is just to say, "How can I get from this text to Jesus Christ?" and then go preaching all the way along it.' 'Well, but,' said the young man, 'suppose I find a text that has not got a road to Jesus Christ.' 'I have preached for forty years,' said the old man, 'and I have never found such a Scripture, but if I ever do find one I will go over hedge and ditch to get to him, for I will never finish without bringing in my Master.'

FOR MEDITATION: (*Our Own Hymn Book* no. 478 v.2—Isaac Watts, 1709)
   'The volume of my Father's grace
   Does all my griefs assuage;
   Here I behold my Saviour's face
   Almost in every page.'

SERMON NO. 1503

7 DECEMBER (1884)

A wonder explained by greater wonders

'Thou drewest near in the day that I called upon thee: thou saidst, Fear not.' Lamentations 3:57
SUGGESTED FURTHER READING: John 7:25–52

Jesus was the most manlike of all men. I could propound to you today the theory that Jesus was an Englishman, and prove it from many points of his character, if I did not know that he was of the seed of Abraham. Jesus of Nazareth is a Jew, but there is no Jewish peculiarity about him. He is a man in the broadest, truest sense. It matters not to you or me what nationality he actually came from, for the most cosmopolitan of men was the Christ of God. I know several excellent men whom I love and revere, but I despair of imitating them: the colour of their virtue has a tint in it peculiar to themselves: I am not made of such stuff as would ever work up into their fashion, admirable though it be. But I never thought thus concerning the Lord Jesus: I always feel that by his grace I can become like him. He is infinitely superior to those admirable friends of whom I have spoken, and yet he is more imitable. The hill is higher, but in his case there are ways and steps which invite, whereas in the other case there are crags which warn us off. I have known good men with whom I shall never be thoroughly at home until we meet in heaven: at least, we shall agree best on earth when they go their way and I go mine. One never feels so with regard to the all-glorious Lord Jesus. There our cry is, 'Nearer, my Lord, to thee. Nearer to thee.' He draws us to himself, and the nearer we come the more fully we appreciate him. If Jesus came thus near to men in his life on earth, do you wonder that he draws near to them now?

FOR MEDITATION: (*Our Own Hymn Book* no. 627 v.2—William Cowper, 1779)
   'Friend of the friendless and the faint,
   Where should I lodge my deep complaint?
   Where, but with Thee, whose open door
   Invites the helpless and the poor?'

8 DECEMBER (UNDATED SERMON)

A plain answer to an important enquiry

'Jesus answered and said unto them, This is the work of God, that ye believe on him whom he hath sent.' John 6:29
SUGGESTED FURTHER READING: Psalm 32:1–11

Faith is the creature acknowledging its God. While a man says, 'I do not care about my soul,' he lives in atheism, disowning God, living as if there were no God. When a man says, 'I need no saving,' that is contradicting God's testimony, wherein he declares that we 'are all gone out of the way' and have altogether become abominable. When a man says, 'I may be wrong, but I can get right of myself. My own good deeds will save me,' he is setting himself up in independence of his God, in fact, making himself his own God, and so, practically, setting up another God. But when the man cries, 'I have sinned,' there is an acknowledgment that the law is 'holy, and just, and good.' When he then adds, 'I have so sinned that I deserve punishment, and I submit myself to it,' there is a recognition of the court of heaven, and an admission of the righteousness of its sentences. The rebellious heart submits itself to the authority of God. When he further says, 'But I have heard, great God, that thou hast given thy Son to bleed and die for sinners, and that he is able to save to the uttermost them that trust him, and I do trust him,' the submission of the man to God is complete. Before, he said, 'I do not believe it. It does not stand to reason'; that is proud reason still a rebel. Or he said, 'It may or may not be so, but I do not see the peculiar beauty of an atoning sacrifice.' There again is the proud heart kicking against God. But the man comes into his right place when he believes. When he believes in Jesus Christ and accepts mercy through the great sacrifice, God is well pleased because his poor erring creature has come into its right place, and God sees in the act of faith the restitution of rectitude.

FOR MEDITATION: (*Our Own Hymn Book* no. 533 v.1a—Joseph Hart, 1759)
'The moment a sinner believes,
And trusts in his crucified God,
His pardon at once he receives,
Redemption in full through His blood.'

9 DECEMBER (UNDATED SERMON)

The plain man's pathway to peace

'Two blind men followed him, crying, and saying, Thou Son of David, have mercy on us. And when he was come into the house, the blind men came to him: and Jesus saith unto them, Believe ye that I am able to do this? They said unto him, Yea, Lord. Then touched he their eyes, saying, According to your faith be it unto you. And their eyes were opened.'
Matthew 9:27–30
SUGGESTED FURTHER READING: 1 Thessalonians 1:1–10

There are all the essentials of salvation in the simple, pleasant, happy way of coming to Jesus just as you are; what are they? The first is *repentance*; these dear souls, though they feel no remorse, yet hate the sin they once loved. Though they know no dread of hell, yet they feel a dread of sin, which is a great deal better. Though they have never stood shivering under the gallows, yet the crime is more dreadful to them than the doom. They have been taught by God's Spirit to love righteousness and seek after holiness; and this is the very essence of repentance. Those who thus come to Christ have certainly obtained true *faith*. They have no experience to trust in, but are all the more fully driven to rest in what Christ has felt and done. They rest not in their own tears, but in Christ's blood, not in their own emotions, but in Christ's pangs, not in their consciousness of ruin, but in the certainty that Christ has come to save all that trust him. They have faith of the purest kind. See, too, how certainly they have *love*. 'Faith worketh by love', and they show it. They often seem to have more love at first than those who come so dreadfully burdened and tempest-tossed, for, in the calm quiet of their minds, they get a fairer view of the beauties of the Saviour, burn with love to him and commence to serve him, while others are having their wounds healed, and are trying to make their broken bones rejoice. I do not wish to depreciate a painful experience, but I only want to show that simply coming to Christ, as the blind men came, simply believing that he could give them sight, is not inferior to the other, and has in it all the essentials of salvation.

FOR MEDITATION: The unregenerate heart lacks repentance, love towards God and genuine faith (2 Timothy 2:25; 3:4,8). These essentials are all gifts from God (Romans 5:5; Ephesians 2:8; 2 Timothy 2:25). What a change occurs when he supplies them (1 Thessalonians 1:3,9). Do you have them?

SERMON NO. 1560

10 DECEMBER (UNDATED SERMON)

The bird escaped from the snare

'Our soul is escaped as a bird out of the snare of the fowlers: the snare is broken, and we are escaped.' Psalm 124:7
SUGGESTED FURTHER READING: Psalm 40:1–17

This text ought to teach us, first, to *sing*, for if a bird gets out of the net, does it not sing? How glad it seems to be when once it flies away! Oh, you that have been delivered from sin and Satan, sing unto the Lord! Praise and bless his name. Be as happy as possible. Be something more than full of happiness; be so full of it that it overflows and cheers others. Let us communicate our joy as far as we can, for we are escaped and will praise the blessed God who broke the snare. Next, let us *trust*, for if the Lord has saved us from the dreadful snare of sin and Satan, he will save us from everything else. It is sad that any should trust the Lord with their souls, yet cannot trust him for their daily bread, or for help in their daily trials. This must not be. If the Lord has given our soul so great an escape, depend upon it he will take care of our bodies. He that gave us Jesus will give us 'food and raiment', and 'let us be therewith content.' Lastly, let us *watch*. If we have fallen into the snare once, let us keep our eyes open not to go there again. May the Holy Spirit prevent any child of God from turning aside even for a moment from the straight way. 'Let them not turn again to folly', is one of God's own cautions to his people. He has brought you up out of the horrible pit; do not play near the edge of it. He has set your feet on a rock; what have you to do with the miry clay? Get away from the slippery ground, and on the rock let your goings be established.

FOR MEDITATION: (*Our Own Hymn Book* no. 124 vv.4&5—John Ryland, 1775)
    'As when the fowler's snare is broke
    The bird escapes on cheerful wings;
    My soul, set free from Satan's yoke,
    With joy bursts forth, and mounts, and sings.
    She sings the Lord her Saviour's praise;
    Sings forth His praise with joy and mirth;
    To Him her song in heaven she'll raise,
    To Him that made both heaven and earth!'

11 DECEMBER (UNDATED SERMON)

The golden lamp and its goodly lessons

'*And I answered again, and said unto him, What be these two olive branches which through the two golden pipes empty the golden oil out of themselves? And he answered me and said, Knowest thou not what these be? And I said, No, my lord. Then said he, These are the two anointed ones that stand by the Lord of the whole earth.*' Zechariah 4:12–14
SUGGESTED FURTHER READING: Hebrews 11:31–40

Read Hebrews chapter 11, and notice on what strange men God set the seal of his approbation, because they had faith. Samson may be quoted as an extreme case: speaking after the manner of men, we might have thought that God would have set him aside altogether, because there were such serious flaws in his character. Yet he was a great child-man, who, with all his faults, believed in God perhaps more than many who were far better than he in other respects. With a thousand foemen before him, think of that one man daring, through his confidence in God, to fling himself upon them all with no weapon except an ass's jawbone. See, he leaps upon the crowd. 'Heaps upon heaps, with the jawbone of an ass have I slain a thousand men.' He never counted the odds. He just went at it, believing that God would help him, however tremendous the struggle might be. So when they put him, blind as he was, into that huge temple of the Philistine gods, where everything was so strong and massive that it could bear up all the Philistine lords up in the gallery, he begins feeling for the pillars: this poor blind man, whose hair had been shorn, and who had been made a prisoner by his bitter adversaries, feels for the huge columns, believing that God would enable him to snap them like reeds, or rock them to and fro as bulrushes. What a desperate and glorious tug was that, what a transcendent act of faith when he bowed himself with all his might, and pulled the structure down upon the heads of his oppressors! A glorious faith animated him. He was a poor specimen of propriety in many respects: strange stuff he was made of; but there was grandeur in his faith, and that saved him. If you can believe God, God can use you.

FOR MEDITATION: In Samson's story note the source of his strength (Judges 14:5–6,19; 15:14–15), the sapping of his strength (Judges 14:15–17; 16:5,15–21) and his supplication for strength (Judges 15:18–19; 16:28–30). What he knew bodily, Christians know spiritually (Ephesians 6:10–13,18).

SERMON NO. 1569

12 DECEMBER (1880)

Alive

'The righteousness of thy testimonies is everlasting: give me understanding, and I shall live.' Psalm 119:144
SUGGESTED FURTHER READING (Spurgeon): Romans 8:1–13

Is it life to live without *light*? You may have been in the dungeons of Venice, where not a ray of light ever came to the unhappy prisoner. To linger there, do you call that life? To live without the light of God is such an existence. We have heard of men who have been in dungeons for forty years, wearing constantly the manacles, never breathing the fresh air; do you call that life? Can there be life where there is no *liberty*? Some men have never been free, but have remained captives to their lusts, never knowing the liberty wherewith Christ makes men free. Call you such bondage life? Another essential of life is *love*. To have nobody to love, and nobody to love you, is that life? Yet many a soul feels that it cannot be contented with earthly love, and if it has not the love of God, of Christ and of the Spirit, it is loveless. Call you that life? Infinite love is a necessity of an immortal spirit. Without light, liberty and love there is no life. Many exist without *peace*, driven to and fro like a sere leaf by the tempest. Never resting, they are as a rolling thing before the whirlwind. Call you that life? 'There is no peace, saith the LORD, unto the wicked.' Is that life? And then to have no *grand object*, to be living merely to get enough bread and cheese to eat, just keeping yourself and your family breathing, is that life? No heavenly object, no ambition worthy of an immortal spirit, do you call that life? Death before you, which you dare not think of! No hope, unless it be the ghastly figment of annihilation! Dreadful hope! To me a thought most horrible! To live without hope is not life; call it death. Lord, give me understanding of thy everlasting testimonies; then 'I shall live.'

FOR MEDITATION: Being without faith in the living God (Hebrews 11:6) means being without God, without Christ, without hope (Ephesians 2:12), without strength (Romans 5:6) and without holiness (Hebrews 12:14), being dead while appearing alive (1 Timothy 5:6). Is that still your 'life'?

N.B. This sermon was occasioned by a rumour the previous day that Spurgeon had suddenly died of heart disease. 'The other day' several workmen had been killed on the line by a train in dense fog near Milan.

SERMON NO. 1572

13 DECEMBER (PREACHED 14 DECEMBER 1884)

Jonah's resolve, or 'Look again!'

'Then I said, I am cast out of thy sight; yet I will look again toward thy holy temple.' Jonah 2:4
SUGGESTED FURTHER READING: Psalm 94:12–23

There is a text that Jonah could never have heard, which I commend to you against the time when you get to be where Jonah was. I do not suppose you ever will be buried alive in a fish literally, but you may spiritually sink as deep as the prophet did. What is that text? 'Him that cometh to me I will in no wise cast out.' Jonah said, 'I am cast out', but that was not true. Poor Jonah! The mariners 'cast him' out, but God did not; he was cast out of the ship, but not out of the sight of God. The Lord of old was faithful, and it was his rule never to cast away his people, even as Jeremiah says, 'For the Lord will not cast off for ever: but though he cause grief, yet will he have compassion according to the multitude of his mercies.' Mark the text I quoted from our Lord's own lips: 'him that cometh to me I will in no wise cast out.' Never question this sacred word. He will never, never cast out a single one that trusts him. So that if ever you should be in a condition which seems to you quite as forlorn as that of this prophet in the midst of the sea, you may yet be sure that you are not cast off, nor cast out. He who says he is cast out, says more than can possibly be true, since the infallible promise is, 'him that cometh to me I will in no wise cast out.' It is not for us to forge a lie against the God of the whole earth. He does not speak that which is false, but out of his mouth proceeds truth. Even if all things in earth and hell should swear that the Lord has cast away one of his own believing people, it will be our duty to disbelieve them all, for it is impossible that he should cast out any believer, in any wise, for any reason or motive whatsoever.

FOR MEDITATION: Like Jonah, David had fears about being cast away from God's presence (Psalm 51:11). As well as John 6:37, there are other verses which give Christians an eternal assurance which Jonah and David were lacking (e.g. John 5:24; 6:39–40; 10:27–29). But the very thing Jonah and David were afraid of is assured to all who forsake God (1 Chronicles 28:9).

SERMON NO. 1813

14 DECEMBER (1884)

Cords and cart-ropes

'Woe unto them that draw iniquity with cords of vanity, and sin as it were with a cart rope.' Isaiah 5:18
SUGGESTED FURTHER READING: Mark 5:1–20

I remember reading a famous writer's description of a wretched cab-horse which was old and worn out and yet kept on its regular round of toil. They never took him out of harness for fear they should never be able to get his poor old carcase into it again. He had been in the shafts for so many years that they feared if they took him out of them he would fall to pieces, and so they let him keep where he was accustomed to be. Some men are just like that. They have been in the shafts of sin so many years that they fancy that if they were once to alter they would drop to pieces. But it is not so, old friend. 'We are persuaded better things of you, and things that accompany salvation'. The Lord will make a new creature of you. When he cuts the traces and brings you out from between those shafts which have so long held you, you will not know yourself. When old things have passed away you will be a wonder unto many. Is it not said of Augustine that after his conversion he was met by a fallen woman who had known him in his sin, and he passed her by? She said, 'Austin, it is I;' and he turned and said, 'But I am not Austin. I am not the man you once knew, for I have become a new creature in Christ Jesus.' That is what the Lord Jesus Christ can do for you. Do you not believe it? It is true, whether you believe it or not. Oh that you would look to Jesus and begin to live! It is time a change was made, is it not? Who can change you but the Lord Jesus?

FOR MEDITATION: (*Our Own Hymn Book* no. 553 v.3—William Hiley Bathurst, 1831)
    'Burdened with sin's oppressive chain,
    Oh, how can I get free?
    No peace can all my efforts gain,
    But Jesus died for me.'

15 DECEMBER (UNDATED SERMON)

Bad lodgers, and how to treat them

'*O Jerusalem, wash thine heart from wickedness, that thou mayest be saved. How long shall thy vain thoughts lodge within thee?*' Jeremiah 4:14
SUGGESTED FURTHER READING: Luke 9:57–62

Many who love the Lord have never done much for him because 'the time of figs' is not yet. Leaves only have they produced. They are live branches of the vine, although they have not brought forth many grapes; but they cheer themselves with the persuasion, that one of these days—they do not know quite when—they will bring forth clusters as famous as those of Eshcol [see Numbers 13:23–24], though hitherto they have been poor specimens of Christian professors; their mind is made up to rise to a higher life; they will grow in grace; they will give more time to Bible-reading and prayer; they will live nearer to God; they will grow quite strong Christians, and when that happens then they are going to do some great thing. I do not know quite what form their resolution is to take, but they will do something extraordinary. They will enter the Sunday-school and bring scores of little children to the Saviour's feet. They will commence a class for young men: the class is sure to grow, and out of it many will come to build up the church of God. They will become fathers or mothers in Israel, and their children will be many: or they are going to preach at the village stations, draw large congregations, and lead hundreds to the Saviour. They are going to serve the Lord by personal exertion, or give to the cause of God very largely of their substance. It has been on their hearts a long time to be bountiful benefactors to the poor, to the church at home, and to missionaries abroad. They have not given much yet, but before long they intend to overflow like gushing fountains which send forth rivers of water. They are resolving: when will they come to acting? If any of us had done about half what we thought we should do, we should have been tolerably fruitful branches of the vine; but we spend so much of our time in this proposing, and then proposing again, that we have little left for the actual performance of anything.

FOR MEDITATION: (*Our Own Hymn Book* no. 119 song 3 v.2—Isaac Watts, 1719)
   'I need the influence of Thy grace to speed me in Thy way,
   Lest I should loiter in my race or turn my feet astray.'

SERMON NO. 1573

16 DECEMBER (UNDATED SERMON)

The dromedaries

'Barley also and straw for the horses and dromedaries brought they unto the place where the officers were, every man according to his charge.'
1 Kings 4:28
SUGGESTED FURTHER READING (Spurgeon): Psalm 62:1–12

You cannot better your circumstances as a servant of Christ by diminishing your charge. If you say, 'I shall not attempt quite so much,' you will not improve your circumstances by that course, for if you diminish work, the Lord will diminish the strength. Our great Solomon will stop some of the supplies if you have fewer dromedaries to feed, and so you will be no better off. If you have to keep six he will give you provision for six; if you take to keeping three he will only give you supplies for three, and you will be poorer rather than richer. Neither can you improve your circumstances by entirely and only increasing the supply, for, if you receive more straw and barley, certainly our Solomon will send you more dromedaries. When you have more strength you will have more trials. When God's children do not discharge their service with the means which he entrusts to them, he frequently lets them take shares in a 'limited liability company,' which is the same thing as throwing your money into the river, or he leaves them to become shareholders in a breaking bank, with unlimited catastrophe as its capital, and this is more terrible still. It often happens to a man who has scraped and saved, and stinted the cause of Christ, that in his later years he is in straits, and he cries to himself, 'It is all gone, and I wish I had used it better before it went. It would have been far better to give it to the Lord than to see the lawyers devour it.' Ah, your sin has found you out. Your Master could not trust you, and so he has taken away his goods from you, and now you wish that you had behaved yourself. Let us take warning from such bad managers, and let us see that, as our charge is, so we cry for supplies, and that as the supplies come we use them wisely.

FOR MEDITATION: (*Our Own Hymn Book* no. 681 v.1—Isaac Watts, 1709)
  'Let me but hear my Saviour say,
  Strength shall be equal to thy day!
  Then I rejoice in deep distress,
  Leaning on all-sufficient grace.'

SERMON NO. 1504

17 DECEMBER (UNDATED SERMON)

The waterpots at Cana

'Jesus saith unto them, Fill the waterpots with water. And they filled them up to the brim.' John 2:7
SUGGESTED FURTHER READING: Proverbs 23:29–35

Jesus was at a wedding feast, and when the wine ran short, he provided for it right bountifully. I do not think that I should do any good if I were to enter upon the discussion as to what sort of wine our Lord Jesus made on this occasion. It was wine, and I am quite sure it was very good wine, for he would produce nothing but the best. Was it wine such as men understand by that word now? It was wine, but there are very few people in this country who ever see, much less drink, any of that beverage. That which goes under the name of wine is not true wine, but a fiery, brandied concoction of which I feel sure that Jesus would not have tasted a drop. The fire-waters and blazing spirits of modern wine manufacturers are very different articles from the juice of the grape, mildly exhilarating, which was the usual wine of more sober centuries. As to the wine such as is commonly used in the East, a person must drink inordinately before he would become intoxicated with it. It would be possible, for there were cases in which men were intoxicated with wine, but, as a rule, intoxication was a rare vice in the Saviour's times and in the preceding ages. Had our great Exemplar lived under our present circumstances, surrounded by a sea of deadly drink, which is ruining tens of thousands, I know how he would have acted. I am sure he would not have contributed by word or deed to the rivers of poisonous beverages in which bodies and souls are now being destroyed wholesale. The kind of wine which he made was such that, if there had been no stronger drink in the world, nobody might have thought it necessary to enter any protest against drinking it. It would have done nobody any hurt, be sure of that, or else Jesus our loving Saviour would not have made it.

FOR MEDITATION: Within a few days many will mark the birth of the Lord Jesus Christ with drunken parties. Spurgeon went on to say, 'I abstain myself from alcoholic drink in every form, and I think others would be wise to do the same; but of this each one must be a guide unto himself.' What is your attitude? The following verses should help you: Proverbs 20:1; Isaiah 5:11–12,22; Romans 14:21; Ephesians 5:18; 1 Peter 4:3.

SERMON NO. 1556

18 DECEMBER (1884)

A sweet silver bell ringing in each believer's heart

'My God will hear me.' Micah 7:7
SUGGESTED FURTHER READING: Psalm 4:1–8

In Scripture we do not often find the expression, 'My God will answer me.' We do read that he answers prayer, but more frequently God is said to be the God that *hears* prayer. It is better for us to have a promise that God will hear us than a promise that God will always answer us. In fact, if it were a matter of absolute fact that God would always answer the prayers of his people as they present them, it would be an awful truth. I should shrink from ever praying again if I were absolutely sure that the Lord would answer my prayer, whatever it might be. I might curse myself seven times deep by a prayer within the next seven minutes, if there were no safeguards and limits to the promise of prayer being answered. It is neither desirable nor possible that all things should be left to our choice: so much do I feel this, that if my Lord should say to me, 'From this hour I will always answer your prayer just as you pray it,' the first petition I would offer would be, 'Lord, do nothing of the sort', because that would be putting the responsibility of my life upon myself, instead of allowing it to remain upon God. It would, in fact, make me the master of the house, and make me my own shepherd: the very first thing I should wish would be to strip myself of such a power. I would cry, 'Lord, do as thou wilt about answering me; I will be well content if thou wilt hear me.' I like that kind of hearing prayer of which Ralph Erskine says:

> 'I'm heard when answered, soon or late,
> Yea, heard when I no answer get:
> Most kindly answered when refused,
> And treated well when harshly used.'

It is enough for a praying heart that it has a hearing God.

FOR MEDITATION: (*Our Own Hymn Book* no. 999 v.1—Henry Bateman, 1862)
  'Let us pray! The Lord is willing, ever waiting, prayer to hear;
  Ready, His kind words fulfilling, loving hearts to help and cheer.'

SERMON NO. 1819

19 DECEMBER (WRITTEN SERMON)

The best of all sights

'But we see Jesus.' Hebrews 2:9
SUGGESTED FURTHER READING: Revelation 21:22–22:5

'We see Jesus' with gladdest expectation. His glorious *person* is to us the picture and the pledge of what we shall be: for 'it doth not yet appear what we shall be: but we know that, when he shall appear, we shall be like him; for we shall see him as he is.' In infinite love he condescended to become one with us here below, as says the apostle, 'Forasmuch then as the children are partakers of flesh and blood, he also himself likewise took part of the same;' and this descent of love on his part to meet us in our low estate is the assurance that his love will lift us up to meet him in his high estate. He will make us partakers of his nature, inasmuch as he has become partaker of our nature. It is written, 'both he that sanctifieth and they who are sanctified are all of one: for which cause he is not ashamed to call them brethren.' What bliss is this that we should be like to the incarnate God! It would seem too good to be true, were it not after the manner of our Lord to do for us 'great things and unsearchable'. Nor may we alone derive comfort as to our future from his person; we may also be made glad by a hope as to his *place*. Where we see Jesus to be, there shall we also be. His heaven is our heaven. His prayer secures that we shall be with him where he is, that we may behold his glory, and we know that ere long we shall dwell in the palace of the great King. The glory of Jesus strikes the eye at once, and thus we are made to exult in his *position*, for it, too, is ours. He will give to us to sit upon his throne, even as he sits upon the Father's throne. He 'hath made us kings and priests unto God', and we shall reign for ever and ever.

FOR MEDITATION: As Christmas approaches, take time to share in something of the anticipation and joy of those who were among the first to 'see Jesus' (Matthew 2:1–2,10–11; Luke 2:15–20,25–32). The apostles never got over the wonder of *the best of all sights* (John 1:14; 2 Peter 1:16; 1 John 1:1–3). Do you wish to 'see Jesus' (John 12:21)?

N.B. This undated sermon written at Mentone was issued with no. 1510 and a 'letter from Mr Spurgeon' dated Mentone, Dec. 19, 1879.

SERMON NO. 1509

20 DECEMBER (UNDATED SERMON)

The key-note of a choice sonnet

'My soul doth magnify the Lord.' Luke 1:46
SUGGESTED FURTHER READING: John 14:15–23

I might not be straining words if I were to say to many a sister in Christ, 'Hail, thou that art highly favoured, the Lord is with thee: blessed art thou among women.' And I might say the same to many a brother: 'Hail, thou that art highly favoured, the Lord is with thee: blessed art thou among men. The Lord hath done great things for thee, and let thy spirit be glad.' True, there is one point in which we cannot be compared to Mary literally. She was to be the mother of the human nature of our Lord; but there is a parallel case in each one of us in which a higher mystery, a more spiritual mystery, gives us a like privilege, for, behold, the Holy Spirit dwells in each believer. He lives within us as within a temple, and reigns within us as in a palace. If we are partakers of the Holy Spirit, what more can we desire by way of favour from God, and what greater honour can be bestowed upon us? It was by her that the Word became incarnate, but so also is it by us, for we can make God's Word stand out visibly in our lives. It is ours to turn into actual, palpable existence among the sons of men the glorious Spirit of grace and truth which we find in the Word of God. Truly did our Lord speak when he called his disciples, 'my brother, and sister, and mother.' We bear as close a relationship to Christ as did the Virgin mother, and we in some sense take the same position spiritually which she took up corporeally in reference to him. May he be formed in us 'the hope of glory'.

FOR MEDITATION: (*Our Own Hymn Book* no. 775 v.3—John Mason, 1683)
   'My soul doth magnify the Lord,
   My spirit doth rejoice;
   To Thee, my Saviour and my God,
   I lift my joyful voice.'

SERMON NO. 1514

21 DECEMBER (1884)

Exceeding gladness

'For thou hast made him most blessed for ever: thou hast made him exceeding glad with thy countenance.' Psalm 21:6
SUGGESTED FURTHER READING: Luke 1:39–56

This joy of the believer *comes to him through many channels*. Heaven has many windows, and out of each one of them the Lord pours out benedictions upon his chosen. Let me read a part of Psalm 21. 'The king shall joy in *thy strength*, O Lord'. Oh, it is a great thing, when you are weak, to be strong in God, for then you will be happy. Divine strength brings divine gladness with it. 'And in *thy salvation* how greatly shall he rejoice!' God's salvation, the election that brings us into it, the redemption that makes us full possessors of its blessings, the effectual calling which leads us to accept it, the eternal love which holds us fast in it, why, in all these how greatly do we rejoice! Next, *answers to prayer* make us rejoice. 'Thou hast given him his heart's desire, and hast not withholden the request of his lips.' When a man comes from the mercy-seat, like Luther, saying, 'I have conquered; I have won my suit with God,' what gladness has the Lord given him! 'For thou preventest him with the blessings of goodness'. God is beforehand with us: he outruns us in love. Here is another source of joy, when God *gives us mercies before we seek them*, when he lays them in our road, and there they are ready for us before we come to the spot. When David was made a king, I am sure he said, 'I never thought, nor sought, nor wrought to be a king.' Many of us have received choice blessings, of which we said when we obtained them, 'Whence is this to me? I never dreamed of this. This was not in my programme. I never proposed this to my soul in her hours of largest desire. Thou preventest me with the blessings of thy goodness.' Brethren, such things as these tend to make God's people glad in their hearts.

FOR MEDITATION: (*Our Own Hymn Book* no. 720 v.1—Isaac Watts, 1709)
    'Come, we that love the Lord,
    And let our joys be known;
    Join in a song with sweet accord,
    And thus surround the throne.'

SERMON NO. 1827

22 DECEMBER (PREACHED 21 DECEMBER 1884)

The great birthday and our coming of age

'*Even so we, when we were children, were in bondage under the elements of the world: but when the fullness of the time was come, God sent forth his Son, made of a woman, made under the law, to redeem them that were under the law, that we might receive the adoption of sons. And because ye are sons, God hath sent forth the Spirit of his Son into your hearts, crying, Abba, Father.*' Galatians 4:3–6

SUGGESTED FURTHER READING: Luke 1:26–38

God sent his Son in real humanity, 'made of a woman'. The Revised Version properly has it, 'born of a woman'. Perhaps you may get nearer to it if you say, 'made to be born of a woman,' for both ideas are present, the being made and the being born. Christ was really and truly of the substance of his mother, as certainly as any other infant that is born into the world is so. God did not create the human nature of Christ apart, and then transmit it into mortal existence by some special means, but his Son was made and born of a woman. He is, therefore, of our race, a man like ourselves, and not man of another stock. You are to make no mistake about it; he is not only of humanity, but of your humanity, for that which is born of a woman is brother to us, be it born when it may. Yet there is an omission, I doubt not intentional, to show how holy was that human nature, for he is born of a woman, not of a man. The Holy Spirit overshadowed the Virgin, and 'that holy thing' was born of her without the original sin which pertains to our race by natural descent. Here is a pure humanity though a true humanity, a true humanity though free from sin. 'Born of a woman', he was 'of few days, and full of trouble'; born of a woman, he was compassed with our physical infirmities, but as he was not born of man he was altogether without tendency to evil or delight therein. I beg you to rejoice in this near approach of Christ to us. Ring out the glad bells, if not in the spires and steeples, yet within your own hearts, for gladder news never did greet your ear than this, that he that is the Son of God was also 'made of a woman.'

FOR MEDITATION: (*Our Own Hymn Book* no. 260 v.2—Edward Caswall, 1858)
'Oh joy! There sitteth in our flesh, upon a throne of light,
One of a human mother born, in perfect Godhead bright!'

23 DECEMBER (PREACHED 2 DECEMBER 1883)

'He shall be great'

'He shall be great.' Luke 1:32
SUGGESTED FURTHER READING: Philippians 2:1–11

There was never such a being as our Well-Beloved. He is peerless and incomparable. He is divine, and therefore unique. He is 'Light of light, very God of very God.' Jesus is truly equal with God, one with the Father. Oh, the greatness of Godhead! Jehovah is a being infinite, immeasurable, incomprehensible, inconceivable! He fills all things, and yet is not contained by all things. He is indeed great beyond any idea of greatness that has ever dawned upon us. All this is true of the Only-Begotten. 'In the beginning was the Word, and the Word was with God, and the Word was God. The same was in the beginning with God. All things were made by him; and without him was not anything made that was made.' 'For of him, and through him, and to him, are all things: to whom be glory for ever. Amen.' 'He is before all things, and by him all things consist.' But our Lord Jesus is also man, and this makes the singularity of his person, that he should be perfectly and purely God, and as truly and really man. He is not humanity deified: he is not Godhead humanized. I have admitted latitude of expression, but there is, in fact, no confusion of the substance. He is God. He is man. He is all that God is, and all that man is as God created him. He is as truly God as if he were not man, and yet as completely and perfectly man as if he were not God. Think of this wondrous combination, a perfect manhood without spot or stain of original or actual sin, and then the glorious Godhead combined with it! Said I not truly that Jesus stands alone? He is not greatest of the great, but great where all else are little. He is not something among all, but all where all else are nothing. Who shall be compared with him?

FOR MEDITATION: (*Our Own Hymn Book* no. 414 v.1—Isaac Watts, 1709)
    'What equal honour shall we bring
    To Thee, O Lord our God, the Lamb,
    When all the notes that angels sing
    Are far inferior to Thy name?'

SERMON NO. 1760

24 DECEMBER (1882)

The star and the wise men

'Behold, there came wise men from the east to Jerusalem, saying, Where is he that is born King of the Jews? for we have seen his star in the east, and are come to worship him.' 'When they had heard the king, they departed; and, lo, the star, which they saw in the east, went before them, till it came and stood over where the young child was. When they saw the star, they rejoiced with exceeding great joy.' Matthew 2:1–2, 9–10
SUGGESTED FURTHER READING: John 1:1–13

If we would cause others to belong to Jesus, we must belong wholly to Jesus ourselves. Every beam in that star shone forth for Jesus. It was his star, always, only and altogether. It shone not for itself, but only as his star: as such it was known and spoken of: 'we have seen his star.' There is no note taken of any peculiarity that it had except that it was the star of the King. I wish that you and I, whatever our eccentricities or personalities may be, may never make so much of them as to attract men's attention to them. May people never dwell upon our attainments or deficiencies, but always observe this one thing, that we are men of God, ambassadors of Christ, Christ's servants, and do not attempt to shine for ourselves, or to make ourselves conspicuous, but labour to shine for him, that his 'way may be known upon earth,' his 'saving health among all nations.' It is well for us to forget ourselves in our message, to sink ourselves in our Master. We know the names of several of the stars, yet they may each one envy that star which remains anonymous, but can never be forgotten because men who sought the King of Israel knew it as '*his* star'. Though you are only a very little star, twinkling for Jesus, however feeble your light may be, make it plain that you are *his* star, so that if men '*wonder what you are*', they may never wonder whose you are, for on your very forefront it shall be written, 'whose I am, and whom I serve'. God will not lead men to Christ by us unless we are Christ's heartily, wholly, unreservedly.

FOR MEDITATION: Andrew and Philip soon learned to point others to Jesus (John 1:40–46). Sometimes we have to go the extra mile and also point away from ourselves, like John the Baptist (John 1:19–30; 3:27–30), Peter (Acts 3:12–16; 4:8–10) and Paul (2 Corinthians 4:5). May we have the same effect as they did this Christmas (John 1:35–37; Acts 4:13).

SERMON NO. 1698

25 DECEMBER (1881)

Chastened happiness

'They shall fear and tremble for all the goodness and for all the prosperity that I procure unto it.' Jeremiah 33:9
SUGGESTED FURTHER READING: Romans 11:13–27

Israel became a people scattered and on the brink of national extinction, for their iniquities had hidden the face of the Lord from them. Yet the Lord had entered into a covenant concerning them with Abraham his friend, which he had afterwards renewed with his servant David. This latter covenant the Lord is said by the prophet Jeremiah to remember even when Jerusalem is desolate. We read in Jeremiah 33:20–21: 'Thus saith the LORD; If ye can break my covenant of the day, and my covenant of the night, and that there should not be day and night in their season; then may also my covenant be broken with David my servant, that he should not have a son to reign upon his throne'. Even in Israel's worst days, when her representative man was the weeping prophet Jeremiah, and when her sorrows were greater than even he could express, yet the Lord revealed his love, and promised that blessed days should dawn for the seed of Abraham. These days have not yet come, but they shall surely arrive, for 'God hath not cast away his people which he foreknew.' There is yet a history for Israel; her sun is clouded, but it has not set. As surely as stands the covenant with day and night, so shall the chosen people return from captivity and possess the land which the Lord has given to them. In those days the Lord will build them as at the first, and cleanse them from all their iniquities. Then they shall not be arrogant, for his goodness shall startle and astound them, and they shall be amazed when they see what great things Jehovah has done for them. The memory of their great national offences, and especially of their long rejection of the Messiah, shall cause them to wear their high dignity without pride; they shall be subdued by love to a childlike fear of again offending; they shall tremble as they see the Lord God of their fathers glorifying all his grace in them.

FOR MEDITATION: The Saviour came to the Jews first (Matthew 15:24) as did the gospel (Matthew 10:5–7; Romans 1:16). On this Christmas Day meditate on his intended relationship to them as in the Christmas story (Matthew 2:2–6; Luke 1:33,54–55; 2:32–34), note their initial response (John 1:11) and pray for their spiritual restoration (Romans 10:1).

SERMON NO. 1636

26 DECEMBER (INCORRECTLY DATED 2 JUNE 1884)

A great gospel for great sinners

'This is a faithful saying, and worthy of all acceptation, that Christ Jesus came into the world to save sinners; of whom I am chief.' 1 Timothy 1:15
SUGGESTED FURTHER READING: Matthew 1:1–17

In the genealogy of our blessed Lord we find the names of certain of the chief of sinners. Three women especially hold a position in it, who were each notorious for sin. Not many women are mentioned, but among the first is Tamar, guilty of incest. The next is Rahab the harlot, and a third is Bathsheba the adulteress. This is a crooked pedigree, an ancestral tree whose branches are more than a little gnarled and twisted. Admire the condescension of our Lord in coming of such a stock. He came of sinners, because he came for sinners. According to the flesh he comes of sinners that sinners may come to him. There was mixed in the veins through which flowed his ancestry the blood of Ruth the Moabitess, a heathen, brought in on purpose that we Gentiles might see how truly he was bone of our bone, and flesh of our flesh. I say not that there was any defilement in his humanity, for he was not born after the manner of men, so as to be polluted in that fashion, but still I say that his genealogy includes many great sinners in order that we may see how closely he allied himself with them, how thoroughly he undertook their cause. Read the roll of his ancestry, and you will see that David is there, who cried, 'Against thee, thee only, have I sinned,' and Solomon, who loved 'strange women', and Rehoboam, his foolish son, and Manasseh who 'shed innocent blood very much,' and worse men than they, if worse could be. Such sinners as these are in the genealogy of the Saviour of sinners. 'He was numbered with the transgressors'. He was called 'a friend of publicans and sinners.' It was said of him, 'This man receiveth sinners, and eateth with them.' Still he delights to save great sinners. It will delight him to save you!

FOR MEDITATION: (*Our Own Hymn Book* no. 551 v.4—Charles Wesley, 1740)
    'Plenteous grace with Thee is found, grace to cover all my sin;
    Let the healing streams abound, make and keep me pure within;
    Thou of life the fountain art, freely let me take of Thee!
    Spring Thou up within my heart, rise to all eternity!'

SERMON NO. 1837

27 DECEMBER (PREACHED 20 AUGUST 1882)

Out of Egypt

'When he arose, he took the young child and his mother by night, and departed into Egypt: and was there until the death of Herod: that it might be fulfilled which was spoken of the Lord by the prophet, saying, Out of Egypt have I called my son.' Matthew 2:14–15
'When Israel was a child, then I loved him, and called my son out of Egypt.' Hosea 11:1
SUGGESTED FURTHER READING: Matthew 1:18–2:6

Mary and Joseph may have known of this prophecy, but I greatly question whether they perceived that it referred to their son at all, or to the Son of the Highest: but now they must do the very thing that God says shall be done, without knowing that they are fulfilling a Scripture. One of the worst things you and I can ever attempt is to try and fulfil a prophecy. Good mistress Rebecca wanted to fulfil a prophecy, and what a mess she made of it! She endeavoured to make her second son the heir, and in the attempt she brought upon him and herself a world of sorrow. Had she not better have let the prophecy alone? Surely, if a prophecy is made of God, God will see that it comes to pass. If it is a Chaldaic prophecy, a prophecy of soothsayers and magi, no doubt they will try to make their own oracle true, but the Lord, who sees the end from the beginning and ordains all things, can speak positively of the future. If any of you set up for prophets, beware of prophesying till you know that you can make it good. God does not need such petty provision: he wants no help from us: his word will surely be established. Mary and Joseph did not try to fulfil the prophecy, for they could not have understood it to mean what it did mean. It was purposely put in a dark and cloudy form, but still the Lord knew what he was doing: 'that it might be fulfilled which was spoken of the Lord by the prophet, saying, Out of Egypt have I called my son.'

FOR MEDITATION: Through his prophets God revealed several details concerning the birth of the Lord Jesus Christ—his person (Isaiah 9:6), his parent (Isaiah 7:14), his progenitors (Isaiah 11:1) and the place (Micah 5:2). Notice how God acted both independently (Luke 1:31–35) and through world events (Luke 2:1–7) to fulfil these prophecies.

28 DECEMBER (1884)

The Ascension and the Second Advent practically considered

'And while they looked stedfastly toward heaven as he went up, behold, two men stood by them in white apparel; which also said, Ye men of Galilee, why stand ye gazing up into heaven? this same Jesus, which is taken up from you into heaven, shall so come in like manner as ye have seen him go into heaven.' Acts 1:10–11

SUGGESTED FURTHER READING: Acts 3:17–26

Jesus is gone into heaven. Jesus is gone! Jesus is gone! It sounds like a knell. Jesus is taken up from you into heaven! That sounds like a marriage peal. He is gone, but he is gone up to the hills whence he can survey the battle, up to the throne, from which he can send us succour. The reserve forces of the omnipotent stood waiting till their Captain came, and now that he is come into the centre of the universe, he can send legions of angels, or he can raise up hosts of men for the help of his cause. I see every reason for going down into the world and getting to work, for he is gone up into heaven and 'All power is given unto' him 'in heaven and in earth.' Is that not a good argument: 'Go ye *therefore,* and teach all nations, baptizing them in the name of the Father, and of the Son, and of the Holy Ghost'? *Jesus will come again.* That is another reason for girding our loins, because it is clear that he has not quitted the fight, nor deserted the field of battle. Our great Captain is still heading the conflict; he has ridden into another part of the field, but he will be back again, perhaps in the twinkling of an eye. You do not say that a commander has given up the campaign because it is expedient that he should withdraw from your part of the field. Our Lord is doing the best thing for his kingdom in going away. It was in the highest degree expedient that he should go, and that we should each one receive the Spirit. There is a blessed unity between Christ the King and the commonest soldier in the ranks. He has not taken his heart, nor his care, nor his interest from us: he is bound up heart and soul with his people and their holy warfare, and this is the evidence of it: 'behold, I come quickly; and my reward is with me, to give every man according as his work shall be.'

FOR MEDITATION: (*Our Own Hymn Book* no. 319 v.5—Emma Toke, 1851)

'Thou art gone up on high; but Thou shalt come again,
With all the bright ones of the sky attendant in Thy train.'

SERMON NO. 1817

29 DECEMBER (UNDATED SERMON)

Till we meet again

'The grace of our Lord Jesus Christ be with you all. Amen.' Revelation 22:21
SUGGESTED FURTHER READING: John 1:14–18

Read the text and pause a while in the middle to enjoy 'The grace of our *Lord*'. Whatever familiarity we have with him, we call him Master and Lord, and he says, 'ye say well; for so I am.' Let us never forget that. The grace that comes from his majesty, the grace that comes from his headship, the grace that comes from his divinely human supremacy over his church, which is his body, this is the grace which we desire for you all. Read the next word: 'The grace of our Lord *Jesus*': may that be with you, that is to say, the grace of our Saviour, for that is the meaning of the word Jesus. All his saving grace, all that which redeems from guilt, from sin, from trouble, all that which saves us with an everlasting salvation, may that be yours to the full. Then comes the other word: 'The grace of our Lord Jesus *Christ* be with you'; may he, as the Anointed One, visit you. May the grace of his anointing be with you; may the holy anointing which was poured upon the Head come down upon you, as the sacred nard dropped from Aaron's beard and perfumed all his robes. May you have that anointing from the Holy One which shall make you know all things. I am tempted to linger over each one of these words, but I may not, for time would forbid. Yet must we tarry on that word 'our': 'The grace of *our* Lord'. Catch at that sweet word. It may not perhaps be genuine in this case, for it is not in the Sinaitic manuscript, but whether it is so in this particular instance or not, it is in the Word, and stands for ever true. Jesus is our Lord, 'our Lord Jesus Christ', both yours and ours. May the fullness of his grace be with you and with us.

FOR MEDITATION: (*Our Own Hymn Book* no. 1053 v.1—John Newton, 1779)
'May the grace of Christ our Saviour
And the Father's boundless love,
With the Holy Spirit's favour,
Rest upon us from above!'

30 DECEMBER (PREACHED 16 DECEMBER 1883)

The New Year's guest

'*I was a stranger, and ye took me in.*' Matthew 25:35
'*But as many as received him, to them gave he power to become the sons of God, even to them that believe on his name.*' John 1:12
SUGGESTED FURTHER READING: Luke 19:1–10

I lately received a New Year's card, which suggested to me the topic on which I am about to speak. The designer of the card has, with holy insight, seen the relation of the two texts to each other, and rendered both of them eminently suggestive by placing them together. There is freshness in the thought that, by receiving Jesus as a stranger, our believing hospitality works in us a divine capacity and we thereby receive power to become the sons of God. The connection suggested between the two inspired words is really existent, and by no means strained or fanciful, as you will see by reading the context of the passage in John: 'He was in the world, and the world was made by him, and the world knew him not.' So he was a stranger in the world which he himself had made. 'He came unto his own, and his own received him not.' So he was a stranger among the people whom he had set apart for his own by many deeds of mercy. 'But as many as received him,' that is to say, gave entertainment to this blessed stranger, 'to them gave he power to become the sons of God, even to them that believe on his name'. I thought that this might prove to be a suitable and salutary passage to discourse upon at the beginning of a New Year, for this is a season of hospitality, and some among our friends will think it well to commence a New Year by saying to the Lord Jesus, 'Come in, thou blessed of the Lord; wherefore standest thou without?' This divine stranger has knocked at many doors, till his 'head is filled with dew, and' his 'locks with the drops of the night', and now I trust there are some who will rise up and open unto him, so that at the end of the year they may say with Job, 'The stranger did not lodge in the street: but I opened my doors to the traveller.'

FOR MEDITATION: Some have entertained angels unawares (Hebrews 13:2) and some even managed to entertain the Saviour unawares (Luke 24:13–18,28–31). Others shut him out when he came (Luke 2:7; John 1:11) and one was too slow to let him in (Song of Solomon 5:2–6). How have you responded to his call for entry (Revelation 3:20)?

SERMON NO. 1757

31 DECEMBER (1882)

'Supposing him to be the gardener'

'Supposing him to be the gardener.' John 20:15
SUGGESTED FURTHER READING (Spurgeon): Luke 13:6–9

I am sometimes troubled by the question, what if roots of bitterness should spring up among us to trouble us? We are all such fallible creatures; supposing some brother should permit the seed of discord to grow in his heart, then there may be a sister in whose heart the seeds will also spring up, and from her they will fly to another sister, and be blown about till brethren and sisters are all bearing rue and wormwood in their hearts. Who is to prevent this? Only the Lord Jesus by his Spirit. He can keep out this evil, 'supposing him to the gardener'. The 'root that beareth ... wormwood' will grow but little where Jesus is. Dwell with us, Lord, as a church and people: by thy Holy Spirit reside with us and in us, and never depart from us, and then no 'root of bitterness' shall spring up to trouble us. Then comes another fear. Suppose the living waters of God's Spirit should not come to water the garden, what then? We cannot make them flow, for the Spirit is a sovereign, and he flows where he pleases. Ah, but the Spirit of God will be in our garden, 'supposing' our Lord 'to be the gardener'. There is no fear of our not being watered when Jesus undertakes to do it. He 'will pour water upon him that is thirsty, and floods upon the dry ground'. But what if the sunlight of his love should not shine on the garden, if the fruits should never ripen, if there should be no peace, no joy in the Lord? That cannot happen 'supposing him to be the gardener', for his face is the sun, and his countenance scatters those health-giving beams, nurturing warmths, and perfecting influences which are needful for maturing the saints in all the sweetness of grace to the glory of God. So, 'supposing him to be the gardener' at this the close of the year, I fling away my doubts and fears, and invite you who bear the church upon your heart to do the same.

FOR MEDITATION: (*Our Own Hymn Book* no. 995 v.2—Isaac Watts, 1709)
'Like trees of myrrh and spice we stand,
Planted by God the Father's hand;
And all His springs in Sion flow,
To make the young plantation grow.'

SERMON NO. 1699

Subject Index

Summary of Subject Index

Section 1	**The Godhead**
	The Trinity
	God the Father
	God the Son: His Person
	God the Son: His work
	God the Holy Spirit
	The Law of God
	The Word of God
Section 2	**Man in his natural sinful state**
Section 3	**The Gospel**
	Salvation—of God
	Proclamation
	Responses & Effects
Section 4	**The Church**
Section 5	**The Christian Life**
	Blessings from God
	Duties & Fruitfulness
	Spiritual warfare
Section 6	**Life in society**
Section 7	**Biographical**
Section 8	**Times & Seasons**
Section 9	**Death & the future state**

Subject Index

Section 1   **The Godhead**

The Trinity   18 Apr

God the Father
Beauty   14 Jan
Care for children   24 Nov
Consuming fire   15 Jan
Economy   30 Oct
Emotions   2 Mar
Greatness   16 Nov
Joy   29 Aug
Judge   18 Aug
Love   18 Feb
Mercy   6 Mar; 17 Aug; 2–4 Dec
Omnipresence   26 Sep
Thought-reading   5 Oct

God the Son—His Person 24 Jun
Calmness   9 Feb
Condescension   9 Jun
Conqueror   28 Jan
Covenant   22 Sep
Deity   13 Apr; 2 Jun; 6 Nov; 23 Dec
Example   17 May
Friend   8 Aug
Genealogy   26 Dec
Greatness   13 Feb
Humanity   7,23 Dec
Judge   25 May
Lord   6 Oct
Love   26 Mar; 23 May
Messiah   6 Nov
Physician   19 Jun
Prophet   2 Aug

373

Subject Index

	Sinless	12 Feb
	Titles	21 Aug; 29 Dec
	Weeping	28 Nov
	Welcoming	7 Nov
	Word	8 Jul

God the Son—His work

Birth	22 Dec
Preaching	10 Feb
Sufferings & Death	8,20 Feb; 15,17 Mar; 27 Jul; 8 Oct
Resurrection	28 Mar; 9 Apr
Ascension	28 Dec
Intercession, mediation & Priesthood	30 May; 26 Sep
Second coming	28 Dec

God the Holy Spirit   25 Feb; 11 Apr; 1 Jun; 14 Jul; 18 Sep

The Law of God   29 Oct

The Word of God   3,5–6,17,22 Jan; 28 Feb; 13 Mar; 8 Jul; 27 Dec (prophecy)

Section 2

Man in his natural sinful state

Abuse of knowledge	18 Jan
Blindness	7 Sep
Demon-possession	10 Jun
Dishonouring God	11 Oct
False assurance	21 Jan; 3 Sep
Idolatry	27 Oct
Impenitence	29 Nov
Iniquities	31 Aug
Judging others	23 Aug
Lifelessness	12 Dec

Subject Index

Modern thought	15 Feb; 25 Jul
Profanity	13 Apr
Self-righteousness	19 Mar; 18 Apr; 27 Sep
Self-sufficiency	16 Sep
Self-trust	2 May
Spiritual ignorance	25 Aug
Spiritual poverty	17 Jun
Unbelief	22 Apr; 3 Oct
Vain hopes	26 Oct
Warnings	26 Feb
Weariness of God	7 Oct
Woe	30 Nov
Worldly wisdom	5 Dec

Section 3   **The Gospel**

Salvation—of God	22 Mar; 24 May
Calling	23 Jul
Cleansing	17 Nov
Cures	9 Jan
Election	31 Jul
For sinners	5 May
Forgiveness	29 Aug; 22 Oct
Freedom	6 Jul
Grace	13,18 Jun; 4 Jul; 12 Aug; 29 Dec
Love to the world	4 May
New birth	29 Jul
New creation	14 Dec
Quickening	30 Aug
Redemption	30 Jan; 14 Nov
Substitutionary atonement & Justification	16,24 Mar; 2–3,29 Apr; 11 May; 29 Jun; 6 Aug; 24 Sep; 13,19 Oct

Subject Index

	Proclamation	
	Invitation	10 Jul
	Preaching	2 Jan; 1 Apr; 12 May; 4 Jun; 21 Jul; 10,15 Nov; 6 Dec
	Testimony	6 Apr; 16 Nov; 24 Dec
	The cross	30 Jul
	Responses & Effects	14 Aug
	Acknowledgement of sin	18 Oct
	Apostasy	19 Jan; 5 Feb
	Assurance	19 Jul
	Child salvation	16,20–21 Oct
	Conversion	5,25 Apr; 31 May
	Conviction	25 Feb
	Cry for mercy	22 Feb
	Desperation	14 Oct
	Excuses	21 Apr
	Faith	29 Jan; 22 Mar; 12 Jun; 18 Jul; 13 Aug; 8–9 Dec
	Fear	13 Aug
	Feelings	26 Jun
	Humility	17 Aug
	Opposition	21 Mar; 23 Oct
	Procrastination	1 Aug
	Receiving	4 Jan
	Rejection	19 Feb; 5 Mar
	Repentance	10,29 Aug; 9 Dec
	Ridicule	17 Apr
	Seeking	8 Jan; 13,27 May; 26 Nov
	Unbelief	21 Jun
	Wrong motives	17 Oct
Section 4	**The Church**	
	Apostasy	20 Jan
	Defending the faith	10 Apr; 26 Jul

Subject Index

Division	14 Apr
Follow-up	20 Apr; 28 Jun
Foundation	14 Sep
God's presence	4 Mar
Idolatry	2 Oct
Jewish nation	14 Jun; 25 Dec
Lord's Day	28–29 Mar; 11 Aug
Martyrs	11 Sep; 15 Nov
Ministry	5, 11 Jul
Ministry—hearing	15 Apr; 25 Jun
Ministry—training	16 Jul
Mission	11 Sep
Outreach & witness	25 Mar; 19 Apr; 16 Jul
Ownership	5 Jun
Prayer meeting	30 Jun; 4 Oct
Public worship	14 May
Reputations	19 May
Revival	18 May
Sabbath	21 May
Sacraments	23 Mar
Singing	7 Aug
Sunday School	7 May; 15 Oct
Sustenance	31 Dec

Section 5   **The Christian life**

Blessings from God	8 May
Acceptance	15 Jul
Certainty	15 May
Chastisement	12 Jan; 4 Aug
Comfort in affliction	13 Jan; 23 Feb; 7 Jul; 5 Aug; 20 Sep; 8 Nov
Communion	24 Jan; 23 Apr; 9 Aug
Expectation	16 May
Firstborn	5 Nov

Subject Index

Guidance	3 Aug; 27 Nov
Healing	10 Jan
Indwelling	2 Jul; 20 Dec
Knowing the truth	16 Jan
Presence	1 Feb; 3 Jun
Preservation	16 Aug
Promises	1 Oct
Provision	15 Sep
Quickening	3 May
Redirection	10 Sep
Security	11 Feb; 20 Aug; 13 Dec
Strengthening	12 Mar
Union with Christ	8 Jun; 19 Dec
Upholding	24 Feb
Duties & Fruitfulness	28 May
Attention to truth	17 Jan
Bodily care	9 Jul
Bodily sanctity	22 Aug
Character	24 Jul
Childlikeness	18 Mar
Christlikeness	21 Aug
Dependence	4 Nov
Desires for God	24 Oct
Desires for holiness	27 Feb
Discipleship	21 Sep
Expectancy	21 Nov
Fear of God	23 Jan; 1 May; 9 Oct
Freshness	16 Feb
Fullness	25 Oct
Good works	7 Feb; 22 May
Graciousness	29 Feb
Heavenly-mindedness	30 Apr
Holiness	8 Sep
Honourableness	1 Mar

Subject Index

Humility	14 Feb; 12 Sep
Imitation	7–8 Mar; 12 Oct
Joy	2,6 Feb; 21 Dec
Love for Christ	6 Sep
Love for God	25–26 Jan; 23 Apr; 15 Aug; 9 Dec
Love to others	26 Mar; 26 May; 5,9 Sep
Obedience	27 Jan; 15 Jun
Patience	21 Feb; 20 Sep
Peace	31 Jan; 17 Sep
Praise	1 Jan; 16 Jun; 1 Sep; 10 Dec
Prayer	11,13 Mar; 11 Apr; 9 May; 7,22–23 Jun; 30 Sep; 1 Oct; 18 Dec
Priesthood of all believers	12 Nov
Righteousness	3 Feb
Service	6 Jun; 20 Jul; 25 Sep; 12 Oct; 20 Nov
Stewardship	26 Apr; 16 Dec
Temples of God	9 Nov
Trust	27 Apr; 22 Jul; 3 Oct; 10–11 Dec
Truthfulness	22 Nov

Spiritual Warfare

Appreciation, lack of	10 Mar
Complaining	10 May
Cowardice	20 Feb
Distrust	28 Sep
Evil days	1 Nov
Fears	23 Jan
Human weakness	2 Dec
Inconsistency	3,12 Jul
Judging others	29 May
Persecution	9 Mar; 4 Sep

Subject Index

	Presumption	1 May
	Pride	14 Feb
	Resisting sin	19 Nov
	Resolving	15 Dec
	Scandal-mongering	17 Feb
	Self-satisfaction	20 Mar
	Sickness	11 Jun
	Sleepiness	10 Oct
	Sorrow	11 Jan
	Speech	3 Jul
	Steadfastness	27 Aug
	Strength	19 Sep
	Trials & Temptations	4 Feb
	1. The Devil	8 Apr; 10,27 Jun; 1 Jul
	2. The World (worldliness)	14 Mar; 24 Apr; 28 Jul; 2 Sep; 31 Oct; 18 Nov
	Unbelief	28 Oct
	Watchfulness	10 Dec
Section 6	**Life in Society**	
	Alcohol	17 Dec
	Amusements	4 Apr
	Children	24 Nov
	Citizenship	13 Jul
	Friendships	23 Nov
	Memorials	20 Jun
	Parenting	10 Aug; 25 Nov
	Salary	29 Mar
	Unemployment	16 Apr
	War	22 Jan
	Women's godliness	28 Apr
Section 7	**Biographical**	
	General	13 Nov
	Abney	4 Oct

Subject Index

Augustine	14 Dec
Burns	5 May
Butler	6 Apr
Cook	19 Apr
Cruden	13 Jan
Darling	26 Aug
Drake	23 Feb
Hawker	5 Jul
Higgs	7 Jan
John (King)	29 Aug
Livingstone	11 Sep
Luther	11–12 Nov
Moravians	21 Jul
Napoleon	16 Mar
Puritans	19 Aug
Richard I (King)	29 Aug
Richmond	6 Apr
Spurgeon	2 Jan; 6,16,21 Jun
Stuart	11 May

Section 8 — **Times & Seasons**

Start of year	1–2 Jan
Christmas	19–27 Dec
End of year	30–31 Dec
Young men	2 Sep
Elderly men	18 Nov
Past, present, future	3 Jan

Section 9 — **Death & the future state**

Burial	3 Nov
Death	7 Jan; 3 Mar; 24 Aug; 13 Sep
Destruction	17 Jul
Exclusion	27 Mar
Glory	20 May
Heaven	31 Mar; 6 May; 23 Sep; 19 Dec

Subject Index

Judgment	1 Dec
Resurrection body	28 Aug
Rewards	26 Aug
Sinless perfection	7 Apr
Vanity of life	30 Mar

Scripture Index

Index of original texts and suggested further readings (Spurgeon's complete texts are identified below by an asterisk*).

Genesis		30:11–16*	30 Jan	**Joshua**	
3:1–19	1 Jul	32:26*	4 Apr	24:4*	13 Nov
4:1–7	19 Nov	33:14*	27 Nov		
7:16*	16 Aug	38:26–27*	30 Jan	**Judges**	
18:1–15	28 Apr			1:19–20*	28 Sep
18:22–32	29 Nov	**Leviticus**		2:4–5*	10 Aug
19:12–26	24 Aug	1:4–5*	16 Mar	6:22–24*	17 Sep
19:24–29	29 Nov	1:5*	17 Mar	14:8–9*	28 Jan
21:8–21	2 Dec	4:6–7*	11 May		
22:14*	13 Oct	23:4–21	1 Jun	**Ruth**	
28:15*	1 Feb	24:10–23	13 Apr	2:12*	28 Jun
28:10–22	7 Jun				
31:3,5*	1 Feb	**Numbers**		**1 Samuel**	
32:1–2*	20 Jun	11:1–23	28 Oct	1:1–20	5 Oct
32:10*	22 Jun	14:11*	3 Oct	1:15*	11 Jan
32:22–28	31 May	14:11–20	29 Aug	2:3*	26 Aug
35:1–15	20 Jun	19:1–22	29 Jun	2:30*	11 Oct
39:2*	24 Jul	21:4–9*	10 May	9:27*	3 Jan
45:16–28	29 Sep	21:9*	19 Oct	12:23*	9 May
48:21*	1 Feb	23:21*	4 Mar	14:24–31	9 Jul
49:22–26	8 May			17:12–58	10 Mar
		Deuteronomy		17:36–37*	25 Sep
Exodus		4:1–31	10 Aug	30:6,8*	22 Jul
8:25,28*	25 Nov	6:1–9	28 Feb		
10:8,11*	25 Nov	8:1–20	14 Mar	**2 Samuel**	
10:24,26*	25 Nov	18:15–19*	2 Aug	1:17–18*	13 Jan
12:1–2*	1 Jan	21:15–17	5 Nov	15:21*	23 Nov
14:19–20*	3 Aug	29:4*	8 Jan	17:27–29*	20 Jun
15:19–16:12	10 May	30:1–20	25 Jan		
15:26*	11 Jun	32:20*	22 Apr	**1 Kings**	
24:1–10	14 Nov	33:26–29	24 Feb	2:30*	23 Mar
30:7–8*	11 Mar			4:20–28*	16 Dec

Scripture Index

8:38–40*	29 Jul	19:28*	15 May	42:1–11	26 Sep
14:13*	21 Oct	22:1–3	6 Jun	46:1–11	4 Mar
18:12*	20 Oct	22:3–11	23 Aug	49:1–15	17 Jun
18:36*	10 Nov	23:11–12*	7 Mar	50:15*	8 Nov
19:12–13*	9 Jul	29:20*	16 Feb	51:1–19	5 May
		33:19–28	16 Feb	57:4*	4 Sep
2 Kings		35:1–7	6 Jun	62:1–12	16 Dec
3:15*	7 Aug	35:10–11*	26 Sep	65:11*	19 May
17:41*	2 Oct			66:8–20	13 Jan
		Psalms		68:20–21*	15 Feb
1 Chronicles		1:1–6	28 May	71:1–18	20 Oct
12:16–18*	17 Feb	2:8–9*	25 Apr	73:1–28	22 Jul
21:28*	9 Nov	4:1–8	18 Dec	73:28*	11 Jul
22:1*	9 Nov	7:1–8	4 Sep	78:1–8	7 May
29:10–13	1 Sep	8:2*	27 Jun	78:10–59	28 Sep
		10:1–18	3 Sep	80:1–19	3 May
2 Chronicles		10:17*	5 Oct	83:1–18	18 Sep
20:1–30	27 Nov	19:7–14	22 Jan	84:11–12*	14 May
21:1–20	25 Nov	20:1–9	2 Feb	85:1–13	18 May
24:1–22	19 Jan	21:6*	21 Dec	86:1–17	9 Oct
34:1–33	27 Feb	22:8*	9 Feb	86:17*	5 Jan
35:2*	10 Mar	22:14–31	11 Sep	89:1–2*	4 Dec
		23:1–6	19 Sep	89:1–8	18 Feb
Ezra	–	23:4*	5 Aug	90:15–17*	14 Jan
		25:1–22	22 Feb	92:10*	16 Feb
Nehemiah		27:1–14	14 Jan	94:12–23	13 Dec
1:1–11	22 Jun	31:1–24	4 Nov	95:7–8*	1 Aug
		31:22*	8 Mar	96:1–13	7 Aug
Esther		32:1–11	8 Dec	99:1–9	16 Nov
4:13–14*	26 Apr	34:1–22	26 Nov	103:3*	31 Aug
		38:9*	24 Oct	103:13*	2 Mar
Job		39:1–13	30 Mar	107:1–32	8 Nov
6:6*	5 Jul	40:1–3*	13 Aug	107:17–20*	17 Jul
18:12*	13 Mar	40:1–17	10 Dec	110:1–7	21 Sep
19:20–27	11 Jun	40:4*	22 Apr	112:1–10	20 Sep

Scripture Index

116:1–16	20 Apr	**Ecclesiastes**		47:8–11	4 Apr
116:12–29	26 Apr	7:1*	3 Mar	50:6*	27 Jul
116:16*	2 Sep	11:1–6	19 Apr	51:2*	28 Apr
119:20*	27 Feb	11:9–12:14	2 Sep	51:2–3*	27 Apr
119:27–35	7 Mar			52:12*	3 Aug
119:41*	22 Feb	**Song of Solomon**		53:1–12	11 May
119:50*	7 Jul	2:2*	29 Feb	53:5*	2 Apr
119:54*	28 Feb	2:16*	24 Jan	53:7*	15 Mar
119:71*	11 Jul	3:1–4	3 Jun	54:11–17	1 May
119:88*	3 May	5:1–8	23 Apr	55:1*	17 Jun
119:89–92*	23 Feb	5:2*	10 Oct	55:1–5	10 Jul
119:117*	24 Feb	5:9–16	8 Aug	55:6–13	5 Apr
119:144*	12 Dec	6:13*	9 Aug	57:14*	22 Mar
119:145–152	13 Mar	8:13*	15 Apr	57:16–18*	17 Aug
119:162*	22 Jan			57:19*	31 Jan
124:7*	10 Dec	**Isaiah**		58:6–14	11 Aug
126:1–6	21 Nov	1:16–20	17 Nov	58:8*	3 Aug
138:5*	11 Aug	5:18*	14 Dec	59:1–13	31 Aug
143:1–12	23 Feb	25:1–9	28 Jan	59:12–20	30 May
143:10*	27 Jan	28:12*	17 Apr	61:1*	19 Jun
145:6–7*	16 Nov	28:17*	26 Oct	63:7–16	2 Mar
145:10*	20 Mar	28:25*	25 Aug	64:3*	16 May
146:1–10	16 Jun	30:18*	21 Feb	65:5*	27 Sep
147:15*	8 Jul	30:21*	23 Jul	66:2*	1 May
		32:1–8	15 Apr		
Proverbs		33:15–16*	2 Feb	**Jeremiah**	
1:1–19	27 Aug	40:1–11	28 Jun	2:32*	4 Aug
16:1–11	26 Aug	40:31*	12 Mar	3:1–14	3 Dec
18:24–19:7	23 Nov	41:8–14	1 Feb	3:12–13*	18 Oct
22:13*	21 Apr	42:3*	21 Jun	3:16*	22 Sep
23:29–35	17 Dec	42:9*	30 Jun	4:14*	15 Dec
26:13*	21 Apr	43:4*	1 Mar	5:3*	22 Nov
26:13–16	10 Oct	43:25*	22 Oct	8:11*	5 May
26:17–28	17 Feb	43:26*	7 Oct	8:20*	17 Oct
		44:21–28	22 Oct	11:1–17	19 Feb

Scripture Index

13:1–11*	17 Nov	**Hosea**		**Haggai**	–
13:15–17*	4 Nov	5:15*	13 Jul	**Zechariah**	
14:7–9*	3 Dec	5:15–6:6	18 Oct	4:1–3,12–14*	11 Dec
14:10–22	15 Feb	10:12*	4 Jan	6:13*	21 Sep
17:12–14*	16 Jun	11:1*	27 Dec	8:6*	28 Oct
17:14*	5 May	14:3*	24 Nov	10:12*	19 Sep
30:17*	2 Dec				
30:21*	6 Aug	**Joel**	–	**Malachi**	
31:33*	29 Oct			1:6–14	7 Oct
31:34*	22 Oct	**Amos**		3:3*	12 Jan
32:39*	9 Oct	5:1–15	8 Jan		
33:9*	25 Dec	7:10–17	10 Sep	**Matthew**	
44:1–30	26 Feb			1:1–17	26 Dec
45:1–5	11 Jan	**Obadiah**	–	1:18–2:6	27 Dec
50:4–5*	26 Nov			2:1–2,9–10*	24 Dec
		Jonah		2:14–15*	27 Dec
Lamentations		1:1–17	3 Aug	2:23*	9 Jun
1:12*	11 Sep	2:1–9	24 Jan	5:6–20	3 Feb
3:22–33	4 Dec	2:4*	13 Dec	5:15–16*	24 Apr
3:57*	7 Dec			5:18*	21 May
		Micah		6:10*	30 Apr
Ezekiel		6:8*	12 Sep	7:1–5	29 May
14:1–11	27 Oct	7:7*	18 Dec	7:7*	27 May
14:20*	29 Nov	7:19*	19 Nov	7:13–27	17 Jul
18:23,32*	18 Aug			8:27*	6 Oct
33:11*	18 Aug	**Nahum**	–	9:10–31	6 Mar
34:30–31*	2 Nov			9:21*	7 Nov
37:11–13*	30 Aug	**Habakkuk**		9:27–30*	9 Dec
40:4*	17 Jan	2:4*	11 Nov	9:35–10:7	23 Jun
43:12*	8 Sep	3:2*	18 May	10:5–16	29 Feb
				10:16–31	9 Mar
Daniel		**Zephaniah**		10:32–40	6 Sep
2:1–23	30 Sep	3:2*	30 Nov	11:16–30	7 Nov
9:1–21	13 Jul			11:28*	12 Jun
9:24*	24 Sep				

Scripture Index

12:3,5,7*	6 Dec	5:30–31*	9 Jan	10:21–22*	5 Dec		
12:10,13*	24 May	6:20*	19 Jan	10:38–11:13	1 Oct		
13:9–17	17 Jan	6:34–44	30 Oct	11:27–32	25 Jun		
13:12*	28 Jul	8:19–21*	30 Oct	11:31*	13 Feb		
14:22–33	24 May	9:14–29	10 Jun	11:37–52	30 Nov		
15:21–28	25 Mar	9:23*	14 Oct	12:1–12	23 Jan		
15:24–25*	31 Jul	10:13–16	16 Oct	13:6–9	31 Dec		
17:5–7*	24 Jun	10:49*	6 Mar	14:15–24	21 Apr		
17:14–21	29 Jan	12:28–34	9 Sep	15:4–6*	26 Mar		
18:1–14	24 Nov	12:34*	25 Jan	15:4–7*	29 Sep		
18:20*	4 Oct	14:6*	3 Nov	16:19–31	13 Sep		
21:15–16*	7 May	14:53–15:5	15 Mar	17:10*	6 Jun		
22:15–22	10 Feb	14:64*	8 Feb	17:12–14*	26 Jun		
25:1–13	27 Mar	15:20–21*	8 Oct	17:32*	24 Aug		
25:21,30*	6 Jun	15:43–46*	26 Jul	18:1–27	27 May		
25:35*	30 Dec			19:1–10	30 Dec		
26:62–68	27 Jul	**Luke**		19:41*	28 Nov		
27:1–26	22 Apr	1:26–38	22 Dec	21:5–33	1 Nov		
27:19*	26 Feb	1:32*	23 Dec	22:24–30	20 Jul		
27:24–25*	5 Mar	1:39–56	21 Dec	22:31–62	20 Feb		
27:27–30	27 Jul	1:46*	20 Dec	23:8–9*	19 Feb		
27:45–54	13 Aug	2:44*	3 Jun	24:25–47	6 Dec		
28:16–20	16 Jul	2:48–49*	25 Jun	24:28–29*	23 Apr		
		4:16–30	19 Jun	24:47*	14 Jun		
Mark		5:5*	16 Apr				
1:21–28*	10 Feb	5:17–32	19 Mar	**John**			
1:35–39*	14 Feb	6:32–34*	20 Feb	1:1–13	24 Dec		
2:23–3:6	21 May	6:46–49*	21 Jan	1:12*	30 Dec		
3:8*	21 Mar	7:38*	8 Jun	1:14–18	29 Dec		
4:26–29*	19 Apr	7:42*	16 Sep	1:43–46	9 Jun		
4:33–34*	16 Jul	8:4–18	24 Apr	1:50–51*	7 Jun		
4:35–41	9 Feb	8:26–39	6 Apr	2:7*	17 Dec		
4:41*	6 Oct	9:11*	16 Oct	3:1–18	19 Oct		
5:1–20	14 Dec	9:42*	10 Jun	4:1–15	4 Jul		
5:25–34	14 Oct	9:57–62	15 Dec	4:16–26	14 May		

Scripture Index

4:27–30*	10 Sep	14:21–31	26 Jan	9:8–19	12 Mar
5:11*	15 Jun	14:28*	6 Sep	9:36–43	7 Feb
5:19–30	25 May	15:1–17	26 May	10:14*	3 Jul
5:24*	29 Jan	15:5*	23 Oct	10:34–43	2 Aug
5:39–47	11 Oct	15:14*	8 Aug	10:42*	25 May
6:6*	2 Jun	16:7*	28 May	10:42–43*	30 May
6:29*	8 Dec	16:8–11*	25 Feb	12:1–24	15 Nov
6:35–47	31 Jul	16:25–33	17 Sep	13:1–4	11 Apr
6:37*	20 Aug	17:6–19	6 Jan	13:12*	31 May
6:47*	29 Jan	17:22–23*	4 May	13:26–41	8 Oct
6:60–71	2 Jun	17:26*	2 Jul	15:1–11	11 Feb
6:66–69*	5 Feb	18:38*	12 Feb	16:16–34	22 Mar
7:25–52	3 Dec	19:1–16	5 Mar	18:9–10*	15 Nov
7:38–39*	28 May	19:17*	8 Oct	19:2*	14 Jul
8:31–36	6 Jul	20:1–26	28 Mar	20:17–21:14	7 Jan
8:34–47	12 Feb	20:15*	31 Dec	20:24*	12 Aug
9:3–4*	23 Aug	20:24–31	21 Jun	22:1–16	2 May
9:39*	14 Aug	20:28*	13 Apr	24:1–21	25 Apr
10:7–30	16 Aug	20:30–31*	6 Nov	24:5*	9 Jun
10:16*	25 Mar	21:15*	15 Oct	24:22–27	1 Aug
11:3*	10 Jan	21:15–19	9 Aug	26:1–29	20 Nov
11:24–26*	13 Sep	21:20*	23 May	26:16–20*	6 Apr
11:26*	21 Nov			27:21–44	12 Jun
11:32–44	28 Nov	**Acts**			
11:43–44*	20 Apr	1:10–11*	28 Dec	**Romans**	
12:1–19	3 Nov	2:1*	1 Jun	1:7–15	2 Jan
12:20–36	13 May	2:2–4*	18 Sep	1:20–21*	18 Jan
12:32–33*	21 Jul	2:37–42	1 Apr	2:1–11	18 Aug
12:35–46	7 Sep	3:1–16	18 Jul	2:4*	1 Apr
13:1–17	6 Oct	3:17–26	28 Dec	2:17–3:8	19 Aug
13:3–5*	12 Oct	4:1–31	21 Mar	3:19–26	12 Aug
13:21–35	23 May	5:27–42	8 Feb	3:27–4:8	16 Sep
13:31–14:6	6 May	8:9–24	21 Jan	4:13–25	27 Apr
14:1–4*	23 Sep	8:26–39	1 Jan	5:1–11	31 Jan
14:15–23	20 Dec	8:30–33*	12 May	5:12–19	6 Aug

Scripture Index

5:15*	3 Apr	7:32*	29 Mar	2:21*	18 Apr		
6:1–11	9 Apr	8:1–13	18 Jan	3:1*	20 Jan		
6:3–4*	31 Oct	9:16–23	12 May	3:2*	11 Feb		
6:12–19	22 Aug	9:22*	1 Dec	3:6–14	11 Nov		
6:14–15*	19 Aug	10:1–12	23 Mar	3:23–4:7	24 Jun		
6:18*	6 Jul	10:14–22	2 Oct	4:3–6*	22 Dec		
7:12–25	29 Oct	11:1–22	8 Mar	4:12–20	17 Apr		
8:1–13	12 May	13:7*	5 Sep	4:19–31	18 Mar		
8:15–16*	23 Jan	14:1–25	14 Jul	5:6*	15 Aug		
8:24–25*	28 Aug	15:35–57	28 Aug	5:6*	12 Nov		
8:26–27*	11 Apr			5:13–26	12 Oct		
10:5–9*	7 Jan	**2 Corinthians**		5:22*	6 Feb		
10:5–13	4 Jan	1:3–11	5 Aug	5:22*	26 May		
10:14–21	23 Jul	1:9*	2 May	6:11–18	30 Jul		
11:1–12	14 Jun	2:12–17	14 Aug				
11:13–27	25 Dec	3:12–18	4 Jun	**Ephesians**			
12:1–13	8 Sep	4:3–4*	4 Jun	1:3–4*	9 Sep		
12:12*	23 Jun	4:6*	7 Sep	1:3–14	30 Jan		
13:11–14*	21 Aug	5:1*	6 May	1:6*	15 Jul		
14:7–18	15 Jul	5:1–10	23 Sep	1:7*	29 Aug		
14:10–12*	29 May	5:11–21	24 Sep	1:15–23	25 Jul		
15:1–6	7 Jul	8:1–17	24 Oct	2:1–10	30 Aug		
15:13–29	25 Oct	8:24*	26 Jan	2:7*	18 Jun		
		9:15*	25 Jul	2:8*	18 Jul		
1 Corinthians		10:5*	5 Apr	2:10*	7 Feb		
1:10–17	5 Jun	11:5–33	14 Feb	3:7–19	18 Jun		
1:17–2:5	5 Dec	12:1–10	2 Nov	3:19*	25 Oct		
1:18*	30 Jul	12:14–21	12 Jul	3:20–21	16 May		
2:6–13	20 May	13:1–14	14 Apr	4:7–14	13 Nov		
2:14–3:4	18 Nov	13:3–5*	12 Jul	4:15–25	22 Nov		
3:6–9*	5 Jun			4:25–5:2	5 Sep		
3:10–17	9 Nov	**Galatians**		5:1*	12 Apr		
3:11*	14 Sep	1:1–12	20 Jan	5:3–14	25 Feb		
6:9–11	9 Jan	1:11–24	11 Jul	6:7*	20 Jul		
6:19–20*	22 Aug	2:20*	22 May	6:10–17	8 Apr		

389

Scripture Index

6:18–20	30 Jun	**2 Thessalonians**		7:23–28	24 Mar
		1:1–12	19 Jul	8:1–6	29 Apr
Philippians		1:10*	7 Apr	8:6–9:5	22 Sep
1:12–18	5 Jul	2:16–17*	13 Jun	8:12*	22 Oct
1:19–26	3 Mar	3:6–13	16 Apr	9:6–14	13 Oct
2:1–11	23 Dec			9:11–28	17 Mar
2:12–18	25 Sep	**1 Timothy**		9:13–14*	29 Jun
3:2–9	18 Apr	1:1–7	25 Aug	9:20*	14 Nov
3:8–16	20 Mar	1:13*	20 Nov	10:1–10	16 Mar
4:1–13	6 Feb	1:15–17*	26 Dec	10:10*	24 Mar
4:19*	15 Sep	2:1–7	3 Apr	10:11–22	11 Mar
		2:3–4*	16 Jan	10:17*	22 Oct
Colossians		4:6–16	10 Nov	10:26–31	15 Jan
1:9–10*	30 Sep	6:6–12	29 Mar	11:8–16	31 Mar
1:11–23	13 Feb			11:13–14*	8 May
1:23*	27 Aug	**2 Timothy**		11:31–40	11 Dec
1:24–2:10	15 Sep	2:8*	9 Apr	11:37*	14 Mar
1:27*	13 May	2:15–22	1 Mar	12:5–11	12 Jan
2:8–15	2 Apr	3:1–9	23 Oct	12:12–17	17 Oct
2:20–3:5	30 Apr	3:10–17	15 Oct	12:22–24*	5 Nov
3:1–2*	28 Mar	4:1–18	10 Apr	12:28–29*	15 Jan
3:5–17	21 Aug			13:7–16	12 Nov
3:15*	14 Apr	**Titus**		13:17–21	27 Jan
4:2–12	9 May	2:11–3:7	13 Jun		
4:7–17	24 Jul			**James**	
		Philemon		1:2–4*	4 Feb
1 Thessalonians		1–7	21 Oct	2:14–26	22 May
1:1–10	9 Dec			3:1–12	3 Jul
1:9–10*	27 Oct	**Hebrews**		4:1–10	17 Aug
2:1–13	21 Jul	1:1–2:4	8 Jul	4:2–3*	1 Oct
2:13–20	19 May	2:9*	19 Dec	4:14*	30 Mar
3:8*	2 Jan	3:7–19	3 Oct	5:7–11	21 Feb
3:11–4:10	26 Mar	6:13–20	20 Aug	5:13–16	10 Jan
		7:2*	3 Feb		
		7:20–22*	29 Apr		

Scripture Index

1 Peter		2:13–14*	8 Apr	14–23	1 Dec		
1:3–9	15 Aug	2:13–14*	18 Nov	24–25	7 Apr		
1:9–12*	22 Feb	2:15–17	28 Jul				
1:22–2:2	29 Jul	3:1–18	2 Jul	**Revelation**			
2:4–10	14 Sep	3:8*	1 Jul	1:1–8	3 Jan		
2:18–25	17 May	3:19–4:1	26 Jun	1:5–6*	1 Sep		
3:6*	28 Apr	4:1–17	4 May	1:9–20	8 Jun		
3:18–4:6	31 Oct	4:10–11*	18 Feb	1:17*	9 Mar		
4:12–19	4 Feb	4:19–5:3	15 Jun	3:8,10*	6 Jan		
5:1–7	12 Sep	5:1–12	6 Nov	3:14–22	4 Aug		
5:6*	19 Mar	5:13*	19 Jul	3:17–18*	3 Sep		
5:10*	20 May	5:13–21	15 May	6:12–17	26 Oct		
				7:16–17*	20 Sep		
2 Peter		**2 John**		11:19*	22 Sep		
1:1–11	4 Oct	1–4	16 Jan	12:1–17	27 Jun		
1:16–2:3	5 Jan			12:12*	1 Nov		
2:17–22	5 Feb	**3 John**		21:6*	4 Jul		
		1–12	12 Apr	21:22–22:5	19 Dec		
1 John				21:27*	27 Mar		
1:5–10	27 Sep	**Jude**		22:3*	31 Mar		
2:6*	17 May	1–4	26 Jul	22:17*	10 Jul		
2:12–13*	18 Mar	3*	10 Apr	22:21*	29 Dec		

Where Spurgeon Preached

Where Spurgeon preached

1. Location of numbers (in order of appearance)

The Metropolitan Tabernacle, Newington (349)

1472–1505, 1507–8, 1510–7, 1519, 1521–32, 1534–95, 1597–1696, 1698–1733, 1738–9, 1741–9, 1751–3, 1755–6, 1758–61, 1763–77, 1779–84, 1786–91, 1793–1815, 1817, 1819, 1821–34, 1837, 1851, 1871–2, 2000, 2065–6, 2071

Mentone (3)

1509 (written), 1518, 1757

Shoreditch Tabernacle (1)

1533 (Tuesday 9/3/1880)

Exeter Hall (11)

1596, 1734–7, 1740, 1750, 1754, 1762, 1778, 1792

Unplaced (1)

1634(b)

Union Chapel, Islington (1)

1785 (Wednesday 7/5/1884)

2. Time of numbers

The time of most sermons is given on the title page; that of the undated sermons is in most cases indicated by internal references. Most of the sermons were preached on **the Lord's Day in the morning**; the exceptions are as follows:—

Sunday afternoon (1)—1757

Sunday evening (37)—1475, 1489, 1508, 1511, 1579, 1600, 1620, 1635, 1640, 1646, 1657, 1688, 1691, 1712, 1717, 1740, 1746, 1750, 1754, 1760, 1762, 1768, 1770, 1792, 1811, 1821, 1826–7, 1830–2, 1834, 1851, 1871, 2000, 2065–6

Tuesday evening (1)—1533

Wednesday morning (2)—1596, 1778

Wednesday evening (1)—1785

Thursday evening (49)—1485, 1496, 1517, 1566, 1588, 1595, 1605, 1615, 1626, 1629–30, 1632–4(a), 1649–50, 1670, 1680, 1686, 1690, 1692–6, 1706, 1722, 1729–30, 1732, 1755, 1761, 1769, 1796–8, 1805, 1809–10, 1819, 1822–5, 1828–9, 1833, 1872, 2071

Undated afternoon (1)—1518

Where Spurgeon Preached

Undated evenings, probably Sunday or Thursday (34)—1503, 1507, 1512-4, 1516, 1521, 1527, 1543, 1547-8, 1556, 1558-9, 1563, 1565, 1573, 1577, 1580, 1583, 1585, 1589, 1628, 1651-2, 1661, 1733, 1756, 1758-9, 1763, 1767, 1814, 1837 (wrongly dated—see below)

Undated & untimed (probably Sunday or Thursday evenings) (16)—1504, 1510, 1515, 1519, 1522, 1546, 1560, 1569, 1574-6, 1578, 1634(b), 1656, 1671, 1718

Written (1)—1509

3. Sermons preached on behalf of societies etc.

London Hospitals—1479 (15/6/1879), 1542 (13/6/1880), [1664 (11/6/1882), 1725 (10/6/1883), 1786 (15/6/1884)]

Centenary of Sabbath Schools—1545 (27/6/1880)

Baptist Missionary Society—1596 (Wednesday 27/4/1881), 1655 (23/4/1882), 1778 (Wednesday 30/4/1884)

Luther commemorations—1749-50

Sunday School Union—1785 (Wednesday 7/5/1884)

4. Dating of undated sermons (see revised appendix)

N.B. One evening sermon seems to be incorrectly dated—1837 is unlikely to have been preached on 2 June 1884, which would have been a Monday, when the weekly Prayer meeting was held. It may be the missing sermon preached on the evening of Sunday 22 June 1884.

5. Contents of volumes used in this compilation

Vol. 25 nos. 1472-1505, 1507-1510

Vol. 26 nos. 1511-1519, 1521-1574

Vol. 27 nos. 1575-1636

Vol. 28 nos. 1637-1696

Vol. 29 nos. 1698-1756

Vol. 30 nos. 1757-1815

Vol. 31 nos. 1817, 1819, 1821-1834, 1837, 1851, 1871, 1872

Vol. 33 no. 2000

Vol. 35 nos. 2065, 2066, 2071

393

Dating of undated sermons (revised and expanded)

72–73: Both of these sermons are dated Sunday morning 30 March 1856 and contain internal references to being preached in the morning. G.H. Pike, *The life and work of Charles Haddon Spurgeon*, vol. 2, pp. 223–6 preserves an eye-witness account which confirms that **72** is correctly dated; the evening sermon on that day was not **73**. Possibly this was preached on the next Sunday morning 6 April 1856 which is unusually unrepresented.

616: This evening sermon indicates that the sermon preached in the morning considered God's calling to receive Christ and to walk in him, which was the theme of **483,** the sermon on Colossians 2:6 preached on the morning of 7 December 1862.

766: A footnote to **3017,** preached on Thursday 1 August 1867, identifies **766** as the sermon preached on the previous Sunday evening, thus dating it to 28 July 1867.

767–768: G.H. Pike, *The life and work of Charles Haddon Spurgeon,* vol. 4, pp. 200–1 records that, during the renovations carried out at the Metropolitan Tabernacle in March and April 1867 when the Agricultural Hall was used instead on Sunday mornings, an offer of Surrey Chapel for the weekday meetings was gladly accepted. **756,** preached at Surrey Chapel on 21 March 1867, would have been the first of the Thursday sermons and the undated evening sermons **767–8,** also preached there, must have been on subsequent Thursday evenings. The sermon preached at Surrey Chapel on Thursday 4 April 1867 appears in *The Sword and the Trowel,* March and April 1899.

993: A footnote identifies **980,** preached on 12 March 1871, as the other sermon about Jeremiah mentioned as having been preached recently. Spurgeon's absence through sickness for most of April and the whole of May and June means that **993** must have been preached in late March or early April 1871.

1022: In this undated sermon published in 1871 Spurgeon indicates that he had spoken on the words 'Ye shall die in your sins' (John 8:21,24) 'the other Sunday night'. This clearly relates to the striking last section of **3043,** the Sunday evening sermon of 8 October 1871. **1022** must have been preached between mid October and late November 1871 when Spurgeon left for the continent.

1037: In this undated sermon published in 1872 Spurgeon indicates that on the previous Sunday evening he had spoken on the fact that Christians are saved with great difficulty. This appears to relate to **3047,** the sermon on 1 Peter 4:18 preached on the evening of 15 October 1871. **1037** seems to be the evening sermon of 22 October 1871.

Dating of undated sermons (revised and expanded)

1117: This evening sermon includes a reference to a hymn quoted earlier that day in the morning sermon; the same hymn is quoted in **1112,** preached on the morning of 18 May 1873.

1123: A suggestion that Luke 19:10 was considered 'not long ago' appears to refer back to **1100** preached on 9 March 1873. **1123** was published in July 1873 and would seem to have been preached in the period between.

1174: This evening sermon is said by Spurgeon to be exactly 24 years since his baptism which was on 3 May 1850, thus dating it to 3 May 1874.

1212–1213: A footnote to **1213** indicates that **1212** was preached on the previous Thursday evening, thus dating **1213** to either the following Sunday evening or Thursday evening. **1212** also contains a reference to the likeness of a child to its father being in some points a caricature, a point mentioned in **1194** (Sunday morning 20 September 1874) as also having been made on the previous Thursday. Thus **1212** was preached on Thursday 17 September 1874 and **1213** on the evening of either Sunday 20 or Thursday 24 September 1874, no other sermons of Spurgeon being allocated to either of these. However, a newspaper report on 23 September 1874, quoted by G.H. Pike, *The life and work of Charles Haddon Spurgeon,* vol. 5, pp. 138–9, would appear to rule out the sermon preached on the evening of Sunday 20 September.

1239: G.H. Pike, *The life and work of Charles Haddon Spurgeon,* vol. 5, p. 154 dates this sermon to the evening of Sunday 16 May 1875.

1259: This evening sermon includes a reference to a point made in the morning sermon of the same day to the effect that that 'the more grace a man has the lower he lies before God'. The same point is found in **1256** (Sunday morning 26 September 1875) where Spurgeon likens good men to ships—'the fuller these are the lower they sink'.

1265: A footnote to this evening sermon links it to **1207,** the sermon preached that morning (Sunday 13 December 1874).

1336: A reference to a sermon preached on Matthew 11:28 'the other night' appears to point back to **1322** preached Sunday evening 22 October 1876. **1336** was probably preached on Thursday 26 October 1876, no other sermon being attributed to that evening.

1393: A footnote to this evening sermon links it to **1388,** the sermon preached that morning (Sunday 9 December 1877).

1466: This sermon, published early in 1879 and preached on an occasion when the

395

Dating of undated sermons (revised and expanded)

Tabernacle was vacated by the regular hearers, probably relates to such an occasion on the evening of 11 August 1878, as noted in *The Sword and the Trowel*, September 1878.

1506: A footnote to this evening sermon links it to **1416,** the sermon preached that morning (Sunday 26 May 1878).

1511: This short evening sermon published at the very beginning of 1880 was followed by a farewell address by Spurgeon's son Thomas. Such a valedictory address appears in *The Sword and the Trowel,* January 1896 and was delivered on 28 September 1879 just before Thomas Spurgeon's second voyage to Australia. Thomas Spurgeon referred to his father's morning sermon, identified by a footnote as **1497**, preached earlier that Sunday.

1520: Footnotes to this evening sermon link it to **1439,** the sermon preached that morning (Sunday 20 October 1878).

1574: In this sermon published at the end of 1880 Spurgeon says 'almost the last time I stood here' he 'spoke of Peter from the words—"When he thought thereon, he wept"'. This refers to Mark 14:72, the text of **2735,** preached on the evening of Sunday 24 October 1880. **1574** would appear to have been preached at the end of October or early in November 1880.

1577: Spurgeon had 'lately' spoken on the words 'Who forgiveth all thine iniquities', the theme of **1492**, preached on 31 August 1879.

1652: During this undated evening sermon published in 1882 Spurgeon remarks, 'I cannot get at any of my books, for they are all packed away', probably identifying this as one of the evening sermons unaccounted for at or around the time of his move to Norwood in the first half of August 1880.

1656: This undated sermon, published at about the end of April 1882, contains a reference to the gospel still being true 'in the year "eighteen hundred and eighty-two"', thus dating it to early 1882.

1693: In this undated Thursday evening sermon published in 1882 Spurgeon refers to the difficulties householders had been experiencing while completing their census forms; he also describes his reading of Colossians 3 on the previous Sunday morning. However, his description of his reading of Colossians 3:15 aptly reflects the exposition of that chapter attached to **2679**, preached on Sunday evening 10 April 1881, which was a week after the taking of the 1881 census. Allowing for a slight editorial lapse some twenty months after the event, **1693** would seem to be the missing sermon preached on Thursday 14 April 1881.

Dating of undated sermons (revised and expanded)

1694: In this Thursday evening sermon, published at the end of 1882, reference is made back to the prayerful response to the 'fearful assassinations in Ireland.' G.H. Pike, *The life and work of Charles Haddon Spurgeon* vol. 6, p. 262 indicates that on Sunday 14 May 1882 Spurgeon prayed for Ireland in the wake of the murders of Lord Cavendish, the new Chief Secretary to the Lord-Lieutenant of Ireland, and of Burke, the permanent Irish Under-secretary, in Phoenix Park, Dublin. This sermon was therefore preached on one of the unrepresented Thursdays between late May and November 1882.

1697: This sermon was preached at the opening of the original Trinity Road Chapel on the afternoon of Thursday 27 September 1877.

1717: This sermon, for which 'the regular hearers left their seats to be occupied by strangers', was published in 1883 and seems to relate to such an occasion on the evening of 11 June 1882. *The Sword and the Trowel*, July 1882 notes that the event gave 'proof that when Christ is lifted up, men are drawn to him', a clear vindication of the text of **1717** (John 12:32–33).

1762: This undated evening sermon was preached at Exeter Hall. From 12 August to 2 September 1883 Sunday services were held at Exeter Hall during repairs to the Metropolitan Tabernacle. The four morning sermons (**1734–7**) are all dated, as are two of the evening ones—**1754** (12 August 1883) and **1740** (2 September 1883). **1762** appears to be the evening sermon of either 19 or 26 August 1883. The Thursday meetings seem to have been held at Christ Church, Westminster Bridge Road where **2597** and **2599** were preached on Thursdays 23 and 30 August respectively. **2600** (Thursday 6 September 1883) marked the reopening of the Metropolitan Tabernacle.

1997: A footnote to **2492**, preached on 7 November 1886, indicates that **1997** (dated Autumn 1886) was the sermon mentioned as having been preached in the evening two weeks previously, thus dating it to Sunday evening 24 October 1886.

2000: The 'two thousandth published sermon' is dated 9 May 1880 in C.H. Spurgeon, *Messages to the multitude,* and was the evening sermon on that day.

2021: This undated evening sermon is identified in a footnote to the exposition attached to **2375**, preached on 24 June 1888, as another sermon on Nathanael preached 'a short time ago'. It was published about the end of April 1888 and probably relates to one of the unrepresented dates in that month.

2177: This undated sermon, published after the death of William Olney in October 1890, is said to have been preached on a Thursday evening before Spurgeon left

Dating of undated sermons (revised and expanded)

for his winter's rest. Internal references indicate that William Olney was present and that Spurgeon had known the congregation for 36 years. He first preached at New Park Street Chapel in December 1853 and the various factors would seem to date **2177** to Thursday 21 November 1889 just before his winter holiday at Mentone. A letter attached to **2117** and dated Mentone, Nov. 28 1889 announced his safe arrival. However, G.H. Pike, *The life and work of Charles Haddon Spurgeon,* vol. 6 p. 312 states 'On November 17 he preached for the last time before going to his winter retreat'.

2210: This sermon on Ephesians 2:9–10 contrasts 'not of works' with 'created in Christ Jesus unto good works', and can be dated to Thursday 30 August 1888 by a reference at the start of **2042**, preached on 2 September 1888, to the effect that this theme had been dealt with 'last Thursday evening'. Spurgeon had discussed the supposed difference between the doctrines of faith and of the new birth 'not long ago', in fact only the previous Sunday evening, 26 August 1888 (no. **2386**)!

2288: This sermon was preached 'On a Christmas Day Evening' and is described internally as being 'on this last Sabbath night of another year'. All but one of the relevant years in which Christmas Day fell on a Sunday can be ruled out: 1859 by a reminiscence of the New Park Street days, 1864 and 1881 by already being accounted for, 1887 by Spurgeon's absence abroad. By process of elimination **2288** seems to have been preached on the evening of Christmas Day 1870.

2448: Spurgeon's description of a burial at Abney Park Cemetery the previous day matches that of Mrs Orsman, as described by G.H. Pike, *The life and work of Charles Haddon Spurgeon,* vol. 4 p. 305. Mrs Orsman died in mid-January 1869 and the sermon appeared in *The Baptist Messenger* in 1870.

2651: Though dated Autumn 1857, due to its appearance in the 1857 *Baptist Messenger*, this sermon had been added to an editorial leader in the *Patriot Newspaper* and there dated Sunday evening 23 September 1855.

2664: In this evening sermon preached early in 1858 Spurgeon reports that on the next Sunday a place with disreputable connections would be opened for a Sabbath concert in connection with the preaching of the gospel and that 'The Messiah will be performed as the great inducement for attracting them.' A footnote identifies the venue as the 'Alhambra Palace' and adds that the experiment was abandoned after one attempt as being likely to do more harm than good. The Alhambra palace had once been used for exhibitions but first opened as a theatre on 18 March 1858. Beyond that it has proved impossible to track down the date of the concert. I

Dating of undated sermons (revised and expanded)

am grateful to Jane Pritchard of the Theatre Museum for providing a reference from *The Globe*, 6 April 1858, which reports that 'A week or two there was preaching, but the Nonconformist minister who undertook to conduct the special services, did not like his name being mixed up with applications for spirit licenses, dancing, and such secular affairs, and he withdrew his countenance and his oratory.'

2703: A footnote to this Thursday evening sermon (dated 1855) identifies **47**, preached 21 October 1855, as the sermon preached on the same text on a former occasion, thus placing **2703** towards the end of the year.

2815: In this sermon, preached at New Park Street Chapel on a Sunday evening early in 1861, Spurgeon remarks that he had lately been in Glasgow, which he had visited during a tour of the North and Scotland in March 1861. The only Sunday evening unaccounted for between this tour and the move to the Metropolitan Tabernacle at the end of March is 17 March 1861. **2811**, preached on Sunday evening 24 March 1861, was the final sermon at New Park Street Chapel (but see **3242** below); **368**, preached on Sunday morning 31 March 1861, was at Exeter Hall.

2836: This sermon is said to have been preached at the 100th anniversary of Amersham Baptist Chapel in November 1857. I am grateful to Sarah Charlton, Archivist at the Centre for Buckinghamshire Studies, for providing more specific details from *The Buckinghamshire Advertiser,* 28 November 1857. The history of the Baptist churches in Amersham is quite complex and 1857 does not seem to have been a centenary for any of them, but it is recorded that 'the Anniversary Sermons of "The Old Baptist Chapel" were to be preached by the Rev. C.H. Spurgeon, at two and six o'clock, on Tuesday, the 24th of November.' **2836** was the sermon preached in the evening; the description of the afternoon sermon on 1 Thessalonians 5:6 seems to indicate that it was a repetition of **163,** preached on 15 November 1857 at the Music Hall, Royal Surrey Gardens.

2875: This sermon's original appearance as an 1854 *Penny Pulpit* narrows it down to the opening months of Spurgeon's ministry that year.

2896: This sermon (dated August 1854) was the first of Spurgeon's sermons to be printed. G.H. Pike, *The life and work of Charles Haddon Spurgeon,* vol. 1, pp. 135–143, dates it to Sunday morning 20 August 1854 and describes the occasion at length.

2924: This sermon is dated 1862 and was preached on a Sunday evening. Spurgeon indicates that he had preached in the morning to the chief of sinners and

Dating of undated sermons (revised and expanded)

notes that some of his congregation may have been in London to visit the Great Exhibition, which opened on 1 May 1862, or to attend the Handel Festival, which took place on 23, 25 and 27 June 1862 (see Michael Musgrave, *The musical life of the Crystal Palace* (C.U.P. 1995) pp. 215–6). **2924** would appear to be the evening sermon of 29 June 1862, the morning sermon on that day being **458**, entitled 'The friend of sinners'. I am grateful to the Gerald Coke Handel Collection (housed at the Foundling Museum, London) and to the curator of the Crystal Palace Museum for providing the dates of the 1862 Handel Festival.

2929: This sermon is dated 1862 and was preached on a Sunday evening. Spurgeon indicates that he had preached in the morning on 'Repent ye, and believe in the gospel', the text of **460,** preached on Sunday morning 13 July 1862.

3048: This sermon was preached on a Sunday morning in 1856 and entitled 'The Holy Spirit in the Covenant'. Spurgeon looks back to two earlier sermons, 'God in the Covenant' (**93**) and 'Christ in the Covenant' (**103**) preached on 3 and 31 August 1856 respectively. Only the evening sermons of Sundays 21 and 28 September are accounted for; **3048** may have been on the morning of either of these. No sermons are recorded for Sundays 5 and 12 October.

3050: This sermon is dated 1863, but Spurgeon's comment that he commenced his pastorate eleven years earlier would place it in 1865. The publishers inserted a footnote referring to those eleven years as 1854–1865. **3050** also appears in the 1865 volume of the *Baptist Messenger,* the periodical which seems to have been the source for many of the partly-dated posthumously-published sermons from Spurgeon's early years.

3114: This sermon's original appearance as an 1854 *Penny Pulpit* narrows it down to the opening months of Spurgeon's ministry that year.

3120: This undated morning sermon was preached at New Park Street Chapel and entitled 'A view of God's glory'. G.H. Pike, *The life and work of Charles Haddon Spurgeon,* vol. 1, pp. 125–6 refers to it as one of the earliest published sermons and includes an excerpt derived from *The Penny Pulpit,* 1854. The sermon appears in the first volume of a representative collection of sermons from *The Penny pulpit* published in 1886 and is there dated 17 September 1854.

3137: Spurgeon's call for a day of prayer and fasting in respect of 'this cattle disease' may relate to the cattle plague of 1865 which prompted J.C. Ryle to write his famous tract *The finger of God*. This sermon appears in *The Baptist Messenger* for 1866.

Dating of undated sermons (revised and expanded)

3155–3156: These were the first two sermons in an unfinished series on the Beatitudes in 1873. The third sermon (second Beatitude) is not represented in the published sermons, but the fourth to sixth (**3065, 3157, 3158** on the third to fifth Beatitudes) were preached on the evenings of Thursday 11, Sunday 14 and Sunday 21 December 1873 respectively. It is likely that **3155–6** were preached around the end of November 1873.

3167: This sermon is dated 1866 and was preached on a Sunday evening. Spurgeon indicates that in the morning he had spoken about 'the hope that salvation was possible', which seems to relate to **684**, entitled 'Hope, yet no hope. No hope, yet hope', preached on Sunday morning 8 April 1866.

3170: During this sermon Spurgeon relates that on the previous day, after months of prayer, he was talking with a friend when a letter arrived giving notification of an anonymous gift of £1,000 for the Stockwell Orphanage. The event is recorded in *C.H. Spurgeon's Autobiography,* vol. 3, p. 175 as having taken place on 20 November 1867, thus dating **3170** to Thursday 21 November 1867.

3185: This undated evening sermon, first published in the 1867 *Baptist Messenger*, refers to 'limpets clinging to the rocks.' In **3454**, preached on Thursday 6 September 1866, Spurgeon indicates that on the previous Sunday he had spoken of 'limpets at the seaside, sitting on the rocks.' Thus **3185** appears to have been preached on the evening of Sunday 2 September 1866.

3231/3283: Internal references indicate that both these Metropolitan Tabernacle sermons were preached on a New Year's Day. The only relevant Sunday and Thursday services not accounted for by dated sermons are Thursdays 1 January 1863 and 1874. **3231** also refers back to the building of the Orphanage, which was founded in 1867. Thus it would appear that **3231** was on Thursday 1 January 1874 (the previously published sermon was **3230**, preached on Sunday evening 28 December 1873); **3283** would have been on Thursday 1 January 1863.

3242: New Park Street Chapel is given as the location of this sermon, preached on Tuesday 17 November 1863, well over two years after the move to the Metropolitan Tabernacle. This is not a mistake! New Park Street Chapel continued to be used until the end of the summer of 1866, when the now small congregation 'finally took leave of the building' (see G.H. Pike, *The life and work of Charles Haddon Spurgeon,* vol. 3, pp. 179–80).

3283: See 3231 above.

3291: Extracts from this evening sermon on Psalm 95:5, preached at the

Dating of undated sermons (revised and expanded)

Metropolitan Tabernacle on behalf of the British and Foreign Sailors' Society, are reproduced in *Sunday at Home,* 1880 pp. 738–41 and the date is given as 6 May 1880. A brief footnote at the end of **1539** reveals that this special sermon was also published separately at the time in May 1880. Other sermons preached on behalf of the society are **2206** and **3321**.

3294/3300: These Thursday evening sermons are wrongly dated 1886, but fit naturally into a chronological sequence of sermons from 1866 posthumously published in volume 58 of the *Metropolitan Tabernacle Pulpit* (see also **3369**).

3309: This is said to be the seventh sermon in a series on Christ's glorious achievements. In Spurgeon's book of the same title the fifth sermon is an addition to the original series, being **273** from the *New Park Street Pulpit* and listed in a footnote to **3309**, while the sixth sermon was originally presented by Spurgeon as the fifth in the series (**1325–1329**), preached on consecutive Sunday mornings from 19 November to 17 December 1876. **3309** would appear to have been originally the sixth and last sermon in the series, but to have been renumbered seventh posthumously to allow for the addition of **273**; the text of **3309** (Luke 19:10) would have been appropriate for the evening of Christmas Eve 1876, the morning sermon having been on a Christmas theme instead of the then current series.

3323: In this evening sermon Spurgeon refers back to the previous Sunday evening when his text had been Romans 13:11. This could be a reference to **857**, preached on Sunday evening 27 December 1868. Internal remarks such as 'during the past year' and 'Here is a blessed thing to think of all the year round' suggest that **3323** was preached at the turn of the year, either on Thursday 31 December 1868 or Sunday 3 January 1869. It appears in the 1869 *Baptist Messenger*.

3350: This was the inaugural address at the Annual Conference of the Pastors' College Association at Devonshire Square Chapel, Stoke Newington and dated 1887. G.H. Pike, *The life and work of Charles Haddon Spurgeon* vol.6, p. 285 indicates that the conference began on 18 April 1887.

3369: This sermon is confirmed as being on Thursday 4 October 1866, not 1886 as printed, by a reference to the forthcoming day of prayer and fasting on Monday 5 November 1866 (see G.H. Pike, *The life and work of Charles Haddon Spurgeon,* vol. 3, p. 187).

3370: A note in *The Sword and the Trowel,* August 1890, dates this address at the 1890 Mildmay Park Conference to the morning of Thursday 26 June.

Dating of undated sermons (revised and expanded)

3389: In this evening sermon on John 5:25 Spurgeon indicates that he had preached on the same chapter in the morning—'we saw in the chapter a three-fold gradation of life-giving in the person of Christ'. The three points involved the raising of the physically dead, the giving of life to the spiritually dead and the universal resurrection. This three-fold description can be found in **896,** preached on John 5:28–29 on Sunday morning 17 October 1869.

3397: This sermon was preached in June. The morning sermon had been on the subject of the Holy Spirit and could have been either **574** (Sunday 12 June 1864) or **754** (Whit Sunday 9 June 1867). The latter appears more likely as the publishers incorporated several sermons from 1867 at this time (e.g. **3373, 3384, 3392, 3401**), but none from 1864.

3412: On the previous Sunday night Spurgeon had mentioned that a young person had attended the Tabernacle for two years without anybody ever speaking to her and he had said that he was ashamed of some of his congregation. The point is to be found in **790,** preached on Sunday evening 29 December 1867. **3412** was preached on Thursday 2 January 1868, said to be a wintry and snowy night.

3434: This sermon is said to have been preached at the Metropolitan Tabernacle on Sunday evening 21 February 1861. However, 21 February was a Thursday and services did not commence at the Metropolitan Tabernacle until the end of March 1861! (**886** is also described as being on a Sunday but carries a correct date for a Thursday, while **3398** and **3531** are described as being on Thursdays but carry correct dates for Sundays.)

3441: A footnote indicates that **512** (preached 31 May 1863) had been more than 8 years previously. The presence of **3441** at the end of the *Baptist Messenger* for 1871 places it late in that year.

3443: This Thursday evening sermon is dated 9 September 1896, an obvious misprint for 9 September 1869!

3446: This sermon appeared in advertisements in 1856.

3457: A footnote to this Sunday evening sermon indicates that the morning sermon on the day was **678,** preached on Sunday morning 25 February 1866. **3457** certainly refers back to **678,** but **3296** is also dated Sunday evening 25 February 1866! (Duplication of dates also occurs on 30 March 1856 (see **72–3** above), 22 April 1860, 29 July 1866, 16 January 1870 and 26 February 1871. **3415** and **3509** are double-booked for Sunday 27 June 1868, a totally incorrect date!)

ATTU4: This is the only dateable sermon among the twenty undated evening

403

Dating of undated sermons (revised and expanded)

sermons comprising Spurgeon's *Able to the Uttermost,* published in 1922 as a follow-up after publication of the *Metropolitan Tabernacle Pulpit* had ceased in 1917. Spurgeon says that the previous Friday was exactly 22 years after his baptism, which was on 3 May 1850, thus dating this communion sermon to Sunday evening 5 May 1872. The likelihood that **ATTU11** was the as yet unpublished sermon on Psalm 85:8 preached 'on a Thursday evening in June 1872' (see W. Williams, *Personal Reminiscences of Charles Haddon Spurgeon,* p. 24) raises the possibility that the publishers of *Able to the Uttermost* continued to use sermons from 1872, the year which accounts for twelve of the last seventeen dated sermons in the final two volumes of the *Metropolitan Tabernacle Pulpit.*

Spurgeon's one hundred best hymns

In September 1866 Spurgeon's *Our Own Hymnbook* was published, but it was not until June 1873 (sermon 1116) that the published weekly sermon began to include the numbers of the hymns sung on each occasion. This practice continued for the vast majority of the sermons published for the remainder of Spurgeon's lifetime and for some years continued into the sermons published after his death. However, the regularity of sermons carrying hymn numbers gradually decreased until volume 53 (1907) which contained only one sermon with hymns (no. 3031). Thereafter hymn numbers were again absent from the final ten volumes of the *Metropolitan Tabernacle Pulpit*.

The following tables show the one hundred most used hymns at those services for which the relevant information is available, beginning with the most frequent. Thirty of the top hundred are by Isaac Watts! His hymns account for no less than 249 (22%) of the entries in the book.

31 times (1)
538   There is life for a look at the Crucified One—(Amelia Matilda Hull)

30 times (1)
708   My heart is resting, O my God—(Anna Laetitia Waring)

27 times (1)
658   Oh happy day, that fixed my choice—(Philip Doddridge)

25 times (2)
551   Jesu, lover of my soul—(Charles Wesley)
670   I'm not ashamed to own my Lord—(Isaac Watts)

24 times (1)
674   Stand up! Stand up for Jesus!—(George Duffield)

23 times (5)
196   Awake my soul, in joyful lays—(Samuel Medley)
229   The God of Abraham praise—(Thomas Olivers)
282   When I survey the wondrous cross—(Isaac Watts)
660   When I had wandered from His fold—(John S.B. Monsell)
668   Lord, through the desert drear and wide—(Mary Bowly)

Spurgeon's one hundred best hymns

21 times (1)
552	Rock of Ages, cleft for me—(Augustus M. Toplady)

20 times (5)
30	I will exalt Thee, Lord of hosts—(Charles H. Spurgeon)
416	Glory to God on high!—(James Allen)
728	Behold what wondrous grace—(Isaac Watts)
775	Where God doth dwell, sure heaven is there—(John Mason)
785	Jesus, these eyes have never seen—(Ray Palmer)

19 times (2)
202	Great God of wonders! all Thy ways—(Samuel Davies)
605	Come, let us to the Lord our God—(John Morrison)

18 times (4)
257	Hark, the glad sound, the Saviour comes—(Philip Doddridge)
607	Lord, I hear of showers of blessing—(Elizabeth Codner)
766	When wilt Thou come unto me, Lord?—(Thomas Shepherd)
917	My Lord, my love, was crucified—(John Mason)

17 times (9)
191	Praise, everlasting praise, be paid—(Isaac Watts)
233	Grace! 'tis a charming sound!—(Philip Doddridge & A.M. Toplady)
289	Nature with open volume stands—(Isaac Watts)
331	Jesus, the name high over all—(Charles Wesley)
397	Jesus, Thy blood and righteousness—(Count Zinzendorf tr. Wesley)
412	Behold the glories of the Lamb—(Isaac Watts)
427	Come, let us sing the song of songs—(James Montgomery)
645	Oh for a heart to praise my God—(Charles Wesley)
649	I want a principle within—(Charles Wesley)

16 times (11)
214	When all Thy mercies, O my God—(Joseph Addison)
262	My dear Redeemer and my Lord—(Isaac Watts)
483	Christ and His cross is all our theme—(Isaac Watts)

488	Let every mortal ear attend—(Isaac Watts)
533	The moment a sinner believes—(Joseph Hart)
544	Mercy is welcome news indeed—(Joseph Hart)
560	I heard the voice of Jesus say—(Horatius Bonar)
686	Give to the winds thy fears—(Paul Gerhardt tr. Wesley)
734	Begone, unbelief, my Saviour is near—(John Newton)
797	O love divine, how sweet Thou art!—(Charles Wesley)
912	Lord of the Sabbath, hear our vows—(Philip Doddridge)

15 times (5)

249	Ere the blue heavens were stretched abroad—(Isaac Watts)
486	Let everlasting glories crown—(Isaac Watts)
555	Not all the blood of beasts—(Isaac Watts)
663	Jesus, spotless Lamb of God—(James George Deck)
909	This is the day the Lord hast made—(Isaac Watts)

14 times (10)

317	Sing, O heavens! O earth, rejoice!—(John S.B. Monsell)
395	Jesus, in Thee our eyes behold—(Isaac Watts)
492	Come, ye sinners, poor and wretched—(Joseph Hart)
546	Just as I am—without one plea—(Charlotte Elliott)
554	No more, my God, I boast no more—(Isaac Watts)
639	Do not I love Thee, O my Lord?—(Philip Doddridge)
720	Come, we that love the Lord—(Isaac Watts)
738	A debtor to mercy alone—(Augustus M. Toplady)
786	Jesus, the very thought of Thee—(Bernard of Clairvaux tr. Caswall)
907	Welcome, sweet day of rest—(Isaac Watts)

13 times (14)

152	Blessed be the Father, and His love—(Isaac Watts)
181	The Lord is King; lift up thy voice—(Josiah Conder)
195	My God, how wonderful Thou art—(Frederick William Faber)
327	Where high the heavenly temple stands—(Michael Bruce)
406	Christ exalted is our song—(John Kent)
537	When wounded sore the stricken soul—(Cecil Frances Alexander)

Spurgeon's one hundred best hymns

548	The wanderer no more will roam—(Mary Jane Deck)
549	My hope is built on nothing less—(Edward Mote)
550	My faith looks up to Thee—(Ray Palmer)
606	Gracious Lord, incline Thine ear—(William Hammond)
681	Let me but hear my Saviour say—(Isaac Watts)
733	O Zion, afflicted with wave upon wave—(James Grant)
916	To Thy temple I repair—(James Montgomery)
957	Revive Thy work, O Lord—(Albert Midlane)

12 times (12)

176	Unto the Lord, unto the Lord—(Edwards A. Park)
193	How oft have sin and Satan strove—(Isaac Watts)
230	Indulgent God! how kind—(John Kent)
296	The Son of God, in mighty love—(Horatius Bonar)
435	I bless the Christ of God—(Horatius Bonar)
499	Come, poor sinner, come and see—(Hewett)
531	Jesus, th' eternal Son of God—(Thomas Gibbons)
556	Jesus, the sinner's Friend, to Thee—(Charles Wesley)
561	In evil long I took delight—(John Newton)
711	My God, the spring of all my joys—(Isaac Watts)
732	How firm a foundation, ye saints of the Lord—(George Keith)
972	O Spirit of the living God—(James Montgomery)

The following alternative versions or parts of some of the Psalms should probably appear higher in the above table, but accurate figures are not possible because it was not always indicated which particular version or part was actually sung.

At least 12 times (3)

23 ver. 3	The Lord my Shepherd is—(Isaac Watts)
103 ver. 2	O bless the Lord, my soul!—(Isaac Watts)
119 song 2	Oh that the Lord would guide my ways—(Isaac Watts)

At least 11 times (4)

23 ver. 2	The Lord's my Shepherd, I'll not want—(Scotch Version)
34 ver. 1	Through all the changing scenes of life—(Tate & Brady)

Spurgeon's one hundred best hymns

42 ver. 1   Like as the hart for water-brooks—(Scotch Version)
103 ver. 3   Praise, my soul, the King of heaven—(Henry Francis Lyte)

At least 10 times (4)
63 song 3   O God, Thou art my God alone—(James Montgomery)
84 song 2   Great God, attend while Sion sings—(Isaac Watts)
136 song 1   Let us, with a gladsome mind—(John Milton)
136 song 2   Give to our God immortal praise—(Isaac Watts)

At least 8 times (1)
92 part 1   Sweet is the work, my God, my King—(Isaac Watts)

At least 7 times (1)
103 ver. 1   My soul, repeat His praise—(Isaac Watts)

At least 6 times (3)
34 ver. 2   Lord, I will bless Thee all my days—(Isaac Watts)
45 ver. 1   O Thou that art the mighty One—(Scotch Version)
51 ver. 2   Lord, I am vile, conceived in sin—(Isaac Watts)

N.B. In addition the occurrences of the above Psalms where parts, songs or versions have not been specified are as follows:—23 (4), 34 (10), 42 (3), 45 (6), 51 (7), 63 (6), 84 (4), 92 (5), 103 (11), 119 (3), 136 (12).

Unused hymns
Of the 1,130 hymns in *Our Own Hymnbook* (1,060 numbers plus 70 extra versions of Psalms) as many as 283 (almost exactly one quarter) are not recorded as having been used at all. Some of these relate to special occasions such as burials, baptisms, mothers' meetings, weddings, inductions of pastors and the opening of places of worship. Many of the unrepresented hymns are quite obscure today, but these eleven are among the most notable absentees:—

169   Lead us, heavenly Father, lead us—(James Edmeston)
253   Angels, from the realms of glory—(James Montgomery)
323   Jesus, hail! enthroned in glory—(John Bakewell)
374   Come, Thou long-expected Jesus—(Charles Wesley)

Spurgeon's one hundred best hymns

892	Blest be the tie that binds—(John Fawcett)
939	Amidst us our Belovèd stands—(Charles H. Spurgeon)
1017	Jesus, where'er Thy people meet—(William Cowper)
1023	Awake, my soul, and with the sun—(Thomas Ken)
1031	Glory to Thee, my God, this night—(Thomas Ken)
1052	Lord, dismiss us with Thy blessing—(Walter Shirley)
1060	Jesus! and shall it ever be?—(Joseph Grigg & Benjamin Francis)

Other hymnbooks used

In addition over twenty other hymns from the following collections are recorded as having been sung on various occasions:—

  Charlesworth's *Flowers and Fruits of Sacred Song*
  Sankey's *Sacred Songs and Solos*

About Day One:

Day One's threefold commitment:

- TO BE FAITHFUL TO THE BIBLE, GOD'S INERRANT, INFALLIBLE WORD;

- TO BE RELEVANT TO OUR MODERN GENERATION;

- TO BE EXCELLENT IN OUR PUBLICATION STANDARDS.

I continue to be thankful for the publications of Day One. They are biblical; they have sound theology; and they are relative to the issues at hand. The material is condensed and manageable while, at the same time, being complete—a challenging balance to find. We are happy in our ministry to make use of these excellent publications.

JOHN MACARTHUR, PASTOR-TEACHER, GRACE COMMUNITY CHURCH, CALIFORNIA

It is a great encouragement to see Day One making such excellent progress. Their publications are always biblical, accessible and attractively produced, with no compromise on quality. Long may their progress continue and increase!

JOHN BLANCHARD, AUTHOR, EVANGELIST AND APOLOGIST

Visit our website for more information and to request a free catalogue of our books.

www.dayone.co.uk

365 Days with C H Spurgeon

TERENCE PETER CROSBY

HARDBACK

CROSBY, TERENCE PETER

VOLUME 1: 978-0-902548-84-8, 384PP

VOLUME 2: 978-1-903087-08-4, 384PP

VOLUME 3: 978-1-84625-006-4, 384PP

VOLUME 4: 978-1-84625-090-3, 448PP

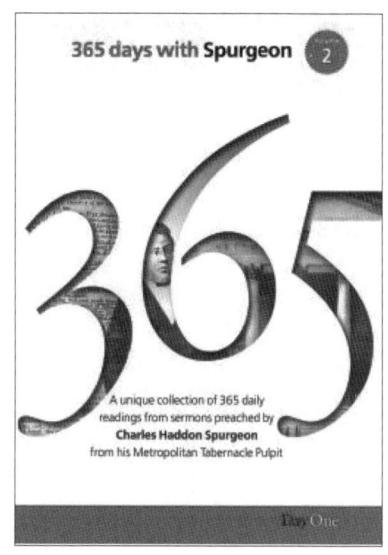

A unique collection of 365 daily readings from sermons preached by Charles Haddon Spurgeon from his New Park Street Pulpit

These excellent book will help if you are looking for something more challenging in your daily readings. From the archive of Charles Haddon Spurgeon's Park Street sermons Metropolitan Tabernacle sermons we have true pearls of Biblical wisdom. What is particularly striking when reading these extracts is how appropriate they are to the ears of the modern Christian in need of genuine spiritual insight.

In this C H Spurgeon compilation, Charles Haddon Spurgeon—the 'Prince of Preachers'—needs little introduction! Terence Peter Crosby holds a PhD in Classics (Greek and Latin) from London University. He lives in south London with his wife, Daphne.

I recommend this without hesitation.
English Churchman

365 days with Calvin

JOEL R BEEKE

416PP, HARDBACK

ISBN 978-1-84625-114-6

A unique collection of 365 readings from the writings of John Calvin, selected and edited by Joel R. Beeke.

John Calvin exercised a profound ministry in Europe, and is probably one of the most seminal thinkers ever to have lived. A godly pastor, theologian and preacher, he led his flock by example and worked hard to establish consistent godliness in his city. A prolific writer, his sermons, letters, and, of course, his 'Christian Institutes' have been published again and again. His writings—once described as 'flowing prose'—are characterized by clarity, simplicity, and yet profoundness, too. In these heart-warming pieces, drawn from his commentaries and sermons, Calvin brings us to Christ, the glorious Savior of all his people.

Dr Joel R. Beeke is president and professor of systematic theology and homiletics at Puritan Reformed Theological Seminary, and a pastor of the Heritage Netherlands Reformed Congregation in Grand Rapids, Michigan.

Daily devotionals—spiritual aids to help us be accountable for a life of disciplined reading of Scripture and prayer—have been around for centuries and need a certain caliber of excellence and insight if they are to prove of lasting value through 365 days! Of those I'd like to spend a year with as my spiritual guide and mentor, John Calvin is most certainly one of them. Joel Beeke guides us through the Reformer's writings to help us discover the help and insight that every Christian needs to live a God-honoring life for Jesus Christ.
—*Derek W. H. Thomas, John E. Richards Professor of Theology, Reformed Theological Seminary, Minister of Teaching, First Presbyterian Church, Jackson, MS, Editorial Director, Alliance of Confessing Evangelicals*

365 Days with Newton

MARYLYNN ROUSE

384PP, HARDBACK

ISBN 978-1-903087-92-3

John Newton was a rich and princely teacher, a sensitive and caring Pastor, and a straight, outspoken guide. His whole ministry bore the marks so evident in his lovely hymns: it was consistently biblical (to share the Word of God), spiritual (to promote walking with God), simple (to make biblical truth and principles plain) and practical (to inculcate personal holiness and sound relationships in church and society). In this collection, every day bears these marks, so useful to every believer, so instructive for those called to minister.

Marylynn Rouse has for many years done extensive research into the life and work of John Newton. She is at present working on the publication of The Complete Works of John Newton through The John Newton Project, a charity of which she is executive researcher. She has published an annotated edition of the original biography of Newton and *The Searcher of Hearts*, Newton's sermon notes on Romans 8.

In Marylynn Rouse, Newton has found a true disciple and a skilled publicist. By enormous diligence, and self-sacrificing application, she has made herself a leading 'Newton expert', and in this sensitive compilation all that expertise is put at our disposal. Come, enjoy and profit!

From the Foreword, J Alec Motyer

365 Days with Wilberforce

KEVIN BELMONTE

384PP, HARDBACK

ISBN 978-1-84625-058-3

William Wilberforce (1759–1833) led the twenty-year fight to abolish the British slave trade. He championed medical aid for the poor, prison rehabilitation, education for the deaf and restrictions on child labour. Wilberforce found 'nothing more effectual than private prayer, and the serious perusal of the New Testament.' He maintained 'All may be done through prayer, almighty prayer.' He insisted that 'in the calmness of the morning, before the mind is heated and wearied by the turmoil of the day, you have a season of unusual importance for communing with God and with yourself.' He seized upon such opportunities, believing 'God will prosper me better if I wait on him.'

365 Days with Wilberforce is a collection unlike any other. Drawing directly from Wilberforce's writings, the selections in this book illustrate how God sustained and guided him. Those who seek to walk their pilgrim's progress aright will find much to ponder, pray over and treasure.

Kevin Belmonte resides in the seaside village of York, Maine, USA—his birthplace. His is a literary family, of British descent, including the poets Robert Frost and Henry Wadsworth Longfellow. For the last five years he has been the principal historical consultant for Amazing Grace, a feature film on the life of Wilberforce produced by Walden Media. He has served as a script consultant for the BBC and his book, *Hero for Humanity: A Biography of William Wilberforce*, is the winner of the John Pollock Award for Christian Biography. He and his wife, Kelly, are the proud parents of a son, Samuel.